# A Failed Parricide

# Historical Materialism Book Series

The Historical Materialism Book Series is a major publishing initiative of the radical left. The capitalist crisis of the twenty-first century has been met by a resurgence of interest in critical Marxist theory. At the same time, the publishing institutions committed to Marxism have contracted markedly since the high point of the 1970s. The Historical Materialism Book Series is dedicated to addressing this situation by making available important works of Marxist theory. The aim of the series is to publish important theoretical contributions as the basis for vigorous intellectual debate and exchange on the left.

The peer-reviewed series publishes original monographs, translated texts, and reprints of classics across the bounds of academic disciplinary agendas and across the divisions of the left. The series is particularly concerned to encourage the internationalization of Marxist debate and aims to translate significant studies from beyond the English-speaking world.

*For a full list of titles in the Historical Materialism Book Series available in paperback from Haymarket Books, visit:*
https://www.haymarketbooks.org/series_collections/1-historical-materialism

# A Failed Parricide

## *Hegel and the Young Marx*

Roberto Finelli

Translated by
Peter D. Thomas
Nicola Iannelli Popham

Haymarket Books
Chicago, IL

First published in Italian by Bollati Borighieri Editore as *Un parricidio mancato. Il rapporto tra Hegel e il giovane Marx* (Turin, 2004).

First published in 2015 by Brill Academic Publishers, The Netherlands


Published in paperback in 2017 by
Haymarket Books
P.O. Box 180165
Chicago, IL 60618
773-583-7884
www.haymarketbooks.org

ISBN: 978-1-60846-706-8

Trade distribution:
In the US, Consortium Book Sales, www.cbsd.com
In Canada, Publishers Group Canada, www.pgcbooks.ca
In the UK, Turnaround Publisher Services, www.turnaround-uk.com
All other countries, Ingram Publisher Services International, ips_intlsales@ingramcontent.com

Cover design by Jamie Kerry of Belle Étoile Studios and Ragina Johnson.

This book was published with the generous support of Lannan Foundation and the Wallace Action Fund.

Printed in Canada by union labor.

10 9 8 7 6 5 4 3 2 1

Library of Congress Cataloging-in-Publication data is available.

# Contents

# Preface

How does hegemony fail?

How was the force of consent that the values and the culture of the Italian Left had conquered since 1968 and throughout the 1970s extinguished, by a capillary diffusion, radically changing the common sense of the country? How and why was that cultural and moral hegemony exhausted, giving way to a sense of radical uncertainty, in the best of cases, when not a complete recantation and a rapid reversal of direction in the face of the rise of other principles and values, which were only apparently manipulatory and misleading but, in fact, very profound and hegemonic?

The book gives what might be regarded as a bizarre answer to these questions of our present history by narrating an episode of the past. It does so not in relation to social and political history or to sociological analysis, as the question would seem to require, but rather, in relation to the history of philosophy and in particular to the specific relationship that was established for a few short years between the young Marx and the philosophy of the old Hegel.

## 1

The rise of new collective and individual values is always fundamental for hegemony. I believe that the most noble and original attempt of the culture of 1968 and of at least the early 1970s was that of a cross fertilisation of the two fundamental components of modern culture: on the one hand, anti-authoritarianism, which aimed at an education and socialisation of the person as free as possible from repressive institutions and the negation of individuality; and, on the other hand, egalitarianism, which fought all the inequalities produced by the economic mechanisms of social reproduction. What was attempted was a mediation between, on the one hand, the principles of communitarianism and of solidarity that had traditionally animated the working-class movement and its political institutions, and, on the other hand, those parts of European culture which, at least since Kierkegaard and Nietzsche through to Sartre's existentialism and the Frankfurt School, had claimed the values of the uniqueness of each single individuality, of the profound interiority of each self and the liberation of body and desire. In other words, it was an attempt to make thinkable a form of society and civilisation in which the universality of rights and duties – an undeniable achievement of modernity – would lose the abstract and rhetorical features that in the real history of women and men has often become a screen for the dissimulation of inequalities and asymmetries, and would become a genuine condition of equal opportunities for each individual to express their own deepest, incomparable self.

If we were to say that this was the most generous and intelligent spirit of 1968 and of consequent transformations of behaviour and ways of thinking, we would be making a very synthetic and reductive judgement, in the light of a distanced observation of those years. Those years were actually much more confused and complex, with a multiplicity of conflicting characteristics, arrogant and haughty, as well as generous and sympathetic. Whoever tries to ascribe today's clarity to the intentions and projects of many of us then, very young protagonists of those events, would be making a great mistake. Those years were rich, not just in ideas and projects, but also in immaturity, personalism and protagonism, in exaggerations, and in violence both suffered and enacted. Nevertheless, the attempted integration of culture and values, although faltering and partially unaware of itself and contradicted by old-fashioned behaviour and ideologies, was still the most continuous and significant axis of meaning with which the best part of the generation of 68 tried to identify and to represent itself.

The history of those years, at least with regard to the consequences we are currently living with and paying for today, ended up in a failure, when judged by the standards of their most profound and original goals. This is not to say that various examples of, on the one hand, more individualism and, on the other, more radical egalitarianism, have not penetrated into many different aspects of national life, in both individual and collective forms. During the decade of the 1970s, the ultimate effect of this process was a genuine transformation of Italy's common sense, which turned into a general modernisation of our country's sensibility. It resulted, in particular, in the significant phenomenon of women's achievement of a new, matured consciousness of themselves, which has now been historically and socially consolidated. However, on the wider front of other forms of life, the culture of the 1970s was unable to remain at the level of the problems generated and opened up by its own needs.

The historically unavoidable duty that such a culture failed to fulfil was that of bringing together the various traditions of its multiple and diverging elements with comprehensive coherence, not just by using easy juxtapositions and mere declarations of intents, but by means of experiments with praxis and thought. Such a failure grew from the inability to find those places and the most delicate and complex forms of mediation between the culture of individualisation and the culture of solidarity. Only their connection would have been capable of enabling the extension and organic unity of theory and ethical life – that is, of philosophy with a high level of universality and strong practical intentionality – wherein lies the heart of every hegemony and every true revolution and which, as such, can only signify intellectual and moral reform.

The causes and obstacles that led to that failure were of various and different kinds. It is sufficient to think of the way that the so-called (not incorrectly) state terrorism first, and then subsequently, in a reflective way, red terrorism, dramatically regressed to the archaic and barbaric dimensions of blood and violence.

Nonetheless, because of the intrinsically cultural substance of the issue, here we will discuss other kinds of considerations, which focus on the inadequacy of the ideal inspirations of those forces. The crucial point seems to lie in a structural asymmetry of a theoretical nature or, in other words, in the different weight and importance given to those cultural galaxies that the work of mediation and equilibrium should have brought together. Central here was the cultural identity of the Italian Communist Party (PCI), which was based almost absolutely and univocally on the values of egalitarianism and communitarianism. It quickly saw in the anti-authoritarian examples of 1968 not a hypothesis to be welcomed or discussed, but only an extraneous issue to refute and deny.

One of the major obstacles – if not the most important – to an adequate maturation of the ideas of 68 was the political and cultural resistance opposed by communist humanism, educated within an anthropological perspective firmly based on the priority of the physical and material needs of human beings and on the egalitarian requirement for these to be satisfied. Such an anthropology – perhaps justified in times of shortages and during the first period of modernity – had difficulty in understanding life programmes that were more articulated and differentiated, and also more consonant with that second phase of modernity that Italy was approaching through the circulation of commodities and mass consumption.

It was effectively this anthropology of poverty, together with materialism and egalitarianism of needs, and the corresponding interpretation of the cultural-symbolic world, that provided an answer that remained deaf to a demand for a new humanism and a new universalism of difference. However, in election times, the very same bureaucratic and intellectual apparatus of the PCI took advantage of the anthropological and behavioural transformation that had spread throughout the entire country since the explosion of the student movement in 1968–9 and the new structure of industrial workers' councils, which in some ways had been triggered by the former. Enrico Berlinguer's Eurocommunism was then able to turn the radical need for new forms of life and social organisation into an abstract and moralistic rigourism, looking to working-class and popular self-limitation of consumerism as the key-stone of a rising nation governed by the popular masses and the alliance between working and productive classes, including both labour and capital. In effect, this initiative merely inverted the meaning of the anthropology of poverty that has always been an integral part of communist spirituality.

The PCI intentionally avoided the historical opportunity to start a process of deconstruction-reconstruction of communist traditions, beginning from the ability to criticise its own dogmatisms and to engage with other anthropologies. Only an evaluation of its own opening-up and acceptance of otherness would have been able to generate real and effective hegemony on the part of a political and intellectual class that had the historical merit of having lived and interpreted the twentieth century as the emergence into social and cultural life of immense masses of human beings, who, until then, had been forced into such a subordinate and almost extra-historical life that was often not dissimilar to the rhythms and conditions of animal life.

Unfortunately, this did not happen. Its most evident consequence was not the elaboration of the self and its own identity, which is by definition one of the abilities of a hegemonic subject, but was rather the conversion undertaken by that political personnel, in order to return to a virginal and intact praise of the commercial-entrepreneurial culture and a vision of politics as a mere technical-administrative mediation between the interests of supposedly autonomous subjects, regarded as individually free at the moment when they join the social pact. However, we know, as Hegel taught, that overturning into the opposite of oneself is the most explicit expression of the stubbornness of a subject that, in order to reaffirm its inalterable identity as a subject of power, passes on from one form to another, never letting the real other penetrate into itself.

## 2

The present book is a conceptual biography and is based on the same kind of problems mentioned above, even if it might not seem so. It returns to an issue that appeared to have already been fully discussed and settled: the relationship between the young Marx and Hegel's philosophy. However, today's increased availability and philological precision of Marx's texts, mainly due to the new *MEGA* edition, as well as the improvement of research on German literature and on Hegel over the last thirty years, allows us to return to the meaning of that relationship, so often thematised, when not even canonised, in Marxist texts.[1]

1 The new *Gesamtausgabe* (cited here as *MEGA*$^2$) is published by the International Marx-Engels

In my opinion, the great theoretical innovation is the chance to challenge the canonical way in which this relationship was considered and evaluated in the past. According to this narrative, the transition from Hegel's idealism to Marx's materialism could not, and should not, mean anything but the result, following a linear progression, of a theory of becoming, initially confined to an abstract level of Idea and Spirit, and then finally found in the real activity of human beings and of their relations, in a historically concrete horizon.

The underlying thesis of my reconstruction breaks the order and the progressive dimensions of such deductions and proposes an interpretation of the relationship between Hegel and the early Marx as characterised by a permanent and structural subordination of the young revolutionary intellectual to the great philosopher from Stuttgart. This subordination lasts for a long time, for a whole period of Marx's life; when denied and repressed, it became the origin of many hasty and not very rigorous aspects of Marx's first theoretical paradigm.

Therefore, as the reader will see, the substance of the connection between Hegel and the first Marx will basically result in a failed act, a *failed parricide*, and in an asymmetric confrontation between two anthropologies. Marx's early anthropology, it seems to me, has a symbiotic-fusional, organicistic and spiritualist nature, despite its claim of materialism and concreteness. This becomes particularly clear when compared with the very original concept of the individual as '*werden zu sich*' and '*bei sich im andern sein*' [to become one's self through the relation with alterity] that Hegel inscribed under the – only apparently – traditional denomination of Spirit [*Geist*].

As the young Marx's philosophy of subjectivity is regulated only by the theme of equality and the organic unity of species – of the 'human species' – it rejects any possible meaning regarding the value of a differentiated individualisation. Passing through Feuerbach's deceptive materialism, it undertakes what amounts to an anthropological regression, when compared to the complexity achieved by Hegel's theory of subjectivity. Such backwardness and archaism will turn up even in the subsequent materialist conception of history developed by Marx and Engels. This conception, despite the profound

Foundation, participants in which include, among others, the International Institute of Social History of Amsterdam (where large number of Marx's manuscripts are held) and the Berlin-Brandenburg Academy of Sciences and Humanities. The new publishing house is Akademie Verlag of Berlin [now De Gruyter]. A first attempt to produce a historical-critical edition of Marx and Engels's writings (cited here as *MEGA¹*) was undertaken by David B. Rjazanov between 1927 and 1935. On the history of the new *MEGA*, see Mazzone 2002.

originality of its interpretation of the history of human societies, fails to mediate between the legitimate acknowledgement given to material needs in the life of human beings, and to the organisation of labour established to order to satisfy them, and that immaterial need of acknowledgement of each person's single and incomparable identity by another human being, which for Hegel's *Phenomenology of Spirit*, and later for psychoanalysis, reveals an unavoidable research programme for modern anthropology.

Nevertheless, I believe that this radical deficit of subjectivitism is the basis for the most singular and fertile paradox of all Marx's work. The indifference towards individual history, upon which young Marx's whole communitarian anthropology is based, allows Marx to succeed in that interminable undertaking that is his later drafting of his mature critique of political economy. In order to construct a science of modern society and its economic laws, Marx assumes that individuals, far from being free and autonomous, should be conceived of as nothing more than masks or mere *dramatis personae*, that is, personifications and bearers of the reproductive functions of the true subject of modernity, namely, capital. Capital, being made of merely quantitative wealth, can have no other aim than that of increasing its quantity *ad infinitum* within its monetary and productive circuit, in a forced process of growth that manipulates the whole qualitative side of life and of human beings in order to guarantee its own accumulation.

However, in order to understand how an abstraction could constitute reality and concretely organise social life – that is, to understand how, in modern times, an economic principle could count as a principle of material production as well as a principle of symbolic production – the mature Marx needed to modify the nature of the deep relationship he had with Hegel all his life. Marx had to distance himself from a master-father, whose complexity and theoretical superiority he could only repress during his juvenile immaturity – that is, negate in a compulsive and forced way. He needed to acquire, after the work of mourning following the defeat of the 1848 revolutions in Europe and the long years of study in London, the ability to recognise such a master-father and use him in the differentiation and autonomy of conception of his mature work. Here I can only refer to what I wrote a number of years ago in a text on the Marx of the *Grundrisse* and *Capital*.[2]

---

2 See Finelli 1987.

## 3

For the above reasons, I trust it is sufficiently clear that going back to the Hegel-Marx connection could be useful in understanding our present. Marxism's founding anthropology had a very idealistic and reductive vision of the human being, and its limitations affected the entire theoretical and practical history of communist tradition.

Furthermore, I believe that inside the multiform and sometimes even contradictory laboratory of Karl Marx's work we can identify two fundamental theoretical tendencies.

The first tendency, perceptively defined by Giovanni Gentile at the end of the nineteenth century, is that of a philosophy of praxis founded upon a subject of an idealistic type, a subject that moves through history by means of the negation, and then the negation of the negation, of its originary fullness. This is a philosophy of history where a subject necessarily loses and alienates itself through labour; but, equally necessarily, and in accordance with a predefined result, it reconciles itself with itself and with its irreducible and irrepressible essence. This theory of praxis generates a paradigm that reduces reality in its entirety to labour. It represents a substantial anti-naturalism, or rather, the valorisation of nature only to the extent that it is elevated and inscribed in the horizon of the historicity of human beings. It thus produces the simplistic vision of symbolic and political superstructures as mere reflections of the productive structure.

The second tendency, which effectively coexists with the first, is instead a sociology of modernity alone, and, thus, not extended to the entire history of humanity, as in the case of historical materialism. It is based upon capital as a principle of totality. In other words, capital is considered as a vector of the universalisation and assimilation of the whole, which progressively transforms, throughout its history, every element of prior reality and civilisation. Presupposed [*presupposto*] elements are transformed into elements posited [*posto*] by its logic, into products of its accumulation. At the same time, as a totalising principle of social integration, it is, precisely in its nature as an element producing material goods that satisfy human needs, a producer of relations between human beings and of the whole process of decomposition of a social ensemble into classes and orders, as well as a producer of the symbolic imaginary and theoretical rationalisations of the various social actors, by means of a singular relation of dissimulation between content and surface.

The profound heterogeneity of these two theoretical paradigms, opposed on so many levels of mediation and contact, will later need to be analysed by means of a philologically informed understanding of the history of Marx's thought. What it is necessary to highlight here is the extent to which, from the beginning, it was the first paradigm that was imposed in a dominant fashion in the history of Italian theoretical and political Marxism in the twentieth century. It was conjugated in the terms of the philosophy of praxis and of a humanism that, despite its own claims to materialism, was instead intrinsically spiritualist and anti-naturalist. It was so dominant that the entirety of Italian Marxism could be substantially described, in my view, as a Marxism without *Capital*.

This book, dedicated to the anthropology of the early Marx, would like to make a contribution to understanding the dynamics of this process, beginning with the multifaceted and contradictory soul of Marx's philosophy, whose limitations need to be discussed again in order to understand, alongside the dramatic inadequacies of the history of communism in the twentieth century, also the limitations and difficulties of more recent history.

This means that there is no possible re-actualisation of Marx's critique of political economy, with its persistent ability to explain the world of today, without a radical self-critique of Marxism with regard to its major and fundamental anthropological and juridico-political weaknesses. Drawing in part upon a revival of Marxological studies, I believe that it will be possible to understand better the reasons for the exhaustion of what was in the end, due to its own limitations, only an attempt at hegemony. Its inevitable failure could only leave the field clear to the miserableness and boredom of our present. However, its most fertile and acute instances will inevitably return to haunt the unresolved problems of future history.

CHAPTER 1

# Between the Ancient and the Modern

## 1 Science and Utopia

One of the less obvious geopolitical consequences of the fall of the Berlin wall, although very important for a limited group of experts, was the end of a honourable man's extended military service. The duration of the service, almost a century, may sound amazing, but is less surprising when we know the man's name is Karl Marx. The philosopher, economist and political organiser, all fields in which he seems to have excelled, was called up to guard the defences of those unfortunate and luckless regimes answering to the name of real communism and of their vulgar state philosophy, called 'dialectical materialism'. Marx was finally given back his freedom when he was retired from military exile on the eastern borders. This freedom meant he could once again walk amongst all those who frequent the peaceful gardens of thought and respond to their questions, liberated from the military obligation to answer in a warlike, schematic and propagandistic way on serious issues concerning the history and life of human beings. The so-called liberation of Eastern Europe is relevant to the following pages only insofar as it concerns Karl Marx's liberation, at the end of his military service and the opportunity this provides to return to discussions with him, over and above any presumed alignments. This will permit a renewed pleasure to be taken from the complex and original richness of his mind, without being dismayed by the limits and profound backwardness that, at times, appear to overshadow some of his thoughts.

Recommencing a productive examination of Marx's thought means, primarily, discarding every myth regarding his heroic figure and his alleged, uncorrupted love of truth, his unconditional dedication to the good – myths subsequently distorted and betrayed by his followers. It means instead to find within Marx's theoretical weaknesses the principle of those rigidities and extremisms that very often characterised later forms of Marxism.

One of this book's objectives is to find within the contradictory history of Marx's thought the multiple sources of the history of Marxism or, preferably, of the history of Marxisms. This requires an analysis of all the theories, even in their most difficult interpretations, which consistently choose to highlight partial and exclusive aspects of Marx's work, without undertaking the patient, global reconstruction demanded by the tortuous progression of his thought. The point of Marx's regained freedom is essentially his liberation from Marxism and the introduction of a new methodological approach that releases Trier's philosopher from apologetic rituals which, for over a century, have considered him immune to error, but thereby end up only handing him over to the turbulent freedom of his own contradictions.

However, humanising the hero, removing him from a celebrative alienation and returning him to the effective time and space of his work, also needs to avoid falling prey to the opposite approach of demonisation. Particularly in recent years, and despite a few formal acknowledgements, this is effectively what happened to Marx's thought, inasmuch as it is seen as lacking substantial theoretical dignity. He is frequently accused of being unable to abandon ideology's passionate and deforming vision and of raising things to the objective and dispassionate level of theory. Furthermore, it has been argued that he was never able to raise his thoughts to the levels of science and philosophy. This study instead aims to examine more mediated, concrete and human configurations, avoiding demons and gods and the celebrations of absolute evil and good.

It is undeniable that Marx himself, from the very start, claimed an entirely special status for his work or, in other words, one that was both theoretical but also immediately practical, in terms of its value as a tool for the organisation and the liberation of the modern proletariat. So much so that, beginning with this claimed non-speculative but fundamentally practical-political nature, the most profound criticisms made of Marx's theoretical works are that they have created an undesirable mixture of description and prescription, or, in other words, of cognitive application (that aims to describe reality as it is) and practical application (that aims to transform reality as it is hoped it will be). The intrinsically ideological nature of Marx's work thus supposedly consists in the prevailing of desire over thought, which means that, even when acknowledging his brilliant ability to identify elements valuable for the interpretation of history and social life, he also stands accused of generating one of the most extreme and damaging combinations of all time, that of science and utopia.

The clearest conceptual formulation of this type of criticism, according to which the levels of real and substantial analysis in Marx are combined with those of the imagination and its abstractions, had already been made by Benedetto Croce, at the end of the nineteenth century, in his *Historical Materialism and the Economics of Karl Marx* [*Materialismo storico ed economia marxistica*], with a specific reflection concerning the well-known Marxian theory of value. This theory, which Marx introduces at the beginning of *Capital*, famously hypothesises that commodities in the modern market are exchanged on the basis of the amount of labour contained within them and interprets the reality of the society in which we live by reference, as Croce notes, to an entirely ideal and imaginary one: a society, precisely because it is composed, it is presumed, only of members who work and exchange their products in accordance with the equality of the work they contain, is an imaginary one, conceived by means of abstractions with respect to the effective complexities of each real, social form of life.

> Let us, instead, take account, in a society, only of what is properly economic life, i.e. out of the whole society, only of economic society. Let us abstract from this latter all goods which cannot be increased by labour. Let us abstract further all class distinctions, which may be regarded as accidental in reference to the general concept of economic society. Let us leave out of account all modes of distributing the wealth produced, which, as we have said, can only be determined on grounds of convenience or perhaps of justice, but in any case upon considerations belonging to society as a whole, and never from considerations belonging exclusively to economic society. What is left after these successive abstractions have been made? Nothing but economic society in so far as it is a society of labour. And in this society without class distinctions, i.e. in an economic society as such and whose only commodities are the products of labour, what can value be? Obviously the sun, of the efforts, i.e. the quantity of labour, which the production of the various kinds of commodities demands. And, since we are here speaking of the economic social organism, and not of the individual persons living in it, it follows that this labour cannot be reckoned except by averages, and hence as socially (it is with society, I repeat, that we are here dealing) necessary labour.[1]

The basic error behind the criticisms of political economy presented in *Capital*, Croce claims, consists in the fact that Marx has confused the abstract with the material. In other words, he conceived, in the abstraction of his mind, a world created according to a utopian and simplifying paradigm and surreptitiously turned this into the principle and measure of the real world. The very concept of surplus value, on which the entire Marxian concept of the exploitation of unpaid labour is based, is, therefore, only the result of an 'elliptical comparison' or the arbitrary and forced comparison between the real economy, diversified into the multiplicity of its consistent elements, and the abstract economy of an ideal society based on a single element consisting of labour.

1 Croce 2001, p. 76; Croce 1914.

The abstraction of the materiality of human history and its multiform motivations, the exclusively ideological and imaginary concept of the law of value, the criticism of economic science according to the rules of the same abstraction, the lack of foundations for the theory of profit as the accumulation of unpaid labour: these are the most significant elements criticised by Croce more than a century ago. He accused Marx, in his construction of *Capital*, of demonstrating a pernicious lack of distinction between that which pertains to knowledge and that which pertains to the desirable or the hoped for. The material world of economics, conversely, is only explained, according to Croce, by beginning with the material usefulness of the single individual, as established by the most credited economic sciences based on marginal utility theory. Therefore, the Marxian theory of value, which refutes the idea that the price of economic goods is based on utility to the individual, is on principle excluded from economic science. It is, therefore, impossible not to conclude that the entire system expressed in *Capital* is erroneous and, in particular, that the theory of the irreversible crisis of capitalism that is expressed in the tendential law of the fall of the profit rate is unsustainable.

The same abstraction of reality, according to Croce, further characterised Marx's ideas in relation to the more general concept of history, in which so-called historical materialism, in an attempt to define a consistently uniform structure of events and by replacing spirit with matter, positions the economic factor as the essential and determining basis for all human life. For Croce, the most authentic form of knowledge is historical and aims both to judge and to distinguish the particular form of human activity that characterises any historical event, which is, due to its unrepeatable nature, always determined and new. Thus, Marx's reflections on history can make sense for Croce only when they are separated from any strong and systematic theoretical claim, and when they do not presume to present themselves as a new vision of the world animated by a philosophy that, with its all embracing and abstract structure, cannot but cancel out the consistently original events of history.

As a consequence, historical materialism only makes sense as 'canons', as an exhortation to the historian to widen his or her interpretative horizons and, therefore, to take into greater account the importance of economic factors in human events. Marx's great merit was supposedly the fact that he theorised

> the assertions of the dependence of all parts of life upon each other, and of their origin in the economic subsoil, so that it can be said that there is but one single history; the rediscovery of the true nature of the State (as it appears in the empirical world), regarded as an institution for the defence of the ruling class; the established dependency of ideologies on class

> interests; the coincidence of the great epochs of history with the great economic eras; and the many other observations by which the school of historical materialism is enriched.[2]

If this is the opinion of one of the most eminent representatives of European idealist philosophy at the end of the nineteenth century, it is not very different from the judgement of Marx made by one of the twentieth century's main philosophers of science, Karl Popper. In *The Open Society and its Enemies*, Popper profoundly criticised Marx as a theorist of historical determinism, of an assumed and anticipated vision of history that has nothing in common with the dignity and seriousness of science. According to Popper, Marx, as a historicist ideologue, did not remain within the limits of the effective prediction of science but expressed historical prophecies that claim to anticipate the course of the future with absolute necessity. It is no coincidence that behind Marx stands Hegel who, for Popper, is one of the greatest theorists of obscurantism and totalitarianism. As an anti-scientific and irrationalist thinker, Hegel effectively posited as the basis of truth those contradictions that science instead absolutely excludes from the genuine progress of knowledge. Imagining dogmatic and improvable hypotheses such as dialectical progress, the conflict of opposites, their synthesis and unity, he celebrated an optimistic philosophy of history aimed at the progressive development of the Idea. In so doing, he linked his concept of Spirit [*Geist*] to Plato's doctrine of ideas and tried to push modern thought, against the Enlightenment and all scientific knowledge, back into authoritarianism and totalitarianism. As a disciple of Hegelian historicism, Marx necessarily fell into abstract generalisations that were far removed from reality and proposed theories such as the claim that the history of all societies hitherto is the history of class struggle, or that social life is organised according to a division between a sphere of essence and one of appearance (base and superstructure), or that politics is entirely unable to condition the laws moving the economy. Nor was Marx able to avoid becoming a false prophet, foreseeing the inevitable historical passage from capitalism to communism through the opposition between increasingly simplified and radical classes, thereby assuming fallacious laws about economic cycles such as the tendential fall of the profit rate and the accumulation of capital based on the concentration of ever greater wealth, on the one hand, and increasing poverty, on the other. All these predictions turned out to be false (or only valid for partial periods that have now been superseded by modern history). Equally false, due to its spiritualist and

2 Croce 2001, p. 28; Croce 1914.

metaphysical nature, is the Marxian theory of value that claims to replace the material causality of supply and demand with essentialist abstractions within which, for Marx (who through Hegel regresses to Plato), 'the Platonic "essence" has become entirely divorced from experience'.[3] Nonetheless, there can be no doubt, Popper adds, regarding the fundamental and irreplaceable role played by Marx in the development of the social sciences and their investigative methods – but obviously, only once Marx's emphasis on the importance of the economic sphere for social existence is subtracted from the evolutionist dialectics of Hegelian origin.

From one century to the other or, in other words, from the judgements of Benedetto Croce to those of Karl Popper, the figure of Karl Marx, with every concession to his merits, appears to be crushed beneath the weight of his abstractions and his naive relationship to Hegel. According to Croce, he is guilty of not correcting the Hegelian theory of opposites with that of distinctions and thereby confusing the theoretical with the practical. For Popper, he is blamed for having wanted to conjugate science and Hegelian dialectics, presuming that dialectical categories such as essence, appearance and contradictions can effectively grasp the material progress of events.

The opposition claimed by Popper between the methods of the natural sciences and the cognitive assumptions of dialectics is also operative in the liquidation of Marx effected towards the end of the 1980s in Italy by Lucio Colletti and other theorists, many of whom had initially subscribed to the school of study and critical diffusion of Marxism set up in the post World War II period around the figure of Galvano Della Volpe. Hegel's modern dialectics, these writers claimed, found its origins and most characteristic concepts in the ancient and mystical context of the Neo-Platonism of the third century. This resulted in instruments whose substantially religious purpose was that of subjecting the world of finite and material elements to the spiritual dominion of the Absolute. The idealism of Hegelian philosophy consists in the non-recognition of the finite's dignity and autonomy of existence, reducing it to being merely a phenomenal manifestation of the Infinite and the Idea.[4] Thus, Marx's work, or at least the part of it that is built on dialectics, becomes, of necessity, part of an obscurantism that rejects science, underestimates the principles of contradiction in relation to every scientific truth upon which it is based and presumes to

3 Popper 2011, p. 383.

4 For this kind of interpretation, see Colletti 1976, pp. 3–76; Bedeschi 1972, pp. 9–56; Albanese 1984, pp. 55–146. The most significant works by Della Volpe on this topic are Della Volpe 1972, particularly pp. 138–210 and 1969, particularly pp. 52–146.

explain the modern world with theoretical inconsistencies such as the identity of opposites, the inversion of subject and predicate, fetishism and alienation.

## 2 Hegel and the Epistemological 'Circle'

From both an idealistic and an empirical and neo-positivist cultural point of view, the deficit of theoretical and scientific dignity in Marx's thought, therefore, has generally been traced back to the excess of dialectics and the Hegelian philosophy of history present in his works; or, in other words, to the excess of the dialectics of opposition and contradiction that force Marxist theory towards an aprioristic and meta-historical system. The interpretative hypothesis proposed in this book, in an overall rethinking of Marx, is different. It aims to demonstrate how the dialectic of opposition and contradiction is undoubtedly a theme that is present, but which is insufficient to clarify the problems of the relationship between Marx and Hegel. For a more in-depth evaluation, we need to examine this theme in the context of the 'epistemological circle' of the 'presupposed-posited [*Vorausgesetztes-Gesetztes*]', which constitutes the most original and innovative element of Hegel's theory of truth. This represents, in my opinion, the most problematic methodological reference in Marx's entire work, despite the various positions that his thought assumes in the transition from his youthful writings to those of the years of maturity.

It is undoubtedly true that Marx eventually dealt explicitly with epistemological and gnoseological subjects – the question of what knowledge and science really are – only in the relatively late writings from the 'Introduction' of 1859 to the *Grundrisse* (Notebook M). It is equally true that, in his life, the problems of doing always dominated those of knowing, but it is also unquestionable that a profound and passionate bond with Hegel's philosophy marked the start of his thoughts. Furthermore, due to the highly original combination that Hegel effected between doing and knowing in his theory of the Idea, it was impossible for Marx, from the very beginning of his research and as a result of this combination, not to pose the question of the nature of theory in its relation to practice, and what the identity might be of the subjectivity that such a relation implies. This is precisely the theme that Hegel attributes, *par excellence*, to science, and which, using the terminology and concepts of Hegel, we will define as a circular paradigm of the 'immediate-mediated-immediate' or, better still, of the 'presupposed-posited'.

This book is written in the conviction that reviving the discussion of Marx today only makes sense if it starts with the problematic issue of this Hegelian circle. A contrast between Marx's thought and science can only be maintained if the new criteria of truth and awareness that Hegel attempted to introduce into the tradition of western thought are repressed and banished from our knowledge of modern philosophy and culture. The various attempts to set this new epistemological structure to work are, in my opinion, the history of Marx's intellectual development. They explain, both in their inconsistencies and their successes, the complex evolution and stratification of this thought.

The new criteria of truth and research initiated by Hegel in his *Phenomenology of Spirit* find their most explicit formulation in the section of *The Science of Logic* entitled 'With what must the beginning of science be made?'[5] Hegel claims here that true knowledge is obtained only when the process of cognition and knowledge assumes the form of a circle: or, in other words, when what appears to be a simple and immediately certain experience, alongside having universal validity, reveals through its very simplicity the effective presence of dualisms and contrasts whose opposing natures require mediation and reconciliation. What, at the beginning, is immediate therefore gradually proves its intimate nature to be mediated, consisting of various levels and mediating figures. The radical nature of this division is tempered and discovers a terrain that is increasingly closer to unification. It eventually finds the greatest and most complete level of mediation that, by repairing the division, returns it to the initial immediacy. It is identical, in its simplicity, to the original state; but, at the same time, it is enriched by all the oppositions-mediations that it has triggered. In this sense, what is presented at the start is, in effect, only an appearance that alludes to the interior structure that creates and produces it precisely as an appearance. As a consequence, the true nature of what is a beginning can only be appreciated as a result.

> Essential to science is not so much that a pure immediacy should be the beginning, but that the whole of science is in itself a circle in which the first becomes also the last, and the last also the first. [...] In this advance the beginning thus loses the one-sidedness that it has when determined simply as something immediate and abstract; it becomes mediated, and the line of scientific forward movement consequently turns into a circle.[6]

Knowledge is, therefore, precisely the passage from the well-known to the known. It is the process of studying in depth a reality that from its appearance passes to its essence, and then returns back again, to the state of its appearance.

5 Hegel 2010, p. 45.
6 Hegel 2010, p. 49.

Now, however, its explanatory connections have been grounded and clarified, by means of a series of transitions in which the explanation never looks for external causalities but always looks for internal ones.

> Further, the advance from that which constitutes the beginning is to be considered only as one more determination of the same advance, so that this beginning remains as the underlying ground of all that follows without vanishing from it. The advance does not consist in the derivation of an other, or in the transition to a truly other: inasmuch as there is a transition, it is equally sublated again. Thus the beginning of philosophy is the ever present and self-preserving foundation of all subsequent developments, remaining everywhere immanent in its further determinations.[7]

At first glance, and considering its formulation in such a schematic way, it is understandable that this Hegelian circle can be seen as both paradoxical and regressive, given that it would seem to revive a concept of truth that, claiming to be objective and beyond the reasoning subject, returns us to the forms of realism and objectivity that Kant's critical philosophy and theory of knowledge, structured around the synthetic activity of subjectivity, definitively superseded in the history of modern philosophy. In this case, Popper's criticisms of Hegel (and, consequently, of Marx), as an essentialist and pre-modern thinker, would appear to be entirely justified.

However, this is only valid at first glance, since, if Hegel's discourse is studied in more depth, we can see that his theory of truth has a phenomenological-dialectical structure that locates it firmly within modern subjectivism, although within the context of an entirely specific and original vision of the subject. In effect, the start of Hegel's circle is always a fact of individual experience that is simultaneously universal, insofar as it is present in the experience of everyone, something that is inevitably and necessarily present in each of us, something that is obvious and unquestionable in the immediacy and simplicity of its presence (such as the fact that we are all sensible subjects at the start of the *Phenomenology of Spirit*, or such as the assumption of the faculty of thought in general, not limited to determinate thoughts, in the *Science of Logic*). However, its content, precisely due to its characteristic simplicity, is so poor and fragile that it is unable to satisfy the identity and sense of self of subjectivity in any way. Thus, the initial fact in some way makes its own insufficient

7 Hegel 2010, p. 49.

nature evident and, as a consequence, transforms itself and overtakes itself in the experience of a subject who aims to look for something more substantial through which it can effect a coincidence with itself. This generates a long and complex path through a multitude of figures of identification that are progressively less partial and insufficient and at the end of which the subject achieves a perfect form of identity and reconciliation with itself.

This process of constant transformation-alteration, which goes from the abstract towards the material and which is teleologically orientated in the direction of a full maturation of the self, is what Hegel calls spirit [*Geist*] – a Subject-Spirit which, because able to pass through and unite the multitude of various, partial forms of its identity, is presented as a universal. However, it is not *a logical-analytical* universal, such as that of a mind that constructs a concept, abstracting from a complex multitude of entities the elements common to individual differences. It is, rather, a practical-experiencing universal that is produced through the obstacles that the subject is obliged to experience within itself.

The subject who is presumed, at the beginning, to be sufficient and coincident with itself – but, in effect, in a merely subjective presupposition and representation of itself – is actually only such at the end of the journey. It has become such by means of a process of production and becoming itself in which, finally, it meets up again with the beginning. This is because only at the end do identity and coincidence with itself, initially naively assumed and taken as given, acquire completeness and effective meaning.[8]

In order to better appreciate the characteristics of this epistemological model, I refer the reader to the chapter in this book dedicated to a brief summary of Hegelian philosophy. However, what must be noted immediately is that

8 Naturally, the philosophical source from which Hegel's thematisation of truth as a circle begins cannot be other than Fichte's *Doctrine of Science* [*Wissenschaftslehre*]. This work provides the fundamental origin for all of German idealism. Fichte, as is well known, by studying in depth the Kantian lesson of the autonomy of practical reason and its unconditional freedom, resolves the theoretical element of the 'I think' in an entirely practical dimension, finding the true identity of the subject in its ability to remove every 'presupposition [*Vorausgesetztes*]' that it finds outside and before itself as a pre-given world, and to transform it, by means of its own elaboration, into the outcome of its own production, of its own positing [*Gesetztes*]. That the identity of the I is risked in this translating of the non-I into the I, of the transformation of everything that is posited by the Other into something that is posited by the Self in a removal of every outer limit, is the key to Fichte's freedom and the practical-dynamic dimension that is the basis of the theory of the subject in all German idealism, whatever its subsequent deviations and speculative closures may have been. On the peculiar nature of the Hegelian concept of the truth as a circle, see Rockmore 1989.

this circular theory of truth and, equally, of subjectivity is rendered aporetic (in the manner in which Hegel expresses it) by the contradictions that are opened up between the spirit seen as an open subject, whose identity is capable of transforming and becoming something other than itself, and spirit that is conclusively conceived of as the perfect self-consciousness of itself in whose completed transparency every vital and prospective difference with itself disappears. The original and new concept of spirit inaugurated by Hegel, a synonym for the vital praxis that produces subjectivity through its own obstacles, is in reality simultaneously deformed and subordinated to the horizon of the more traditional concept of Spirit-Subject as synonymous with self-consciousness, conceived of as that in which there is complete identification between subject and object, between thought and existence, without any residual differences. This is the position of the most consolidated ancient and modern philosophical traditions that assign to self-consciousness – and to its immediate coincidence of 'thinking thought' and 'thought thought' – the supreme value of absolute evidence and transparency. Going back before the time of Kant's 'I think', via Descartes's 'cogito', this position links back to the identity of the Aristotelian 'unmoved mover', conceived precisely as a pure and immaterial knowledge of knowledge, pure *nóesis noéseos*.[9] This is to say that the circularity between beginning and result, in Hegel's works, is profoundly intertwined – with the risk of seeing the significance of its epistemological innovation radically annulled – with the conclusive and metaphysical circularity of a subject whose identity is provided only by thought, of an Absolute, that is, which is singularly theoretical and whose end is to lead its life from an immediate existence lacking in consciousness to an existence that is completely marked and illuminated by the light of awareness.

The basic interpretive thesis regarding Marx proposed in this book is that all his work moves in opposition to this double circle – though in a manner,

9 'And thought in itself deals with that which is best in itself, and that which is thought in the fullest sense with that which is best in the fullest sense. And thought thinks itself because it shares the nature of the object of thought; for it becomes an object of thought in coming into contacts with and thinking its objects, so that thought and object of thought are the same. For that which is capable of receiving the object of thought, i.e. the substance, is thought. And it is active when it possesses this object. Therefore the latter rather than the former is the divine element which thought seems to contain, and the act of contempolation is what is most pleasant and best' (Aristotle, *Metaphysics*, Λ 1072 b 18–30). Hegel of course concludes the last page of his *Encyclopedia of Philosophical Sciences in Outline*, at the end of the section on 'Absolute Spirit', with the quotation (in Greek) of this passage from Aristotle in which the divine is defined as thought that thinks itself.

it should be highlighted, never sufficiently explicated and formalised. I am convinced that the more fragile and less mature Marx always remained subaltern to and inscribed within the Hegelian double circularity, whilst the more mature and self-assured Marx broke with it. Rejecting the metaphysical circle, he was able to use only the epistemological circle, valorising it in a new thematic continent, within a new horizon of concepts and reality. My hypothesis is, therefore, that there is a Marx who is still to be discovered and appreciated not only because he can, at last, be extracted from the ideological fixation that has rendered him rigid and militarised; but, above all, because the different image that the more serious studies over the past thirty years have rediscovered in the figure of Hegel and his idealism reflects on the image of Marx,[10] bringing out of the shadows a new figure that surprises and encourages us to consider his thought again. Thus, it is possible to see – and the key to this suggested reading lies in this crucial passage – that, as long as Marx, despite his great emphasis on praxis, allows an essentially theoretical-contemplative identity of the human subject to triumph (in the above-mentioned sense of a subject whose fullness of life is only realised through the mirror of self-consciousness), he does not escape from a metaphysical and spiritualist vision of history, and thus remains subaltern to Hegel's conception of spirit as theoretical-speculative Idea. It is only the abandonment of such an aristocratic form of anthropology, which privileges seeing over doing and which confines the subject within the circle of self-reflection and the unconditional possession of the self, that allows him to conceive of a science of modernity based on the centrality of praxis and the realisation, without omnipotent and mythological presuppositions, of the circle between beginning and result.

However, proposing this reading means returning to the myth of the hero and asking oneself why it was Marx himself who cultivated such a heroic aura, giving himself up to the fortune of posterity by means of such a self-representation. The image of himself to which Marx was always faithful is precisely that of a person who has committed an absolute transgression, a person who has overturned the entire structure of western culture and who, as a result of this overturning, was able to propose the eschatology of communism.

---

10 I am thinking in particular above all, among the by-now vast wealth of critical literature about Hegel, of the deepening of *Hegelforschung* in Germany in the work of scholars such as Pöggeler, Henrich, Schüler, and Nicolin, linked to the activities of Bochum's *Hegel-Archiv*, the publications of the *Hegel-Studien* and Hegel's *Gesammelte Werke*, edited since 1989 by the *Nordrhein-Westfälische Akademie der Wissenschaften* and published by Meiner of Hamburg.

Marx saw himself essentially as re-establishing historical being in its most radical nature, making the material, rather than spirit, the principle and basis of reality. In this overturning, he executed the most classic parricide of which a young German intellectual in the first half of the nineteenth century could ever think; in other words, the parricide of Hegel, who with his thought in the Germany of that period did not represent simply a philosophy, but rather philosophy as such. Marx always remained tied to this archetype of the pure revolutionary without residues (in the sense of he who enacts radical changes without any form of mediation). By so doing, he fell into a profound self-misinterpretation of his own theoretical work even when his thought, above all with his mature criticism of political economy, took paths different from that of the overturning of one thing into its opposite, constructing a theoretical system mediated to a much greater extent by the great European cultural traditions at both the philosophical-epistemological and historical-economic levels. It often happens that the great spirits who inaugurate and explore new lands and who throw up bridges between the past and the future become aware of and possess the new territories in accordance with types and forms of thinking that belong to the world which, in reality, they have already abandoned. Thus, to use a significant example, all Freud's work laboured under the burden of the self-misunderstanding of claiming to legitimise the new human relationships revealed by the clinical study and theories of psychoanalysis according to the classic deterministic-quantitative model of natural science.[11] In a similar way, in my opinion, all Marx's work is tarred by the self-misunderstanding of an author wanting to legitimise his thoughts and, in particular, his fundamental discovery of the social unconscious of an accumulation of abstract wealth and of an impersonal principle of modern society, based on an absolute overturning and the primacy of sensuous and material praxis over that which is spiritual and intelligible.

However, the fact is that the young Marx, like many of his contemporaries, in a crucial period of his formation found in Hegel's philosophy the absolutely best theoretical system for thinking the world. This occurred to such an extent that it was virtually inevitable that, following his youth, the achievement of theoretical autonomy occurred under the banner of a rejection and metaphorical murdering of such a dominant and imposing authority. In other words, it was a drastic and resolute parricide.

This, therefore, is the subject of this book: the conceptual and psychological themes of the overturning that the young Marx enacted with regard to Hegel,

---

11 On the subject of Freud's self-misinterpretation, see Habermas 1987. See also Finelli 1998.

but also with regard to himself and his previous, very strong, identification with that philosopher. The capacity and fertility of early theoretical Marxism cannot but measure the level of truth of its conceptual co-ordinates not only on a level of logical consistency, but also on that of its psychological consistency; that is, in terms of Marx's mastery of the motivations and the methods with which he presumed to enact that murder of the father and his idealistic sophistries. Anticipating the outcome of this research and revisiting what has already been said previously in relation to the circle of beginning and result, my hypothesis is that all the theoretical works of the young Marx are essentially involved in a failed parricide or, in other words, in a negation of Hegel. Its violence and radical nature expresses, both on a psychological level and on that of theoretical concepts, rather than a genuine overcoming, the reconfirmation of Marx's subalternity and Hegel's dominance. The negation was so sudden and immediate that it could not but be considered as an overturning which did not modify the substance of its constitutive principles on a theoretical level. The more mature and more responsible Marx appeared only later, when the bitter defeats suffered in life and in history forced him into the work of mourning, into a burdensome toil of solitude and theoretical refinement that brought him, amongst other things, to a more serene and meditated distance from Hegel.[12] The liberation of the more original part of his mind could only take place with the initiation and consolidation of this distancing, albeit in a manner that remained contentious up to the bitter end, given that, even in Marx's mature work, the presence and function of the stereotypes of his youthful work continue to exist, divided and contradictory, regressive and deforming.

The moment has now arrived to enter, *in medias res*, into a philosophical consideration of the profound nature of the identification of Marx, as a young student, with Hegel and his concept of the Idea.

## 3 The 'Idea' as an Organising Principle of Reality. Marx's Anti-Materialism

The story is well known. At the age of 17, in the autumn of 1835, Karl Marx matriculated at the University of Bonn to study law, but on 22 October 1836 he had already transferred to the University of Berlin where, with his father's

12 In relation to the maturity of Marx's thought, see Finelli 1987, 1989, 1996b and Bellofiore and Finelli 1998.

permission, he continued his studies. The early engagement to Jenny von Westphalen, who lived in Trier, Marx's home town close to Bonn, and the somewhat disorderly life led by the young Karl in his first year of study, perhaps encouraged his father, Heinrich, not to oppose his son's desire to transfer to the political and cultural capital of Germany at the time, thus creating a degree of distance between the young student and the frivolities of the Rhineland. Marx remained for five years in the more serious Berlin where, over nine semesters, despite studying intensely, he only attended eleven courses, mainly concerned with legal subjects.[13] After giving up law for political journalism, he graduated on 15 April 1841 at the age of 24 in the more modest University of Jena, without attending the discussion of his thesis entitled *The Difference Between the Democritean and Epicurean Philosophy of Nature*.

This dissertation, together with its seven Berlin notebooks of preparatory work compiled by Marx between 1839 and 1840, as well as the eight Berlin notebooks of *Excerpta*, are significant for the purposes of this study for two basic reasons. First, they throw light on the work method that Marx adopted for the rest of his life; and second, they are the only and therefore invaluable evidence of the great theoretical depth of Marx's early Hegelianism. Negated and repressed for the practical and propagandistic reasons of the political battle, these themes only re-emerged 25 years later with the drafting of the *Grundrisse* and *Capital*. The importance of these first writings by Marx justifies the relatively extended consideration that I will give to them.

*The Difference Between the Democritean and Epicurean Philosophy of Nature*, of which there remains a copy of the manuscript written by another hand but reviewed by Marx with corrections and additions, is evidence of the young student's good command of Greek and Latin. He prepared his dissertation by means of a vast and humble work of translation and extracts. He used faithful and more or less extensive quotations from the texts he had read and to which he often added personal reflections as comments. The seven preparatory notebooks (the so-called *Vorarbeiten*) contain texts on the Democritean and Epicurean philosophies by Diogenes Laertius, Sextus Empiricus, Plutarch,

13 The certificate from the University of Berlin, needed by Marx to take his degree at Jena, certifies that he had completed the following courses. Winter Semester 1836/37: Pandects (Savigny), Criminal Law (Gans), Anthropology (Steffens); Summer Semester 1837: Ecclesiastical law, Civil Procedure (Heffter), Prussian Civil Procedure (Heffter); Winter Semester 1837/38: Criminal Procedure (Heffter); Summer Semester 1838: Logic (Gabler), General Geography (Ritter), Prussian Civil law (Gans); Winter Semester 1838/39: Inheritance Law (Rudorff); Summer Semester 1839: Isaiah (Bauer); Winter Semester 1839/40 and Summer Semester 1840: no courses attended; Winter Semester 1840/41: Euripides (Geppert).

Lucretius, Seneca, Stobaeus, Clement of Alexandria and Cicero, as well as summary tables of Hegel's philosophy of nature contained in the *Encyclopaedia of Philosophical Sciences*. The eight *Excerpta* notebooks, dated Berlin 1840 and Berlin 1841, contain translations of book I (chapters 1 and 2) and the whole of book III of Aristotle's *De Anima*, as well as references to Leibniz,[14] Hume's *A Treatise of Human Nature*, Spinoza's *Tractatus theologico-politicus* and *Letters* and Karl Rosenkranz's *Geschichte der Kant'schen Philosophie*. Furthermore, many more authors both ancient and modern are quoted, sometimes only once in both the notebooks and the dissertation. These include ancient and medieval commentators on Aristotle such as Thomas Aquinas, John Philoponus, Themistocles, and Simplicius, as well as modern historians of philosophy such as Pierre Bayle, Heinrich Ritter and Johann Schaubach. All this demonstrates the breadth of Marx's reading, the patience and philological scrupulousness with which he undertook his studies, equipped with the virtue of compilation typical of a good German student of the time and already demonstrating a surprising speed and intelligence in his reading.[15]

But what is now of interest is above all the extent to which Marx explicitly uses the Hegelian theory of philosophical science in his dissertation, organising his thought in accordance with four, basic epistemological-ontological principles that will reappear in an explicit and systematic way only in the logic that underlies the drafting of *Capital*. These four principles claim that:

---

14 Marx made extracts from Vol. II of Leibniz's *Opera omnia* in the edition of Dutens, apud Frates de Tournes, Genevae 1628, 6 volumes. He also reads Leibniz's *Meditationes de cognitione, veritate et ideis, De primae philosophiae emendatione et de notione substantiae, Principia philosophiae, Principes de la Nature et de la grace fondés en Raison*.

15 Marx's mother sent Karl money for his 'promotion' to the title of Doctor on 22 October 1838 (see *MEGA*, III, 1, p. 334). Between the end of 1838 and the start of 1839, Marx began to study Epicurean philosophy, of which there are seven remaining *Hefte* (notebooks). The comparison with Democritean philosophy is fairly marginal, almost non-existent in these notebooks. This leads us to assume that Marx's original plan to dedicate his studies to Epicureanism as part of a broader investigation into all the post-Aristotelian philosophies was gradually modified due to the possibility of obtaining a lectureship in Bonn with the assistance of Bruno Bauer, using the material previously collected for a briefer and more rapidly written text. The quotations contained in the Dissertation from the writings of Lucretius, Plutarch, Seneca, Sextus Empiricus and Clement of Alexander are the same as those present in the notebooks. The quotations from Aristotle and his commentators, Semplicius, Themistocles and Philoponus, as well as those concerning Eusebius and that taken from the *De placitis philosophorum*, are different.

1) Science is conceivable only as the 'realisation of the principle itself',[16] or, in other words, in accordance with Hegelian terminology, as the circle of continuity between the beginning and the result. That which is the beginning of something true, in order for it not to remain only a subjective and mental hypothesis, an abstract idea, must demonstrate that it is capable of generating, beginning with itself, the articulation and multiplicity of the various levels of reality. If must, therefore, be able to unify what is real, producing thereby the various figures and demonstrating the internal thread that supports and assigns to them a systematic form. The alternative is merely empiricism that collects the data of the experience without really unifying it. The hypotheses it puts forward are reduced to mere abstract unifications that the individual subject wishes to impose on reality from outside its own reflection.
2) It follows that reality consists not only of material determinations, those that are empirical and able to be experienced by the senses, but also and more importantly, of ideal determinations or more precisely, according to Marx's terminology, of 'formal determinations' that structure and unify empirical reality precisely because they are not visible and perceivable within it, as would be the case if they were determinate and particular segments of it.
3) Standing between material determination [*materielle Bestimmung*] and formal determination [*formelle Bestimmung*] is heterogeneity. The former belongs to the ambit of particular and finite things, the second to that of a totalising principle of connections and syntheses, a systematic principle of universalisation. Such heterogeneity passes into contradiction when a determinate and finite figure of the first ambit claims to embody and exhaust in its limits the quality and universal extension of the second. Contradiction, therefore, here means that the idea, in its totalising universality, cannot be confined by the limits of the material and its figures. As a consequence, when this occurs or when the finite claims to present itself in its particular nature as a universal and absolute, it cannot help but come into conflict with itself and, therefore, negate and sublate itself. The idea is, therefore, the non-material but objective principle of reality that binds and connects the multiple by means of the negation and sublation of all the inadequate and partial figures of it that claim to realise and to exhaust it.
4) The ontological centrality of *Formbestimmung* – or, in other words, its ability, through its ideal nature, to organise and structure reality – imposes on

16 *MECW* 1, p. 58. On the drafting of Marx's Dissertation and the state of the manuscript in handwriting different from Marx's, see *MECW* 1, p. 735. See also Marx 1983.

the level of knowledge the distinction between objective appearance [*objektive Erscheinung*] and subjective semblance [*subjektiver Schein*], between the shaping of the *sensible* world whose surface refers to appearance and making visible an objective principle of reality that is neither sensible nor visible, and a taking form of the world that depends, instead, on mere subjective opinion, which stops at its perception of the content and the more immediate facts of its own sensibility.

These four principles, as a whole, constitute the keystone of Marx's early thought and, since all four are philosophemes of unquestionable Hegelian origin and conception,[17] they demonstrate just how deeply the young student in Berlin adhered to Hegel's idealism.

Furthermore, given the impossibility of basing science on empirical and material elements, Marx, throughout all his works and despite what is generally thought about him, was never a materialist thinker precisely because materiality and thought, as evidenced by these first important Marxian manuscripts, are expressions that are entirely opposed and incompatible. To think effectively means, in the pages of the *Vorarbeiten* and the dissertation, to refute every pos-

17 The significance of the 'formal' in Hegel, as often occurs to this term in philosophical use, is polysemous. As well as being synonymous with exterior and superficial, or in other words, that which is produced by the abstract and non-concrete activity of the intellect, it refers to the more precise and Hegelian meaning of 'form', as that which expands and exceeds the self-imposed limit of determinate and material being. The form is that which identifies the determinate but, at the same time, reflects and relates it to something else. As such, it is that which opens to being otherwise, that which declares its non-autonomous subsistence and its relationship to the other than itself. In this sense, 'form' means for Hegel that which does not permit the coincidence of something with itself but, on the contrary, forces it to shun itself and opens it up to a relationship with what is beyond it. It designates the way in which negation works and takes shape in the horizon of determinate reality, having left behind it the indeterminacy in which, like absolute Nothing, it operated in the first triad (Being-Nothing-Becoming). 'The negation – no longer as the abstract nothing but as a determinate being and a something – is only form for this something. It is being something else. The quality, because this being something else is its actual determination but is distinct before it. It is the being for an other – an expansion of the determinate being, of the something' (Hegel 1975a, p. 48; § 91, translation modified). Thus, while ancient Greek philosophy saw form, as *morphé* or *eidos*, as the greatest function of identity, because it is what circumscribes any particular thing and assigns it consistency in the autonomy of its limit, in Hegelian philosophy, very probably through the mediation of Leibniz and Kant, the dynamic function of form assumes importance because it resolves the determinate in something that is ulterior to itself.

sible materialism and empiricism; or, in other words, to reject every perspective that begins from facts and particular determinations to proceed then by means of associations and comparisons to generalisations that are inevitably exterior to the initial assumptions. To think means, on the contrary, to conceptualise and universalise facts, unifying them by means of an immanent vector of reality which, in its being ulterior to the given material, is, therefore, always concept or idea. In this sense, Marx, from the very outset, is – and will be whatever the identity he assigns to the principle of the real – an idealistic thinker. I mean this in the sense that he belongs to the theoretical tradition of the valorisation of ideality that connects such profoundly different, pure philosophies such as those of Plato or Spinoza or Kant or Hegel, who, whatever their differences, agree that perception and consciousness of the real is impossible without the unified or synthetic action of an idea as an integrating principle that cannot be reduced to the segments of reality that it unifies and informs. Otherwise, due to the absence of this ideal or transcendental principle, the very existence of reality is rendered inconceivable, as inevitably occurs to any empirical formulation that claims to resolve reality into a succession of atomistic and punctual elements which, without a true unity immanent and objective to them, remain entirely external to each other.[18] Obviously, what distinguishes Marx from the other philosophers of ideality and what, in turn, in Marx's own journey, distinguishes the various phases of his thought, are the very different methods used to identify this principle of synthesis and integration.

---

18 In relation to Marx's idealism in the doctoral dissertation, even the words of the dedication that Marx addresses to Baron Ludwig von Westphalen, an elderly functionary of the provincial Prussian government, who was the half-German and half-Scottish father of Jenny, are significant. For the young Marx, he was a figure of fundamental cultural reference and of education as a free spirit. 'May everyone who doubts of the Idea be so fortunate as I, to be able to admire an old man who has the strength of youth, who greets every forward step of the times with the enthusiasm and the prudence of truth and who, with that profoundly convincing sunbright idealism which alone knows the true word at whose call all the spirits of the world appear, never recoiled before the deep shadows of retrograde ghosts, before the often dark clouds of the times, but rather with godly energy and manly confident gaze saw through all veils the empyreum which burns at the heart of the world. You, my fatherly friend, were always a living *argumentum ad oculos* to me, that idealism is no figment of the imagination, but a truth' (*MECW* 1, p. 28). On the character of J.L. von Westphalen and his cultural and political openness, see Monz, von Krosigk and Eckert 1973, and, in particular, the letter of 7 April 1831 sent by von Westphalen to F. Perthes in Gotha (pp. 13–19). The father of von Westphalen had been the head of the armed forces during the Seven Years War, while his mother, the Scottish Anne Wishart, descended from the counts of Argyll, a family with a considerable role in Scottish history.

However, let us return to the young Marx's doctoral dissertation and ask ourselves what the deepest motivations are in its composition, over and above the conclusion of a young philosopher's university studies and plans for future employment.

## 4 Democritus and Epicurus: The Empiricism of the Sciences and the Idealism of Philosophy

Why did the young Marx write a dissertation on ancient philosophy, choosing the subject of the comparison between the atomism of the fifth century BCE Democritus and that of the fourth century BCE Epicurus? The answers to this question may be multiple.

One may be that a thesis on ancient philosophy, given Marx's good classical education, could have provided the easiest solution for the conclusion of his troubled path of study. Another may have been because a 'young Hegelian' such as Bruno Bauer, with whom Marx had established an intense relationship during his Berlin period, had already valorised, in the wake of Hegel, Greek post-Aristotelian philosophy and Christianity itself as the cultural context within which, after the objectivism of the great systems of Plato and Aristotle, the meaning of the subject as an individual and a person were opened up. Yet another reason may have been that Epicurus's atheism was part of that radical critique of religion in which all the young Hegelians found the most unifying sense of their theoretical and civil commitment, over and above the compromises which, in their opinion, their master, Hegel, had made on the terrain of the connections between religion and philosophy.

These are all possible answers, which are partially credible; but the most profound reason lies in the fact that Marx used the ancient to think about and problematise the modern. He studied the post-systematic philosophies of classical Greece to meditate on the contemporary situation closest to himself.[19] In particular, it was used to reflect on the cultural-political experiences that he was personally undergoing, as a budding German intellectual caught in a force field between, on the one hand, the Hegelian system with its theory of

---

19 The dissertation on Greek atomism was part of a work that Marx wanted to write on post-Aristotelian philosophy in general. See the fragment written by Marx in which he says that 'The treatise that I herewith submit to the public is an old piece of work and was originally intended as part of a comprehensive exposition of Epicurean, Stoic, and Sceptic philosophy. At present, however, political and philosophical arrangements of an entirely different kind prevent me from bringing such a task to completion' (*MECW* 1, p. 106).

the concluded maturation of modern history within the developed framework of reason, and, on the other, the followers and continuers of Hegelian philosophy, with their need for further revolutions and rationalisations of reality, such as, for example, the *Junghegelianer* of the Berlin *Doktorclub* of which Marx quickly became an assiduous member with a not inconsiderable role.[20] Thus, Marx writes about the past in order to write about the present. In his opinion, what allows the association of post-Aristotleanism and post-Hegelianism, on a philosophical level, is precisely the fact that both were historical and theoretical times characterised by subjective self-valorisation. The dissertation, in its entirety, is an intense reflection on the value of individuality and on its capacity, or lack thereof, to move and transform reality. The outcome to this problematic is resolved, for the graduating Marx, in the conclusion, which is also of Hegelian inspiration: namely, the claim that the forces of individual conscience are entirely insufficient for grasping and shaping the forces of reality.

After the famous letter to his father of 1837 and the self-criticism of his first romantic identity (to which I will refer later on), the dissertation, the *Vorarbeiten* and the Berlin *Excerpta* therefore constitute the most explicit document of the young Marx's rejection of a supposed capacity attributed to the individual subject to confront reality. Nonetheless, it should be noted that this very claim on Marx's part of a non-individualistic idealism, capable of effectively tapping into the complexity of the real, at the same time expresses a not unconditional adhesion to Hegel, at least insofar as Hegel's idealism already appeared to the early Marx to tend towards an unequivocal, speculative and contemplative polarity marked, due to its excess of theoreticity, by the absence of a practical and transformative dimension that – for the young man from Trier, at least – cannot but be present in a principle of totality.

What the dissertation and the *Vorarbeiten* present in the framework of the ancient is the dilemma of how to continue the anti-individualist dimension of Hegelian idealism while subtracting it from the theoretical asymmetry that risks deforming the objectivity of the Idea into the abstract and separate character of an Idea that is far from the world of actions. This would appear to be

20 The small Hipper café in Berlin on Französische Strasse was the meeting point of young Hegelians such as Bruno Bauer, Carl Friedrich Köppen and Adolf Rutenberg, who had founded the *Doktorclub* in 1837. The letters sent to Marx between 1839 and 1841 by Bauer and Köppen give an account of the role played in the group by the young man from Trier. See Bauer's letters (11 December 1839 and 31 March 1841) and Köppen's (3 June 1841) in, respectively, *MEGA*, III, 1, pp. 335–51, 360–3.

for Marx the most relevant characteristic of the whole of Greek philosophy, the development of which, from the pre-Socratic to the post-Aristotelians, followed the various identities that the figure of the scholar, the *sophòs*, took on in turn with respect to the community of which they were part. This establishes a relationship between the intellectual and the community, a relationship that, for the young Marx in Berlin studying antiquity, contains insufficient mediation throughout the entire development of Greek philosophy. It is understood as an indicative expression of a knowledge that, by remaining apart from the lives of the majority, is unable to become praxis and a collective habit of life.

But let us take one problem at a time. Let us primarily consider what the four theoretical points are by means of which Marx valorises, in terms of a theory of physics, idealism and Epicurean philosophy over empiricism and Democritus's positive knowledge.

a) Democritus is not a thinker in the most rigorous sense of the expression. He is only a materialist and an empiricist. For him, the atom is only a material principle from which it is impossible to deduce and develop the reality of the world as it materially appears to our eyes: 'Sensuous appearance, on the one hand, does not belong to the atoms themselves. It is not objective appearance [*objektive Erscheinung*], but subjective semblance [*subjektiver Schein*]. "The true principles are the atoms and the void, everything else is opinion, semblance"'.[21] Democritus does not posit any continuity between the atom and the world that appears to the senses, because a materialistic principle posits outside itself, outside its materiality, all the other sensible entities and phenomena. A merely material principle is passive, it cannot generate, by its own volition, the concreteness and polymorphous nature of the world; as such, it remains only an abstract hypothesis, a merely intellectual and not concretely real principle of universality. If anything, because it derives from a reflection that is only exterior to the sensible multiplicity, it presupposes the latter rather than founding and explaining it. 'For Democritus [...] the atom is only the general objective expression of the empirical investigation of nature as a whole. Hence the atom remains for him a pure and abstract category, a hypothesis, the result of experience, not its active [*energisches*] principle. This hypothesis remains therefore without realisation, just as it plays no further part in determining the real investigation of nature'.[22]

21 *MECW* 1, p. 39. The quote contained in Marx's passage is taken from Diogenes Laertius, *De clarorum philosophorum vitis*, IX, 43–4.

22 *MECW* 1, p. 73.

Epicurus, on the other hand, is a proper philosopher because he sees the atom as an *arché*, a non-material principle from whose actions he necessarily deduces the forms and happenings of the world of phenomena. 'For Democritus the atom means only *stoichèion*, a material substrate. The distinction between the atom as *arché* and *stoichèion*, as principle and as foundation, belongs to Epicurus'.[23]

b) Epicurus constructs a science, in contrast to Democritus, because he conceives of a system of the real in the light of the contradiction between essence and existence or, in other words, between formal determination or universal determination and particular determination or material determination. The real is such, therefore, only insofar as it is the realisation of a principle that contradicts every determinate and partial realisation of itself. 'Epicurus objectifies the contradiction in the concept of the atom between essence and existence. He thus gave us the science of atomistics. In Democritus, on the other hand, there is no realisation of the principle itself. He only maintains the material side and offers hypotheses for the benefit of empirical observation'.[24]

c) The atom, considered conceptually and not materialistically, signifies pure individualism – which is the negation of any relativity, of every possible relationship with another existence. The consequent realisation of this principle occurs in Epicurus's physics, which is distinct from the atomism of Democritus due, above all, to its theory of *clinamen*. The deviation or declination of the atom from the straight line is the realisation of the formal determination of the atom, which is synonymous with pure individuality. The atom, its vertical fall though the void due to its weight and the deviation from the straight line of its fall are the material and sensible stages by means of which the principle of pure individuality gives life and form to the world. The atom, as an abstract individuality, is entirely autonomous from any relationship with anything other than itself. The line of its fall removes autonomy and self-reference from the atom:

'Every body, insofar as we are concerned with the motion of falling, is therefore nothing but a moving point, and indeed a point without independence, which in a certain mode of being – the straight line which it describes – surrenders its individuality [*Einzelheit*]'.[25] However, if the line in its extension suppresses the autonomy of the atom as a point, the movement of the clinamen,

23 *MECW* 1, p. 61.

24 *MECW* 1, p. 58.

25 *MECW* 1, p. 48.

with its deviation, in turn opposes the fall in a straight line and re-establishes the independence of the atom from every external force and influence. 'But the relative existence which confronts the atom, the mode of being which it has to negate, is the straight line. The immediate negation of this motion is another motion, which, therefore, spatially conceived, is the declination from the straight line'.[26] The Epicurean theory of the declination of atoms is, therefore, the consequent realisation of the concept of the atom. The atom is, on principle, defined as an absolutely autonomous singularity. In order to posit the existence in reality of its essence, it must render itself autonomous from every possible relationship, denying every possible link with alterity.

Furthermore, in a world made only of atoms and voids, the otherness of the atom can only be another atom or, within the perspective of egoistic individuality, the other can only be an *alter ego*. For this reason, the deviation from the parallelism of the vertical straight lines becomes repulsion, a clash between the atoms and thus their combination on the basis of their strength, size and weight. The reciprocal repulsion of atoms, as a consequence of their deviation from the straight line, is the even more consistent realisation of their presupposed autonomy: the even more explicit organisation of the material world on the basis of the non-material principle of absolute individuality.

> In it [the declination] is expressed the atom's negation of all motion and relation by which it is determined as a particular mode of being by another being. This is represented in such a way that the atom abstracts from the opposing being and withdraws itself from it. But what is contained herein, namely, its negation of all relation to something else, must be realised, positively established. This can only be done if the being to which it relates itself is none other than itself, hence equally an atom, and, since it itself is directly determined, many atoms. The repulsion of the many atoms is therefore the necessary realisation of the *lex atomi*, as Lucretius calls the declination.[27]

d) Epicurus's theoretical strength as a thinker is, therefore, that of conceiving of reality as the system of a principle that posits itself. But the strength for the universalisation of this principle, of abstract individuality, is insufficient, according to Marx, to carry out this realisation. The self-referential singularity has no need, on principle, for mediation with otherness in order to define itself,

26 *MECW* 1, p. 49.
27 *MECW* 1, p. 51.

while universalisation is synonymous with mediation and consubstantiality with otherness. Marx concludes that: 'the domain of the atom is immediacy'.[28] Thus, it is a still too naturalistic and materialistic sphere in which the conclusivity of each body in its own individual and autonomous figure prevails over the relationship and mediation with otherness. In such a perspective of immediate identity, even opposition cannot be other than immediate – the repulsing elimination that does not seek any point of contact and relationship with what it rejects.

## 5 Humanity as the Negation of Nature

Not only Epicurus's physical doctrine but also his entire philosophy represents, according to Marx's dissertation, the coherent application of the principle of a subjectivity that constructs its identity on the basis of separateness and abstraction. Even morals and religion – the former with the theory of virtue as an absence of physical pain that eliminates the troubling of the soul, the latter with the doctrine of the gods as beatific and heedless of human beings and the world – realise within their specific fields a principle of subjectivity that claims to be absolutely autonomous.

> The purpose of action is to be found therefore in abstracting, swerving away from pain and confusion, in ataraxy. Hence the good is the flight from evil, pleasure the swerving away from suffering. Finally, where abstract individuality appears in its highest freedom and independence, in its totality, there it follows that the being which is swerved away from, is all being; for this reason, the gods swerve away from the world, do not bother with it and live outside it.[29]

Even more Hegelian than Hegel, the young Marx uses in his thinking nothing other than Hegelian categories. At the same time, however, he assigns to the work of Epicurus a systematic nature, beginning with the principle of atomistic individuality, that is even more stringent and cohesive than that applied by Hegel in his *Lectures on the History of Philosophy*.[30]

---

28 *MECW* 1, p. 49.

29 *MECW* 1, p. 51.

30 On the presence of Hegel's lectures in Marx's doctoral dissertation, see the careful analysis in Cingoli 2001.

Other reflections are thus added, in particular, on the human subjectivity-nature connection that will be of fundamental importance for the understanding of Marx's other youthful writings and their presumed materialism. Singularity, or 'self-consciousness', as Marx also calls it,[31] can universalise itself only through abstraction, through separating itself from every otherness that can influence and determine it. A truly real and not just a fleeting relationship with otherness, however, can be guaranteed only by a capacity for penetration and tolerance, which are inherent to the universalising strength of knowledge and the idea.

> As a matter of fact, abstract individuality can make its concept, its formal determination, the pure being-for-itself, the independence from immediate being, the negation of all relativity, effective only by abstracting from the being that confronts it; for in order truly to overcome it, abstract individuality had to idealise it, and only universality can do this.[32]

It is for this reason that singularity, closed as it is within its presumed self-sufficiency, enters into a relationship with another outside itself, even if only to reject it. Nonetheless, it does this only with respect to another that is entirely equal to itself, confirming thereby, by means of a repulsing identification, its identity. However, this absolute non-dependence on the other requires that abstract objectivity also cannot depend on that internal otherness that

31 However, it is Hegel who, as is known, in his *Lectures on the History of Philosophy*, defined post-Aristotelian philosophies as the philosophies of self-consciousness. Stoicism, Epicureanism and Scepticism belong to an age in which the organic unity of the Greek culture of the polis and the great philosophical systems broke down. Thus, individuality removed from mediation with universality withdraws and is reflected solely in itself. 'Therefore, for all these philosophies, the principle is the pure reference of self-consciousness to itself since it is only satisfied by this idea […]. Since the principle of this philosophy is not objective but dogmatic and is based on the impulse of self-consciousness to satisfy itself, it follows that it is the subject that must provide it. The subject searches for a principle of its own freedom by itself, of its own imperturbability'. Born in Greece, these constitute the philosophies of the Roman world and became increasingly abstract and separate from the political universe. 'The living individualities of the geniuses of the peoples have been compressed and killed in their intimate natures; an extraneous power hangs over the individual, an abstract universality. In this lacerated state arose the need to retreat to this abstraction as in the thought of an existing subject, to this interior freedom of the subject as such' (Hegel 1995a, vol. 2, p. 230 et sqq., translation modified).

32 *MECW* 1, p. 50, translation modified.

corresponds to its natural determination. The human being thus acquires, for Marx, the first consciousness of itself, attaining to self-consciousness only by denying itself as a natural existence.

Nature is, for Hegel, the space of maximum exteriority of the spiritual subject with respect to itself and, consequently, it is the place of its greatest dependence on what does not appear to be born of its own will. Marx, here again, faithfully takes on board the Hegelian lesson. Material needs and natural desires keep the human being from its most genuine humanity, so that it is only by freeing itself from its natural neediness that it can begin to posit its identity in relation to other human beings, even if this is, initially, only in the most elementary manner of confrontation:

> the singularity existing in an immediate way is realised conceptually, inasmuch as it relates to something else which actually is itself, even when the other thing confronts it in the form of immediate existence. Thus man ceases to be a product of nature only when the other to which he relates himself is not a different existence but is itself an individual human being, even if not yet the spirit [*Geist*] of a man. But in order for man, as such, to become the only real object in itself, it must have broken the relative existence within it, the strength of its desires and mere nature. Repulsion is the first form of self-consciousness, it corresponds therefore to that self-consciousness which conceives itself as immediate-being, as abstractly individual.[33]

The human being, in other words, becomes aware of itself as such only when it escapes nature and takes on, as a constituent element of its identity, not physical needs but the relationship, even if initially only one of opposition, with another human being.

This is what Epicurus, a genuine philosopher, appreciated. He translated the principle of self-consciousness into the metaphor of the atom and thereby spiritualised the atom, removing the heavily naturalistic identity in which the immediate and anything but metaphorical materialism of Democritus had constrained it. For this reason, in Epicurus's physics, if every natural connotation that fixes the atom at a determinate size, form and weight is established and affirmed, on the one hand, it is denied and negated, because it contradicts, as a material determination, its most intrinsic formal determination, on the other. The latter, the pure concept of the atom, resolving itself

33 *MECW* 1, p. 52, translation modified.

into absolute self-reference, does not tolerate qualitative determinations that, in contrast, are created only from the relationship and confrontation of itself with the other of itself and the need, therefore, to take into account the differentiated multiplicity of the atoms and, with these, the variations in the sensible world.

> Through its qualities the atom acquires an existence that contradicts its concept; it is posited as an alienated being different from its essence. It is this contradiction that mainly interests Epicurus. Hence, as soon as he posits a property and thus draws the consequence of the material nature of the atom, he counter-posits at the same time determinations that again negate this property in its own sphere and validate instead the concept of the atom. He therefore determines all properties in such a way that they contradict themselves. Democritus, on the other hand, nowhere considers the properties in relation to the atom itself, nor does he objectify the contradiction between concept and existence that is inherent in them. His whole interest lies rather in representing the qualities in relation to concrete nature, which is to be formed out of them. To him they are merely hypotheses to explain the plurality that makes its appearance. It follows that the concept of the atom has nothing to do with them.[34]

## 6 Contradictions and Meteors

By means of such an idealistic interpretation of Epicurus's philosophy – idealistic also in the peculiar sense that the principles of material reality, like the atoms, are nothing more than projections of the manner in which man represents and conceives of himself (representing himself here as individual self-consciousness) – the young Marx ultimately clarifies the sense of what he means in these pages by contradiction. Once again, he refers, as will be seen forthwith, to the original sense in which this classical term in the history of philosophy is used in Hegel's works, alongside the traditional sense. Contradiction means, for this Marx, that a principle, an essence, of universal character – in other words, of such a nature that its breadth embraces and structures a systematic totality of entities – is represented as embodied and completely realised in an entity or in an existence that is particular and finite. As a consequence, this representation (as the constraining of a universal in a particular)

34 *MECW* 1, p. 54, translation modified.

is obliged, intrinsically and necessarily, to renounce, to negate itself, in order to give space to an existence and a realisation that is more consistent with the infinite one.

In the Aristotelian tradition, contradiction mainly concerns the ambit of the logical-communicative formulation of thought, according to which it is impossible to predicate and non-predicate the same attribute to the same subject in a judgement at the same time and according to the same point of view ('it is impossible that the same attribute, at one moment, belongs and does not belong to the same subject in the same respect').[35] In Marx's dissertation, contradiction, on the other hand, concerns the sphere of the visible and representable in the sense that it concerns the experience of a subject who claims and presumes to see and encapsulate the universal in a particular, to embody the infinite in a finite element. Thus, while for Aristotle contradiction means binding to the subject of a judgement a predicate that is both affirmed and contemporaneously denied, for the Marx of this period, under the influence of Hegel, contradiction means the establishment of a dialectical situation. The process takes place, first, by means of a dogmatic and reified representation or existential incarnation of the universal in a particular and, then, by overcoming that fallacious infinitisation of a finite element, in the need for a more adequate realisation consistent with the nature of a principle of totality.

The specific contradiction that Marx uses in the dissertation concerns the connection in the atom between form and matter or, in other words, between the spiritual and immaterial essence of the atom that expresses itself in its concept, and its material nature that is expressed in its sensible qualities and determinations. The most true and profound sense of this contradiction is that between the founding principle of abstract, individual self-consciousness and its concrete and sensible existence. Marx thus uses the metaphor of physical atomism to make explicit and criticise the contradictory fate of a subjectivity that claims to be unrelated and abstract: 'the atom is nothing but the natural form of abstract, individual self-consciousness'.[36] What is derived from reflecting on the contradiction inherent to the atom between its essence and existence is that the result of a subjectivity that claims to find the basis of its identity in nothing other than its own self-consciousness is the dramatic negation of itself, its own dissolution and the impossibility of coinciding with any kind of determinate and concrete figure of its existence. For the existence

35 Aristotle, *Metaphysics*, Γ 1005 b 19–20.

36 *MECW* 1, p. 65, translation modified.

of each individuality, in its concreteness, precisely in order to be determined, needs the relationship with the other, which is, however, entirely incompatible with the nature of absolute non-relativity and autonomy that is its principle. Size, form and weight are qualities that Epicurus attributes to the atom but which, at one and the same time, he removes because 'the abstract individuality is the abstract equal to itself'. In this absolute identification with itself, it cannot bear any determination that distinguishes it and relates it to the other. Here, the difference in philosophical depth between Democritus and Epicurus emerges once again, for while the former assigns differences of size and form to atoms in an extrinsic and empirical way, simply by a statement of facts, the latter establishes a profound connection between concrete determinations and their removal, and the absolutely, self-referential and individual essence of the atom itself.

On the basis of these fundamental arguments in his dissertation – that Epicurus had effectively philosophised about autonomous and abstract subjectivity by means of his treatment of the atom – Marx ultimately evaluates the coherence and peculiarity of the Epicurean doctrine of the meteor: namely, that part of Epicurus's philosophy which, as demonstrated by the *Letter to Pythocles*, contradicts what Aristotle and a large number of the Greek thinkers had argued regarding the nature of the sky and the celestial bodies. They were considered as eternal, immutable and perfect insofar as they were in their circular motion without a beginning, an end and any discontinuity. They were thus seen as consisting of a specific element – ether – that, unlike the other four elements of the material world, was not subject to the force of gravity. For Epicurus, on the other hand, the celestial bodies are explained in many ways [*pollachós*] and, therefore, according to a plurality of causes and explanations rather than in one way [*aplós*], or according to a single and objective model of truth. As Marx notes, for Epicurus the purpose of all knowledge and, therefore, also knowledge of celestial phenomena, consists in happiness and the avoidance of any disturbance. Therefore, in relation to this aim of ataraxy, it is natural that, for him, having placed the divine within human self-consciousness, the same divinity cannot be distanced and placed in the sky and in what is assumed to be the perfect and always identically the same nature of its phenomena. It is precisely the opposite that occurs – that is, the greatest disturbance of the soul – when men believe the celestial bodies to be beatific and indestructible entities, and then compare them with their own life on earth with such different characteristics. Therefore, to claim that, in contrast to the unambiguousness of physical science founded on atoms, the metaphysics of the celestial bodies does not allow for a single objective truth but rather a plurality of opinions – notes Marx in his firm intention of bringing back some consistency to

Epicurus's entire theoretical system – means nothing other than refuting the assumed autonomy of reality attributed by the majority to outer-worldly bodies. It makes their existence instead dependent upon the variety of meanings that the human eye confers on them. This theoretical transition, Marx emphasises, is 'the profoundest knowledge achieved by his system, its most thorough consistency'.[37]

If the idea of the eternal and immutable nature of the celestial bodies, due to the exceptionality of such characteristics when compared to the birth and death and human lives, disturbs the ataraxy of the human subject and its centre in self-consciousness – this being the single true principle of Epicurus's philosophy – it is entirely consistent to deny and refute the metaphysics and autonomy of the celestial bodies. This is also because, Marx claims (here providing us once again with unquestionable evidence of his Hegelianism), the celestial bodies, if truly eternal and immutable, would represent a true universal, in the Hegelian sense of the term or, in other words, the non-abstract, concrete singularity. For they would constitute the perfect fusion and mediation of material and ideal determination, that is, a nature not determined mechanistically by external causes but capable, spiritually, of self-determination. Marx comments that, in the celestial bodies,

> all antinomies between form and matter, between concept and existence, which constituted the development of the atom, are resolved; in them all required determinations are realised. The celestial bodies are eternal and unchangeable; they have their centre of gravity in, not outside, themselves. Their only action is motion, and, separated by the void of space, they swerve from the straight line, and form a system of repulsion and attraction while at the same time preserving their own autonomy and also, finally, generating time out of themselves as the form of their appearance. The celestial bodies are therefore the atoms become real. In them matter has brought individuality into itself.[38]

The atom would therefore here have a completed reality, to be incarnated finally in matter, without contradictions. This is why Epicurus's rebuttal of the presumed single and true nature of the celestial bodies is the clearest confirmation, for Marx, that the real principle at the centre of Epicurus's thought is only apparently the atom and the physical world built around atomism. In reality,

---

37 *MECW* 1, p. 71.

38 *MECW* 1, p. 70, translation modified.

beyond the metaphor of the atom, it is instead the singular and abstract self-consciousness of the human being.

What Epicurean atomism really studies is the question of the singularity that includes reality within the circle of its own thought and which, as a consequence, in relation to an abstract and immaterial universality of its own mind, is terrified of a universal that is really such or, in other words, of a principle of reality that embraces the whole of life in its circle, in both its spiritual and material dimension. Such a universal, still using the metaphorical language of the natural world, would find its symbols in the celestial bodies conceived according to the Aristotelian schema, in their perfect and intimate fusion of form and matter.

> But now, when matter has reconciled itself with the form and has become autonomous, individual self-consciousness throws down its mask and proclaims itself to be the true principle and opposes nature, which has become autonomous. [...] In the meteors, therefore, abstract-individual self-consciousness is met by its contradiction, shining in its materialised form, the universal which has become existence and nature. Hence it recognises in the meteors its deadly enemy, and it ascribes to them, as Epicurus does, all the anxiety and confusion of men. Indeed, the anxiety and dissolution of the abstract-individual is precisely the universal.[39]

The unconditional nature and freedom of the self-consciousness of the individual is the dominant theme in Epicurus, 'the greatest representative of Greek Enlightenment'. In order to be consistent with its absolute nature, this principle must deny any other principle that is transcendent and superior to human consciousness. Just as the gods, conceived as living in the *intermundi* without body or blood and entirely ignorant of and disinterested in human issues, must not condition the freedom of the human being in any way, so the physics of the celestial bodies in Epicurus is the most explicit confirmation that the centre of reality in his vision is the singularity that conceives of itself as universality, and thus does not tolerate any other place of autonomy outside itself.

39 *MECW* 1, pp. 71–2, translation modified.

## 7 Ancient Atomism between Hegel and Marx

If these are the essential lines that Marx follows in his interpretation of Epicurus in his dissertation, it is impossible not to ask how and why the discussion by the young student distinguishes itself from that of his master in Berlin, since he was evidently the source of his inspiration, as even a cursory examination of the treatment that Hegel dedicated to Epicurean philosophy in his *Lectures on the History of Philosophy* demonstrates. Marx's reading in fact is so different as effectively to overturn Hegel's interpretation. For Hegel's reconstruction of ancient philosophy, it is the figure of Democritus that is outlined with a depth and philosophical profundity that is not given to Epicurus – precisely the opposite of the connections that Marx established in his dissertation.

Nonetheless, all the speculative and conceptual – and, therefore, not physical-materialistic – determinations that Marx attributes to Epicurus in his comparison of the two Greek atomists are taken from the pages that Hegel dedicated to Leucippus and Democritus in his first volume of the *Lectures on the History of Philosophy*. For Hegel, these were the first atomists who investigated the natural and material world in accordance with non-material but conceptual and ideal fundamentals by means of principles such as atoms and the void.

> Leucippus and Democritus present more ideal principles, the atom and the void, and penetrate the objective with greater determination of thought, beginning, in this way, a metaphysics of bodies. Or, in other words, in them, pure concepts assume the meaning of corporality and, therefore, thought becomes objective form.[40]

The first atomists were genuine philosophers because they read the material world through the immaterial profoundity of essence and the concept, gaining for the history of humanity with the concept of the atom the logical-anthropological configuration of 'being one' and 'being for itself', figures of the maturation of a subjectivity that conquers its own self through the overcoming of all the alienations that had rendered it dependent on the other, outside itself. It is precisely in this sense – of a physical metaphor for a spiritual configuration – that the atom is not perceivable by the senses but is the expression of a purely intellectual-speculative reflection.

---

40 Hegel 1995a, vol. 1, p. 298, translation modified.

> Instead of being for itself, as a being, it is simply a relationship with itself but through the negation of its alienation from itself. When I say that I am for myself, I not only am but I also negate every other in me, I exclude it from me insofar as it appears as external. The being for oneself, as a negation of being another, which is the same negation in front of me, is the negation of the negation and is, therefore, an affirmation. I call this absolute negation which, although it contains mediation, it is a mediation that, at the same time, has been surpassed.[41]

The principle of one, therefore, corresponds to a fundamental, if not definitive, mode of the construction of subjectivity: that of the certainty of the self procured by means of a relationship of autonomy-opposition with others, a certainty that is the basis upon which the world of the subjective free will, of right and the law is built.

However, Epicurus is characterised in Hegel's lectures as a thinker who privileges the sensible, immediate dimension of experience much more intensely than that which is philosophical-speculative.

> Epicurus's philosophy is not the affirmation of a system of concepts but, on the contrary, as a system of representation, or even of sensitive existence which, looked at from the ordinary point of view as perceived by the senses, Epicurus has made the foundation and criterion of truth.[42]

Considering the practice of philosophy more from the perspective of gnoseology rather than from the theory of the atoms, Epicurus remains for Hegel closed within the world of the senses and the finite. If anything, with his theory that makes truth depend on sensation and with his concept of representation as the mere repetition and confirmation of sensations, he is a thinker who, through the reflection of thought, works against the force and profundity of that thought itself.

> This absence of thought is not itself without thought, but the use made of thought is to keep thought away; thought thus takes up a negative position in relation to itself. The philosophical activity of Epicurus that consists in the reconstruction and affirmation of the sensuous, removing it precisely from the concept that disturbs it.[43]

41 Hegel 1995a, vol. 1, p. 302, translation modified.
42 Hegel 1995a, vol. 2, p. 281, translation modified.
43 Hegel 1995a, vol. 2, p. 279, translation modified.

Nor does Epicurus make significant theoretical progress in relation to metaphysics or with respect to the genuine theory of atoms, where – here again fairly differently from what Marx attributes to Democritus and Epicurus – he does nothing more for Hegel than to re-propose the difficulties of the ancient atomists, such as the attribution to atoms of a difference by figure, size and weight that are entirely incompatible with their nature, which, due to their absolute simplicity, are wholly identical the one to the other. Thus, Epicurus also does not allow any steps to be taken past atomism in what is his fundamental theoretical aporia, that is, the immanent and non-intrinsic transition from the presupposition of the atoms, as metaphysical and ideal principles, to the construction of the concreteness of the sensible world.

> The chief thing is now to clarify the relationship of the atoms with sensuous phenomena, to make the essence pass into the negative [...]; however, at this point, Epicurus envelops himself in indeterminate expressions that say nothing. In fact, like the other physicists, he cannot offer anything but an unconscious mixture of abstract concepts and reality.[44]

Furthermore, since Hegel does not attribute any importance at all to the Epicurean theory of the clinamen as the deviation of the atom from the perpendicular line of fall, the only valorisation of Epicurus in Hegel's *Lectures* (which anticipates the much more positive reconstruction subsequently made by Marx) is the recognition of his enlightenment. With his theory of nature, of the gods as a place of beatitude indifferent to the human passions, and with his concept of morality as the pursuit of pleasure in quietness and in the absence of anything unpleasant, he profoundly contributed to the criticism of superstition and vulgar representations, particularly when Epicurianism was popularised by the Romans. But, even here, Hegel detects structural limitations that accompany the struggles of enlightenment and secularism for freedom. It certainly justifies the reasons of the material and finite world of the senses with respect to the supersensible stupidities of irrational credence, but without ever managing to rise above the finite horizon and mediate it with principles and values of greater significance for reality and spirituality:

> now, precisely in the not moving away from the field of the finite consists the so-called enlightenment. It searches for a connection to another finite, in conditions that are themselves conditioned [...]. On the other

44 Hegel 1995a, vol. 2, p. 289, translation modified.

> hand, in this same field, the concept is already something superior; but this more elevated manner of considering that we have found in previous philosophers is effectively eliminated by Epicurus who, together with superstition, also removes every connection in himself and the world of the ideal.[45]

The overturning of the relation between pre-Socratic and post-Aristotelian atomism that the young Marx undertakes in his dissertation therefore assumes even greater significance and theoretical dignity. Since this is an authentic overturning, Marx leaves substantially unaltered the interpretative categories of atomism, which he takes largely intact from Hegel. He limits himself to dislocating them in time, assigning to the *postea* that which Hegel had conceptualised in the *prius* (except for the more personal reflection, although, once again, this is none other than a Hegelian concept, that Marx makes on the Epicurean doctrine of the *clinamen*).

The reason for this theoretical operation – and, it should be added, for the interpretative exaggerations that are derived from a text that is already resolutely interpretative (in the context of the history of Greek philosophy) such as Hegel's *Lectures on the History of Philosophy*, though this does not take anything away from the intelligent originality and argumentative coherence of Marx's writings[46] – consists in the young Marx's need, after having given up any attempts at a legal career or academic position, to present the primal scene of his ethical-political present, albeit in a disguised form. The study of a post-systematic and post-classical philosophy such as that of Epicurus (in relation to the classical systems of Plato and Aristotle) enables him to attempt to think the connections and problems between the already classical philosophy of Hegel and the philosophical and political fate of Marx's own post-Hegelian present.

The intensification and dislocation of sense that Marx projects onto Epicurean atomism and its role as a metaphor for an era of theoretical and practical

---

45 Hegel 1995a, vol. 2, p. 298, translation modified.

46 When Lassalle sent his book on Heraclitus to him, Marx commented in 1857–8, in two letters to Lassalle, that he had written in his youth on Epicurus due to 'political' rather than 'philosophical reasons'. In a comparison with Lassalle's Heraclitus, Marx said that he had undertaken 'a similar work on a far easier philosopher, Epicurus – namely the portrayal of a complete system from fragments, a system which I am convinced, by the by, was – as with Heraclitus – only implicitly present in his work, not consciously as a system' (K. Marx to F. Lassalle, letters of 21 December 1857 and 31 May 1858, in *MECW* 40, respectively p. 226 and p. 316).

behaviour based on the autonomy and critical spirit of the individual subject, after an era of systematic and universal inspiration, fundamentally allows him (regardless of whether intentionally or consciously) to study the urgent issues of his time, cooling down emotionality by means of historical regression.

Nonetheless, the discussion of the young Marx as a theoretician and student of ancient philosophy is not yet complete. To conclude it, we must take a further step.

## 8 The Comparison of Idealisms. Ancient Idealism

Physics, theories of the heavens and religion, the doctrine of ataraxy and morality: according to Marx, Epicurus's entire philosophy systematically links to the principles of self-consciousness conceived of as individual subjectivity. Alongside this thesis, we must now consider two other of Marx's arguments, from the pages of the preparatory notebooks and one of the notes appended to the dissertation. These reveal two other theses that, intrinsically linked to the first, study in depth and expand the problematic to the point of encountering the heart of the cultural and political debate of modernity. These theses claim that:

1) Epicurus's philosophy, with its exaltation of the *sophós* [the sage or wise man] and his ataraxy, is not a partial and separate episode in the history of ancient thought but, rather, represents the epilogue, the consistent synthesis of the constituting principle of all Greek philosophy: the extraneousness, when not the opposition, of the moment of conscious reflection with respect to the unopposed value of objective and collective reality;
2) This extraneousness of objectivity from the subjective finds its resolution only in the development of modern thought whose highest outcome in Hegel's idealism assigns to philosophy the function of overcoming every opposition of subjectivity and consciousness, on the one hand, and of objectivity and the world, on the other.

Marx deals with the first point in a very dense page of history of philosophy found in the third of the preparatory notebooks. Its originality is expressed (again, with an implicit reference to the Hegelian interpretation of Hellenism) in the significance that the young student assigns to the figure of the *sophós*, synthesising the entire journey of Greek spirituality. 'Greek philosophy begins with seven wise men, among whom is the Ionian philosopher of nature Thales, and it ends with the attempt to portray the wise man conceptually. The beginning and the end, but no less the centre, the middle, is one *sophós*, namely

Socrates'.[47] Greek life is characterised – Marx writes, following Hegel's model – by 'free substance': by the belonging of each individual to a community in which all participate equally without this whole coming under the domination of a despot, as instead occurred in the empires and monarchies of the East. But this community, even if free, is still substantial and not spiritual, in the sense that the adherence of the individual to the community is still instinctive, unconditional and spontaneous. It therefore lacks the reflection on the self, the valorisation of individuality, which connotes modern subjectivity. This is why, Marx adds, the Greek community needs the sage: because, being still unable to acquire consciousness of itself in the singularity of each of its members, in contrast to modern communities it is obliged to devolve and singularise this function in the figure of the *sophós*. The sages, as individual personalities, are counterposed to the community, but their knowledge contains nothing other than the problems, the ways of living, the most fundamental and structuring dictates of the community itself. The sage is thus an individual in whom the community incarnates the consciousness of its own substance. The first sages and philosophers, from the Seven Sages to the Ionian naturalists, to the Pythagoreans and Eleatics, are all incarnations of the communitarian substance. They are only apparently individualities; in reality, they are the bearers and representatives of a truth and an objective behaviour that relates to the most genuine needs of a people seen in its entirety rather than according to the particular, arbitrary needs of each one. They represent the demands of a people's collective interests, its united and common spirit in contrast to a life lived by the same people according to only material and particular demands. The truth of which they are testimonies and symbols, beyond a merely naturalistic and utilitarian existence, is therefore an ideal truth. They are identified with this ideality without any residual elements, almost like statues of the Olympian gods, whose images express, beyond the earthly troubles of human beings and their material passions, harmonic inclusiveness within themselves and the coinciding of each of them with the universal, with the spirit of the whole.

> This embodiment of the ideal substance occurs in the philosophers themselves who herald it; not only is its expression plastically poetic, its reality is this person, whose reality is its own appearance; they themselves are living images, living works of art which the people sees rising out of itself in plastic greatness [...]. Hence these wise men are just as little like ordin-

---

47 *MECW* 1, p. 432.

> ary people as the statues of the Olympic gods; their motion is rest in self, their relation to the people is the same objectivity as their relation to substance.[48]

In the most ancient periods of Greek civilisation, the community therefore found in the sage the expression of its most authentic, intimate and unified nature, even if expressed through semi-mysterious and esoteric or even initially abstract and formal language. In its obscurity is expressed the slow emergence of a supra-individual essence and the overcoming of an elementarily naturalistic life-interest. With the exception of the Ionian philosophers of nature, the ancient *sophós* was generally also a legislator, an active leader of political life.

But, Marx notes, all the pre-Socratic philosophers, the Ionians, the Pythagoreans, the Eleatics, are substantial individuals: individuals who have escaped from nature and its coarse particularity and who have elevated themselves to the universal. However, in their archaic nature, they continue to conceive of the universal, the whole, in the manner of nature or, in other words, in the form of an objectivity that does not need and is not mediated by subjectivity and its reflective consciousness. As a passionate disciple of Hegel, Marx uses both meanings that Hegel gave to the concept of nature. Nature, in these pages, means both the objective, that which merely exists insofar as it is lacking in self-reflectiveness – in other words, matter without spirit – and also, as a consequence, the merely individualistic-utilitarian dimension of experience, insofar as it is the existent that immediately and blindly coincides with itself, without the consciousness of self that is such only if, at the same time, it is consciousness of otherness and the universal.

Archaic and pre-Socratic Hellenism is still closed within the horizon of the natural, both from the point of view of the materialism of the people's life and from that of the substance that opposes the sage to it. So much so that, here, spirit is still unable to establish itself, is still unable to damage and destroy (these expressions reveal the intense anti-materialism that characterises Marx's thought in the dissertation) nature's energy and the forces of life.

> If the first Greek wise men are the real spirit, the embodied knowledge of substance, if their utterances preserve just as much genuine intensity as substance itself, if, as substance is increasingly idealised, the bearers of its progress assert an ideal life in their particular reality in opposition to the reality of manifested substance, of the real life of the people, then the

48 *MECW* 1, p. 436.

> ideality itself is only in the form of substance. There is no undermining of the living powers; the most ideal men of this period, the Pythagoreans and the Eleatics, extol state life as real reason; their principles are objective, a power which is superior to themselves, which they herald in a semi-mystical fashion, in poetic enthusiasm; that is, in a form which raises natural energy to ideality and does not consume it, but processes it and leaves it intact in the determination of the natural.[49]

With the sophists and Socrates,[50] in contrast, it is abstractly individualised subjectivity, that which detaches itself from identification with the community and its norms and traditions, which represents the symbol and value of wisdom and knowledge. But, this too, in its distance from popular life, continues to be linked to the community, because it is only in this context that it can find the space where it can employ its criticism and intelligence.

> Not of the people, this subjectivity, confronting the substantial powers of the people, is yet of the people, that is, it confronts reality externally, is in practice entangled in it, and its existence is motion. These mobile vessels of development are the Sophists. Their innermost form, cleansed from the immediate dross of appearance, is Socrates, whom the Delphic oracle called the *sophòtatos* [the most wise].[51]

The purpose of acting and living in this subjective spirit is the achievement of virtue, of the good. However, this ideal result, due to the opposition of the sage to his own community, cannot but appear as an abstract universal, as a 'must'. The sage calls the entire living spirit of the people to the realisation of this universal by means of education and teaching (and, in particular, through the strengths of judgement and reasoning). Socrates's tragic death perfectly expresses all the aporetic nature of this type of sage who has his roots in the substantive, unfree community, which he wants to criticise freely according to the power of his reasoning.

> Finally, inasmuch as this individual pronounces the judgment of the concept on the world, he is in himself divided and judged; for while he has his roots for one part in the substantial, he owes his right to exist

49 Ibid.

50 On the significance of Socrates in these pages, see Cingoli 2001, pp. 110–32.

51 *MECW* 1, p. 437.

> only to the laws of the state to which he belongs, to its religion, in brief, to all the substantial conditions which appear to him as his own nature. On the other hand, he possesses in himself the purpose that is the judge of that substantiality. His own substantiality is therefore judged in this individual himself and thus he perishes precisely because he is born of the substantial, and not of the free spirit which endures and overcomes all contradictions and which need not recognise any natural conditions as such.[52]

That the universality of thought, represented by the type of sage like the sophists and Socrates, is an abstract universal is confirmed by Plato's philosophy where the world of ideas, distinct and in contrast to the real world, is precisely the projection and objectification on a metaphysical level of the philosopher's subjectivity. Rejecting the life of common experience, the philosopher wishes to subject it to an external and autonomous reign of ideas. But, in this way, knowledge, or philosophy, condemns itself to a incongruous doubling of reality – empirical reality on one side and the reality of the idea on the other – such as occurs in Plato's idealism according to Aristotle's criticism, here recalled by Marx. Ideality is not comprehended as the self-understanding and self-returning to unity of the real itself, but as the criterion and norm that, when confronted by it, constitute themselves as transcendent and coercive.

> The real will of the philosopher, the ideality active in him, is the real 'must' of the real world. Plato sees this his attitude to reality in such a way that an independent realm of ideas hovers over reality (and this 'beyond' is the philosopher's own subjectivity) and is obscurely reflected in it. […] The philosopher as such, that is, as the wise man, not as the motion of the real spirit in general, is therefore the truth-beyond of the substantial world facing him.[53]

If the division between the sage and the community is a constant in Greek culture, between the practices of life and forms of knowledge, then Epicurean philosophy, together with Stoic and Sceptic philosophy, turns out to be for Marx the most consistent conclusion of Greek culture, in its most extreme and radical form. Epicurus's philosophy expresses to the highest degree the condition of a subjectivity that wants to completely isolate itself from the

52 Ibid.

53 *MECW* 1, pp. 439–40.

community. It no longer even wants to make the community an object to be educated, but only the term of a negation. However, at the same time, it is isolated in the presumed self-sufficiency of its individuality and does not renounce turning its own separate and imperturbable image into the keystone of a systematic vision by means of which to re-think and re-design the entire structure of reality. For Marx, therefore, the Greek *sophós* embodies a meaning of idealism that does not refer to the clarification of the idea in the sense of movement and the immanent law that determines and synthesises, *ab intra*, the multiple of a totality. In other words, it does not refer to the meaning of real universalisation as the life that all the members of a community, consciously and intentionally, live not according to nature but according to the spiritual interests of the whole. Rather, it refers to the sense of a universal that lives only within the space of individual consciousness and, as such, cannot but crystallise itself in an abstract idea of the world.

In all this, Marx has undoubtedly followed the Hegelian interpretation of the Greek world as one in which the principle of the community, the principle of *ethos*, is the dominant motif in relation to singularity. At the same time, however, he has originally conjugated this motif according to the various relationships of belonging, critical relation and autarchic rejection – in other words, the forms in which the figure of the sage-philosopher presented himself to the community in the various eras of Greek culture. Marx has deduced, with implicit reference to his contemporaneity, an essential typology for the evaluation of what, a few years later, he will define as the 'critical intellectual'. The moralistic idealism of the latter is realised, due to the opposition of his knowledge to the world, in the presumed imposition of a rigid and intrinsic 'must' that is nothing more than the projection of the abstract and idealised way in which subjectivity conceives of and, at the same time, deforms itself. It is precisely this that Epicurean atomism has demonstrated, as a reflective metaphor at a profound level of conceptualisation of an individualistic anthropology deprived of relationality.

## 9 Modern Idealism

With respect to the second question – the value that the young Berlin student ascribes to modern idealism – what Marx highlights in both the preparatory notebooks and the dissertation is the quality and the breadth of the modern universal, a view that coincides with that of Hegel's. The universal in modern times, in contrast to that in antiquity, effectively avoids every incarnation and identification with a naturalistic content that could fix it in a limited and crystallised figure. Its special characteristic is that of being a spirit that becomes the principle of a truly universal relationship and synthesis precisely through its refusal to coincide with any material determination and in thereby overcoming nature as a condition and horizon of meaning of human life. Ancient philosophy, from Ionian philosophy to the Platonic doctrine of the idea, to Aristotle's theory of substance, to Epicurean atomism, always assigns its principles with an objectivist-naturalist configuration, far from the modern concept of freedom as a principle of universality this is not limited by anything in particular, be it nature, geographical space, community or determinate human peoples and races. Thus, while ancient idealism cannot, despite all its best efforts, conceive of a universal that is really such and, therefore, can only conclude and exhaust itself in a battle against nature and its necessarily limited and particular world of existences, modern idealism, rather than remaining in this state of contrast and opposition, resolves reality as a whole and, therefore, nature, in the textures of a universal that gathers together and integrates every detail in its immanent dynamic.

> The premise of the ancients is the act of nature, that of the moderns the act of the spirit. The struggle of the ancients could only end by the visible heaven, the substantial nexus of life, the force of gravity of political and religious life being shattered, for nature must be split in two for the spirit to be one in itself. The Greeks broke it up with the Hephaestan hammer of art, broke it up in their statues; the Roman plunged his sword into its heart and the peoples died, but modern philosophy unseals the word, lets it pass away in smoke in the holy fire of the spirit, and as fighter of the spirit fighting the spirit, not as a solitary apostate fallen from the gravity of Nature, it is universally active and melts the forms which prevent the universal from breaking forth.[54]

Ancient philosophy leads to the contradictions of a consciousness that wants to be ideal and other than reality but which, in this contrast, continues to find its own foundation in the opposite; in this contradicting of itself, it produces its own ruin. Modern philosophy, on the other hand, looks for a universal capable of effectively being such and of recognising in the real not the fixity and finite and unrelated determinations of naturalistic-material figures, but the vital dynamics of its own activity of relationship and synthesis.

---

54 *MECW* 1, p. 431.

> His [the sage's] own substantiality is therefore judged in this individual himself and thus he perishes precisely because he is born of the substantial, and not of the free spirit which endures and overcomes all contradictions and which need not recognise any natural conditions as such. The reason why Socrates is so important is that the relation of Greek philosophy to the Greek spirit, and therefore its inner limit, is expressed in him. It is self-evident how stupid was the comparison drawn in recent times between the relation of Hegelian philosophy to life and the case of Socrates, from which the justification for condemning the Hegelian philosophy was deduced. The specific failing of Greek philosophy is precisely that it stands related only to the substantial spirit; in our time both sides are spirit and both want to be acknowledged as such.[55]

Nonetheless, even modern philosophy that is capable of achieving the greatest freedom of the universal suffers a deficit of realisation, an insufficiency of reality. Even its universal, despite not being confined within the limits of ancient objectivism and naturalism, manifests in its mode of relating to the exterior all its difficulties and structural limits, in the moment in which, having completed its conceptual world, it turns towards the non-conceptual and non-philosophical world that lies outside it. Since this is the fate of philosophy as such, its 'overturning [*Umschlagen*]', as Marx calls it here, 'its transubstantiation into flesh and blood',[56] its becoming practical, either remains an idea or theoretical system, however articulated and complex but real only in the conclusion of thought, or it faces the world with the intent of transforming and bringing it round to its own reasoning, thereby translating its theoretical universal into a multiplicity of individual consciousnesses that criticise the world abstractly and externally. It is precisely on the nexus philosophy-world and on the overturning of theory into praxis that Marx makes some penetrating comments in the fifth of the preparatory notebooks for his dissertation.

> As in the history of philosophy there are nodal points which raise philosophy in itself to concretion, apprehend abstract principles in a totality, and thus break off the rectilinear process, so also there are moments when philosophy turns its eyes to the external world, and no longer apprehends it, but, as a practical person, weaves, as it were, intrigues with the world, emerges from the transparent kingdom of Amenthes and throws itself

55 *MECW* 1, pp. 438–9.

56 *MECW* 1, p. 492, translation modified.

> on the breast of the worldly Siren. That is the carnival of philosophy, whether it disguises itself as a dog like the Cynic, in priestly vestments like the Alexandrian, or in fragrant spring array like the Epicurean. It is essential that philosophy should then wear character masks. As Deucalion, according to the legend, cast stones behind him in creating human beings, so philosophy casts its regard behind it (the bones of its mother are luminous eyes) when its heart is set on creating a world; but as Prometheus, having stolen fire from heaven, begins to build houses and to settle upon the earth, so philosophy, expanded to be the whole world, turns against the world of appearance. The same now with the philosophy of Hegel.[57]

The history of philosophy is *ipso tempore* also the history of the relationships between philosophy and the world. For Marx, this history is marked by moments of great theoretical intensity in which the subjectivity of the individual philosopher dissolves into the transformation of a universal philosophical principle into a finished theoretical world. It is also marked by moments of practical expansion in which the philosophical Idea, renouncing its purely thought-world and a self-sufficiency that is only theoretical, emerges into the world that is other than theory. However, precisely for this reason, by abandoning the supra-personal unity of its system, it multiplies in the ideas of the individual philosophies that now, in the world outside philosophy, try to transform and not just contemplate it. Just as the post-systematic Greek philosophies that renounced a single theory (the eyes of philosophy) attempted, like Prometheus, to develop methods or ways of knowing how to behave amongst men, so too do the various representatives of the Hegelian school after the death of their master. Paradoxically, the more philosophy turns its principle into a system or, in other words, the more it becomes a consistent theoretical world enclosed within itself, the more it distances itself from and contrasts with the world, thereby dividing reality into two worlds and opposing totalities.

> While philosophy has sealed itself off to form a consummate, total world, the determination of this totality is conditioned by the general development of philosophy, just as that development is the condition of the form in which philosophy turns into a practical relationship towards reality; thus the totality of the world in general is divided within itself, and this division is carried to the extreme, for spiritual existence has been

57 *MECW* 1, p. 491.

> freed, has been enriched to universality, the heart-beat has become in itself the differentiation in the concrete form which is the whole organism. The division of the world is total only when its aspects are totalities. The world confronting a philosophy total in itself is therefore a world torn apart.[58]

This leaving the world outside itself on the part of philosophy, in its being spiritual universality – the intrinsically contradictory nature of philosophy that is a part precisely when it constructs itself as a whole – cannot but manifest itself even when, for the completeness of life, it abandons its merely theoretical life and is converted into 'a practical relationship with reality'. It then effectively ceases to live just as an Idea, as a spirit that cannot be reduced in its universality either to facts or empirical-individual existences, and translates itself from theory into praxis, living as a thinking and critical activity of individuals and multiple individualities. However, in this way, a period of crisis is necessarily generated since philosophy, obliged to individualise itself, loses the universal perspective and finds its meaning in subjectivity, making its object no longer the Spirit but individual existence.

> This philosophy's activity therefore also appears torn apart and contradictory; its objective universality is turned back into the subjective forms of individual consciousness in which it has life. But one must not let oneself be misled by this storm which follows a great philosophy, a world philosophy. Ordinary harps play under any fingers, Aeolian harps only when struck by the storm.[59]

Thus, if world-philosophies are necessarily followed by philosophies of crisis, we need to know how to see the latter as the drama of the laceration between philosophy and reality in all its significance. We need, that is, to understand that this unhappy, subjective and negative approach to the way of understanding philosophy derives from the failure of a period of theoretical systematicity. At the basis of these subjectivist theories the motif of the universal and of a pacific reality continues to operate, precisely by means of its absence. Otherwise, disconnecting them from their principle of meaning that is systematic philosophy, ones falls into the fairly superficial perspective of judging the crisis periods as positive and normal modes of the presence of an Absolute, whose

---

58 *MECW* 1, p. 491.

59 Ibid.

typology of existence, marked by relationships of reciprocal division and exteriority, would be configured only as wretched and mediocre.

> He who does not acknowledge this historical necessity must be consistent and deny that men can live at all after a total philosophy, or he must hold that the dialectic of measure as such is the highest category of the self-knowing spirit and assert, with some of the Hegelians who understand our master wrongly, that mediocrity is the normal manifestation of the absolute spirit; but a mediocrity which passes itself off as the regular manifestation of the Absolute has itself fallen into the measureless, namely, into measureless pretension. Without this necessity it is impossible to grasp how after Aristotle a Zeno, an Epicurus, even a Sextus Empiricus could appear, and how after Hegel attempts, most of them abysmally indigent, could be made by more recent philosophers.[60]

Those who do not begin from the structural limits of systematic philosophies, due to their intrinsic theoretical nature, and, therefore, of their inevitable fate of overturning themselves into praxis, cannot understand the history of philosophy and its temporal evolution. They thus fall into the trap of making the end of history coincide with the totalising self-positing of a world-philosophy, which cannot be followed by either other philosophies or other philosophers. They cannot understand that the way of overturning into praxis and, therefore, the particular nature of the various philosophies of subjectivity, is always anticipated and presupposed by the specific individual configurations of the theoretical principle of the totalising philosophy from which these derive. Nor can they grasp the titanic, tragic nature of the periods of crisis when every presence of the divine – or the universal – disappears from the horizon of human beings; tragic but also, in some ways, blessed by fortune. For in the continuity of this kind of philosophy of history that the young Marx extracts from the history of philosophy, there is a positive side, an element of fortune, to each philosophy of crisis and subjectivity, which is the other side of the negative, of the misfortune of the thought of totality as a monad which, closed within itself, has the bad fortune of not acknowledging the existence of a reality outside itself. This positive side is the fortune of turning itself, even if within the impotency of subjectivity, towards a reality other than itself.

60 *MECW* 1, pp. 491–2.

Neither must we forget that the time following such catastrophes is an iron time, happy when characterised by titanic struggles, lamentable when it resembles centuries limping in the wake of great periods in art. These centuries set about moulding in wax, plaster and copper what sprang from Carrara marble like Pallas Athena out of the head of Zeus, the father of the gods. But titanic are the times which follow in the wake of a philosophy total in itself and of its subjective developmental forms, for gigantic is the discord that forms their unity. Thus Rome followed the Stoic, Sceptic and Epicurean philosophy. They are unhappy and iron epochs, for their gods have died and the new goddess still reveals the dark aspect of fate, of pure light or of pure darkness. She still lacks the colours of day. The kernel of the misfortune, however, is that the spirit of the time, the spiritual monad, sated in itself, ideally formed in all aspects in itself, is not allowed to recognize any reality which has come to being without it. The fortunate thing in such misfortune is therefore the subjective form, the modality of the relation of philosophy, as subjective consciousness, towards reality. Thus, for example, the Epicurean, [and the] Stoic philosophy was the boon of its time; thus, when the universal sun has gone down, the moth seeks the lamplight of the private individual. The other aspect, which is the more important for the historian of philosophy, is that this turn-about of philosophy, its transubstantiation into flesh and blood, varies according to the determination which a philosophy total and concrete in itself bears as its birthmark. At the same time it is an objection to those who now conclude in their abstract one-sidedness that, because Hegel considered Socrates' condemnation just, i.e., necessary, because Giordano Bruno had to atone for his fiery spirit in the smoky flame at the stake, therefore the philosophy of Hegel, for example, has pronounced sentence upon itself. But from the philosophical point of view it is important to bring out this aspect, because, reasoning back from the determinate character of this turn-about, we can form a conclusion concerning the immanent determination and the world-historical character of the process of development of a philosophy. What formerly appeared as growth is now determination, what was negativity existing in itself has now become negation. Here we see, as it were, the curriculum vitae of a philosophy in its most concentrated expression, epitomised in its subjective point, just as from the death of a hero one can infer his life's history. Since I hold that the attitude of the Epicurean philosophy is such a form of Greek philosophy, may this also be my justification if, instead of presenting moments out of the preceding Greek philosophies as conditions of the life of the Epicurean philosophy, I reason back from the latter to draw conclusions

> about the former and thus let it itself formulate its own particular position.[61]

On the basis of these arguments, it is easy to understand the chosen subject and the research methods used by the young Marx as a student of ancient philosophy. Between the Idea and ideas, between a 'total philosophy' and the philosophies of self-consciousness, in the discontinuity of the overturning of the first into the second there is a substantial continuity. It is precisely this continuity that allows the generation of a philosophical historiography based on the *après coup* and on retrospection. It is not only that the viewpoint of the more concrete and vivid of the philosophies of the particular enable the nature and character of the Idea and the universal that preceded them to be comprehended better. It is also in the broader sense that retrospection allows a dislocated mirroring in time. This is what occurs to the young Marx, who sees in the comparison of the universal philosophies and philosophies of self-consciousness the reflection of the more current and pressing problem for him of the relationship between the Hegelian system and post-Hegelian philosophy, of the connection, that is, between the completed philosophy *par excellence* of the Idea and the illuminated and subjective promotion of ideas.

It is precisely the anchoring of the question of the relationship between Hegel's philosophy and the post-Hegelian school in the problem of the theory-praxis nexus that is treated in the most significant of the surviving notes that Marx appended to his dissertation: the second note of the fourth chapter of the first part. Evaluating Hegel's philosophy from a position that does not correspond to its constitutive theoretical principle – namely, not assessing its validity or insufficiency from the height of its supra-personal nature – means falling into moralism or to consider Hegel's limits only as the yielding of his individual and private consciousness to the powers of his time. This is what his followers did (above all on the Hegelian Left), incapable of comprehending this principle. After unconditionally endorsing Hegel's philosophy, they became his fiercest critics due to the compromises that he was supposed to have made with the Church and the Prussian state.

> Also in relation to Hegel it is mere ignorance on the part of his pupils, when they explain one or the other determination of his system by his desire for accommodation and the like, hence, in one word, explain it in terms of morality. They forget that only a short time ago they were

---

61 *MECW* 1, pp. 492–3.

> enthusiastic about all his idiosyncrasies [*Einseitigkeiten*], as can be clearly demonstrated from their writings. If they were really so affected by the ready-made science they acquired that they gave themselves up to it in naive uncritical trust, then how unscrupulous is their attempt to reproach the Master for a hidden intention behind his insight! The Master, to whom the science was not something received, but something in the process of becoming, to whose uttermost periphery his own intellectual heart's blood was pulsating! On the contrary, they rendered themselves suspect of not having been serious before. And now they oppose their own former condition, and ascribe it to Hegel, forgetting however that his relation to his system was immediate, substantial, while theirs is only a reflected one. It is quite thinkable for a philosopher to fall into one or another apparent inconsistency through some sort of accommodation; he himself may be conscious of it. But what he is not conscious of, is the possibility that this apparent accommodation has its deepest roots in an inadequacy or in an inadequate formulation of his principle itself. Suppose therefore that a philosopher has really accommodated himself, then his pupils must explain from his inner essential consciousness that which for him himself had the form of an exoteric consciousness. In this way, that which appears as progress of conscience is at the same time progress of knowledge. No suspicion is cast upon the particular conscience of the philosopher, but his essential form of consciousness is construed, raised to a definite shape and meaning and in this way also transcended.[62]

Furthermore, not problematising a world-philosophy at the level of its Idea means not managing ever to overcome it, but instead to remain within the confines of its system. Above all, it means imagining the overturning into praxis as criticism – that is, paradoxically and contradictorily, to consider it still only as theory. It means to maintain an extrinsic and moralistic approach in which, having taken up the basic structure of a philosophy unquestioningly, one turns to the world solely in order to measure the world's relative consistency or inconsistency in relation to this philosophy, in 'a relationship of reflection' – once again Marx emphasises the Hegelian dimensions of his argument. Such a relation demonstrates the degree to which philosophy and the world continue to remain divided and opposed.

62 *MECW* 1, pp. 84–5.

> It is a psychological law that the theoretical mind, once liberated in itself, turns into practical energy, and, leaving the shadowy empire of Amenthes as will, turns itself against the reality of the world existing without it. (From a philosophical point of view, however, it is important to specify these aspects better, since from the specific manner of this turn we can reason back towards the immanent determination and the universal historic character of a philosophy. We see here, as it were, its curriculum vitae narrowed down to its subjective point). But the practice of philosophy is itself theoretical. It is the critique that measures the individual existence by the essence, the particular reality by the Idea. But this immediate realisation of philosophy is in its deepest essence afflicted with contradictions, and this its essence takes form in the appearance and imprints its seal upon it. When philosophy turns itself as will against the world of appearance, then the system is lowered to an abstract totality, that is, it has become one aspect of the world which opposes another one. Its relationship to the world is that of reflection. Inspired by the urge to realise itself, it enters into tension against the other. The inner self-contentment and completeness has been broken. What was inner light has become consuming flame turning outwards. The result is that as the world becomes philosophical, philosophy also becomes worldly, that its realisation is also its loss, that what it struggles against on the outside is its own inner deficiency, that in the very struggle it falls precisely into those defects which it fights as defects in the opposite camp, and that it can only overcome these defects by falling into them. That which opposes it and that which it fights is always the same as itself, only with factors inverted.[63]

Thus, for Marx in this fundamental note, the dilemmas of philosophy in its relationship with the world are explained according to two insuperable difficulties, the one complementing the other. One is objective, the other subjective. This objectivity, as seen above, consists in philosophy contradicting itself, that is, in it making itself, from a totality, into a partiality. If philosophy, despite achieving its most systematic theoretical maturity, lives in a world that is not yet philosophical, for Marx this means that if it should attempt to realise itself, to become a world, from the whole that is in theory, it cannot help but reduce itself to part against part, in a confrontation between inevitably external and irreducible ambits the one against the other. The second difficulty concerns

63 *MECW* 1, p. 85.

the becoming worldly of philosophy in terms of the subjective aspect, that is, in relation to the diffusion and multiplication of a theoretical system through the use made of it by its continuers, since, as seen from the pages of the fifth notebook, the insufficient objectivity, however systematic, of a universal philosophy necessarily overturns it into subjective philosophies.

> But this [the realisation of the philosophy] has also a subjective aspect, which is merely another form of it. This is the relationship of the philosophical system which is realised to its intellectual carriers, to the individual self-consciousnesses in which its progress appears.[64]

Here, each one, precisely because a single subject, singularises the theoretical system of which it is the bearer, bringing into force only one aspect to the detriment of the others, also because, in some way, it wishes to personalise the system of which it feels itself to be prisoner. However, in this way, it falls into the contradiction that, if it wants to free the world from non-philosophy, what it effectively demonstrates is that it wants to liberate itself from the philosophy of which it is the spokesperson.

> This relationship results in what confronts the world in the realisation of philosophy itself, namely, in the fact that these individual self-consciousnesses always carry a double-edged demand, one edge turned against the world, the other against philosophy itself. Indeed, what in the thing itself appears as a relationship inverted in itself, appears in these self-consciousnesses as a double one, a demand and an action contradicting each other. Their liberation of the world from unphilosophy is at the same time their own liberation from the philosophy that held them in fetters as a particular system. Since they are themselves engaged merely in the act and immediate energy of development – and hence have not yet theoretically emerged from that system – they perceive only the contradiction with the plastic equality-with-self [*Sich-selbst-Gleichheit*] of the system and do not know that by turning against it they only realise its individual moments.[65]

As a result, Hegel's theoretical system cannot help but divide into the two camps of the 'liberal party' and those who support 'positive philo-

64 Ibid.

65 *MECW* 1, p. 86.

sophy'.[66] In other words, it is divided into the intellectuals of the Hegelian Left who want to transform the world in accordance with the reason of philosophy, and the theoreticians of the Right who defend the positivity of the real, accusing the liberal philosophers of blindness in relation to the rationality provided by the existing order and institutions.

> This duality of philosophical self-consciousness appears finally as a double trend, each side utterly opposed to the other. One side, the liberal party, as we may call it in general, maintains as its main determination the concept and the principle of philosophy; the other side, its non-concept, the moment of reality. This second side is positive philosophy. The act of the first side is critique, hence precisely that turning-towards-the-outside of philosophy; the act of the second is the attempt to philosophise, hence the turning-in-towards-itself of philosophy. This second side knows that the inadequacy is immanent in philosophy, while the first understands it as inadequacy of the world which has to be made philosophical. Each of these parties does exactly what the other one wants to do and what it itself does not want to do.[67]

Thus the same objective contradiction, already present in a philosophy's claim to acquire reality and become a world, manifests itself when it takes on the form of a subjective contradiction in the overturning of each position into its opposite. The liberals, who posit philosophy's rationality against the real in the world, instead ensure that philosophy comes out of itself and becomes worldly; they therefore begin from the world. The positivists, on the other hand, who posit the rationality of reality before that of the philosophers, claim that it is philosophy that recognises reality; they therefore begin from philosophy.[68]

---

66 In the German philosophical-cultural debate of the 1830–40s, positive philosophy meant all the theoretical positions of those who saw in the historically existing institutions (above all those of the Christian religion) the existence and manifestation, positive and concrete, of the Absolute (we are thinking here of figures such as von Baader, Fichte, Fischer, Weisse and, finally, Schelling). However, it would seem that here Marx's distinction refers to the opposing positions, within Hegelianism, of the Left who valorised the criticism of the idea against the irrationality of the real, and the Right who, maintaining the rational reality of the institutions against the critical-philosophical radicalisation of the young Hegelians, interpreted the conservative positions of positive philosophy and made them their own within the Hegelian school.

67 *MECW* 1, p. 86.

68 One of the most illuminating exegeses of these fairly difficult pages by the young Marx (Notebook V and the second note) can be found in Rossi 1977, pp. 174–210.

What therefore results from this double aporia, objective and subjective, is the confirmation for the young Marx that, given the heterogeneity of philosophy and the world, it is impossible that their reconciliation be effected by philosophy itself. The structural partiality of the latter, when faced with the limitations posed by the non-philosophical world, are confirmed and duplicated in the partiality of the individual philosophical consciousnesses which, although participating in a single theoretical system, cannot but bring into force abstract determinations separate the one from the other, due to the individuality of the perspective that defines them. 'That which in the first place appears as an inverted [*verkehrtes*] relationship and inimical trend of philosophy with respect to the world, becomes in the second place a diremption of individual self-consciousness in itself and appears finally as an external separation and duality of philosophy, as two opposed philosophical trends'.[69]

## 10 Philosophy, World, 'Young Hegelians'

When posing the question of philosophy as praxis or the becoming worldly of philosophy, the young Marx made the fundamental question that animated the so-called *Junghegelianer* movement his own. These were the 'young Hegelians' of which Marx was an organic and very lively member, at least in the period when he frequented the Berlin *Doktorclub*. For personalities such as, amongst others, Bruno and Edgar Bauer, August von Cieszkowski, Theodor Echtermeyer, Georg C. Jung, Carl Friedrich Köppen and Arnold Ruge – all figures of a new intellectual scene composed of essayists and journalists no longer linked, at the time or in the near future, to universities or state and ecclesiastically-owned cultural institutions, in contrast to traditional intellectuals – Hegel's philosophy represented the greatest claim for and radicalisation of freedom carried out by human thought in any period of history. For the *Junghegelianer*, even in their opposition to the so-called 'Hegelians of the Right', the ultimate meaning of Hegelian spirit, in its unconditionality of the Absolute, is freedom. This freedom is not transcendental and metaphysical but immanent; it constructs and develops itself in the history of the world and humanity. Hegel's *Weltgeist*, or world-spirit, is not a theological and creationist spirit, separate from human beings, but is the very history of humanity in its becoming gradually independ-

69 *MECW* 1, p. 86.

ent from every external limitation and conditioning. It is the history of the gradual realisation of self-consciousness as the progressive becoming of human beings who become conscious of their strength and autonomy of reason and their capacity to cast off every bond of authoritarianism through the process of the development of civilisation.

For a scholar of religion such as Bruno Bauer, the theory of freedom as the development of infinite self-consciousness thus constitutes the most profound nucleus of Hegel's philosophy and its conception of spirit. The identity of spirit consists in passing from a condition of passively subaltern, naturalistic existence to that of a subjectivity which, freeing itself from any form of coercion both from nature and any authoritarian human institution, increasingly deepens its own power and autonomy as universal reason. By increasingly recognising itself as free self-consciousness, it takes only from itself, as a rational and universal subject, the criteria and principles of its own action; but without forgetting, as Bauer himself maintains, that this identification of the universal with self-consciousness can only occur through the finite spirit.[70] This is the case in the sense that only the human being who, overcoming the natural and sensible content of its life and filling it with an increasingly less individualistic content and interest, makes the universal spirit live concretely, by becoming universal itself. Thus the history of spirit is the history of human self-consciousness – or, of those amongst men who have gained a perspective of the universal – and of their inexhaustible battle with all the human, cultural, political and social institutions that constrain and impede the universalisation of freedom, even to the point of conflicting with the mass of men who, closed in

70 'The universal is that which opens up to consciousness only in the finite spirit, removing the latter from its finitude and introducing it into the entire movement [...]. Infinite consciousness is an external form that the absolute, the substance, has taken on, it is the internal difference that the universal posits in itself and that it must posit because it can mediate itself only with consciousness and the finite spirit and, only by rendering itself finite can it arrive at becoming knowledge of itself' (Bauer 1960, p. 120; see Bauer 1989). Infinite self-consciousness in Bauer, as freedom that has overcome any type of division and determinacy (and which thus refers to the figure of 'absolute knowledge' at the conclusion of the *Phenomenology of Spirit*) is a permanent and metahistorical dimension that turns polemically (by means of the criticism of finite consciousnesses and intellectuals) against all the forms of the past that still endure in the present, despite their intrinsic lack of actuality. On this and the way in which Bauer introduced a conception of history based on ruptures that are not linked to that which preceded them (in relation to the continuity of the philosophy of history of Hegel), on the basis of the critique of historical communism of Strauss in his *Life of Jesus* (1835), see the accurate analysis in Tomba 2002.

their egotistic-naturalist existence and bound to the passive values of tradition, resist any attempts at enlightenment.[71] Philosophy, free self-consciousness, has to aim to explain the incoherence between an epoch and the now inadequate

---

71 Bruno Bauer's activities (1809–82), which in the years 1840–2 included editorial and university projects in collaboration with Marx, took place at least up until the early 1840s more in terms of the critique of religion than in terms of the critique of politics. This contrasts with Arnold Ruge (1802–80), the other figure of the Hegelian Left with whom the young Marx had most contact. For Bauer, the real meaning of Hegel's philosophy of religion, the lectures on which Bauer published together with his teacher Marheineke in 1842, consists in the fact that 'Hegel preaches only atheism, and has made self-consciousness the tomb of religion and the entire universe', affirming that 'self-consciousness is the only power of the world, the creator, the lord, the tyrant of the world' (Bauer 1960, p. 179). For Bauer, Hegel's message is thus atheism, and definitely not the reconciliation of religion and philosophy, according to the theory proposed by Hegel himself in which religion and philosophy express the same content of truth, the first in the concrete and plastic forms of representation, the second in the more elevated garb of the concept. The Hegelian theory should, for Bauer, be read by radicalising the terminology and distinguishing between that which belongs to 'substance', as truth based on an external principle of authority, and what is precisely 'self-consciousness', as the translation of every universal value into the convictions and affirmation of free subjectivity. The giving in of the self to the universal for Bauer can only be temporary, for the purposes of overcoming the limits of individualism. But the true purpose cannot but be the consolidation of the universal in the most intrinsic and least extrinsic form of self-knowledge. Hegel 'permits the substantial relationship only for a moment, insomuch as the moment in the process of which the finite consciousness renounces its finitude; substance is only the momentary fire in which the self sacrifices its finitude and its limitation. The conclusion of the process is not substance but self-consciousness that is posited really as infinite and which has accepted into itself the universality of substance as its own essence. Substance is only the power that consumes the finitude of the self in order then to be the prey of infinite self-consciousness' (Bauer 1960, p. 125). Furthermore, we should not forget the substantial continuity and exchangability between the critique of religion and the critique of politics for all the radical German intellectuals of the *Vormärz*, in a historical-cultural horizon in which the philological-philosophical discussion of Christianity put in question an entire system of constituted authority. This was even more the case for Bauer, whose first criticisms of the Bible (from the first two volumes of the *Kritik der Geschichte der Offenbarung* of 1838 to the *Kritik der evangelischen Geschichte der Synoptiker* of 1841), with the contraposition of the Old and New Testaments and the epochal opposition of the figure of Christ to the 'old', anticipated the radicality of the historical discontinuity of which self-consciousness needed to be capable in its refutation of everything that pushed for the maintainence and repetition of the past. On this and the way in which Bauer and post-Hegelian thought is considered in the political theology of Carl Schmitt (in terms of the affinity between religion and politics), see Tomba 2002, pp. 63–93 and 113–36.

forms (because more traditional, but therefore also more diffused) of the way in which the majority represent it and are conscious of it.

This is the basis of the essentially critical character of philosophy, as claimed by Bauer and others such as Ruge. Its nature consists in overcoming all that which came before the present and actual moment of spirit, and in the attempt to sublate the present in turn into the future.[72] For this reason, genuine philosophy, or Hegelian philosophy, which in Germany found its basis firstly in the spirit of Reformation and subsequently in liberal and enlightened Prussianism, turned primarily, as Ruge states in the essay *Der Protestantismus und die Romantik* [*Protestanism and Romanticism*] written in collaboration with Echtermeyer, against the romantic irrationalism that finds its maximum expression is Schelling's thought. However, the Prussian state of the present increasingly distanced itself from the principles of free rationality. Philosophy therefore had to take on as the subject of its criticism the existing institutions, to operate within history and in practice in order to make the state the place of rationally and freely self-determining universal will. If our times are essentially political, as Ruge writes in his essay *Die Hegelsche Rechtsphilosophie und die Politik unserer Zeit* [*Hegel's Philosophy of Right and the Politics of Our Time*], philosophy must cease to be only cognitive and justifying of existing conditions and must instead address the insufficiencies of the present, the passions of men about what is lacking. It must lead 'the state to the form of the state'.[73]

To realise philosophy, leading it from theory to praxis, therefore means for the young Hegelians to diffuse and to realise within the entire social, political

---

72 It is no coincidence that Hegel's *Logic*, for Ruge, consists in the great task of having presented and connected, in their progressive sublation, the thought of all philosophies, and of having demonstrated that the essence of dialectics coincides with the eternally enacted structure of thought that never stops at any of its content but is always open to broader and newer determinations. 'This work is a great work. In fact, it connects all the principles of all preceding philosophies, all the thoughts that have ever been claimed as germs or principles of the universe and in such a way that the legitimacy of thought, in its real situation, and of superior, more concrete thought in which the former is necessarily dissolved, is clarified. The passage from one thought to another is incessant, the dialectic never stops, at any moment. Every new word is critical of that which has preceded it but only to be criticised in turn by that which follows' (Ruge 1960, p. 10). Arnold Ruge founded together with Theodor Echtermeyer in 1838 the most radical journal of the Hegelian left, the *Hallische Jahrbücher für deutsche Wissenschaft und Kunst*, printed in Leipzig by Otto Wigand; after the intervention of the Prussian government censor, it was then printed in Dresden, in Saxony, with the title *Deutsche Jahrbücher für Wissenschaft und Kunst*.

73 Ruge 1981, pp. 213–14.

and cultural organisation of modern society the absolutisation of freedom achieved by Hegelian philosophy, liberating it from the compromises of the archaic and anachronistic institutions of the time which Hegel had instead acknowledged and legitimised in his theoretical system. The translation of philosophy into praxis effectively and essentially means 'criticism', because it denounces all the figures of the present that are inadequate or contradictory in relation to the principle of the universalisation of freedom. It is a criticism that, in turn, implies a new class of intellectuals, qualified in the universal but outside the academic and institutional establishment. They will be capable of indicating and representing to the mass of the population the discrepancies between the forms of their lives (which particularly in terms of religion and the State are antagonistic to the idea of freedom) and the fullness of the idea of reason and spirituality. Theory is, therefore, in Bruno Bauer's words, 'the most powerful praxis [*die stärkste Praxis*]'.[74]

However, such a theorisation of philosophical praxis as criticism is problematic for the Marx of the dissertation – and here he expresses the peculiar nature of his position within the *Junghegelianer* – due to the aporia of an individual consciousness that claims, from outside the mass of common and popular people, to be a diffuse and collective consciousness.

Furthermore, in the transition from his poetic and literary activities to the study of philosophy (as we will see later in the appendix to this chapter), the young Marx had already lived the crisis of his first identity too intensely, based on the romantic titanism of the individual who wants to purify the world in the light of its own 'must', in order not to be conscious of the vanity of every enlightened and subjective constraint in relation to reality. This awareness, matured in the transition from romanticism to Hegelianism, never abandoned him throughout the rest of his life. Possibly due to the radical nature and speed with which this transition was undertaken, it can help us to explain such a clear absence, and so pregnant with consequences, in the entire breadth of Marx's works of a reflection on the theme of the individual.

Thus, in the dissertation and preparatory notebooks, if Marx is undoubtedly a young Hegelian as he affirms the necessity of the becoming worldly of philosophy, he is also well aware of the intrinsic contradiction in this necessity. Posited and established by means of subjectivity and critical individualism, it ends up making philosophy regress to Fichtean subjectivism and a theory of consciousness that is the reflective and external act of a subject on an object. This is, therefore, a Marx who already began to appreciate how much the inher-

74 Bruno Bauer to K. Marx, 5 April 1840, in *MEGA*, III, 1, p. 346.

itance of Hegeliansm poses the need to draw upon a principle of reality that is not exhausted in the circle of the Idea, but also posits the question of a non-individual subject capable of sustaining and producing the effective universalisation and liberation of reality. However, it is only an embryonic awareness burdened by such a degree of problems that the young Marx, in the still early phases of this thought, is not yet able to resolve it. He can only light the fire in his soul and bear its complex aporicity by dramatising it. That is, he objectivises and projects it by means of the reconstruction of a moment in the history of ancient philosophy in which the abstract categories of the problem are presented using precisely the intrinsically figurative nature of ancient objectivism.

To repeat: through his dissertation, Marx thinks and represents the aporicity of the historical present contained in the drama of post-Hegelianism, displacing it to the distance of ancient times. The post-Hegelian conjuncture simultaneously embraced and refused Hegel's great system of thought, in the sense that Hegelian philosophy had claimed to complete and even to put an end to the becoming of history. It was precisely with the theme of the becoming worldly of philosophy and the criticism of the institutions repressing freedom that the young Hegelians well expressed what appeared to them to be the main limits of the Hegelian system, which were consistent with the claim of ending temporality and, consequently, concluding with the legitimisation of the historically given institutions. Despite being important for the young Marx (and we will see how he carries out this task later), all this could not be enough. A part of his soul believed that his friends, with whom his sentimental and theoretical life was profoundly intertwined, fell beneath the level of the Hegelian lesson, since they did not seek to define a subject capable of an even more extensive and consistent universalisation than that proposed by Hegel.

In this regard, revisiting the significant example of August von Cieszkowski's *Prolegomena to Historiosophy* (1838) helps us to realise how explicit among these intellectuals was the awareness of the aporia that Hegel's system established in relation to an assumed conclusion of history, if not even a complete rationalisation of the real, as well as the degree to which the values of the theme of action was embedded in their perspectives.

Hegel's philosophy of history looked at the only necessary path of the past, which he divided into the four eras of the Oriental, Greek, Roman and Christian-Germanic worlds. Cieszkowski notes that

> In his work he does not mention the future by name at all and he was even of the *opinion* that in exploring history philosophy can only be valid

> retroactively and that the future should be completely excluded from the sphere of speculation.[75]

On the contrary, it is necessary to include the future as an integral part of history and determine the connection of the path already taken by humanity with that yet to come: determination and prevision through that knowledge which, by using the laws of dialectics, must be seen not as philosophy of history looking to the past but as wisdom of history or, in other words, knowledge of the organic nature of the evolution of spirit in the world and also knowledge of its implications, in its organic nature, and thus also of the dimensions of the future. By reshaping Hegel's lesson, Cieszkowski conceives of a philosophy of history that divides the historic process into three periods respectively informed by the principles of being, thought and the deed: the ancient world in which the subject is entirely subaltern to that which is objective and independent of it; the Christian-Germanic world which, on the contrary, is guided by the subject and his thought; and, finally, the world of the present and the future that will be the world of praxis, of transforming action, and which will reconcile realism and idealism in the sense of a real world progressively penetrated and coincident with the world of values and ideality.[76] Hegel's philosophy

---

75 Cieszkowski 1979, p. 52. August von Cieszkowski (1814–94), a Polish Count, moved to Berlin in 1833 and studied logic, philosophy of law and philosophy of history with disciples of Hegel such as H.G. Hotho, E. Gans and L.v. Henning. Together with Carl Michelet he founded in 1843 a *Philosophische Gesellschaft* and from 1860 onwards ran the journal *Der Gedanke*. On the influence that Cieszkowski might have had on the young Marx, see Duichin 1982, pp. 182–99. On the concept of praxis, see Lobkowicz 1976, pp. 193–204; Jakubowski 1992, pp. 155–61. The only reference to Cieszkowski on Marx's part is a fairly late letter to Engels dated 12 January 1882, in which Marx writes that he 'did in fact once call on me in Paris (at the time of the *Deutsch-Französische Jahrbücher*), and such was the impression he made on me [*hatte mir's so angetan*] that I neither wanted nor would have been able to read anything whatever of his contriving' (*MECW* 46, p. 177). The passage, even if it begins with a reference to a small economic work of 1839 by Cieszkowski (*Du crédit et de la circulation*, Treuttel et Wurtz, Paris 1839) is clearly ironic with respect to the philosophy of action [*Philosophie der Tat*] theorised in these years by the Polish Count, whose *Prolegomena* was defined by Engels in a subsequent letter as a 'a book on natural philosophy (botany)' (*MECW* 46, p. 181).

76 'To give the reader a general insight into our position – and a prolegomenon must be confined to general insights – lets us mention that the universal spirit is presently entering the third, synthetic period whose first or thetic period consists of all Antinquity and whose second or antithetic period, radically opposed to the first, is the Christian-Germanic world. Accordingly, in our view, Hegel's first three main periods are only three moments of

concludes the second period in the most elevated way with a system that is capable of translating the whole of reality into the categories of thought. Now, however, in the period of the future, thought must be translated into will, into the outside of itself [*ausser sich*] and lead the history of humanity to its organic totality.[77] Pre-theoretical praxis, dependent on the objective fact, as occurs in the ancient world, must be replaced by post-theoretical praxis. By using the maturity of knowing achieved by Hegel, such a post-theoretical praxis leads to the overturning for which the natural state of givenness no longer precedes and commands the deed, but 'consciousness outpaces the facts and after having advanced beyond them engenders the true deed, namely the post-theoretical praxis that properly belongs to the future'.[78]

---

the first overall period that makes up the ancient world. Hegel's fourth period is our second period and consists of the modern world. Finally, our third period is the future whose proper definition can be gleaned form the one-sided opposition of the two preceding ones' (Cieszkowski 1979, p. 57).

77 An important moment in the reopening of Hegel's philosophy of history that fertilises the philosophical-political themes of the young Hegelians consists in the manner in which E. Gans, first a disciple of Hegel and then a continuer of his teaching in Berlin, rereads the historical-political thought of the master during the 1830s. Gans edited the 1833 edition of the *Grundlinien der Philosophie des Rechts* and, in 1837, the first edition of the *Philosophie der Geschichte*. For Gans and his liberal reasoning, the concept of the state in Hegel must be subtracted from the conclusivity and complete identification with the rationality of the real with which it had been burdened by Hegel and, on the contrary, must be relativised and situated in the broader path of history which becomes, in the varying of the state forms and in their adaptation to the needs of the *Weltgeist*, the true place of rationality, in a reconciliation that proceeds to infinity in time. A key aspect of this move is the criticism that Gans makes of the Hegelian institution of representation by orders, or estates. Gans claims that the collective principle of the estates, of a medieval or pre-modern nature, is incompatible with the system of modern political representation that sees the individual as the basis for the construction of the state. For Gans, the criticism of the *ständisches Prinzip*, attacking the Hegelian system of the state at its most delicate point (but see also on this Marx's criticism in the *Kritik* of 1843) and the positing of an individual basis of the state, liberates the state from the *Sittlichkeit* [*ethical life*] in which Hegel had constrained it, resituating it in the much larger context of history and its varied forms of reconciliation between the individual and universality. On the liberal interpretation of Hegel developed by Gans, see Vaccaro 1980; Wazsek 1992. On the connections and distance between Gans and Cieszkowski, see Matassi 1991. Nor should we forget that the young Marx attended Gans's lessons in Berlin in the winter semester 1836–7 and the summer semester 1938.

78 Cieszkowski 1979, p. 55.

However, this 'practical philosophy' or, more precisely, Cieszkowski's 'philosophy of praxis [*Philosophie der Praxis*]',[79] demonstrates its dependence on and continuity with the Idea, with theory, in the fact that praxis is only conceivable as the realisation of an already completed theory and, therefore, precisely as consciousness that actively unifies the world, going 'out of itself, beginning with itself [*tätig aus sich*]'.[80] Thus, it is only because humanity has already achieved its real self-consciousness that it can carry out deeds that are appropriate to its nature and its original disposition. For this reason, the future era can be that of the deed, an era in which the self-determination of the will exists on the basis of the assumption of a full self-consciousness of thought.

> The deed [*actum*] is [...] something completely different: it is no longer an immediate event to be received and reflected. It is already reflected, already mediated, already cogitated, intended and then accomplished. It is an *active* event that is entirely *ours*, no longer foreign but already conscious before being realised.[81]

Thus, also in Cieszkowski, due to this essentially theoretical nature of the deed, the subject of praxis, which will need to overcome the institutions in which the human being no longer recognises itself, will either remain indeterminate in its generic reference to the progressive evolution of humanity and spirit in the world, or will once again be represented by the enlightenment of those consciousnesses that are thoroughly imbued with that theoretical lesson.

The young Marx, however, is aware that subtracting the world and the time of history from the conclusion imposed upon them by Hegel is only possible by not regressing behind the horizon of thought inaugurated by Hegel himself: in other words, by trying to conceive of a much richer and concrete universal, more comprehensive than Hegel's, thereby explaining the original and intrinsic limits of the Hegelian principle of universality. Otherwise, as we have seen, Hegel is only extrinsically accused of having fallen into compromises, without effectively confronting the essence of his philosophy.

The Marx of the dissertation and preparatory notebooks knows that a great philosophy – such as Hegel's *par excellence* – must be followed by 'titanic' periods in which that philosophy that has thought and conceptualised the world in accordance with a principle of universal systematicity cannot help but

79 Cieszkowski 1979, p. 77.

80 Cieszkowski 1979, p. 75, translation modified.

81 Cieszkowski 1979, p. 55, translation modified. On the overall subject of the figure of Cieskowski, see Tomba 1997.

contradict itself and become a world, precisely because of its intrinsic demand for universalisation. That is, it cannot help but cease to know the world and be itself a world. It must undergo a transubstantiation into flesh and blood that leads it from theory to praxis, to being a practical and real ordering of the world. Neither can this 'converting of itself into a practical relationship with reality' take place through compromises and mediocre negotiation, since it is a matter of the achievement of an 'animating spirit of historic-universal developments'. It is a spirit or subject that must be capable of organising the entire reality of life in accordance with its principle of universalisation and which, in order to do this, must be capable of going beyond speculative philosophy and displacing itself onto the new continent of experience and practical life. This is precisely what Themistocles did in the affairs of ancient Athens when he had the courage to refound the city on an entirely new element.

> At such times half-hearted minds have opposite views to those of whole-minded generals. They believe that they can compensate losses by cutting the armed forces, by splitting them up, by a peace treaty with the real needs, whereas Themistocles, when Athens was threatened with destruction, tried to persuade the Athenians to abandon the city entirely and found a new Athens at sea, in another element.[82]

However, this 'overturning of philosophy', its becoming praxis rather than theory, cannot occur, at least initially, except by paradoxically reaffirming theory as a criticism proposed by an individual and subjective consciousness.

This is the problem for which Marx does not yet have a solution. It is the problem of the overcoming of philosophy, the problem of the connection between theory and praxis. The elaboration of this problem will give rise to the entire thematic of Marx's future work.

It is thus immersed in such problems that the young Marx arrives at the end of his university studies (the degree in philosophy is awarded without his being present at the discussion in the University of Jena on 15 April 1841). He sets off on his journey as a German intellectual, prepared and ready to commit himself to the movement opposing the social, political and cultural institutions of Prussian Germany. This problematic can be summarised in the following terms: how is it possible to translate the philosophy of spirit into a philosophy of deeds without renouncing the fundamental anti-individualist and anti-empirical dimension of Hegelian philosophy?

---

82 *MECW* 1, p. 492.

The next chapter will provide a very rapid summary of Hegel's philosophy in an attempt to make the central themes of the master in Berlin more understandable than has been possible thus far. Before doing so, however, it would be wise to pause for a moment and go back to the first meeting between Marx and Hegel as described in the famous letter of the former to his father. This letter establishes the importance that the category of 'formal determination [*Formbestimmung*]' has in all of Marx's works, even from its very first appearance, and even when it is absent.

## 11 From Poetry to Philosophy. From One Father to Another

The letter that the Berlin student, Karl Marx, sent to his father Heinrich in Trier on 10 November 1837 is the only one remaining from this period of university studies. It is thus even more precious. It also summarises well the encounter with Hegelian philosophy that produced a decisive change in the young Karl's studies and by which, with the abandonment of his legal studies and the certainty of a bourgeois profession, he would be marked for the rest of his life. Heinrich (Heschel or Hirschel) Marx was a cultured lawyer, and, as seems from the letters, a tender, patient father who was profoundly concerned about Karl's physical and spiritual health.[83] He was forced gradually to renounce any illu-

83 Karl's father, Heinrich Marx (1777–1838), was a lawyer owning vineyards on the banks of the Moselle and belonged to the cultured and moneyed bourgeoisie of Trier, the oldest city of the Rhineland. He belonged to an ancient Jewish family that since 1723 had provided the rabbis for the city's community in which the prevailing religion was Roman Catholic. Thus, Marx's paternal grandfather, Meier Halevi Marx, was a rabbi as was his paternal uncle, Samuel Marx. When the Jews of Trier, with a Prussian edict of 1812 that withdrew every liberal concession made by the Napoleonic administration, were denied any opportunity to exercise the liberal professions or gain employment in public service, Hirschel was re-baptised as Heinrich and converted to Lutheranism. His children were baptised in the Christian religion on 26 August 1824 (Karl was six at the time), while his wife, Henriette Pressburg (1788–1863), who had arrived in Trier from a family of Dutch Jewish rabbis, was baptised as a Christian only on 25 November 1825, probably only after the death of her father, the rabbi Isaac Pressburg. Karl's father, Heinrich Marx, was very open to the influence of French culture and European Enlightenment, a frequenter of the Literary Society of the city's Casino, and the promoter of a liberalism that was respectful of both authorities and institutions. He was born in 1777 and died of tuberculosis in 1838. See Monz 1973. Through his paternal grandmother (Eva Levoff) the Marx family descended from the famous rabbi Jehuda ben Elizer ha Levy Minz, professor in the University of Padua in

sion of channelling the intellectual energy of his son, of strong emotions and very clear talent, into the continuation of his own legal profession. Sums of money repeatedly sent; undoubtedly serious studies of legal matters but also a very intense dedication to poetry and literary composition; a very young engagement, when Marx was just eighteen, with Heinrich's consent but unbeknownst to her family, with Jenny von Westphalen, four years older than him and belonging to a noble family of the Prussian ruling class;[84] the transfer after only two terms at the University of Bonn to Berlin; the frequenting of the most extreme and radical intellectual circles in the city; the continuation, after passing to Berlin, of intense poetic-literary activity; a night in prison for drunkenness during his time in Bonn; an investigation for the possession of arms and a duel with a young aristocrat of the Borussa Korps,[85] from which Marx escaped with a slight injury to his left eye: all this must probably have soon convinced Heinrich that his favourite son was very unlikely to become a man of the law. He did not disapprove of the decision that, at a certain stage, matured in the young

---

the sixteenth century. For the genealogical tree of Marx's mother and father, see Raddatz 1975, pp. 422–3. On the relationships between the Marx family and the Jewish community in Trier, see also Karl Marx Haus Trier, 1975. On the Dutch origins of Karl Marx's mother, Henriette, who never learnt the German language, as far as can be seen from her letters, see Gielkens 1999. Henriette Pressburg's relatives emigrated from Hungary to Holland. One of Henriette's sisters, Sophie, had married the banker Lion Philips, the grandfather of the founder of the homonomous modern industrial enterprise. Marx was frequently a guest of this family of the maternal relatives at Zaltbommer, in Holland, from whom he also received financial support during the course of his life.

84 On the von Westphalen family, see the brief presentation in Friedenthal 1981, pp. 38–52. Baron Ludwig von Westphalen, Jenny's father, had an early marriage with Elisabeth von Veltheim (from the old Prussian nobility, dying in 1807), with whom he had four children; one of them, Ferdinand, would become a reactionary Minister of the Interior of the Prussian state. He married a second time to a Rhineland woman of bourgeois origins, Karoline Heubel, the mother of Jenny and Edgar, with whom Heinrich Marx's children were playmates. Jenny, the first born of the younger Westphalen family, was born on 12 February 1814.

85 Karl spent two terms at the University of Bonn. Like any good student, he was not indifferent to good company and beer halls. A member of the *Trierer Landsmannschaft*, in the summer term of 1836 he was one of the five presidents of the *Trierer Kneipverein*. The investigation for possession of arms, ended by his father's intervention and communication with a judge in Cologne, appears to be linked to the possession of a pistol, possibly bought due to the frequent clashes between the Trier band and the young aristocrats of the Borussa Korps, which also led to a duel between the young bourgeois from Trier and a militarily educated aristocrat. See Raddatz 1975, pp. 29–30.

man in Berlin to dedicate himself to university teaching of either law or philosophy. Nonetheless, he encouraged his son to consider, particularly given his commitment to his engagement, the difficulties of access to and the length of a university career, and of the 'vital question in the proper sense' that lay before him, inviting him to think also of a possible career as a government advisor in the field of administration.[86] But the young Marx was, in truth, already destined to be, rather than a man of the law, a man who necessarily lived *extra legem*. Due to his profoundly courageous and passionate character, his strong sense of himself, due to his incorrigible tendency towards creativity and intellectual affirmation, even in his studies during his six years in Berlin it was impossible for him not to transgress against the paternal rules and fill his time with theoretical passions and the writings that most greatly encouraged and interested him. Nonetheless, Heinrich's concern and tender affection were never denied to Karl, despite the bitterness that this prodigal son undoubtedly did not spare his father. It was a protective concern and attention, from a distance and with advice and encouragement and, at times, with complaints and severe reprimands, but never with coldness or authoritarianism. Perhaps due to Heinrich's possibly excessive meekness, nonetheless, the young Marx continued to wander at his pleasure through the various sites of his moral and intellectual formation until he arrived at the determining encounter with this other, metaphorical and spiritual father that was to be Georg Wilhelm Friedrich Hegel. It is undoubtedly no coincidence, proving the intense relationship between the two men of the Marx family, that on the day of Karl's death in 1883, Friedrich Engels wanted a daguerreotype of his father Heinrich to be placed in his dear friend's coffin.[87] Heinrich, in dying a premature death from tuberculosis at the age of 56, was not only removed from life, but possibly also from bitter disagreements with his son. Probably due to the great distance between the Rhineland and Berlin, his son Karl did not attend the funeral.[88]

The conceptual structure of the letter that the young Berlin student sent to his father on 10 November 1837, around one year after arriving in the Prussian capital, is explicitly Hegelian from the very outset. Even the words that the young Marx uses in presenting and justifying to his father the intellectual and sentimental vicissitudes of his student life make clear this inspiration. To the young Marx, these experiences appear not as the expression of a disorderly

86 *MECW* 1, p. 681.

87 See McLellan 1973, p. 21.

88 On the relationship between Heinrich and Karl Marx, see Siegel 1978, pp. 37–59.

life and an arbitrary and superficial personality, but rather – and he wants his father to see them as such – as orderly and progressive stages in a process of maturity which, dislocating and transfiguring his personal biography within the movements of a historical cycle, imposes on a subjective experience of life an objective logic and necessity.

> There are moments in one's life that are like frontier posts marking the completion of a period but at the same time clearly indicating a new direction. At such a moment of transition we feel compelled to view the past and the present with the eagle eye of thought in order to become conscious of our real position. Indeed, world history itself likes to look back in this way and take stock, which often gives it the appearance of retrogression or stagnation, whereas it is merely, as it were, sitting back in an armchair in order to understand itself and mentally grasp its own activity, that of spirit.[89]

If not starting from the synthetic nature and supra-personal view of spirit, of *Geist*,

> What better amends and forgiveness could there be for much that is objectionable and blameworthy than to be seen as the manifestation of an essentially necessary state of things? How, at least, could the often ill-fated play of chance and intellectual error better escape the reproach of being due to a perverse heart?[90]

Marx judges his own life not episodically and in a fragmented way but in the light of a principle that integrates the various episodes of his existence in the circle of its totality.

> When, therefore, now at the end of a year spent here I cast a glance back on the course of events during that time [...] allow me to review my affairs in the way I regard life in general, as the expression of an intellectual activity which develops in all directions, in science, art and private matters.[91]

89 *MECW* 1, p. 10 (Karl Marx to Heinrich Marx, 10 November 1837).

90 Ibid.

91 *MECW* 1, p. 11.

The first phase of his university education, Marx observes, could not help but be idealistic, in the romantic understanding of the word or, in the more intellectual idealist sense that Hegel assigns to the philosophies of division, in the sense of the visions of the world that begin from the presupposition of dualism and the separation of finite and infinite, subject and object, individual and reality and from the endless longing for their impossible reconciliation. The first and most urgent literary expression of this spiritual approach, motivated and centred on his separation from Jenny, to whom he had just become engaged, and his move to the distant and cold Berlin, could not be other than a lyrical versifying created in accordance with the schema and more traditional and external motifs of romantic poetry centred on the idealisation of the hero who battles against the prosaic nature and miseries of the world in order to affirm the purity of his ideas, the first among which is his burning and noble affection for the woman he loves.[92] Eyes of an eagle, passions of the heart and the depth of the sea, the sublime nature of the sky and art, nostalgia and uncontainable ardour, magic harps, sirens, moonlight, follies and extreme spiritual expression: these are the themes and style of the very young Marx's literary work, constantly flamboyant and, in its titanism, lacking in poetic authenticity and intensity, which he himself lucidly admits.

> In accordance with my state of mind at the time, lyrical poetry was bound to be my first subject, at least the most pleasant and immediate one. But owing to my attitude and whole previous development it was purely idealistic. My heaven, my art, became a world beyond, as remote as my love. Everything real became hazy and what is hazy has no definite outlines. All the poems of the first three volumes I sent to Jenny are marked by attacks on our times, diffuse and inchoate expressions of feeling, nothing natural, everything built out of moonshine, complete opposition between what is and what ought to be, rhetorical reflections instead of poetic thoughts, but perhaps also a certain warmth of feeling and striving for poetic fire. The whole extent of a longing that has no

92 Four handwritten notebooks of the young Marx's literary productions have survived. The first three, from the last months of 1836 and possibly the start of 1837, are dedicated to 'my dear, eternally beloved Jenny von Westphalen'. The fourth notebook, of 1837, was sent by Karl to his father. On the other poems of the same years, collected in a notebook and diary, by Marx's sister, Sophie, see *MEGA*, I, 1, pp. 705–67. On Marx the poet, see Johnston 1967; Rose 1978.

> bounds finds expression there in many different forms and makes the poetic 'composition' into 'diffusion'.[93]

Furthermore, the practice of philosophy of the Berlin student is structurally homologous in its exteriority and artificiality with a form of expression and thought that is unable to be the adequate form in which to express a real content. As he expressly states, in moving from Kantian and Fichtean idealism, the young Karl attempted in a first very long manuscript to organise the subject of law in accordance with a first part that is philosophical, made of principles and definitions, and a second part, relating to history, dedicated to positive law and interpreted in the light of the concepts of the first part. However, in compliance with what Hegel claimed in his criticism of Kant and Fichte, he was rapidly forced to appreciate, as he wrote to his father, that a form that is not self-determination and self-production posited by the same content in question is a form that remains exterior and violently imposed by the arbitrary nature of a manipulating subject external to that reality.

> Here, above all, the same opposition between what is and what ought to be, which is characteristic of idealism, stood out as a serious defect and was the source of the hopelessly incorrect division of the subject-matter. First of all came what I was pleased to call the metaphysics of law, i.e., basic principles, reflections, definitions of concepts, divorced from all actual law and every actual form of law, as occurs in Fichte, only in my case it was more modern and shallower. From the outset an obstacle to grasping the truth here was the unscientific form of mathematical dogmatism, in which the author argues hither and thither, going round and round the subject dealt with, without the latter taking shape as something living and developing in a many-sided way. A triangle gives the mathematician scope for construction and proof, it remains a mere abstract conception in space and does not develop into anything further. It has to be put alongside something else, then it assumes other positions, and this diversity added to it gives it different relationships and truths. On the other hand, in the concrete expression of a living world of ideas, as exemplified by law, the state, nature, and philosophy as a whole, the object itself must be studied in its development; arbitrary divisions must not be introduced, the rational character of the object itself must develop as something imbued with contradictions in itself and find its unity in itself. Next, as the second

93 *MECW* 1, p. 11.

> part, came the philosophy of law, that is to say, according to my views at the time, an examination of the development of ideas in positive Roman law, as if positive law in its conceptual development (I do not mean in its purely finite provisions) could ever be something different from the formation of the concept of law, which the first part, however, should have dealt with.[94]

The young student's arrival at fundamentally Hegelian positions, after an idealism 'above the earth' ('nourished with the idealism of Kant and Fichte'), is thus clear.[95] The determinations that structure the real and which render it perspicuous and knowable must be the produced and explained by the real itself, by means of a development driven by contradiction. The poles of this development consist in form and matter (already identified here by Marx, as later in his dissertation, also as formal determination and material determination). The former represents the function of universality and the infinite or, rather, represents the dynamic function of self-knowledge, according to which a reality really exists only when it is conscious of itself and possesses itself in the completed development of all its determinations. The latter represents the function of particularity, or the provisional coincidence of that same reality with one of its configurations or states of development, determined, partial and finite but, precisely for this reason, materially and concretely perceptible. The transition from one configuration to another and the complete development of all the material determinations constitutes the form. The relationship between matter, or content, and form is thus mediated and intrinsic. The form is the content itself that possesses and conceives itself (this is why it is a 'concept') in the totality of its determinations. This is what Marx confirms in the following passage where, once again in an exact Hegelian sense, he uses the term 'quality' as synonymous with finite and particular determination and where, singularly but not randomly, he identifies his fallacious and pre-Hegelian way of thinking and conceptualising with von Savigny's (the founder of the so-called 'historical school of law') manner of conceiving of right and its history.[96] The extrinsic nature of this approach on a conceptual-formal and historical-empirical level

94 *MECW* 1, p. 12.

95 *MECW* 1, p. 18.

96 Friedrich Karl von Savigny (1799–1861) was, together with Gustav Hugo, the greatest representative of the 'historical' school of law, which, opposing a constitutional and liberal interpretation of the spirit of the law, theorised the foundation of law as only that in which the historical tradition of a people is sedimented. Marx's lecturer in Berlin in the winter term 1836–7, he was also the Prussian Minister for legislative reform from 1842 to 1848.

in the consideration of juridical history had already been criticised by Hegel in his *Preface* to the *Outlines of the Philosophy of Right.*

> Moreover, I had further divided this part into the theory of formal law and the theory of material law, the first being the pure form of the system in its sequence and interconnections, its subdivisions and scope, whereas the second, on the other hand, was intended to describe the content, showing how the form becomes embodied in its content. This was an error I shared with Herr von Savigny, as I discovered later in his learned work on ownership, the only difference being that he applies the term formal definition of the concept to 'finding the place which this or that theory occupies in the (fictitious) Roman system', the material definition being 'the theory of positive content which the Romans attributed to a concept defined in this way', whereas I understood by form the necessary architectonics of conceptual formulations, and by matter the necessary quality of these formulations. The mistake lay in my belief that matter and form can and must develop separately from each other, and so I obtained not a real form, but something like a desk with drawers into which I then poured sand.[97]

However, before arriving at Hegel's philosophy and, therefore proceding to seeking 'the idea in reality itself',[98] and abandoning the idealism that instead imposes artificial and formal conceptual constructs on reality (such as that of Kant and Fichte, in Marx's opinion), the young Marx has to suffer the consequences of the exhaustion of this first theoretical consciousness. He has to see the inconclusiveness of his first classifying schema of the metaphysics of right, the artificiality of the triptych into which he tried to order all juridical matters (see the schema relating to private law that he attaches in the letter).[99] He will need to test himself with a second classifying system and, ultimately, fall into a decisive crisis of his spiritual formation that probably occurs between the first winter and the first summer terms of this time at the University of Berlin.

> At the end of the section on material private law, I saw the falsity of the whole thing, the basic plan of which borders on that of Kant, but deviates

97 *MECW* 1, p. 15. Marx quotes, probably from memory, as the citations are not precise, from F.C. von Savigny 1837, *Das Recht des Besitzes. Eine civilistische Abhandlung*, (6th edition), part I, § 1, pp. 4–5.

98 *MECW* 1, p. 18.

99 *MECW* 1, pp. 16–17.

> wholly from it in the execution, and again it became clear to me that there could be no headway without philosophy. So with a good conscience I was able once more to throw myself into her embrace, and I drafted a new system of metaphysical principles, but at the conclusion of it I was once more compelled to recognise that it was wrong, like all my previous efforts.[100]

The conclusion of all this toil lies in his capitulation and the acceptance of Hegel's philosophy, which until then he had considered as foreign and hostile. A period of illness affecting even his language and his body's reflexes expresses the intensity of this crisis and transition. It was during this period that the young man spent time recovering in the fishing village of Stralow on the banks of the river Spree in the Berlin countryside, still using the generous funds made available to him by his father Heinrich, that Karl read 'Hegel from beginning to end, together with most of his disciples'.[101] Thus, at the end of the composition of a philosophical dialogue, the young student, despite himself and with considerable surprise and amazement, sees his original spiritual identity overturned and now configured in accordance with the theoretical structure of Hegelian philosophy. The transformation and self-legitimisation of Marx's *Bildungsroman*, through the comparison of the stages of his formation to the movements of Hegel's *Phenomenology of Spirit* – or, in other words, the failure of a mode of self-representation of consciousness and its unexpected but necessary overturning into the opposite of itself – thus takes place before the eyes of his father and all his future readers.

> I wrote a dialogue of about 24 pages: 'Cleanthes, or the Starting Point and Necessary Continuation of Philosophy'. Here art and science, which had become completely divorced from each other, were to some extent united, and like a vigorous traveller I set about the task itself, a philosophical-dialectical account of divinity, as it manifests itself as the idea-in-itself, as religion, as nature, and as history. My last proposition was the beginning of the Hegelian system. And this work, for which I had acquainted myself to some extent with natural science, Schelling, and history, which had caused me to rack my brains endlessly, and which is so [...] written (since it was actually intended to be a new logic) that now even I myself can hardly recapture my thinking about it, this work, my dearest

100 *MECW* 1, p. 17.

101 *MECW* 1, p. 19.

> child, reared by moonlight, like a false siren delivers me into the arms of the enemy.[102]

Thus, in the end, he arrived at Hegel and the acceptance of his philosophy. With this, the young Marx attains the certainty of a perspective according to which the individual's living and doing must be understood and evaluated within a horizon of supra-individual forces and necessities.

It is obvious that one of the most determining reasons behind the beginning of this way of thinking was, as previously discussed, the psychological and subjective urgency of justifying before the caring and worried eyes of his father the intense but also disorderly and multiform progress of his university studies. However, this affective urgency, lacking any depersonalisation and deresponsibilisation, translated, through the meeting with Hegel, into a philosophical and conceptual theory of reality as the outcome of the actions of a supra-personal and supra-individual spirit, which, in various configurations and meanings, will be so significant throughout all of Marx's works.

As a consequence, and in an obviously unwitting and indirect way, his natural father's attention assisted in leading the young Karl into the arms of a new spiritual father and his paternalism. The identity of Marx in Berlin, therefore, will henceforth be that of a young Hegelian who turns towards the master's works with passion and acumen, as evidenced by the dissertation and its preparatory works.

But the letter from Berlin is not just evidence of Hegel. What it also introduces is the young Karl's enormous capacity for reading and his wide interests. His furious and impassioned study does not mean that he is not also very disciplined, composing patient and laborious extracts in a way that will remain a constant characteristic of his style of work throughout his life. A passage of the letter referring to the phase immediately preceding his conversion of Hegel shows us the interest in aesthetics, history, humanist culture and languages that he cultivated alongside his legal studies.

> In the course of this work I adopted the habit of making extracts from all the books I read, for instance from Lessing's Laokoon, Solger's Erwin, Winckelmann's history of art, Luden's German history, and incidentally scribbled down my reflections. At the same time I translated Tacitus'

---

102 *MECW* 1, p. 18. There has remained no trace of the philosophical dialogue 'Cleante' written by Marx. There are, however, fragments of the tragedy 'Oulanem' and the humorous novel 'Scorpion und Felix' quoted by Marx in the same letter.

> *Germania*, and Ovid's *Tristia*, and began to learn English and Italian by myself, i.e., out of grammars, but I have not yet got anywhere with this. I also read Klein's criminal law and his annals, and all the most recent literature, but this last only by the way.[103]

A later passage provides further evidence of the style and intensity of Marx's methods of study, when he mentions the mountain of reading, of legal and other material, that he had to complete in order to placate his anxiety and troubles.

> Shortly after that I pursued only positive studies: the study of Savigny's *Ownership*, Feuerbach's and Grolmann's criminal law, Cramer's *de verborum significatione*, Wenning-Ingenheim's Pandect system, and Mühlenbruch's *Doctrina pandectarum*, which I am still working through, and finally a few titles from Lauterbach, on civil procedure and above all canon law, the first part of which, Gratian's *Concordia discordantium canonum*, I have almost entirely read through in the corpus and made extracts from, as also the supplement, Lancelotti's *Institutiones*. Then I translated in part Aristotle's *Rhetoric*, read *de augmentis scientiarum* of the famous Bacon of Verulam, spent a good deal of time on Reimarus, to whose book on the artistic instincts of animals I applied my mind with delight, and also tackled German law, but chiefly only to the extent of going through the capitularies of the Franconian kings and the letters of the Popes to them.[104]

But now, beyond all this, there is Hegel, whose name and philosophy profoundly mark the Berlin years of the young Karl Marx.

## 12 '*Formbestimmung*' or 'Formal Determination': The Keystone of Marx's Thought

The category of 'formal determination' plays a central role in the substance of Marx's dissertation and expresses the theoretical site of the maximum impact of the influence that Hegel's thought had on his studies in Berlin. This category, in the preeminently Hegelian sense, indicates in Marx's text all that is active in

103 *MECW* 1, p. 17.
104 *MECW* 1, p. 19.

the non-physical and non-material, as the principle organiser of reality in the physical and material world. 'Form', as a distinct category in contrast to 'matter', is that which, immanently and non-transcendently, organises and relates the phenomena of experience and sensible life in accordance with connections of sense that are themselves non-sensible. It is that which, according to Hegel's conceptual usage, prompts the natural and the sensible to determine themselves by reference to something other than themselves, which forces the determinate to subtract itself from itself and its presumed coincidence with itself.

It is a singular fact, and one central for understanding the entire evolution of Marx's work, that the use of this conceptual category is exhausted and substantially disappears in Marx's subsequent writings. It only reappears, again with a fundamentally theoretical role, in his mature critique of political economy, beginning with the manuscript of 1857–8 known as the *Grundrisse*.

This is clearly not the place, given the limiting of our text to the early Marx, to discuss Marx in his maturity as well. However, in order to better understand the path and the fundamental thesis of this book – which concerns the depth of philosophical and emotional connection that the young man from Trier initially had with what, in Berlin during the years from 1830 to 1840, still represented philosophy as such, and the way that Marx soon after represses that connection when he enters politics, in an overly hasty and relatively unmeditated move from theory to praxis – it may be opportune to mention here, in a very few words, the way in which Marx begins to use once again the category of *Formbestimmung* in *Capital*. The return of the repressed in this sense shapes not only emotional and psychological but also scientific and theoretical experiences.

It is only through the re-proposal of *Formbestimmung*, and the dialectical multiplication of reality between essence and existence that this implies, that the mature Marx manages to avoid, if not always then at least in a significant part of his reflections, the metaphysics of history centred on the progressive self-enlightenment and self-possession of the human species through labour. In my opinion, this, in a nutshell, is the position operative in his philosophy of praxis, from the *Economic and Philosophic Manuscripts* of 1844 to the *Manifesto of the Communist Party* in 1848, via works such as *The Holy Family*, *The German Ideology* and *The Poverty of Philosophy*.

The paradigm of human praxis as nothing other than labour – or, in other words, the reduction of the whole of reality, both as direct production and the most indirect outcome, to nothing more than the elaboration on the part of the human species of natural objectuality – is the particular theoretical model into which the post-Berlin Marx pushes the young Hegelians' desire for a philosophy of action. But, behind the presumption of inaugurating a materialist concept of history, abandoning the mystifications of pure thought and entrusting himself to the simplicity of 'premises [that] can thus be verified in a purely empirical way',[105] there circulates in Marx's anti-idealism a motif of exasperated and omnipotent idealism which is resolved in the celebration of the poetic and Promethean prevailing of humanity over nature. It is as if the radical and unquestionable rejection claimed against Hegelism and its philosophical paternalism should necessarily give rise to a counterpart in Marx's soul, the idea of an *arché* – of a totalising principle of the explanation of the real – that could not help but reflect and change, precisely in its special structure as theoretical principle, the emotive tonality of the demand for self-sufficiency and omnipotence that this repression displaced onto the level of affects and the psychological register of his own life. It is as if a too hasty transition from the idealism of thought to the claimed and much more concrete fecundity of praxis brought with it, in the very heart of praxis, an obviously unstated and unconscious excess of theory, due to the haste of the transition.

Marx's materialist philosophy of praxis results in a theory of historical civilisation conceived as the progressive perfecting of the dominion of the human species over nature, in a celebration of the accumulation of the productive forces of humanity which, only with communism, can overcome the internal divisions that are inseparable from this development, and become truly self-conscious and in control of itself. Thus, the meaning of history will consist in and be unified by the continuity of a substance (the interrupted development from generation to generation of the productive forces of labour) and the variation of an accident represented by the various forms of social life – the social relationships of production – that are born and die in accordance with how they move from being forms that facilitate the growth of that substantial principle to being limits that impede and contradict their development.

It is therefore a substantialist paradigm of historical life. Its paradoxically undialectical and analytical character will become very explicit with the claimed explanation of every moment of individual and collective life, both socio-economic and cultural-ideological, from ancient to modern history, on the basis of the analytical concept *par excellence* – and, truth be told, fairly simplistic concept – of the 'division of labour'. It is by means of this concept that Marx, together with Engels, above all in the pages of *The German Ideology*, attempts to explain every dimension of material, cultural and political

105 *MECW* 5, p. 31.

life of humanity.[106] In this vision, the presupposition of historical events will remain a subject such as the human species, which, however much subjected to class divisions, alienations and expropriations, cannot but finally overcome every division and reaffirm the organic nature of the essence that on principle belongs to it, due to its innate unity and universality.

However, how the philosophy of praxis in the Marx of historical materialism will claim to explain social action in terms of the labouring activities of the human species, beyond these all too brief remarks, cannot be discussed in detail here. This could be done adequately only elsewhere, on the basis of a very specific analysis, both conceptual and lexicographic, that would demonstrate the extent to which the notion of 'human species being [*menschliche Gattungswesen*]' remains a constant in Marx's works of the 1840s, conditioning Marx's concept of economics, history and politics in those years with its logic of alienation and reappropriation.

Here, it must suffice to note that Marx will be able to weaken the hold of such a metaphysics of history on him, and of such a narrative based on a universal and presupposed subject, only when, by returning to the notion of *Formbestimmung*, he is able to theorise modern society according to the articulation and dualism of two worlds: 'world 1', as the sphere of appearance and visibility, animated by concrete things and individuals, and 'world 2', which is the sphere of essence and invisibility, animated only by the abstraction of a merely quantitative wealth which, precisely because it is mere quantity, cannot have any other purpose than becoming its own quantitative accumulation. This will occur, however, only when Marx will have the theoretical strength to really confront the notion of negation, in the sense given to this term by Hegel in the history of philosophy (that is, as the force that removes fixed and rigid determinations from existence), and only when he will be able to translate it into the disanthropomophic and impersonal abstraction that, as mere quantity, lies at the heart of *Capital* and its tendentially infinite accumulations. In other words, this will happen only when, providing an entirely original meaning to it, he will return to the Hegelian notion of *Formbestimmung* and its concern with the infinite and the negation of the world of particulars. On this basis alone will he be able to avoid the limits of his anthropocentrism and the vision of preconceived theories of history from which it necessarily derives.

Marx himself, however, was insufficiently aware and self-conscious of this unfolding of his theoretical journey. Thus, often, even in his mature pages, he will again methodologically and epistemologically express the new perspective

---

106 See Finelli 1990b.

and the new categorical field of research in accordance with forms of consciousness and theoretical reflection that are still linked to the formulation of his youthful years and the 1840s. This is a further problem that should be added to the much-debated question of the connection of continuity or discontinuity that links Marx's thoughts before *Capital* to the subsequent criticism of political economy. This problem, also, necessarily must be reserved for another study, with a breadth of argumentation suitable for the complexity of the problem that can only be indicated here.

Now, we must try to reflect, even if fairly synthetically, on Hegel. Only an clear recognition of the fundamental concepts of truth, spirit and the dialectics of the philosopher of Stuttgart will assist us in understanding how and why the attempts of the young Marx to find a further and progressive solution to the problems left open in Hegel's idealism will conclude, at least in his early works that we will be considering here, in a theoretical system that is much more regressive and naive than that of Hegel himself.

CHAPTER 2

# A Hegelian Sketch

## 1 Negation and Contradiction

Hegel's concept of truth as a circle runs through and structures his entire work. The most explicit theorisation, however, as previously mentioned, is found in the 'Preface' to the *Phenomenology of Spirit* and in the first volume of the *Science of Logic*, in the section 'With what must the beginning of science be made?' Some significant passages from this latter text, published by Hegel in 1812, have already been quoted. But from the *Phenomenology* onwards, in 1807, Hegel had already been particularly clear on the subject.

> Further, the living Substance is being which is in truth Subject or, what is the same, is in truth actual only in so far as it is the movement of positing itself, or is the mediation of its self-othering with itself [...]. It is the process of its own becoming, the circle that presupposes its end as its goal, having its end also as its beginning; and only by being worked out to its end, it is actual [...]. The True is the whole. But, the whole is nothing other than the essence consummating itself through its development. Of the Absolute it must be said that it is essentially the result that only in the end is it what it truly is; and that precisely in this consists its nature, viz. to be actual, subject, the spontaneous becoming of itself.[1]

---

1 Hegel 1977, pp. 10–11. As previously mentioned, this Hegelian concept presupposes the foundation of all German idealism, namely, Fichte's *Wissenschaftslehre* (1794) and his definition of the self as an activity that posits itself. 'The self posits itself and by virtue of this mere self-assertion it exists; and conversely, the self exists and posits its own existence by virtue of merely existing [...]. The self posits itself simply because it exists. It posits itself by merely existing and exists by merely being posited' (Fichte 1970, p. 98). The decisive theoretical articulation that marks the transition from Kantian criticism to German idealism lies in the subtraction of the most profound identity of subjectivity from the intuitive-cognitive immediacy of the Kantian 'I think', and in Fichte's dislocation in praxis and in action that runs through and removes the limitations of the non-I. Fichte, by mediating the two Kantian definitions of theoretical subjectivity and practical subjectivity as respectively constituted on self-consciousness and on the freedom unconditionally to give oneself norms, inaugurates a conception of subjectivity as an Absolute, whose freedom consists in liberating itself from every non-I or, in other words, any limits or conditioning that finds an external and presupposed self, transforming it into something posited and produced by the I itself. Both German

This passage from the 'Preface' to the *Phenomenology* clearly demonstrates that at the basis of the circular concept of truth lies, for Hegel, a circular concept of subjectivity. In effect, he conceives of the spiritual as the self [*Selbst*] capable of opening itself up and experiencing the relationship with otherness without losing itself and being dissolved in it, but, on the contrary, returning and maintaining itself precisely by means of its own identity. Nature, on the other hand, is the place where individuality is subject to a relationship with the other of itself, losing itself in the infinite series of alterations and transformations. In nature, the particular and finite entity assumes, without any consciouness of the universal, that it will immediately coincide and remain in its own self, defending itself and abstracting from the relationship with the other. However, otherness, repressed and not sublated, effectively 'bends' the particular and obliges it to be unceasing in its transformations. In the spiritual, on the other hand, the being in itself of subjectivity cannot but acknowledge its constitutive dependence on otherness. This, initially, translates itself into being-other, but then returns from this otherness to itself or, more precisely, to the in itself and for itself, in a circle that is true infinity, given that it makes the subject the synthesis of the self and the other than the self, rather than the bad infinity of natural metamorphoses that never deviate from the centrality of a *Selbst* [of a self].

'Spirit [*Geist*]' in Hegel therefore means to become one's self precisely through the relationship with the other. It means that the self is not immediately and originally coincident with itself, but rather becomes equivalent with itself only in its mode of relating itself to its other. Spirit is nothing more than the modality of this self-relating.[2] The various fields of reality, from inorganic to organic nature, from human life in its most private and family organisation to social existence established in accordance with the environments of the economy and the state, through to the realisation of the more universal circles of

---

Romanticism and the more specifically idealist culture were profoundly conditioned by this concept of the I as an Absolute which translates the presupposed into the posited and profoundly identifies the nature of knowledge (as consciousness of self or self-consciousness) with the nature of producing or acting. On this last subject in Schelling and Hegel, see what Heidegger writes in his *Nietzsche* (Heidegger 1991, pp. 34–5): 'In one of Schelling's most profound works, the treatise *On the Essence of Human Freedom*, published in 1809, that philosopher writes: "In the final and ultimate instance, there is no other being at all than Willing, Willing is primal being" (I, VII, 350). And in his *Phenomenology of Spirit* (1807), Hegel grasps the essence of being as knowing, but grasps knowing as essentially identical to willing'.

2 See Henrich 1980, pp. 103–18.

human experience such as art, religion and philosophy, correspond precisely to the various degrees of self-affirmation of a spiritual or circular subjectivity of this kind. The extent to which a subject coincides with itself or not is the extent to which its relationship with itself – in what can be called the interior or vertical dimension – is either rich and full or poor and fragmented, to the degree to which it limits or expands its relationship – what might be called horizontal – and its passing through alterity.

This is why nature is defined by Hegel 'as the Idea in the form of otherness'.[3] This is conceived not in the creationist sense that Spirit, by going out of itself, gives rise to a world that before this act had not existed, but in the sense that the dimension most characteristic of the natural world, as it is lived by the entities and beings that are part of it, is that of exteriority or, in other words, that in which the other exists externally and indifferently to the entity in question, without intrinsically contributing to the sense of its identity.

> In nature, not only is the play of forms a prey to boundless and unchecked contingency, but each separate entity is without the Notion of itself. The highest level to which Nature attains is life; but this, as only a natural mode of the Idea, is at the mercy of the unreason of externality, and the living creature is throughout its whole life entangled with other alien existences, whereas in every expression of Spirit there is contained the moment of free, universal self-relation.[4]

The connection between nature and spirit in Hegel's philosophy should not, therefore, be read in the light of the widespread interpretation generally associated with idealism (an idea which, by falling outside itself, generates a subordinate and inferior reality in the form of matter), but rather according to the relationship of 'bad' or 'true' infinity.[5] Here, true infinity is that of a subjectivity that universalises itself and refinds itself in relation to the other of itself, while bad infinity is that of an inexhaustible series of alterations in which a finite figure is replaced by another finite figure without this seriality of forms maturing into the synthesis and mastery of a subject. This is not because in nature there is no regime of laws and supra-individual connections that sustain the exist-

3 Hegel 2004, p. 13 (§ 247).

4 Hegel 2004, p. 17 (§ 248, Remark).

5 For an interpretation of the relationship between the Idea and nature in Hegel that is neither creationist nor dualist, see Wandschneider and Hösle 1983. On Hegel's reading of Schelling, which lies at the origins of a vision of nature as the other of the idea, rather than its being other, see Horstmann 1986.

ence of the singular, but because in nature the single individual, enclosed in the egoism of its confines and in the immediate and absolute need to reproduce itself, knows nothing of the universal and, therefore, cannot express its becoming other, the going out of itself [*Entäusserung*], other than through alienation [*Entfremdung*], or an abandonment to external forces from which there is no return to mastery of oneself.

The various interpretations that have been given of Hegel's idealism have often depended precisely on the meaning of this Hegelian concept of nature, as a world not created by an entity going outside itself, but as a world external to itself. However, those who do not agree with the meaning we have attributed to the manner in which Hegel rereads and reformulates Descartes's *res extensa* instead interpret the exteriority of nature in a creationist sense. They must therefore necessarily equate idealism with theology and transcendental spiritualism, beginning with the reading of Feuerbach.

Movement and the process that leads from the level of natural existence to that of spiritual subjectivity is the 'dialectic' in Hegel, and the motor of this dialectical becoming is 'negation-contradiction'. Every determination is negation, Hegel claims following Spinoza: every determined entity is, in other words, itself insofar as it is not the other entities from which it distinguishes itself. However, negation thus conceived is not limited, for Hegel, to tracing a boundary of difference between the determined entity and the other entities, which would leave everything co-existing in indifference. Negation-determination should, instead, take place and be radicalised in all its implicit sense, meaning, above all within spiritual life, not so much or not only distinction from the other, but rather, exclusion of the determined from every relationship that intrinsically links it to the other.

Already in nature, the relationship between an individual existence and the other forms of life cannot be organised, beginning from that individual's point of view, in accordance with the modality of co-existence and indifferent difference, because that individual lives for the reproduction of its own existence in a condition of permanent suspicion and opposition towards the other. However, it is more precisely within spiritual life that negation, in an existence that dogmatically insists on closing itself within the immediacy of its self, intentionally and clearly becomes an exclusion: not just a distinction between the individual and the other of itself, therefore, but opposition to every connection that intrinsically and essentially refers it to the other.

However, in this way – and this transition is decisive for an understanding of Hegel's philosophy – the subject that conceives of itself and wants to be finite and closed within its individuality, by negating the other, negates itself or, in other words, negates its truest nature, since it represents itself as merely a naturalistic entity, rejecting the profound dynamics that belong to it as a spiritual entity, and which consist precisely in rendering itself infinite and interiorising the other-than-itself within the horizon of its existence. That the finite is the negative means for Hegel, therefore, that the finite is negative self-reference because it is opposed to and divided from its truest nature. As such, therefore, as fracture and discordance with itself, it is a mode and form of existence intrinsically destined to decline and to be sublated into something else.

The Hegelian dialectic thus has its foundation precisely in this radicalisation of the concept of determination-negation: in the assumption, that is, that the negation of the other is at the same time the negation of the self and, therefore, that determinate negation, rather than guaranteeing the pacific co-existence of an entity within a context of other entities, is, on the contrary, in its self-reflective negating, the condition of self-overcoming and self-refutation. It is not, therefore, determination-negation in the sense attributed to it by Plato's *Sophist*, as synonymous with difference – and, therefore, of relationships between entities that positively exist – but in the sense, as mentioned, of an integral repression of every relationship to the other, which is at one and the same time the subtraction of ontological consistency for the self. This is precisely the negation that becomes a contradiction, in the Hegelian sense of a destructive existence that repels itself or, more precisely, repels the fallacious manner of self-representation that corresponds to a dogmatic and partial image of itself. Contradiction effectively corresponds to the moment in which the finite recognises that, by opposing the other, it has the opposition within itself and that, therefore, its existence is not one and simple, as an empirical and naturalist self-representation of the self would have it, but is binary, composed of the interior co-presence of two opposites. Thus, Hegelian contradiction, as the co-presence and reciprocal implication of opposites, is the path by which the finite recognises the abstraction and partiality of its naturalistic, initial configuration. Accepting the links and dependency on the other of itself, in the contemporaneity of exclusion and implication of the other, it arrives at a full and mature, self-conscious figure of subjectivity.

In the sense just indicated, the finite for Hegel is therefore not a real entity or existence. It is a modality *of knowing*. More precisely, it is one of the possible modes of self-representation of a subject and, therefore, in this sense it cannot be claimed that the finite in Hegel's idealism is a nothing. The finite is subjectivity's naturalistic modality of recognising and identifying itself, its primary and primitive way of representing itself. It is therefore the form of self-consciousness that finds the reasons of its own negation and its own self-overcoming not in external constrictions or moralistic duties, or in compliance with an external instance and authority, but in nothing else but its own intrinsic inadequacy and existential fragility.

## 2 Intellectualistic Subjectivity and Its Bad Infinity

There are two possible paths of the sublation of the finite for Hegel: a false path consisting merely in the reversal into the opposite; and another, true path, which consists in the unity or identity of opposites.

The first path, the reversal into the opposite, coincides with the 'destiny' of the finite when it claims to persist in a naturalistic representation of itself. It is the inevitable punishment to which the finite is condemned when it claims to be the immediate and original absolute subject or, in other words, freed from any consubstantial link to alterity. Hegel argues that those who commit the original sin of abstraction and separation from life will soon be obliged to see their claimed autonomy and indifference overturned and negated by life itself, by that alterity that they wished to keep outside themselves, as opposing and extraneous. Such a process happened to the Jews according to Hegel (who, it must be said, acritically accepted the stereotypes of the Christian tradition). He sees them as one of the prime historic examples of a desire for separation from and negation of community with the human species. As a result of this structural inability to maintain the relation with the other of themselves, they are condemned throughout their history to the destiny of an opposite condition of being, to the destiny, that is, of an inferior and subaltern position in all historical contexts.[6] Such a process also occurs to those beautiful souls who, beginning with the figure of Jesus through to the great figures of Romantic literature, want to keep themselves innocent and pure of commerce and any worldly interests, superior to all other men and their terrestrial passions, because they are inspired only by the 'must' of their disinterested ideals. They end up being the victim of the same world they have rejected, witnessing the devastation and profanation of their supposed perfect and beautiful nature.[7] Abstract subjectivity tears itself away from life, but the denied and repressed life returns to persecute it until it wrenches it from its supposed autonomy in a phenomenological process that anticipates, under the guise of the Hegelian metaphor of 'destiny', the psychological processes

6 See Hegel 1948, pp. 182–300.

7 Hegel 1948, pp. 242, 269.

and categories of psychoanalysis. The repression that the finite, as abstract subjectivity, enacts within itself is translated into a projection to the exterior of the connections of life and the relationships that constitute and sustain it. These forces are thus turned from internal into external forces and, in this exteriorisation and autonomisation, contrasting and hostile forces, until they persecute, invade and subordinate the initial finite to themselves. It is clear here that the category of opposition occupying a central role in Hegel's philosophy has nothing whatsoever to do with the 'real opposition' theorised by Kant in his work *An Attempt to Introduce the Concept of Negative Magnitudes into Philosophy*. For Kant, opposing but equally intense forces of nature meet in a point of equilibrium or negation equal to zero, in which both nullify each other (each existing however autonomously in a positive way and without any lack).[8] The opposition theorised by Hegel is not of a physical but a psychodynamic nature, in the sense that it belongs to the context of sentiments and the will of human beings and their processes of repression-projection. Opposition begins with an act of force that the subject exercises over the other and, at the same time, over itself. This force generates a field of tension that, not recognised as a genesis and the responsibility of the subject in question, is taken up and put on the other term of the relationship. Due to this dynamic over-determination, from being the other of the first expression it is transformed into its opposite or, in other words, into that which the subject in question must exclude but, at the same time, include in its horizon of life in order to give meaning to its own existence.

The bad infinitisation of the finite is, therefore, its reversal into the opposite of itself: its being is filled and dominated precisely by the content and determinations that it wanted to leave aside, irrelevant and indifferent, outside itself. This has the consequence that, with this method of infinitisation, by reversing into the opposite of itself, the finite never ceases to finish or, in other words, to be finite. Within this scenario, where experience is structured in accordance with the general method of opposition, even the opposite of the first finite cannot help but represent itself and conceive of itself in compliance with the criterion of finitude and domination. Therefore, it is destined, after having triumphed and dominated the first finite, to be in turn invaded and devastated by another finite – and so forth, in a succession of finite abstractions and reversals in which there is no space for the universal in its most genuine meaning as that which leads to a true universalisation of the finite. It is no coincidence that precisely this thematic is central to Hegel's thought from its first phases, as can be

8 See Kant 1992, pp. 220–36.

seen from a reading of the *Jugendschriften* and, in particular, the decisive text in this sense which is *The Spirit of Christianity and its Fate*.[9]

The second path, the identity or synthesis of opposites, is when the finite truly ceases to finish or, in other words, when it ceases to have a naturalistic consciousness of itself and, as a consequence, goes on to consider the opposite not as external but as internal and consubstantial with itself. It is when subjectivity, by becoming spirit, is able to draw on and sustain contradiction, because the self is contemporaneously the other and, reciprocally, the other is the self. As will be illustrated later, this function of reconciliation and mediation performed by opposites (which coincides with what Hegel defines as Absolute Spirit or the perfect realisation of subjectivity) corresponds to the most problematic and aporetic dimensions of Hegel's philosophy. There are two fundamental reasons for this: first, because the conclusion of the dialectical path, presenting itself as an absolute identity and the co-penetration of an opposite into another without any residue implies an ontological completeness that contains the risk of a greater theological aspect of Hegel's philosophy; and second, because the possibility of rendering opposite poles contemporaneously present is formulated (above all in the mature works) not in accordance with a capacity for a practical-dynamic resolution of contradiction, but in accordance with a negation or, rather, a merely logical-linguistic overwhelming of the principle of the impossibility of contradiction that, from Aristotle onwards, has been defined as the absolute principle of knowledge and science.

## 3 The False Infinity: The Secret of Ideology

The first path in overcoming the finite corresponds to the dialectic in a negative or sceptical sense, because in this there is only an inexhaustible alternation of opposites without this movement ever finding any peace and meaning in an act of synthesis. 'This infinity is the wrong or negative infinity: it is only a negation

9 On the central role of this theme in the early writings of Hegel, see Finelli 1996a. Galvano della Volpe's attempt to attribute to the young Marx, in contrast to Hegel, the original discovery of the defective logic of 'empirical subremption', according to which a given historical detail is acritically justified and legitimised with the filling of an empty and abstract ideal level with its content (see Della Volpe 1969, pp. 208–10), completely represses the Hegelian foundation of the fallacious infinitisation of a finite – perhaps because the attribution to Hegel of the original concept of such a way of proceeding would have entirely avoided the iconography of a young Marx who was already mature and entirely autonomous from Hegelian idealism.

of a finite: but the finite rises again the same as ever and is never got rid of and absorbed'.[10] The second nexus of opposition, as a relationship not of alternation but of co-presence of opposites, is the dialectic in a positive sense, which, by managing to think in the contemporaneity of the very unity of time about one thing and the other, sustains contradiction as an experience of something which, by passing into the other, effectively continues to accompany itself. Here the finite that ceases to finish is that which Hegel defines as the Absolute insofar as it is not transcendent of, but immanent to, reality. The Absolute is none other than the finite itself, in its abandoning of the false absoluteness of naturalness and its pursuit of an identity that is neither transient nor rhapsodic but firm and able to maintain a relationship with alterity. This is precisely the most characteristic function of the sublation of the finite as defined by Hegel with the term *Aufhebung*. Sublation does not mean the annihilation of the finite, as for those, beginning with Feuerbach, who wish to reduce Hegelian philosophy to mere theology; rather, it means raising up and conserving (the true meanings of the German verb *aufheben*) or, in other words, the raising up to a superior and broader perspective in which the finite abandons its presumed autonomy and abstraction and, having confirmed itself within the network of relationships that support it, deprives its existence of contingency and aleatoriness. The process of sublation and *Aufhebung* can also be seen as a circular process because the subjectivity in question never goes out of itself but only passes through the various possible modes of self-representation always based in itself until the supreme return to itself that consists in the removal of every naturalistic presupposition from itself, presuppositions merely found and assigned to its existence. It thus achieves an identity that is the outcome only of its own production and realisation.

We have seen that the productive faculty of the circular structure of subjectivity and truth is, for Hegel, 'dialectical reason'. Outside this and its relationship and synthetic capacities stands the 'intellect [*Verstand*]', the faculty of division, which produces all the abstractions-separations that subjectivity puts into play, both theoretically and practically. Over and above this, as will be seen, this is also, precisely as a faculty of division, the faculty of producing the ideological institutions of history, as organisational and integrative modes of a community based on separation and abstraction.

The intellect is that which separates or makes rigid and fixed as one outside the other the particular and the universal, finite and infinite, terms of relation and relation, content and form, matter and spirit. In the sense of that which

10 Hegel 1975a, p. 137 (§ 94).

breaks away from and rejects unifying mediation, it is synonymous not only with reflective-abstracting thought but, more generally, with a total mode of being of subjectivity that gives importance to one of its faculties, be it sentiment, intuition or sensibility, as something that in its immediacy and separateness from the subject's other faculties presumes to exhaust and understand reality as a whole in itself. Thus, Hegel considers that the various historical forms of culture and civilisation that have characterised the history of humanity are established according to whether the intellectualistic subject privileges one of its faculties of partial approach to reality and according to the pole of any possible relational couple that, in turn, is abstractly privileged with respect to another. These are all affected by some form of incompleteness and partiality, until modern times when the most mature and rational forms of social organisation are realised. The partiality of these historic-social formations – in the context of a theory of the idealistic causation of history,[11] we should recall – consists in the asymmetry with which this intellectualistic subject perceives reality and makes itself an archetypal model, in the generalisation of its mode of being, for the mores of society as a whole.

The intellect, therefore, is the compendium and the keystone for the definition of a subject that finds both reassurance and identity in an only partial use of itself and experience. As a consequence, it generates and organises a world of ideas and of practical and institutional reality consistently characterised by a typology of impoverishment and division. This is also because the intellect, over and above the reversal of opposites and so-called bad infinity, enacts an appearance of mediation and synthesis, a false infinitisation of the finite or an apparent concrete universality, which is the foundation for the production of ideology.

The fallacious infinitisation of the finite is, in effect, the reconciliation that is provided by means of a mere juxtaposition of two extremes rather than through dialectical synthesis. It consists in the attribution or elevation to the value of a universal of a merely finite or particular, at the same time excluding from such dignity all the other particulars. Thus, the function of the universal here is – rather than that of unifying the multiple or, in other words, of relating all the finites – that of putting a merely particular in the form of the universal; without, that is, modifying its real mode of being, but only modifying its way of appearing and seeming to be. Thus, the false infinitisation of a finite consists precisely in the transfiguration of a particular, in its acquisition not of the

11 On the use and meaning of this expression in a context not limited to Hegelian philosophy, see Rodano 1986.

effective reality but only of the symbolic reality of the universal. A mere singularity becomes the symbol of the universal relationship and synthesis. But this occurs – and this is the decisive point of Hegel's argument – because that particular benefits from the symbolic surplus that derives from the cessation that all the other individuals unwittingly apply to their participative and communal nature. The transfiguration of a particular is the outcome of a process of repression-projection-displacement that all the other individuals – that is, which are not that particular – make of their original human-relational nature. This is the process that Hegel designates with the pair of terms 'alienation' or 'estrangement [*Entfremdung*]' and 'thingification' or 'reification [*Verdinglichung*]'.

This pair describes and conceptualises a process that is simultaneously a process of socialisation and of ideological production. In every socio-historical situation in which the members of a community are lacking in conscious participation and passion about the common good as a source of care for and reproduction of their individual well-being, and instead attribute importance only to private interests, abstract and separate from those of others, then the nexus of socialisation or, in other words, the connection with the interests and lives of others, can occur only in a way that is in turn abstract and separate from those individuals. It must be realised and posited outside them, in another place, which, precisely because it is external, can be made concrete and perceivable by means of particular and determinate figures and things. Alienation means, that is, that their repressed sociality, being located externally, is necessarily reified: deposited and embodied in particular realities which, by means of their finite particularity, express and symbolise the valency and authority of the universal. The production of the social nexus is therefore simultaneously the production of its ideological dissimulation, the production, that is, of a simulacrum, in the sense that something, be it person or thing, comes to be valued, transfigured and overdetermined as something universal and suprasensibile precisely in its finite and sensible determination. The production of the visibility of the universal is in this way the enactment of the modes of its effective construction and generation, and at the same time of its concealment.

Hegel's first theorisation of this mechanism appears in his *Early Theological Writings* and, therefore, as for all his works in this period, as part of the philosophy of religion. The divinity in 'positive' religions (such as the figure of Christ, for example) develops as a compensation for social atomism, and thus as a consequence of the disintegration of a community whose members, by now only private individuals, locate the values of autonomy, freedom and the dignity of their communitarian being in the figure of a single individual. Such a figure is overvalued and rendered divine precisely because those private individuals are faced with the degradation and diminishing value of themselves as authentic human beings. The surplus of value of the divine individual is only the other side of the deficit of value that the members of the community, deprived of the value of community and reduced to abstract atoms, unconsciously attribute to each of themselves. However, the mechanism that produces political alienation-reification is analogous, as in the transition from the Roman Republic to the Empire when the Roman *cives*, interested only in personal profit, found themselves faced with the unlimited and vast will of a person such as the Emperor, the autocrat.

> And in the immense empire he was a single being who encapsulated everything. Against this single being stood, as private persons, the individuals, an infinite mass of atoms. They were absolutely equal [...] and without any political rights [...]. What, therefore, stood before the consciousness of man was, on the one hand Fate and the abstract universality of domination, and on the other, individual abstraction which is noted for the fact that the individual in itself is something, not according to its vitality, not according to a complete individuality but as an abstract individual.[12]

It is the same automatism that generates modern economic socialisation based on the exchange of commodities and money: because in what the mature Hegel calls 'the system of needs', individuals, freed from any kind of social extra-economic constraint that predetermines their existence, socialise only by means of the exchange of the fruits of their labour which, in turn, is permitted by something external to them – money – that becomes the representative of social constraint and which, in the determinateness of its metal, expresses the unity of universal measure on the basis of which all specific commodities are compared and equalised. Money is the universal that permits socialisation insofar as it is abstract, external and independent of individuals: precisely because it is a universal deposited in a thing. 'But this money, which has the meaning of all needs', Hegel writes in his Jena Lectures of 1803–4, 'is itself only an immediate thing'.[13] The freedom of the modern subject is based on the separation-abstraction from that which is similar to it. The resultant socialisation can, therefore, itself only be abstract and reified, entrusted to a single

12 Hegel 2001, pp. 334–5, translation modified.

13 Hegel 1979, p. 154, translation modified.

thing which must represent the whole: 'money', state the Jena Lectures of 1803–4 on *Realphilosophie*, 'is this material, existing concept, the form of unity, or the possibility of all things needed'.[14] It is the necessary modality of life and thinking of an anthropological condition characterised by an intellectualistic dimension, which the Hegel of the *Philosophy of Right* defines as the 'external state – the state which satisfies one's needs and meets the requirements of the understanding'.[15]

## 4 The Speculative Closure. From Negation-Division to Absolute Negation

The intellect in Hegel's philosophy is therefore the organ of division-abstraction, a function that contemporaneously refers to the practical and the theoretical. It indicates both a modality of behaving with respect to others and to oneself, and a way of knowing/not knowing oneself and reality as a whole.

The decisive transition in Hegel's philosophy, which gives it its more precisely idealistic character, is that this practical-theoretical link at a certain point becomes only theoretical-speculative. In other words, thought is proposed by Hegel as the supreme unifying element of reality and the knowing subjectivity is posted as the most elevated and universal from of life. The goal of the entire dialectical process, its end point – but one which, due to the structure of the circle, cannot help but condition the beginning and thus shape the entire process according to its demands – is indeed spirit [*Geist*], but spirit as absolute spirit [*absoluter Geist*], in which there is an absolute identity between subject and object and in which the other, the object, is only a mirroring without any further distance between it and the subject, the self. The greatest identity of the subject, in which this experiences its supreme reconciliation, is therefore in Hegel self-knowledge, the sublation of any distance within the self, the removal of any opacity: it is the subject as a 'speculative' identity that finds nothing more than the mirror of itself in the object that it thinks. It is the subject, that is, as reason, as philosophy, which sees in all the determinations of reality, logic, the

14 Hegel 1979, p. 249. In relation to the formal, external nature of the resultant socialisation, Hegel here adds that 'need and labour, elevated into this universality, then form on their own account a monstrous system of community and mutual interdependence in a great people; a life of the dead body, that moves itself within itself, one which ebbs and flows in its motion blindly, like the elements, and which requires continual strict dominance and taming like a wild beast'.

15 Hegel 2005, p. 97 (*PR*, § 183).

natural and the historical only the traces of necessity and universality. It therefore finds in the object that same universal that constitutes it as a conceptual and knowing subject.

According to the more self-referential side of his idealism, Hegel confers the dignity of the authentic universalisation of the human subject, of its mode of relationality and sublation of partial and dogmatic identifications, to thought and its supposed infinitisation independent of sensibility. Of course, thought is not the only element, since Hegel is capable of bringing into play a rich complexity of relations between the self and the other-than-the self, which constitute the vast wealth of his historical and anthropological phenomenology, in a story composed not only of logical-linguistic relations. However, it is undoubtedly thought that is elected as the outstanding factor of universalisation and the real recognition of the subject. Therefore, self-consciousness which, ultimately, concludes absolute knowledge, is no longer the self-consciousness of a subject that knows itself as a person only in the problematical and even conflicting comparison with the other, but is precisely self-consciousness in the more traditional, theoretical-speculative sense, as the 'I that thinks itself' and thereby produces the unconditional identity of subject and object.

However, in this way, Hegel fairly unequivocally and reductively closes and resolves the complexity of the problems tackled and expressed in his youthful writings, where he had set out the practical origins of philosophy in the sense of it being born of the need to bring together the contradictions and divisions of human life, and proposed a universal that coincides with an ample and reconciled anthropology of humanity. In proposing a concept of spirituality whose final outcome is self-consciousness, as the perfect transparency of the subject to itself, without any residues, he falls into the trap of that philosophy of self-referential subjectivity which, in his youth, he had wanted to overcome due to its abstraction and separation from life. Jürgen Habermas thus justly noted: 'with this concept of the absolute, Hegel regresses back behind the intuitions of his youthful period. He conceives the overcoming of subjectivity within the boundaries of a philosophy of the subject'.[16] It is precisely this philosophy of the subject, as thought without body, that begins with Descartes's *cogito*, but which re-actualises in the terminology of modern rationalism the perfect self knowledge and coinciding of the self, the 'being thought of thought' which, as we have seen, for Aristotle defines the essence of divinity, without any form of sensibility.

16 Habermas 1990, p. 22.

It is this closing of the subject into the completeness of self-consciousness, where there is no distance between the object and the subject and where the objective is merely the transparent mirror of the subjective, that legitimates the transition from the *Phenomenology* to the *Science of Logic* in Hegel. It is, namely, the transition from the experience of division and contradiction in the life of the human being, be it as an individual or historic-inter-individual, to division and contradiction being put to work in a system of categories of pure thought whose dynamic factor, rather than the experience of life, is the systematic-dissovling valency of 'absolute negation'.

The Hegelian move from a circular and historical-experiential conception to a merely self-reflective concept of subjectivity makes use, not by chance, of negation-contradiction based on an illegitimate and regressive ontologisation and reification of language. This produces, as a fundamental category, the theorisation of 'absolute negation' which, unrelated to determinate aspects of the real and thought, is conceived as an activity which, by unconditionally negating, negates not only every thing or expression that aims to limit it, but also and above all, self-reflectively, its own self. The linguistic expression 'non-being', ceasing to have any normal meaning related to determinate and specific logical-predicative-semantic contexts, takes on the sense and ontological depth of an absolute 'Nothing', conceived as pure activity whose being is constituted by unlimited negation, which cannot help but negate even its own negation, due to its unlimited unconditioned nature. For by not tolerating any rigidity of structure that can resist it, it cannot help but remove even that constituted by the function of its own negating activity.[17]

---

17 The 'negation of the negation' in Hegel represents the fundamental articulation of every dialectical transition. 'The relation of the negative to itself [*Die Beziehung des Negativen auf sich selbst*]' represents 'the turning point of the movement of the concept. It is the simple point of the negative self-reference, the innermost source of all activity, of living and spiritual self-movement; it is the dialectical soul which everything true possesses and through which alone it is true; for on this subjectivity alone rests the sublation of the opposition between concept and reality, and the unity which is truth. – The second negative at which we have arrived, the negative of the negative [*Das zweite Negative, das Negative des Negativen*], is this sublating of contradiction, and it too, just like contradiction, is not an act of external reflection; for it is on the contrary the innermost, objective moment of the life of spirit by virtue of which a subject is a person, is free' (Hegel 2010, pp. 745–6). This self-reflective movement of negating in its turn has its own foundation, in the *Science of Logic*, in the thematisation of nothingness [*Nichts*] undertaken in the first chapter of the first section of the 'Doctrine of Being'. The possibility of conceving absolute nothingness, as an absolutely negative negating – which, not being relative to an other,

Thus, Hegel's 'non-being' that reifies and substantialises language is not:

a) the non-being of predicative, negative judgement that negates the attribution of a predicate to a subject ('Socrates is *not* Spartan');
b) non-being in the sense of the false opposed to the true, as union or disunion in thought of that which, instead, is not united or disunited in reality ('it is not true that hippogryphs, as the image of horses with wings, exist'); or, in other words, the non-being of existential judgement that negates the conjugation of being to any thing ('the hippogryph *is not*', or, in other words, does not exist).
c) non-being in the sense of difference, as conceived by Plato in the *Sophist* where, in opposition to Parmenides and his prohibition on pronouncing non-being, Plato conceives of relative non-being (as opposed to absolute non-being) as synonymous with otherness or, in other words, of the nexus of relation between two entities that are both positively existent and whose co-presence in space does not imply exclusion or repulsion but only coexistence in distinction.

---

is pure negation, and not negation of the other of the self – is the indispensible condition for conceiving the negation of the negation as negating absolutely reflexive in itself. But precisely the foundation of nothingness, in the first categorial triade of being, nothing and becoming encounters insuperable difficulties in Hegel's exposition. For in order to be able to assign difference and autonomy to nothingness in the face of being (in order to conceive the birth and passing of becoming as transitions, respectively, from nothingness to being and from being to nothingness), Hegel is constrained to use and to cite the category of 'something [*etwas*]', which in that initial context of Hegel's logical argumentation cannot be introduced yet (and, in fact, is conceptualised by Hegel correctly only in the second chapter dedicated to *Dasein*). 'Nothing, pure nothingness; it is simple equality with itself, complete emptiness, complete absence of determination and content; lack of all distinction within. – In so far as mention can be made here of intuiting and thinking, it makes a difference whether something or nothing is being intuited or thought. To intuit or to think nothing has therefore a meaning; the two are distinguished and so nothing is (concretely exists) in our intuiting or thinking' (Hegel 2010, p. 59). However, if a foundation is not given to the 'pure nothingness', not only does the entire movement of the logical categories obviously not begin, but above all there is not constituted the context of concepualisation of a negation that, before the exclusion of the other, is negation directed towards itself, which is to be precisely the negation of the negation, as constant and self-reflexive alternation of any presumed identity. On this original sin of Hegel's *Logic*, see Ilchmann 1992. On negation in Hegel as absolutisation of the 'non' present in the negative judgement, abstracted from any determinate context, see Heinrich 1978.

All these multiple senses of the linguistic expression 'is not' do not refer at all to an emptiness of being but identify positively determined representations or entities, independently of the fact that they are images of reality or only thought/imaginings. Hegelian non-being, as the inexhaustible and self-reflective activity of negation, is, however, the absolute lack and emptiness of being *qua* the absolute repulsion of the self that removes any possible place or margin of coincidence with the self.[18] As such, it is the reproposition of Parmenides's non-being with all its valency of an unexpectedly and arbitrarily hypostatised linguistic term, energised by means of the Fichtean concept of the spirit as an act that removes and negates any presupposed limitation to itself.

Furthermore, I have already discussed how central in Hegel's dialectic is the theme of the transition from a representation of the self of naturalististic individualism to the maturity of an individualisation based instead on a relation with alterity and the extent to which, in the transition from immediacy to mediation, the theory of a determinate negation is central. The meaning of this theory consists not in difference but in exclusion-opposition, with the dynamics of repression-projection that this specific sense of negation in Hegel implies. This is also the case because this theory of negation as the repression of a part of the self into the opposite and external of the self demonstrates the degree to which Hegel's opposite cannot be other than the precise and specific other of the self, or, it cannot be other than its 'own other', thereby expressing an originality in the Hegelian concept of opposition-contradiction that distinguishes it from the way that all the traditions of western philosophy have theorised this theme. However, this concept of negation as repression-projection in Hegel is accompanied by and often made subordinate to a linguistic reification of the concept of negation (as well as other terms of philosophical language), that can produce the most devastating damage to the coherence of individual Hegelian passages. It is no coincidence that the Hegelian dialectic, from its birth in his *Early Theological Writings* through to his mature works, oscillates between an anticipation of the Freudian theory of division-repression-projection in which negation essentially means the refusal of the subject to accede to the totality of relations with its own interior nature and, more generally, with the alterity that constitute it, and a metaphysical theory that is contemporaneously a theory of the constitution of the real and of thought, which utilises a negation that is the onto/logical intensification and over-determination of linguistic non-being.

---

18 See Léonard 1974, particularly the pages dedicated to the 'Doctrine of essence', pp. 131–48.

It is therefore opportune to summarise, referring to a useful text by Landucci,[19] some of the main senses according to which Hegel's doctrine of negation as opposition-contradiction is distinguishable from the classic theories of the philosophical tradition on this theme.

1) Hegelian negation is not the contradictory negative of a term in the sense of the non-A. This would mean, as Hegel says in his *Science of Logic*, 'the pure other of A', implying in its definition the entire universe of determinations that negate A. Thus, if A is the colour black, non-A is not only all the colours different from black but also a tree, an angel, a unicorn, and so on to infinity. But this negation is indeterminate, whereas dialectical negation – Hegel strongly emphasises – is determinate and does not disappear into the void of indeterminateness (A is not non-A).

2) Negation, for Hegel, does not have the meaning of contrariety, at least in the classic Aristotelian conception according to which a pair of opposites, like white and black, constitute the extremes of a genera (in this case, colour) and therefore admit the existence of several intermediary terms, in contrast to contradictory terms, in which *tertium non datur* – that is, where there is no possibility of other terms between the two. The unity of opposites that conclude Hegelian dialectics effectively is never conceivable as a genera within which these terms are included with other intermediary terms, but rather as an ulterior figure whose reality is heterogeneous and not homogeneous to both.

3) Negation, in Hegel, is not synonymous with correlativity as expressed, for example, in the relationship between a mother and a daughter or between siblings, the one older and the other younger. In these relationships, the relative terms have their own determinations and characteristics in themselves, independent of the relationship, and from this point of view, can exist even outside the relationship to the correlative. Dialectical opposites, on the other hand, have no indifferent side that pre-exists before the relationship: 'both essentially have this relationship and outside of this have no meaning'.[20] The dialectical relationship is not a relationship with the other than the self generically understood, but the relationship with one's own other. In the former case, there is only a relationship between different elements that are not intrinsically constituted and exhausted by reciprocal relativity, while, in the latter case, each

19 Landucci 1977. On the polysemy of 'negation' in Hegel's *Logic*, see also Henrich 1978.
20 Hegel 2010, p. 364.

term is uniquely itself insofar as it negates the opposite to itself and, in this way, by including its own other in itself, is the unity of opposites. It can, therefore, be stated that 'to be opposed is not a mere moment, nor [is it] just a matter of comparison, but [...] it is the determination of the sides themselves of the opposition'.[21] All this explains how far Hegel's dialectical opposition is from that which Kant defines as real opposition in which, for example, two forces, autonomous and independent the one from the other, find themselves exercising opposing pressures on the same body.

> [...] in a real opposition one of the opposed determinations can never be the contradictory opposite of the other; for if it were the conflict would be logical [...]. Therefore, in every real opposition, the predicates must both be positive but, in such a way that, in the union of the same subject, the consequences reciprocally rule each other out. In this way, the elements of one considered as the negative of the other are both, taken by themselves, positives.[22]

Thus, as both are positive, real opposites find themselves occasionally and not constitutively to be in contrast and opposing.

4) Dialectical opposition in Hegel, therefore, consists in a relationship whose extremes are exhausted, in reference to the possibility of existence, only by the relationship itself: they have no determination or characteristic of reality beyond the nexus of opposition that bind them together 'That is, each of these two (positive and negative) is stamped with a characteristic of its own only in its relation to the other: the one is only reflected into itself as it is reflected into the other; and so with the other. Each in this way is the other's own other'.[23] Each extreme in the dialectical opposition is itself only insofar as it is both itself and the other. In the dialectical opposition, therefore, the nexus of contraposition is not something that occurs outside, that is added outside the existences that are already in themselves characterised by opposites, but is their immanent and constitutive relation. Their reciprocal contraposition is so exhaustive of their existence that to say dialectical opposition means to say contradiction, because each extreme, by implying in its own self that which it contemporaneously excludes, is, at one and the same time, itself and its own

21 Hegel 2010, p. 370.

22 Kant 1992, pp. 215–16.

23 Hegel 2010, pp. 94–5, translation modified.

opposite. It is, therefore, the unity of the opposites and, as a consequence, the totality of the relation: in other words, its reality consists in being that which is absolutely prohibited by the principle of non-contradiction.[24]

Clearly, the exposition provided here of some of Hegel's essential philosophical ideas has, due to its schematic and synthetic nature, mixed theoretical formulations and categories of works from the various phases of his thoughts, from the youthful writings to the more systematic and mature works. It is thus now appropriate to discuss at greater length, even if in fairly brief outlines, the more significant moments, in chronological terms, of Hegel's philosophy.

## 5 Between Anthropology and Logic

Healing and reconciling any condition of division is the main function that Hegel assigns to philosophy. It is unquestionable that this exigency is explicit from the very first organisation of his thought. The Hegel of the first youthful manuscripts (*Folk Religion and Christianity, The Positivity of the Christian Religion, The Life of Jesus*) assumes as the fundamental problem of his reflections on this topic the question of how to universalise, to extend to all the members of a community, the freedom of modern subjectivity based, philosophically, on Kant's *Critique of Pure Reason* and celebrated, politically, by the French Revolution.[25] In other words, the problem he confronts is that of how to heal the divisions between the minority of enlightened intellectuals – capable, by following the conceptual path, as Kant indicates, of deriving the autonomy of the human being from pure reason – and the majority of humanity, constrained in the immediacy of a sensuous life and ready to subject itself to universals that are merely external and authoritarian. The early Hegel responds to this problem with the idea of a collective and diffuse educational instrument that, in his opinion, is that of a non-authoritarian, non-positive religion. In other words, he proposes the solution of a popular religion [*Volksreligion*] capable of translating and generalising the values and the abstract universal of philosophy into the concrete and figurative, sensuous and personalised language of narration, myth and festivities: in accordance with the civic valency that religion had in the ancient Greek *polis*, which honoured

---

24 On the way in which Hegel's dialectical contradiction necessarily implies a negation of the principle of non-contradiction, see Landucci 1977, pp. 43–61. A different theory is proposed by Longato 1977.

25 See Pöggeler 1986.

through heroes and gods the much more substantial divinity that was the community as an organic unity of its members. The divine, the absolute, in the early Hegel is none other than humanity understood (by means of a radicalisation of Kantianism) as a totality capable of returning back through the autonomy of reason to organic unity and the freedom of an unconditional self-determination without any dependency on the other. This occurs where religion, in all its historic-positive forms and, primarily, Christianity, is the external and alienated projection of this unifying limitation that occurs in history, together with all the authoritarian and extrinsic incarnations and institutionalisations of the universal, every time that human beings, by rejecting the immanent divinity in themselves, cease to identify themselves with communal life and act only in accordance with egoistical-private ends. In effect, the 'positive' (etymologically derived from *positum*), for Hegel at this time, is synonymous with a condition of dependency of subjectivity on an external authority insomuch as it coincides with that which the subject finds to be posited and imposed by tradition or, in other words, as presupposition and conditioning of its activity, rather than produced and generated by its free self-determination.

Very soon, however, by means of various, complex influences and paths, Hegel abandons the two essential presuppositions of this paedagogy that unifies and generalises through the medium of a civic religion: the adherence to Kantianism and the conviction that Kant's universal morality is an authentic universal, and the idealisation of classical Greek ethics as the model for community that could be re-proposed in modern times. The spirit of the Greek *ethos* begins to appear to him as a bond that over-exalts the community without conceding anything to the differences and specificities of individuals. With respect to the value of this undifferentiated collectivity, the value of subjectivity and its autonomy now appears to Hegel so unquestionably to represent the archetypical and founding principle of modernity that it stands as an obligatory expression of the definition of a new model of community. Thus, just like Kant's universal morality (despite the translation that the *Critique of Pure Reason* has made of the principle of authority from outside to inside the subject), the Greek *ethos* no longer appears capable of containing and expressing human subjectivity in the varied complexity of its instances and faculties. Kant's categorical imperative – 'Act only on that maxim whereby you can at the same time will that it should become a universal law' – claims to derive the modalities of human behaviour and praxis from the mere form of reason, without the emotive-sensible elements of the person and the determination of their empirical-historical living playing any part. However, this results in a universal which, due to its rationalist abstraction, necessarily produces a division within subjectivity and assumes the configuration of a domination, within the subject, of the rational component of personality over the empirical-sensuous elements.

What Hegel subsequently studies, in the second phase of his youthful development (*The Spirit of Christianity and its Fate, Fragment of a System 1800*) after having eliminated the hypothesis of an Enlightenment pedagogy based on Kant's rationalism, is a principle of self-determination and freedom of humanity that is the productive whole of two unifications: the ethical-political unity of humanity and subjective-anthropological unity, within each individual person, integrating all its various faculties without the repression or division of any of them. Two unifications, of which the second will become the condition of the first, so much so that it becomes the virtually exclusive subject of Hegel's interest: in the sense that there cannot be any real ethical-political unification without consenting to and guaranteeing an authentic integration and valorisation of subjectivity in all its being. The freedom of the whole, in the sense of a community free from any external authoritarianism, implies the subjective freedom of everyone, in the sense of a rejection of any internal authoritarianism as an asymmetrical domination of any one faculty over all the others. Now the divine is the human community, but no longer as a unity without differences, as in the Greek *ethos*, but as a totality rich with the fullness of being of each of its members, as an articulated and multiple totality in which the differences do not impede unity but are, rather, its conditions. Hegel theorises this with a metaphor derived from the language of St John's Gospel.

> What Jesus calls the 'Kingdom of God' is the living harmony of men, their fellowship in God; it is the development of the divine among men, the relationship with God which they enter through being filled with the Holy Spirit, that is, that of becoming his sons and living in the harmony of their developed many-sidedness and their entire being and character. In this harmony their many-sided consciousness chimes in with one spirit and their many different lives with one life, but, more than this, by its means the partitions against other godlike beings are abolished, and the same living spirit animates the different beings, who therefore are no longer merely similar but one; they make up not a collection but a communion, since they are unified not in a universal, a concept (for example, as believers), but through life and through love.[26]

26 Hegel 1948, pp. 277–8.

What Hegel will later call the 'concrete universal', the unity of differences, is anticipated in the form of an absolute humanism. When faced with such fullness and richness of human life, which is achieved only through the acknowledgement of a common identity of the multiple development of individualities, the unification of the concept is abstract and 'positive'. It is a universal, that is, achieved only through the equalising of the many, or through the imposition of a univocal and undifferentiated unity of common measure. It is clear that the abstraction of the universal and the division of the subject coincide, in the sense that any form of abstract socialisation-universalisation of living individuals internally corresponds in the interiority of any of them to the mortification of an essential part of their selves; more specifically, in the sense that the abstract and univocal prevailing of one faculty of the mind over the others is a condition of the interiorisation on the part of the individual of the abstract and undifferentiated universal that unifies, in a forced and external way, the life of a community. The radical criticism that Hegel makes throughout his thoughts of the culture of the Enlightenment and Kantianism, as well as the representative institutions of modern liberal society, emerges here, in this vision of the realisation of the divine in the human, according to which the highest level of socialisation coincides with the highest levels of individualisation.

Thus, in the *Systemfragment* of 1800, with the formula 'life is the union of union and non-union',[27] the young Hegel already explicitly thinks on the basis of a divinisation that makes the human the Absolute, insofar as nothing falls outside life, even if they are also lacerations, divisions and oppositions. The identity of that Absolute is rather such as to be constituted precisely and solely through contrasts and oppositions so that only in this way can life be the true container of every event and experience belonging and traceable to the human. The young Hegel's Absolute is, therefore, anthropological and its principle is the divinisation of life as a principle that does not tolerate principles external to itself; as such, there cannot be parts that autonomise themselves claiming to be absolute in their separateness. This is evidenced by the fact that every living being that dogmatically wants to be unrelated will rediscover the relations that it represses as projected and objectified outside itself, as forces that persecute and negate any presumed and arbitrary asymmetry. Hegel describes and theorises this using the metaphor of the tragic in Greek drama in his first formulation of the dialectic as destiny: in other words, destiny that strikes as a necessary and unavoidable punishment – as *anànkaia tyche* or *moira* – those

27 Hegel 1948, p. 312. For an interpretation of Hegel's early writings I refer to the illuminating pages of Mirri, particularly in Hegel 1970.

who produce lacerations on the body of the living, obliging it either to succumb or reconcile itself with life.

> Destruction of life is not the nullification of life but its diremption, and the destruction consists in its transformation into an enemy. It is immortal, and, if slain, it appears as its terrifying ghost which vindicates every branch of life and lets loose its Eumenides. […] The trespasser intended to have to do with another's life, but he has only destroyed his own, for life is not different from life, since life dwells in the single Godhead. […] Opposition is the possibility of reunification, and the extent to which in affliction life is felt as an opposite is also the extent of the possibility of resuming it again. It is in the fact that even the enemy is felt as life that there lies the possibility of reconciling fate.[28]

Fate thus inaugurates the dialectic for Hegel insofar as it is undoubtedly the punishment for a wrong but, at the same time, is the reconciliation of two extremes represented by the autonomous and violent action of singularity, on the one hand, and by the universality of broken and wounded life, on the other. With fate as represented by Greek drama, the punishing forces do not take on an impersonal dimension (and, therefore, only abstract and distanced from the law). Rather, they take on the dimension of the concreteness and tangibility of a human figure that is similar, despite its oppositional role, to the subjectivity of the guilty one. In other words, this means that through destiny the guilty person sees not the cogency of the law that is merely extraneous and other than himself, but rather, the enemy which he himself opposes as an enemy, in a nexus where identity transpires through opposition. This leads to the recognition that the harmed life, personified in the figure of fate, is not heterogeneous but is identical with it, or, rather, it is the same but rejected and removed from the self, thus rendered hostile and excluding.

1) The breaking of an original unity due to the dogmatic and violent affirmation of a partiality; 2) oppositional and negating reaction on the part of the excluded and rejected world in relation to this partiality; 3) recomposition of the original unity, present no longer in its naive and primitive simplicity but with the richness and implication in itself of this process of differentiation-opposition-reconciliation: these are already the fundamental terms of Hegel's subsequent dialectic. It will consist precisely in the generalisation of this paradigm to both the entire historical-phenomenological experience of the human

28 Hegel 1948, pp. 229–32.

being and to the totality of the mature idealistic system. Nonetheless, this occurs without ever losing the imprint of the original foundation in the psycho-anthropological background of Greek tragedy. The Hegelian dialectic, even in its most logical-speculative formulation, will continue to filter through the dynamic energy of psycho-anthropological division-projection into the pure forms of conceptuality. It will also continue to promote an overly easy reconciliation of opposites, mechanically inspired by the catharsis which, in Greek tragedy, is the device of a narrative invention, however dramatically coherent and culturally determined. The aporia, the most insuperable difficulty in Hegel's philosophy, does not lie, as is often claimed, at the beginning, in the presupposition of an organic unity that conditions the entire unfolding of reality. It does not lie in the beginning that already anticipates, in its absoluteness, the fullness of the end and which, therefore, renders vain or merely repetitive the differentiation into the various figures of the intermediary path. In fact, the difference between the beginning and the end is too evident in Hegel's philosophy to allow us to retreat to coinciding the latter with the former. The initial Absolute always refers, whatever the various beginnings of it in Hegel's works, to a very miserable and poor condition of existence or experience, of fusion and immediacy, entirely unreflected, in which the presence of subjectivity is thus not yet given. It is synonymous with 'being' as primordial life, which is wholly opaque and ignorant of itself, while the final Absolute is instead synonymous with an existence at the highest level of subjectivity and knowing awareness of the self. As a consequence, above all if seen anthropologically as the birth of the consciousness of a condition of undifferentiated life, the breakup of the primitive unity and its transition to a division of partiality do not appear to create unsustainable problems of plausibility for Hegel's philosophy. This is the case, at least, as long as the question remains within an anthropological-psychological sense, which cannot help but make use for the purpose of greater clarity, beyond Hegel, of psychoanalytical formulations.[29]

However, Hegel's philosophy, despite anticipating, above all in his early writings, such anthropological-psychoanalytical subjects, is not developed within this problematic. The overriding problem for Hegel remains how to reconcile the *ethos* of the ancient community and the freedom of modern subjectivity, how to bring together unity and differences. The distance between the two Absolutes must include, alongside the genesis of consciousness and the maturing of subjectivity, the harmonisation without any residual inconsistency of individual autonomy and communal life. Thus, Hegel needs a vector of social-

29 On this subject, see the indications present in Ferreri 1990 and 1994.

isation and universalisation of the subject that cannot be exhausted in the psychological-emotional forms of an individual consciousness, as still occurs in the dialectic of fate – for no better reason than because the reconciliation of the opposites with their own fate, precisely because within the ambit of feeling, is specifically entrusted to that sentiment of love to which the anti-romantic Hegel never conceded any significant unifying value.[30]

The idealistic bent of Hegel's philosophy is defined when this required vector of real universalisation of particulars (once the insufficient virtues of unification both of moral actions and sentimental actions is discounted) is found in thought as an infinite capacity of transcending limitations and attaining to otherness as an immanent and constitutive structure of determinateness. The Absolute is fundamentally Idea, Consciousness, Knowledge, because only thought is the dynamic force of universalisation that does not find in any possible content a limitation to its immaterial ability to expand and pass through anything. The Absolute, as thought, means precisely this: to remove any assumed autonomy and self-consistency from the world of individual and sensible existences, universalise their determinateness and thereby acknowledge the universality of thought in the objectiveness of a universalised world. The final Absolute consists in the completeness of self-consciousness, in Absolute Knowledge, where the subject and the object are identified because the subject does not see or find in the object anything other than itself. In other words, it is an Absolute which, with respect to the initial Absolute, is a being that has become completely transparent to itself and, therefore, has perfect self-knowledge that is unconditioned and limited by any form of opacity.

However, for this process of universalisation of every particular existence to be possible, it is necessary that the 'difference' that structurally constitutes every determinate in its relation to the other than itself becomes increasingly radicalised, transforming itself into 'diversity' and then into 'opposition', becoming 'contradiction': in other words, the acceptance of alterity not as a limit and external foundation but as an internal principle of infinitisation. It is the force and continuum of negation that permits the transformation of determining difference into infinitising contradiction. Spirit, for Hegel, is not original transparency, equality with itself to be presumed as given, but the 'rendering itself equal to itself' by means of 'removing its being other'. It is recognising oneself in the other or being recognised by the other in oneself. As such, it is the removal of nature, as a condition of existence other than spirit, precisely because in nature the process of recognition and confirmation of itself through

30 On this, see Mirri 1977, particularly pp. 346–9.

alterity is rejected. 'Spirit removes nature or, in other words, its being another, recognising that this other being is itself, that it is nothing more than itself posited as an opposite'.[31] Nature does not acknowledge negation which is the true principle of freedom because in freedom there exists the force of nothingness that removes all conditions of opaque and passive coincidence with itself and makes of being 'a being that has become; a derivate from negation and thus freely moving and enjoying this ideal element, nothingness, that it has taken into itself'.[32]

However, negation, which represents the heart of Hegel's philosophy, is, as we have seen, the source also of its greatest obscurity and aporeticity. This occurs because in his polysemic and overdetermined concept, the mass of forces linked to the early Hegel's anthropological problematic and the logical-predicative-discursive valency of linguistic negation are indiscriminately intertwined. The negation of psychical repression is something completely different from that of logical-linguistic negation. However, in the speculative Hegel, above all in his *Science of Logic*, linguistic negation receives its divisive, expulsive, oppositional and self-denying strength from the implicit forms of psychical negation-repression. Hegel is not aware of this relation, but it constitutes the indispensible premise for conceiving, in the face of the Aristotelian prohibition, of that contradiction whose realisation is in the Hegelian system the source of every spiritual progress of reality. Contradiction in Hegel takes place and is made possible through a quadrupling of the two extremes of an opposition. Each extreme that is initially distinguished from and in contrast to the other of itself, recognises, negating its first form of existence, that the other of itself is inside it. In this way it duplicates itself, infinitises itself and becomes a totality. Nonetheless, this takes place through a network of movements in which logical-discursive negation is constantly supported by a dynamic and ontological economy of negation that belongs to a statute of experience and reality that is profoundly different from its apophantic and predicative statutes.

The weakest part of Hegel's philosophy thus resides in this overdetermination of the contradiction between logic and anthropology, not in its beginning and immediacy of being, unreflexive, fusional and lacking in determinations. Rather, its weakness consists in its final totalisation and all the partial totalisations that precede it in which the divisions, the partialities and the oppositions of existence conclude, by means of the overdetermined and forced automatism of contradiction, in the reconciliation of their synthesis. It is a resolving and

31 Hegel 1998, p. 370.

32 Ibid.

reconciling contradiction in which, furthermore, logical-linguistic argumentation cannot help but appear as constitutive and dominating when faced with the implicit and hidden plan of the psycho-anthropological dynamic, given that Hegel's speculative choice of thought as the preferred factor of universalisation of existence must necessarily imply methods of resolution of opposing figures of an essentially conceptual-discursive nature.

Furthermore, this ambiguous nature of negation, together with the abuse and spread of contradiction, explains the more characteristic and complex aspects of Hegel's mature philosophy. It essentially explains how thought, the mode of conceptualising, is always not only knowing but knowing with a consistent implication of sense linked to action, as a specific way of behaving towards oneself and towards alterity. It explains, that is, why it is so difficult to attribute a merely idealistic-speculative character to Hegel's concept of the Absolute and, for the same reason, how difficult it is to be able to distinguish – a distinction that is precious and indispensible – between the theoretical and the practical moment of experience in the Absolute's progress. We have already seen how schematic and simplifying is the reduction of Hegelian philosophy to the theological epiphany of the Idea which goes out of itself in order to create nature and history and to return, from this fall, to consciousness of self. Nature, like the world of the finite, represents in Hegel a mental attitude more than an objective reality. When he constructs the Absolute on their *Aufhebung*, on their sublation, he does not think of a spiritual destruction of objective and material reality, but the sublation of an archaic and primitive way of relating to oneself and the other by means of a more advanced method rich with relations. The most accurate meaning of Hegel's idealism does indeed consist in deriving reality from the Idea, but not in the creationist sense of expression. It consists, rather, in the meaning that the necessary objective modalities of organisation and configuration of external reality derive from the various modalities of conceiving of the self and the other that traverse the formative path of a subjectivity. Nature and history correspond to the objectivisation of progressively less insufficient and partial modalities of subjectivisation, which begins from a total absence of the subject to itself, as a condition of the immediacy and opacity of life that is exemplified by nature. The idealistic excess of Hegel's philosophy, its reductionism of that which is objective to the subjective, does not lie in a theological and neo-Platonic conception of the Idea, but in a theoreticist extremisation of subjectivity, in the belief that a subject can achieve a condition of total transparency and possession of itself through thought: that the Kantian *Ich denke*, the transcendental self-consciousness in which subject and object coincide, can still be the limit and the foundation of the subject's identity.

Due to the permanence of this rationalistic myth of transparency, the circular theory of the subject, of a subject that is not presupposed but posited and produces itself through mediation with alterity, becomes rigid again and focuses itself in a theory of subjectivity as identity and of the exhaustive and specular mirroring of the subject in the object. The theoretical-contemplative destination of the subject in question prevails over the effectiveness and validity of meaning of every practical-transformational instance. The young Hegel's difficulty in finding satisfactory responses in a dynamic praxis to his need to radicalise modern freedom force him into a resolution dominated by a theoretical dimension. Thus, as a result of this fundamental choice, the dialectic of his concept of spirit, of *Geist*, however articulated through the implication of alterity, is inevitably structured around categories and modalities of development of an essentially theoretical-discursive nature.

It is precisely here, in a dialectic that moves in its logical and phenomenological overturning essentially through linguistic hypotheses, that we encounter the fundamental unsolvable problems of Hegel's entire philosophy. It is much more this dimension, and not in having tacitly presupposed the unity of the Absolute to the multiple and concrete articulation of the real, as the greater part of Hegel's critics have always claimed. On the contrary, the beginning of all Hegel's works coincide with a division, with a breakage in the body of the real or of thought; it is the need for consistency and reconciliation of this breakage that prompts the search for and production of unity and the Absolute. However, there remains the difficulty of finding an authentic division capable of generating dialectical deviations that are effectively real, and not simply linked to verbal games. In other words, as a conclusion to this brief summary of Hegel: what is defective in his philosophy is not the translation of the circle of the presupposed-posited into the vicious circularity of a result that is inappropriately premised on that which it must prove, but rather, the even more strongly speculative (in the original sense of *speculum* as a place of self-reflection) component present in his very original concept of *Subject-Geist*, which, with its myth of transparency without residue, assigns to that subject the function, *par excellence*, of absolute and self-reflective negativity.

## 6 Hegel and the Young Hegelians

There are, therefore, two fundamental theses that Hegel bequeaths to his successors: 1) the theory of reality as systematic totality, and precisely as the self-conscious progress of a subject that produces itself as such only by estranging itself from its immediacy; 2) the concept of 'criticism' as a denunciation of the false rationality of the partial figures of the same process. It is precisely on the basis of the inheritance of these philosophical ideas that debate of post-Hegelianism arises and the problematical nexus between Marx and the young Hegelians assumes significance.

The *Junghegelianer* appear to have substantially taken on board Hegel's lesson on what is critical and instead left aside the question of a non-individual subjectivity capable of realising Hegelian circularity. This, however, as we have seen, was the most delicate question left open by Hegel: that is, to what degree his original theory of a subjectivity that can never be thought as presupposed but always instead as posited can be compatible with the rationalist-speculative subjectivity emerging at the end of his system, in strong continuation with the pre-Hegelian philosophical tradition. Amongst the young Hegelians, it is only Marx who appears to be capable of tackling this problem, attempting to conceive a new subject that is not empirical-individualistic and that is different from the Hegelian idea but, at the same time as in Hegel, to be conceived as a *werden zu sich*, or a realisation of itself.

Nonetheless, taking on the challenge does not mean conquering it. The ability of the young Marx to tackle the Hegelian inheritance will be defined, as we will see, on the basis of the degree (or lack thereof) of acritical presupposition that will accompany his new subject. It is against this theoretical and problematic background that Marx's intellectual life, as a journalist and essayist, began after his university period in Berlin. Democratic radicalism first, and subsequently communism, are the political terms of the questions that enthuse and disturb him. However, underlying this remains the question of the subject, with the proscription of presupposition, since the question of democracy and, even more, the question of communism coincides with the question of the subject. Not resolving the latter, through and beyond Hegel, means returning to a substantialistic theory of occurrence, to a philosophy of history where becoming is only the progress of an already given principle and communism is only the realisation of a monistic and unilateral presupposition – and, therefore, not going beyond but remaining subaltern to the Hegelian horizon.

CHAPTER 3

# Journalism with a Philosophical Soul

## 1 'To the Left and to the Right'

As we have seen, realising philosophy in history was the programme of the 'Young Hegelians'. Philosophy – as knowledge that the Absolute, the essence and principle of every being, is freedom – was completed and finished with Hegel. It was now only possible and necessary to generalise it to society as a whole by means of the praxis that is essentially a criticism of religion and of the state, because religion and the state are the institutions that most alienate and deprive humanity of its faculties for self-determination. When faced with the question of what we can say, schematically, separates rightwing from leftwing Hegelians – whether the Absolute is the God who becomes a man only in order to return to himself and establish complete transparency and intelligibility of himself, or whether man is God; in other words, whether the Idea, in the completeness of its articulations, is presupposed to nature and history or whether it is nothing more than the history of humanity and all the events and civilisations of which it is composed – the young Hegelians replied with reference to an entirely humanistic Absolute. For this current, Hegel's Spirit should be interpreted and understood not in the sense of an Absolute that reflects the perfection of its logical time within the texture of historical time, as the Hegelian Right would have it, but in the entirely immanent sense of being synonymous with the human species seen as a unity of individuals raised up to the level of the universal of reason, since history is, in each of its moments, the struggle of men of reason against the irrationality of the present. All the fundamental categories of Hegelian philosophy, such as essence, alienation, self-consciousness, contradiction and dialectic, are to be preserved and valorised as long as Hegel's humanism is detached from the excesses of the contemplative idealism into which his system falls and the resultant compromise with authoritarian institutions, both religious and political, of its historic present. Thus, while the Right saw in Hegel's philosophy the greatest ever reconciliation undertaken by philosophy with Christianity, due to Hegel's valorisation of Christ as a figure who, by realising the humanisation of God, anticipates and permits a mediation between the human and the divine in each human being, the Left criticised this exaltation of a single individuality in the face of the value of all human beings, contesting the divinity of Christ (including by means of philological critique of the New Testament).[1]

It is precisely this reduction of idealism to humanism that is of particular interest when reconsidering the young Marx. For, if the fundamental meaning of this identification tends towards a process of secularisation and desacralisation of all German culture, it also implies a process of idealisation

---

1 This begins with the work of 1835–6 by Strauss, *Das Leben Jesu kritisch bearbeitet* (Tübingen, 2 vols.) in which the historicity of Jesus as a person is denied and the Gospels are seen as the mythical expression of the needs and aspirations of the Jewish people. In the *Schlussabhandlung* at the end of the second volume, Strauss summarises the meaning of his work: 'The results of our research have by now cancelled out, it would appear, the greater and most important part of Christian beliefs regarding Jesus, all the encouragement which he finds in them having been destroyed and all consolation withered. The infinite treasure of truth which has, for the past eighteen centuries nurtured humanity, appears irreversibly dissolved' (Strauss 1835–6, Vol. 2, p. 591). On the differences between the various positions of the Hegelian Left, see Cesa 1972; Pepperle 1978; Eßbach 1988. The most in-depth work on the subject is Breckman 1999. The distinction between Right and Left within the Hegelian School is owed to Strauss, with reference to the question of the links between Christianity and philosophy and, analogously, with the sub-division in the seats in the French parliament, in the work *Streitschriften zur Verteidigung meiner Schrift über das Leben Jesu*, III, Tübingen 1838. In parallel to the differentiation between Left and Right is the distinction, in the German debate of the time, between 'Old Hegelians' or *Hegeliter*, and 'Young Hegelians' or *Hegelinge*. The old Hegelians had been direct students of Hegel. Their members included right Hegelians strictly conceived (like Göeschel and Gabler), who defended Christianity and the the authentic nature of the Biblical story, disseminators and editors of Hegel's works (such as Hoto, Marheineke, and von Henning), as well as authors belonging more to the so-called 'centre', such as Rosenkranz, Michelet, Haym, Erdmann and Fischer, whose theoretical works aimed to defend Hegel's philosophy in general, not criticising the basic principles but, if anything, generalising the application of its categories and methods to every field of knowledge. The young Hegelians, on the other hand, were not direct students of the master, and were substantially the same as the left Hegelians. They engaged in a radical critique of Christianity and the defence of a rational democratic state, against the confessional monarchical state. In this book, for reasons of expositional synthesis, I utilise the distinction between right and left Hegelians, and its superimposition on that of old and young Hegelians (also used, for instance, by Löwith 1964). In reality, however, it is a distinction that should be at least problematised. See, for example, Stuke 1963. It is not simply that it is difficult to define as conservative direct students of Hegel such as Michelet or Gans, or even like Erdmann and Rosenkranz, but also because it is difficult to locate on the political spectrum some of the young Hegelians themselves. It is enough to think of the transition of Bauer from the right to the left, or the figure of Cieszkowski, whose influence on the left was considerable, but who defined himself always as a 'progressive conservative' close to the right (Cieszkowski 1842, pp. 11–12). On this, see Tomba 2002, pp. 27–35.

and spiritualisation of the human being that risks establishing an anthropology that is angelically oriented as the principle of a renewed humanism. The young Hegelians thus presumed to cut like the Gordian knot the overdetermination and polysemy of the meanings of Hegel's *Geist*, as well as the inherent categories of Hegel's philosophy of spirit. However, they did not appreciate the difficulties (when not the impossibility) of separating the depth and human rootedness of subjectivity in Hegel from its structural torsion towards a dematerialised and self-reflective subjectivity. It is this simplification of Hegelism that the *Junghegelianer* delivered up to Marx: in other words, the belief that Hegel can be used in a process of radical emancipation, taking care only to substitute the subject 'Idea' with the subject 'Man', whilst unaware of the perils of the abstract fusion and spiritualist extenuation that this movement continues to maintain, unaltered, within itself.

It is no coincidence that it was sufficient for them essentially to subtract Hegel's philosophy from the dangers of an over-exposure to and reconciliation with the Christian religion. This occurred, in their opinion, when one proposed to read Hegel's valorisation of Christ's incarnation not as implying an individualised and concrete symbol of the dialectical becoming of the concept and the mediation of the universal and the particular, but instead as a celebration of the most authentic subjectivisation of the spiritual substance ever to be found in a historical individuality, as was proposed by the more traditional Hegelians, to such a degree that, from this point onwards, all history is illuminated and given meaning by the completeness of this model.[2] On the other hand, the

---

2 On this subject of the individualisation of the divine, of the Absolute, the discussion between the Hegelian Left and Right occurred in the context of a wider debate on the relationship between faith and philosophy – and, specifically, of the links between philosophy and Christianity – that involved the authors of the so-called German 'late-idealism' amongst whom were Ch.H. Weiße (*Die philosophische Geheimlehre über die Unsterblichkeit des menschlischen Individuums*, Dresden 1833), I.H. Fichte (*Die Idee der Persönlichkeit und der individuellen Fortdauer*, Elberfeld 1834) and Fr. Stahl (*Die Philosophie des Rechts nach geschichtlicher Ansicht*, Heidelberg 1830–3). They established the value of the 'person' against that of universalism and the pantheism of Hegel's dialectic. On the relevance of the 'person' and a personal God in the German culture of the period, including from the position of Jacobi, with essentially anti-Hegelian implications, see Breckman 1999, pp. 20–89. However, obviously, the 'second' Schelling of the Munich Lectures and the preface to Cousin's *Philosophical Writings* constitutes the keystone of an opposition to Hegelianism and its assumption of resolving the principle of the divine in the immanent texture of a dialectic development. 'When faced with this concept of God seen as an immanent outcome of thought and, therefore, prescribed within the limits of a logical philosophy of which Hegel, with his theory that "it is not so much that God is a simple concept but that the concept is God" had provided the most

fundamental, theoretical requirement of the *Junghegelianer* was that the liberation of the finite, its infinitisation, should not be the privilege of just one out of all human beings but the goal and value of humanity as a whole, in its universality. It is precisely in this humanistic conjugation of *Geist* that their reception-transmission of Hegel's philosophy is basically exhausted, without them feeling the need for an investigation and problematisation of the anthropology from which this spiritualisation derived.

Furthermore, the young Hegelians also demonstrated both an excessively naive and immediate approach with respect to Hegel's conceptualisation of freedom or, in other words, with respect to the circle of the presupposed-posited that, I have argued, is the second element left open by the Hegelian inheritance, together with the problem of the true identity of the subject. Identifying the Absolute with freedom does not necessarily mean accepting the circular equation according to which freedom is truly realised and not merely presupposed only when it is produced through mediation and the return from the other of the self. However, for all the Hegelian Left, despite the range of diversity, freedom is a principle so indisputably and immediately coincident with the human being that every subject participates in it as long as they can abandon egoistic thinking and feeling and move in accordance with the elements of universal humanity within them. This is within a context where even the radical individualism and 'egoism' proposed in Stirner's The *Ego and its Own* clearly constitute the claim for freedom and a vital force that applies originally to humanity, without such an origin requiring confirmation through the objectivisation and mirroring of the external world.[3] The fundamental question of German intellectuals in the *Vormärz* thus appears to be the extent to which those critical and radical intellectuals knew and had effectively appropriated Hegel's work and teaching. The fall into free individualities of the rational and

complete model, it is now Schelling's claim for a God as reality that extends beyond thought as a reality that cannot be reduced to such and deductable from pure thought, a reality that is independent from the world and necessary movement of its governing dialectics, because the world itself is a product of its free act of creation, a reality, therefore, that, insomuch as it is the original fullness of being and free will, is configured as a "free" "person" subject to "free" relationships and, thus, cannot be coordinated with any a priori knowledge' (Donadio 2002, p. 11).

3 The reference here is clearly to Max Stirner, *The Ego and Its Own* (1845). For Stirner, the sense of freedom of the Ego consists in a process of liberation of oneself, for 'freedom is essentially self-liberation' (Stirner 1995, p. 151): in a process of release from generalised charges and from collective identifications that permit the Ego of each person to express all its original and unrepeatable singularity.

infinite self-consciousness, critical of the old representative forms of the past, seems to occur too rapidly with respect to the long journey of mediations between individual and universal that we find in Hegel's work, in such a way that it posits itself too quickly in a historical context of post-Hegelianism and of the translation-incarnation of its absolute of freedom, now it is assumed to be definitively conceptualised in critical individualities. This occurs, however, without thinking enough about the legitimacy of the Hegelian solution of a spirit that has managed to make itself absolute by means of the universalising force of absolute negation and of its theoretical-speculative valency.

However, on this decisive element, Marx differentiates himself from the others. The world and the unifying principle of the world are considered as intrinsically united, to such an extent that the one is the realisation and evidence of the other. The creative activity of the spirit effectively lies not only in critically opposing the world but also in its integration with it; thus, it is by identifying itself in a subjectivity that it can effectively permeate and assimilate all reality with its own unlimited strength of universalisation. The dialectic, therefore, cannot consist in the opposition of single and illuminated self-consciousnesses to religious and political authoritarianism, but in a movement of oppositions between the valency of the whole and rigid and dogmatic partialities that must be immanent to the real, and such that it can develop as a phenomenology in the world of a universal that, in the beginning, is only implicit and latent and which, therefore, requires progressive development of itself. Furthermore, it is precisely with respect to the definition of the identity of the subject in question (the difference between single illuminated individualities and more communitarian and collective instances), that, alongside Hegel, the figure of Ludwig Feuerbach appeared within the horizon of the young Marx's formation, with his philosophy's central proposal: the reduction of all reality to anthropology and the identification of the absolute subject no longer with the Idea or Hegel's *Geist* but, now, explicitly with the collective and anti-individualistic principle of the 'human species [*menschliche Gattung*]'.

The next chapter will be dedicated to Feuerbach's humanism, given the importance of this encounter in the history of Marx's formation. However, what is now of interest is briefly accounting for how Marx, in his own way, in passing from philosophising in a systematic way, such as in his dissertation, with one eye still on the possibility of some kind of academic career, to being an essayist-journalist, combines Hegel and Feuerbach, idealism and humanism, and generates an ethical-political theory whose singularity will be equal to is structural aporeticity.

From 15 October 1842 to 17 March 1843, Marx was the editor in chief [*Chefredakteur*] of the *Rheinische Zeitung für Politik, Handel und Gewerbe*, the Cologne daily paper of liberal persuasion, founded on the initiative of Georg Jung and Moses Hess,[4] and supported by a number of the wealthy bourgeoisie of this western Rhineland city which, at the time, was witnessing strong commercial and productive development. Having abandoned any hope of being nominated as professor of philosophy at the University of Bonn,[5] due to the disgrace into

4 G. Jung, the young Cologne lawyer, member of the *Jünghegelianer*, wrote to Ruge in October 1841 about the young Marx and another possible publication, before the *Rheinische Zeitung*: 'Dr. Marx, Dr. Bauer and L. Feuerbach will come together in a theological-philosophical publication. All the angels can gather around God and He can be merciful with himself given that these three will undoubtedly throw him down from the heavens and, by means of a trial, manage to hang him. At the very least [...] Marx defines Christianity as one of the most immoral religions. On the other hand, despite being an extreme revolutionary, he is one of the most acute witnesses I know' (*MEGA*[1], I, 1/2, pp. 261–2). Moses Hess, in a letter to Auerbach in September 1841, also expressed enthusiasm for Marx: 'He is a man who has made an enormous impression on me, despite us working in the same field of studies; in summary, you can be sure to encounter the greatest, or rather, the only true philosopher currently alive, a man who soon, when he becomes publically known, through his works and courses, will attract the attention of all Germany. Due to his tendencies and philosophical formation, he surpasses not only Strauss but also Feuerbach, which is saying a great deal [...] Dr. Marx, as my idol is called, is very young: he is 24 at the very most; it will be he who delivers the final blow to religion and medieval politics and will strike the decisive blow to the political and religious orientations inherited from the Middle Ages. He brings together the most biting irony and the most profound and serious philosophical spirit: I'm thinking of Rousseau, Voltaire, Holbach, Lessing, Heine and Hegel, I'm not saying all mixed together but fused in a single person and you'll get Dr. Marx' (*MEGA*[1], I, 1/2, pp. 260–1). The *Rheinische Zeitung* started publication in Cologne on 1 January 1842. Financed by members of the Rhineland bourgeoisie, Georg Jung and Moses Hess were instrumental in calling Marx to participate in the venture.

5 In mid April 1841, having obtained a doctorate in philosophy from the University of Jena, Marx left Berlin and returned, via Frankfurt, to Trier whence he moved to Bonn in July while awaiting a possible university position. Here he managed to read Feuerbach's *Das Wesen des Christentums* [*The Essence of Christianity*] that had just been published in Leipzig. He helped Bruno Bauer to write *Die Posaune des jünsten Gerichts über Hegel den Atheisten und Antichristen. Ein Ultimatum* [*The Trumpet of the Last Judgement against Hegel the Atheist and Anti-Christ: An Ultimatum*]. In May of the same year, his brother Hermann died and his relationship with his mother worsened when she denied him access to his paternal inheritance until he had found an economically profitable profession. (Letter of Marx to Ruge of 25 January 1843: 'As I wrote to you once before, I have fallen out with my family and, as long as my mother is alive, I have no right to my property' (*MECW* 1, p. 397)). After the withdrawal of Bruno Bauer's teaching post in October 1842 by the Prussian authorities, Marx returned to Trier participating, at Moses Hess's insistence, in the Cologne meetings for the creation of the daily *Rheinische Zeitung*. In April 1842, he moved back to Bonn.

which his supporter Bruno Bauer had fallen,[6] Marx turned resolutely towards a courageous, acute and surprising activity of criticism by means of journalism and essays. The works in question, whose most significant conceptual outlines will be discussed here, include all the articles that appeared in the *Rheinische Zeitung* from January 1842 to March 1843, plus the two essays that appeared respectively in the *Anekdota zur neuesten deutschen Philosophie und Publicistik* and the *Deutsche Jahrbücher für Wissenschaft und Kunst*.

## 2 Freedom as the Absolute

Having finished his university studies, the philosophy that the young Marx placed at the foundations of his impassioned cultural and political battles during the years 1842–3 can be summarised by the following three philosophical propositions:

1) Freedom, more than an ethical-political value or, in other words, an axiological principle of 'must', is the ontological principle of being. It constitutes the most substantial and constitutive identity of the human being. 'Freedom is so much the essence of man that even its opponents implement it while combating its reality; they want to appropriate for themselves as a most precious ornament what they have rejected as an ornament of human nature'.[7]

---

6 Bruno Bauer (1809–82) had taught courses in the University of Berlin's theology faculty since 1834, assuming a theoretical position organic to the Hegelian Right and publishing *Zeitschrift für speculative Theologie*. In October 1839, due to his criticism of religious orthodoxy (the *Kritik der Geschichte der Offenbarung*, 2 vols., Berlin, 1838, in particular), he was transferred by the Minister Altenstein to the University of Bonn's theology faculty, from where he still hoped to help the young Marx in an eventual academic career, due to their intense relationship established in Berlin. Due to his perseverance in criticising the Gospels and Christianity (undertaken particularly in the *Kritik der evangelischen Geschichte der Synoptiker*, 3 volls, Leipzig, 1841–2), he was definitively removed from the University on 29 March 1842. His theory of the Gospels radicalised that of Strauß in the sense of denying any objective historical truth to the New Testament. The Gospels were not even to be interpreted as an expression of the collective myths of the primitive Christian community that was deeply conditioned by the Jewish messianic tradition. According to Bauer, they were rather the conscious works of individual authors, and not of a community, who expressed through their literary creations a content of values that could not be traced back to tradition but to the advancement of a new and more progressive spirituality. Thus, they are a moment, obviously necessary but ephemeral, of the development of humanity's history towards progress and self-consciousness.

7 *MECW* 1, p. 155. With these *Bemerkungen über die neueste preußische Zensurinstruktion* the

2) The human being is free only insofar as it is a 'communal', 'universal' and 'generic' being or, in other words, a member of that absolute and self-determining totality that is humanity, the *menschliche Wesen*. Humanity is the 'species [*Gattung*]', the principle of generation whose inexhaustible creative strength is translated and expressed in the never-ending totality of its creatures. However, in contrast to the natural species, the human species is not lost in the inexhaustible series of its individuations because it returns to itself and possesses itself.
3) The *menschliche Gattung* [human species] is the presupposed and immanent universal, although only implicitly and potentially, in every single person. In effect, in order to take into account its own humanity, the individual negates itself as an individual entity of nature and, expressing itself as spiritual subjectivity, produces acts and objective universal ambits with its thought and actions, by means of which the species self-reflects and takes possession of itself. The organisation of economic and cultural life, law and the state can only have meaning when compared to this ontological-anthropological structure of reality, which takes on a form and historic concreteness in the totality and self-determination of a people.

---

collaboration of the young Marx began with the *Rheinische Zeitung für Politik, Handel und Gewerbe*. The Cologne paper was originally edited by Höpken, then from February 1842, by Rutenberg (a member of the *Junghegelianer*), and finally, from 15 October 1842, by Marx himself. The basis of the Prussian laws on the press was the 1819 *Zensuredikt*, the restrictions of which were further increased after the July revolution of 1830. The censorship instructions of 24 December 1841, subject of an article by Marx, permitted a degree of relaxation but continued to be extremely severe in relation to any criticism of the Prussian government and its political institutions. The assembly of the provincial Diet [*Landtag*] established in Prussia in 1823 was convened by the King and endowed with an authority limited to local administrative problems. It was formed by representatives of the nobility (princes and knights), the cities and rural municipalities (within which the nobility consistently obtained a majority). The electoral body, as well as being articulated on an ancient structure of classes or Estates [*Stände*], was also greatly reduced by the censorship limitations. The sixth Rhineland Diet, to which Marx refers in his articles, was held in Düsseldorf from 23 May to 25 July 1841 and dealt with the theft of timber, crimes linked to hunting and the questions of censorship and freedom of the press. The problem of the continued presence in Prussia at the time of a constitution still based on the division of society into estates and, as a consequence, the problem of a different institutional 'representation' is the focus of Marx's articles of 1842 and continued to be of great significance, as will be seen, also in the 1843 *Kritik des Hegelschen Staatrechts*.

The young Marx's ontology of freedom thus is based on an explicit divinisation of the human. The human species is the 'great Saint', the 'sacred Human': a self-sufficient totality through which the individual becomes a spiritual subject by participating in its absolute and unconditioned nature: 'the particular can be seen intellectually and freely only in connection with the whole [*das Besondere nur im Zusammenhang mit dem Ganzen*] and therefore not in separation from it'.[8] However, more rapidly than any of the other members of the Hegelian Left with regard to the Hegelian theory of circular becoming, that which Marx later claimed was a specification of identity – of that general basis of reality that is humanity – that permits a reading of reality that is essentially historical and ethico-political: precisely in relation to a principle that is evidenced by means of a procedure that allows for self-reflection and self-consciousness. Thus, the 'species [*Gattung*]', the 'common being [*Gemeinwesen*]', in the Marx of the *Rheinische Zeitung* is explicitly determined as the *demos*, the 'people [*Volk*]'. As a people, the human species establishes itself as the unquestionable cornerstone of the life of the individual, at the same time subtracting its faculty of generation from a reductively ethological-naturalistic significance and repositioning it within an horizon of sense and action that initiates history, beyond nature. It is the people who, in Marx's theory of history and society at the time, makes itself the absolute subject and protagonist, positing its transition from nature to spirit – from an unreflective condition of existence to a reflective and aware one – as the constitutional norm of its actions.

In the *Rheinische Zeitung* articles (and in the pages of the 1843 *Kritik*), the people appears in its spontaneous and unreflective life as the merely exterior unity of individuals, each existing for itself, and such that the life of the whole does not flow into them. So much so that Marx defines this as a 'private mob [*Privatpöbel*]', the masses, whose lack of organicity illustrates a singularity that is conceived as above all private, that is, as abstracted from relation with others. In its most immediate life the people are, therefore, not a spiritual but a natural species – Marx here seeing nature, as previously in his dissertation, in an explicitly Hegelian way, as the horizon of exteriority in which each individual, lacking an awareness of the whole, sees every other individual as distinct from itself and, tendentially, in opposition. In the life of a people, when private interests prevail over general interests, unity occurs only in a mechanical way, without self-determination and freedom. It is the freedom of a people, on the other hand, that becomes manifest and is realised only when it demonstrates the capacity to produce institutions and forms of universal culture that are

8 *MECW* 1, p. 176.

not subject to private interests; that is, when not constrained by its need for physical reproduction, it gives life to a process of realisations (or 'predicates', as Marx also calls them) that are increasingly less naturalistic and more suited to a non-partial sense of life. The most elevated of these is the state since, in it, the people knowingly takes the universal as the object of its own actions, beyond any individualistic and personal activities and interests.

In effect, the state is the predicate that is absolutely suited to the universal and free nature of that human subject that is the people. Here the object wholly manifests the essence of the principle by means of which it was generated, creating thereby a visible and concretely perceivable reality, in contrast to the latent and, therefore, merely ideal existence that the principle possesses when in popular life egoistic and naturalistic needs alone prevail. Thus, it is only in appearance that the unity of reality is divided between the subject and the predicate in the state, that is, between the people on the one hand and political institutions on the other, since the *Volk*, in its own right and only through the generation of and separation of itself from the state, can become aware of its deepest unity. As this is the place where the separations and partialities of the private sphere are overcome, the state mirrors and returns the image of its organic integrity to the people.

The entire development of the real in question is concluded for Marx in this *Rheinische Zeitung* period with the people becoming the state. The 'people' and the 'people-state' are the two poles, reciprocally and circularly implicating each other, of a single subject that proceeds from ways of acting and knowing itself that are profoundly incongruous with its true essence to increasingly coherent forms of self-consciousness. The development of these forms of self-knowledge constitutes the entire phenomenology of the forms of life of such a popular subject as it gradually translates its existence from an extrinsic to an intrinsic nature. Thus, if the state is the place where the people finds its greatest reality, analogous if not essential to it are all the manifestations of the life of the *Volk* where it is able to express itself as a collective subject, rather than an individual and private one. The 'press', 'culture', 'public spirit' and 'rights' are thus the predicative forms *par excellence* and constitute, together with the state, the fundamental and categorial texture of Marx's thought in the *Rheinische Zeitung*.

'The defects of a nation', Marx writes, 'are at the same time the defects of its press'.[9] As he says, 'the press is the ruthless language and manifest image of the

9 *MECW* 1, p. 144.

historical spirit of the people [*Volksgeistes*]'.[10] The free press 'is the ubiquitous vigilant eye of a people's soul, the embodiment of a people's faith in itself, the eloquent link that connects the individual with the state and the world, the embodied culture that transforms material struggles into intellectual struggles and idealises their crude material form. It is a people's frank confession to itself'.[11] The press, therefore, is the *Volksgeist*, the people that becomes spirit, the people that reflects on itself from the perspective of universality. 'The press is the most general way by which individuals can communicate their intellectual being. It knows no respect for persons, but only respect for intelligence'.[12] As such, it is the negation of private interests, of subjective opinion, of the spirit of partiality; in effect, it subtracts the human being from individual needs, from dependence on that which is extrinsic and finite. 'What makes the press the most powerful lever for promoting culture and the intellectual education of the people is precisely the fact that it transforms the material struggle into an ideological struggle, the struggle of flesh and blood into a struggle of minds, the struggle of need, desire, empiricism into a struggle of theory, of reason, of form'.[13]

The press expresses well how the young Marx understood the spirit of the people and just how far this concept for him is from any romantic and anti-Enlightenment inspiration that would see in the *Volksgeist* the primeval but latent strength of all national life. For this tradition – and it is sufficient to consider the 'historical school of law' (the lectures of the greatest representative of which, Friedrich Karl von Savigny, Marx had followed in Berlin) – the spirit of the people is effectively a creative source that remains inaccessible and indefinable in its originary nature. It explains the historical development of a people but cannot be reduced, because it is inexhaustible, to any one determination or manifestation, even the most characteristic of them. However, in Marx, the concept acquires an unmistakeable Hegelian character according to which the *Volksgeist* is the result, the outcome, of a process of elaborations and education that, by means of the various public and cultural institutions, leads the people to the level of an ethical life conceived of as the motivated and conscious participation of all in the life of the whole. *Volksgeist* thus is comprehended not in terms of some ultimate unfathomability, but in terms of the explanation and clarification of its own nature.[14]

10 Ibid.

11 *MECW* 1, pp. 164–5.

12 *MECW* 1, p. 177.

13 *MECW* 1, p. 292.

14 Marx's thought can thus be understood in terms of the distinction between a romantic

The press, taken in its totality, has the same character of an organism as that of the people seen as a unified and universal container of the various manifestations of its members' lives.

> In the natural development of the popular press, each of the different elements which determine the nature of this press must first of all discover for itself its specific form of development. Hence the whole body of the popular press will be divided into different newspapers with different complementary characteristics [...]. But for the press to achieve its purpose it is above all necessary that it should not have any kind of purpose prescribed for it from outside, and that it should be accorded the recognition that is given even to a plant, namely, that it has its own inherent laws, which it cannot and should not arbitrarily evade.[15]

As a consequence, no form of censorship is admissible with respect to the press because this would be applied by an external authority. The correction of its limits and partialities cannot but derive, intrinsically and freely, from the press itself or, in other words, from the dialogue that it enables between various points of view. 'The true censorship, based on the very essence of freedom of the press, is criticism [*die Kritik*]. This is the tribunal which freedom of the press gives rise to of itself'.[16] 'In the struggle with truth, error will of itself be recognised as such, without the need of any suppression by external force'.[17] Thus, every act of censorship, even before being criticisable from a

---

and an idealistic understanding of the concept of *Volksgeist* theorised in Rosenzweig 1976, pp. 38–40.

15 *MECW* 1, p. 314. This text by Marx refers to the debate of the sixth Rhineland Diet on the government proposal concerning the theft of timber and other produce from the woodlands; the debate results in laws even worse for the transgressors. What was in question was the persistence of old community rights, including those relating to timber, in the face of the privatisation and acquisition of ancient feudal areas by new owners. It was undoubtedly Marx's text, in five parts and anonymously signed as 'Von einem Rheinländer', published between 23 October and 3 November 1842, that caused the suppression of the *Rheinische Zeitung*. The *Oberpräsident* of the *Rheinproviz*, von Schaper, writing to the *Regierungspräsident* von Gerlach in Cologne, on 7 November 1842, stated that 'the *Rheinische Zeitung* increasingly demonstrates that it wants to continue in its condemnable practice of being an enemy of the government and the established order, threatening to go beyond every limit, as has already occurred, in particular, with the third article on the debate on the law on the theft of wood' (see *MEGA*, I, 1, p. 1022).

16 *MECW* 1, p. 159.

17 *MECW* 1, p. 191.

moral and political point of view, is unsustainable from an ontological point of view because it claims to exchange the universal basis of reality with a particular individuality. 'The real immodesty consists in ascribing perfection of the species [*die Vollendung der Gattung*] to particular individuals [*besondern Individuen*]. The censor is a particular individual, but the press becomes the embodiment of the whole species [*Gattung*]'.[18]

However, from the ontologically incongruous nature of any codification established by the censor, we not only find a reconfirmation of the centrality, in the young Marx, of the nexus of species-individual. It is also his particular way of understanding right and the nature of the law. For Marx, at that time, the law pertains, singularly, not to praxis but to theory: it is not an act of will but of knowledge. The juridical or normative statutes of the law refer to any presupposition that is the juridical nature of reality or, in other words, the establishment (or not) of every reality, before any juridical codification, in an order and objectively universal horizon. The law is in the nature of things, before being in the will and the mind of humanity. With legislation, therefore, it is only brought to light and given a formal explication.

> The law is not exempt from the general obligation to tell the truth. It is doubly obliged to do so, for it is the universal and authentic exponent of the legal nature of things [*über die rechtliche Natur der Dinge*]. Hence the legal nature of things cannot be regulated according to the law; on the contrary, the law must be regulated according to the legal nature of things.[19]

The universality of the law does not derive from the coercive force of the authorities that issue it, but from the necessity of things ('The standpoint of the legislator is the standpoint of necessity').[20] Universality consists precisely in the theoretical nature of the law which, being placed in a perspective that is free of the private interests and passions of the individual, is able, liberated from the limitations of factional prejudices, to reflect the objective nature of reality. 'The legislator, however, should regard himself as a naturalist. He does not *make*

---

18 *MECW* 1, p. 122, translation modified.

19 *MECW* 1, p. 227. This article, with which the young Marx's essayist and journalist activities began in earnest, and which he, in 1851, dated 'December 1841', was not intended for the *Rheinische Zeitung*, which had not yet started publication. Sent to Ruge's *Deutsche Jahrbücher*, due to the censor, it was only published in 1843 by Ruge in Switzerland in the *Anekdota zur neuesten deutschen Philosophie und Publicistik*.

20 *MECW* 1, p. 310.

the laws, he does not invent them, he only formulates them, expressing in conscious, positive laws the inner laws of spiritual relations'.[21]

Thus the question of law is only conceivable as part of a co-penetration and ontological circularity of content and form which excludes any possibility for an individual subject to make itself the productive and organisational principle of reality. The typically universal form of law must be the self-determination and self-explication of a content that must find in the form of law nothing other than the making evident and attainment of self-consciousness of its own nature. Otherwise, any law is an extrinsic, moralistic and authoritarian imposition on a matter that is not understood in terms of its needs and its necessity but which is overlaid by a merely individual legislative opinion, which is thus inadequate and incongruous.

> Prussian law is based on an intellectual abstraction which, being in itself devoid of content, conceived the natural, legal, moral content as external matter which in itself knows no laws and then tried to model, organise and arrange this spiritless and lawless matter in accordance with an external aim. It treats the objective world not in accordance with the latter's inherent laws, but in accordance with arbitrary, subjective ideas and an intention that is extraneous to the matter itself.[22]

Here, the intellect that clearly produces the juridical abstraction is the Hegelian instrument of the division that separates object from subject and which produces a universal that is only apparent, formal. 'The form is of no value if it is not the form of the content'.[23] Abstract law generates and legitimises in this way, utilising the mere form of law, rather than real universals, only privileges and partiality. In effect, 'The censorship law has only the form of a law'.[24]

## 3 A 'Generic' Ontology

It is, therefore, reality itself that originally, and before any act of legislation, possesses a juridical nature, a structure ordered on the basis of principles and laws. The architrave of this intrinsic statute can be nothing other than that of the

---

21 *MECW* 1, p. 308.

22 *MECW* 1, p. 275.

23 *MECW* 1, p. 261.

24 *MECW* 1, p. 161.

'species' or, in other words, of a texture of reality arranged according to organic articulations and connections. This is clearly shown in the article 'Debates on the Law on Thefts of Wood' in which Marx argues that the ancient, customary right of the gathering of dead wood, although not codified, unquestionably represents a legitimate practice insomuch as it is behaviour that respects and mirrors the intrinsic – and, therefore, objective and true, if considered from an organic perspective – nature of the reality in question. Fallen and dead wood is effectively lacking in any connection to living reality, it does not participate in the organic society of the natural world and, therefore, is the specular complement of the 'elementary class' or 'poor class [*elementarische, arme Klasse*]' or, in other words, the social class that has no place in the society of the human world and lives outside any organic relationship.

> Such wood [fallen] has as little organic connection [*in einem organischen Zusammenhang*] with the growing tree as the cast-off skin has with the snake. Nature itself presents as it were a model of the antithesis between poverty and wealth in the shape of the dry, snapped twigs and branches separated from organic life [*vom organischen Leben getrennten*], in contrast to the trees and stems which are firmly rooted and full of sap, organically assimilating [*organisch*] air, light, water and soil to develop their own proper form and individual life. It is a physical representation of poverty and wealth. Human poverty senses this kinship and deduces its right to property from this feeling of kinship. [...] In these customs of the poor class, therefore, there is an instinctive sense of right; their roots are positive and legitimate, and the form of *customary right* here conforms all the more to nature because up to now the *existence of the poor class itself* has been a *mere custom* [*eine blosse Gewohnheit*] of civil society, a custom which has not found an appropriate place in the conscious organisation of the state.[25]

If the form of the law implies universality and necessity insofar as, by definition, it must necessarily be extended to all the members of the social body, its content cannot be any less necessary and cogent because its validity or lack thereof derives from its participation or non-participation in an organic reality. The customary rights of gathering fallen wood are entirely legitimate, even without any formal legitimisation.

---

25 *MECW* 1, p. 234.

> Their content [of these customary rights] does not conflict with legal form, but rather with its own lack of form. The form of law is not in contradiction to this content, on the contrary, the latter has not yet reached this form [*Die Form des Gesetzes steht ihm nicht gegenüber, sondern er hat sie noch nicht erreicht*].[26]

The customary rights of the nobles, however, cannot be translated from spontaneous and unreflective behaviour into the mediated and aware activity of the law. Its natural practice cannot determine itself according to juridical forms because it is of an unnatural and inessential nature. Formed as it is on the basis of arbitrariness and partiality, its existence cannot be deduced from a perspective of organicity and totality and, as such, its immediacy is not based on any source of validity.

> The customary rights of the aristocracy conflict by their *content* with the form of universal law [*die Form des allgemeinen Gesetzes*]. They cannot be given the form of law because they are formations of lawlessness. The fact that their content is contrary to the form of law – universality and necessity – proves that they are *customary wrongs* and cannot be asserted in opposition to the law, but as such opposition they must be abolished and even punished if the occasion arises.[27]

Thus nature confirms itself as a reality (in the sense of a whole animated by a unitary principle of life) only when its horizon includes a human world that is spiritually one and by means of the unity and self-consciousness of which nature itself expresses and reveals its profoundly organic intimacy. If this is not the case, nature is merely an environment of fragmented and reciprocally hostile life: mere nature whose principle is not the human species but the feral opposition of species to species. Thus, a society such as that in the Middle Ages, in which the fragmentation of the parts has dissolved any spirit of unity, can be defined as belonging to the realm of beasts rather than that of human beings.

> Their [i.e., the customs of the privileged contrary to the law] origin dates to the period in which human history was part of natural history [...]. Mankind appeared to fall into definite species of animals which were connected not by equality, but by inequality, an inequality fixed by laws. The

26 *MECW* 1, p. 232.

27 *MECW* 1, p. 231.

> world condition of unfreedom required laws expressing this unfreedom, for whereas human law is the mode of existence of freedom, this animal law is the mode of existence of unfreedom. Feudalism in the broadest sense is the spiritual animal kingdom, the world of divided mankind, in contrast to the human world that creates its own distinctions and whose inequality is nothing but a refracted form of equality. In the countries of naive feudalism, in the countries of the caste system, where in the literal sense of the word people are put in separate boxes, and the noble, freely interchanging members of the great sacred body, the holy Humanus [*des großen Heiligen, des heiligen Humanus*], are sawn and cleft asunder, forcibly torn apart, we find therefore also the worship of animals, animal religion in its primitive form, for man always regards as his highest being that which is his true being. The sole equality to be found in the actual life of animals is the equality between one animal and other animals of the same species; it is the equality of the given species with itself, but not the equality of the species [*nicht die Gleichheit der Gattung*].[28]

The circularity of nature and law, in the Marx of the *Rheinische Zeitung*, does not therefore refer to a foundation of natural law, at least in the sense in which the sixteenth- and seventeenth-century natural law tradition strongly emphasises the more subjective aspect of natural right with the theory of the individual's innate rights. For, if it is true that the content of law for Marx is nothing other than the nature of humanity and its originary freedom, the human being here, as we have seen, is always a communitarian and generic being and never the individual of the natural law tradition, which, by means of a contract, passes from a precarious and uncertain form of life, precisely as in a state of nature, to civil society as a form of stable and organised life in a juridical-political sense.[29]

---

28 *MECW* 1, p. 230, translation modified.

29 The interpretation proposed in Guastini 1974 (see, in particular, pp. 13–109) is very different from the young Marx's circular theory of law. Highlighting the contradictory and juxtaposed presence, in the Marx of the *Rheinische Zeitung*, of a healthy, empirical-materialistic approach that begins from the 'nature of the thing' and from an interest in an intrinsic constitution of the facts, on the one hand, and, on the other, of an abstract and prevaricating idealism that, based on presupposed values and ideas of reality, bends realism towards an a priori idealism, means repressing, in my opinion, the profound co-penetration that the *Rheinische* Marx achieves between empiricism and idealism. This is because all segments of reality are registered originally in an organic texture which the various cultural institutions and their associated life, through to those of the law and the state, must bring to

A theory of law necessarily refers to a theory of the state. The state, like the law, for Marx in this period is the universal and spiritual translation of reality, the sublation of all particular interests and the affirmation of the whole. The prevalence of partial needs and exigencies, on the other hand, constitutes the negation of the state.

> In a true state there is no landed property, no industry, no material thing, which as a crude element of this kind could make a bargain with the state; in it there are only spiritual forces [*geistige Mächte*], and only in their state form of resurrection, in their political rebirth, are these natural forces [*die natürlichen Mächte*] entitled to a voice in the state. The state pervades the whole of nature with spiritual nerves, and at every point it must be apparent that what is dominant is not matter, but form, not nature without the state, but the nature of the state, not the unfree object but the free human being.[30]

Material life in itself is only a negative, dogmatic naturality. It is synonymous with the need of the individual, of the class, of the part: a need which, abstractly

---

light in a mirroring process. Guastini's reading instead implies the repression of the basic continuity linking Marx to the epistemological and ontological circuit of Hegel.

30 MECW 1, p. 306. This article by Marx concerns the other representative institution that, alongside the provincial Diet, characterised the Prussian legislative activities on a territorial basis in these years. The Estate Committees [*ständische Ausschüsse*] had been established by Frederick William IV from June 1842 in all the Prussian provinces on the basis of the Estate orders represented by the provincial Diets. They enjoyed a consultative power and performed their duties, on the behest of the king, between one Diet and another. The dominance of the nobility in this institution was also guaranteed, as evidenced by the Committees' composition in 1842 throughout the eight Prussian provinces: 44 representatives of the princes and knights, 32 for the cities, 22 for the landowners and peasants (see MEGA, I/1, p. 1061). The creation of these committees, together with the provincial Diets, was the Prussian government's response to the request for representative institutions by the German bourgeoisie and intellectuals. To the demand for a constitutional representation which, on the French model, could stand for all Prussians *qua* citizens, the Prussian monarchy responded with the intensification and diffusion of a pre-modern order characteristic of a society based on estates, founded precisely on the distinction of the juridical status between the various estates. Marx intervened in two articles in the conservative and pro-government Augsburg *Allgemeine Zeitung*. On the contrast between the law of Estates and modern law of the first half of the nineteenth century that, beginning with the establishment of the general Prussian Code [*Allgemeines Landrecht für die preussischen Staaten*] by Frederick II, characterised Prussian history, see Koselleck 1988, in particular pp. 23–129 and pp. 323–72.

valorised for itself, can only oppose the universal and see it as something external to itself and which it can turn to its own advantage: 'for the particular in its isolated activity is always the enemy of the whole, since precisely this whole makes it feel its insignificance by making it feel its limitations'.[31] This occurs, for example, in the case of the landowner who recognises the existence of the state only as a means related to his own private interest.

> The state structure, the purpose of the individual administrative authorities, everything must get out of hand so that everything is degraded into an instrument of the forest owner and his interest operates as the soul governing the entire mechanism. All the organs of the state become ears, eyes, arms, legs, by means of which the interest of the forest owner hears, observes, appraises, protects, reaches out, and runs.[32]

For Marx, however, the state is to be conceived of as 'a realisation of rational freedom' or, in other words, of the freedom that consists in the sublation of interests linked to personal and natural needs and in the acceptance of an interest that is universal, belonging to everyone. This cannot coincide with the mechanical composition of interests because it is 'organic rationality'. As such, the state is where the existence of the *Volksgeist* is at its most intense, precisely because it is where the people becomes spirit, overcoming every form of life linked to individualism and a biologically conditioned mode of existence. However, precisely because this is only conceivable on the basis of the people and its organic destiny, whenever the state abstracts and separates itself from this foundation it necessarily becomes the institution of only one part, of power and arbitrariness, which juxtaposes itself to a civil society disaggregated into particularism. By taking this path, it reflects, with its separate and partial institutional dimensions, the principle of popular life reduced to traces of subjectivity that themselves are also only particular and abstract.

This nexus of reciprocal implication between the people and the state becomes most apparent in the question of representation. For Marx, this constitutes the heart of any state's constitution, given that it summarises not only the relationship between citizens and institutions, but also that of the division of powers and the connections between legislative activity and constituent power. Marx makes a radical declaration in the pages of the *Rheinische Zeitung*.

31 *MECW* 1, p. 305.

32 *MECW* 1, p. 245.

The institution of representation, of delegation to others, is the negation of the autonomy of any spiritual subject.

> In general, to be represented is something passive; only what is material, spiritless, unable to rely on itself, imperilled, requires to be represented; but no element of the state should be material, spiritless, unable to rely on itself, imperilled.[33]

Representation is division, the fracture of the totality of a people into the represented and the representing, into civil society on the one hand and the political state on the other. It therefore corresponds to the genesis of a radical, ontological incoherence that assigns to the few, to a small part, the ability to represent the whole. But the only form of representation that is coherent with the organic destination of the *Volk* is that which universalises the act of representation and which, by removing any distinction between represented and representing, makes each one a representative of the interests of all the others. (The 1843 *Kritik* explains this universalisation as the generalised extension of the active and passive rights of election to all, without any distinctions.) Only in this way is it possible to conceive of political representation that is completely self-representative of a people or, in other words, by means of which each person represents all and a people can achieve the greatest consciousness of itself as a body, not of private individuals, but of organic and universal humanity.

> Representation must not be conceived as the representation of something that is not the people itself. It must be conceived only as the people's self-representation [*Selbstvertretung*], as a state action which, not being its sole, exceptional state action, is distinguished from other expressions of its state life merely by the universality of its content.[34]

Marx critically points out that the institution of provincial German Diets, formed by representatives of the various orders of civil society, nonetheless represents only specific interests in opposition to the general interest. Furthermore, Marx adds, the institution of bodies are generated, but contemporaneously separated by the civil orders, which gives them (introducing this concept in his writings for the first time) a fetishistic effect, making them appear as autonomous and independent from the subject that posits them. In the institu-

33 *MECW* 1, p. 306.

34 Ibid.

tion of representation, the elected detach themselves from those they represent and establish themselves as autonomous subjects, independent of those subjects of whom they should be the emanation.

> Privileges of the estates are in no way rights of the province. On the contrary, the rights of the province cease when they become privileges of the estates [...]. The rights of the Provincial Assembly are no longer rights of the province, but rights against the province, and the Assembly itself would be the greatest wrong against the province but with the mystical significance of being supposed to embody its greatest right [...]. The speaker knows only the province of the estates, not the estates of the province. The Assembly of the Estates has a province to which the privilege of its activity extends, but the province has no estates through which it could itself be active. Of course, the province has the right, under prescribed conditions, to create these gods for itself, but as soon as they are created, it must, like a fetish worshipper, forget that these gods are its own handiwork.[35]

The institute of the Diets is not the place for the self-mirroring and realisation of a people's unity; rather, it is the mirroring of a civil society which, because it is formed of orders or, in other words, of separate social bodies, is interwoven with particular interests that prevent the birth of a true community spirit. A society based on orders, divided into *Stände*, can only have the materiality of private interests as its main principle. 'Landed property is the general condition for participating in the right of estate representation'.[36] But an organisation that is rigidly fixed into divisions of estates corresponds only to a primitive level of human life, very far from understanding the true nature of the modern state and its production of universality. To those who defend a society organised into estates and a state that represents a unity that is only external to the separations of civil society, Marx responds in this way:

> The author [the editor of the *Augsburg Gazette*] does not examine whether this difference which is presumed to exist in the institution in question characterises the estates of the past or those of the present. Instead he discusses the difference between the estates [*den Ständenunterschied*] in general. It will be as little possible to eradicate it, he says, 'as to destroy

35 *MECW* 1, pp. 145–7.

36 *MECW* 1, p. 293.

the difference existing in nature between the elements and to go back to a chaotic unity'. One could reply to the author: just as no one would think of destroying the difference between the natural elements and going back to a chaotic unity, no one would want to eradicate the difference between the estates. At the same time, however, one would have to demand of the author that he should make a more thorough study of nature and rise from the first sensuous perception of the various elements [*von der ersten sinnlichen Wahrnehmung der verschiedenen Elemente*] to a rational perception of the organic life of nature [*zur vernünftigen Wahrnehmung des organischen Naturlebens*]. Instead of the spectre of a chaotic unity, he would become aware of the spirit of a living unity [*einer lebendigen Einheit*]. Even the elements do not persist in inert separation. They are continually being transformed into one another and this transforming alone forms the first stage of the physical life of the earth, the meteorological process. In the living organism [*Im lebendigen Organismus*], all trace of the different elements as such has disappeared. The difference no longer consists in the separate existence of the various elements, but in the living movement of distinct functions, which are all inspired by one and the same life [*die alle von einem und demselben Leben begeistet sind*], so that the very difference between them does not exist ready-made prior to this life but, on the contrary, continually arises out of this life itself and as continually vanishes within it and becomes paralysed. Just as nature does not confine itself to the elements already present, but even at the lowest stage of its life proves that this diversity is a mere sensuous phenomenon that has no spiritual truth, so also the state, this natural realm of the spirit, must not and cannot seek and find its true essence in a fact apparent to the senses. [...] If it would be unfitting to set the people in motion as a crude, inorganic mass, it would be just as much impossible to achieve an organised movement of the people if it were resolved mechanically into rigid and abstract constituents, and an independent movement, which could only be a convulsive one, were demanded of these inorganic, forcibly established parts. The author starts out from the view that in the actual *state* the people exists as a crude, inorganic mass, apart from some arbitrarily seized on differences of estate. Hence he knows no organism [*keinen Organismus*] of the state's life itself, but only a juxtaposition of heterogeneous parts which are encompassed superficially and mechanically by the state. But let us be frank. We do not demand that in the representation of the people actually existing differences should be left out of account. On the contrary, we demand that one should proceed from the actual differences created and conditioned by the internal structure of the state, and

> not fall back from the actual life of the state into imaginary spheres which that life has already robbed of their significance. [...] And those distinctions, which owing to their very essence are dissolved at every moment in the unity of the whole [*in der Einheit des Ganzen*], are free creations of the spirit of the Prussian state, but are by no means raw materials imposed on the present time by blind natural necessity and the dissolution process of a past period! They are members but not parts, they are movements but not states [*Stände*];[37] they are differences of unity but not unities of difference.[38]

This long page taken from the article 'On the Commissions of the Estates in Prussia' perfectly expresses the intensity of the organicist ontology on which the young Marx's thoughts are founded, and the consequences that such a presupposition implies in relation to his theory of the state and politics. It is an explicit metaphysics of organic life, culminating in the unity *par excellence* that is the *Gattung-Volk*, which dominates the more explicitly political arguments of Marx the journalist. 'Dominion of philosophy over politics' here means not to deny the obvious political valency of Marx's activities at the time, as is evidenced by his belonging to the most extreme wing of German intelligentsia before 1848, editing an anti-government paper such as the *Rheinische Zeitung*, his battles against censorship and the defence of various disadvantaged classes such as the Moselle vineyard workers.[39] It is, rather, to say that it is, paradoxically, the same philosophy that underlies the entire discourse that prevents the development of any articulated and concrete theory of politics. The organicity of the people, the prevalence of the value of the universal in it over the individual's lack of value, permits a differentiation of the whole that can be reduced only to its self-reflection. The various segments of the totality, such as the press, legislation, intellectuality, administration and government, through to individuals themselves, have meaning only when they are the vectors and witnesses of the universal. Otherwise, any autonomy and specific nature of existence they might have is only the negation of and opposition to that principle of totality. Organicist humanism prohibits the Marx of the *Rheinische Zeitung* from thinking unity as the synthesis of the multiple, to conceive, that is, of the universal as

---

37 In the sense of 'fixed position'. The other meaning of the term *Stand*, to which Marx refers, is also 'estate'.

38 *MECW* 1, pp. 295–7.

39 On the political significance of Marx's writings in the *Rheinische Zeitung* see, amongst others, Sabetti 1962, pp. 143–61; Fetscher 1965, pp. 125–35; Adams 1972; Zanardo 1966; Cornu 1971.

having a wealth of differentiated individualities. This prohibition also encompasses the impossibility of conceiving of politics as a complex of institutions and powers articulated in a community animated by distinct and autonomous subjectivities. Thus, precisely this same philosophical depth that blesses the journalistic pages written by Marx in 1842–3 with a brilliant and original argumentative line, an extremely effective and critical radical nature, at the same time takes away the depth and breadth from its constructive perspective.

The Marx of this period was searching for a principle of constitution of reality which, although embracing the substance of Hegel's lesson, would sublate the containment of Hegel's philosophy in an excessively idealistic-speculative horizon. It was a search for a philosophy of action, a philosophy that becomes worldly. Thus, from this point of view, he is a young Hegelian who embraces, with an eye on Feuerbach, the translation of Hegel's *Geist* into *menschliche Gattung*, into the human species or, more specifically, into the *Volk* as a principle of historical reality. However, at the same time, giving weight to Hegel rather than Feuerbach, as we will see further on, he could not accept the thesis of the immediate fullness of the reality of this principle, as is instead implied by the strongly organicist-naturalist component of Feuerbach's theory of the *Gattung*. The principle of the people can therefore achieve fullness of itself only in a Hegelian sense, by means of the objectivisation and self-reflection in the most elevated and disinterested realisations of life.

Feuerbach *versus* Hegel, Hegel *versus* Feuerbach: within this intertwining chiasma, the young Marx's first theoretical system comes into play.[40] However, the weight of the original immediacy that distinguishes Feuerbach's humanistic subject can only be compensated for and rebalanced with difficulty – due to a principle of radical incompatibility – by the more rightly mediatory and intrinsically dynamic example of Hegel's *Geist*. The consequence of this asym-

40 Louis Althusser's famous structuralist interpretation in 1960–70s of Marx's work, isolating a first phase of Marx's thought that was supposedly entirely reducible to the influence of Feuerbach alone, does not take into account this chiasmatic structure of the young Marx's philosophy. By attributing only importance to Feuerbach's anthropocentrism, anticipated by a single Kantian-Fichtean moment in 1840–2 (see Althusser 1969, p. 35), he neglects seeing just how much Hegel is indispensible for the articulation, despite the difficulties of its development, that the young Marx is attempting. However, Althusser then attributes to the subsequent Marx, precisely through Hegel, the concept of history as a 'process without a subject': an idea which, in truth, appears to me at least to be foreign to both Hegel's philosophy and Marx's thought, also because the latter, in his maturity, although renouncing the centrality of the subject 'man', does not renounce the centrality of 'capital' as a subject producing reality and the totalising laws of its valorisation (see Althusser 1970).

metry is the immobilisation of Marx's first theoretical organisation in a structural impossibility of thinking and conceiving of society and history's development. Furthermore, there is the impossibility of even imagining the existence of the single human being, since, as seen, the individual either coincides with the universal or does not exist; as an abstract and separated individual, it is reduced to an animal or a thing, subtracting and negating its more properly human identity.

Thus, in Marx's Manichean vision, there are only two alternatives: either a condition of generalised egoism and thus a society tending towards the dimension of naturalness and the conflict of interests from which any pulsation of universality is absent, or a condition of total organicity in which the universal interest permeates and entirely reduces individual interests to itself. In other words, either a society of structurally repulsing atoms where the multiplicities of the 'one' and the radical nature of the conflict of private interests would not even allow us to speak of the presence and conceptualisation of a united and social horizon, or an angelically based and, at the same time, totalitarian society where the fullness of the 'One' does not permit the conception even of the possibility for many 'ones'.

However, Hegel's reflection on this subject developed in a completely different way, as already mentioned, and as will be seen analytically further on in our discussion of the concept of a 'civil society'. What Hegel's dialectics essentially sought on this level, having overcome the extremes of both individualism and collectivism, was the mediation of antiquity and modernity. He tried, that is, to conceive of a type of society that would guarantee both the value of collectivity and common interests (perspectives of the ancient world), and those of freedom and self-determination (belonging to the modern era). For, without the co-presence of the two values, there would be a reversal into the extremes of a despotic and undifferentiated society or into one of unbounded and destructive individualism. Those studying the ethico-political ideas of Hegel thus find that he is the author who, more than any other modern author – far beyond the philologically dubious version that has fed the liberal interpretation of him as a totalitarian thinker – has reflected on modernity as the place where, despite making subjective freedom its fundamental principle, there is no obligation to reject abstractly the heritage of values and civilisation that has been elaborated and sedimented by the pre-modern world. This same problem, in the mature Hegel, also takes on the role of reconciling the tradition of Anglo-Saxon and, more specifically, Scottish economic-political liberalism, with the cameralism of the German tradition, in which political and administrative sovereignty coincides with taking on responsibility for not so much and not only order, but, above all, for the well-being of its subjects. In this tradition, therefore, institutional powers should not only define the rules of the reciprocal exercising of freedom, as in the traditions of Locke and Kant, but also intervene in the life of their subjects in order to guarantee sustainable and comfortable conditions of existence for them all. The problem, therefore, is that of how is it possible to reconcile – according to the classification put forward by Hegel in his early writings – 'French freedom', fundamentally based on the values and defence of subjectivity, with 'German freedom', based on a greater connection between the rights of the individual and community values; or, more precisely, the problem of reconciling the Anglo-French traditions of what constitutes freedom, in the essentially more individual and personal sense of the expression, with the Germanic tradition that, instead, finds the essence of freedom in the ability to see the good of all as not contradictory to that of the self.

We can see the profound difficulties that Hegel's proposed solution faces, above all in the later text of the *The Philosophy of Right* [*Grundlinien der Philosophie des Rechts*]. However, these difficulties do not detract from the richness and originality of Hegel's socio-political philosophy, which problematised modernity as the complexity of a social system constituted not only by individuals and their conscious freedom, but also by the institutions of their collaboration and solidarity.

The young Marx, on the other hand, with the assumption of the principle of the *menschliche Gattung-Volk* [human species-people] as a totality, distinguished by the single voice of integration and organicity, takes the thematic back to a pre-Hegelian stage, inevitably exposing himself through this move to the (in our opinion) simplifying and regressive influence of Feuerbach. This subject, inspired by Feuerbach, does not undergo a development through the Hegelian categories of self-objectivisation and self-reflection, except in the sense of a fruitless and aporetic juxtaposition. The organic nature of the people is not generated by and is not a product of individual differences and their endurance. As a consequence, it remains a merely ideal abstraction, an idea that is only presupposed, an idea that does not bring together in itself the complexity of life and experience.

On 19 January 1843, the Prussian government ordered the cessation of the *Rheinische Zeitung* on the following 1 April. The radical nature of the Cologne daily paper's criticism had become intolerable. Marx, after waiting two months, without the petitions in defence of the paper by the citizens of Cologne and the other Rhineland cities such as Barmen, Düsseldorf, Trier and Wesel having achieved anything at all, left the paper on the 17 March with the following words: 'The undersigned declares that, owing to the *present conditions of censorship*, he has retired as from today from the editorial board of the *Rheinische*

*Zeitung*'.[41] On 19 June of the same year, he married Jenny von Westphalen, after an engagement lasting seven years, in the Protestant church of Kreuznach, a spa town around sixty kilometres from Trier. After a short honeymoon, he remained there until September and most probably composed the manuscript which was only published 50 years after his death, entitled by the publishers: *Critique of Hegel's Philosophy of Right* [*Kritik des Hegelschen Staatsrechts*].

Marx's steps following the *Rheinische Zeitung* period – by now, with the aim of leaving Germany for France – were, as will shortly be seen, a presumptively definitive break with Hegel. They represent his transition from radical democracy to communism. The populism of his *Volksphilosphie*, the valorisation of the collective subject with the rejection of any attribution of meaning to singularity, will constitute the fundamental, theoretical condition that permitted this transition. In carrying out the parricide of Hegel, in his passion for populism and the radicalising of this populism in his first theorisation of communism, the figure of Feuerbach now becomes even more important. The moment has now arrived to turn our attention to this other mentor of the young Marx's work.

41 *MECW* 1, p. 376.

CHAPTER 4

# The Deceptive Materialism of Ludwig Feuerbach

## 1 The Divinisation of Reason

In the canonical iconography of Marxism, Ludwig Feuerbach (1804–72) has been assigned the role of the 'ferryman'. It was he who carried Marx and Engels from idealism to materialism but was himself unable to set foot on the Promised Land due to the limitations of his materialism, too confined to the sensibilities of the individual human and not at all open to history. However, he has all the value of a Charon who, by reversing the primacy assigned by Hegel to the spirit and thought into the primacy of matter, took decisive steps towards the historicist accumulation of truth with which great German philosophy triumphantly overflows into the works of Marx and Engels. It was, after all, the latter who, with his *Ludwig Feuerbach and the End of Classical German Philosophy* (1886), codified a very simplified version of the history of modern philosophy, presented as the outcome of an unstoppable journey towards the light of the truth that, by means of a continuous series of overturnings, goes from Hegel through Feuerbach to Marx.

However, in this sense, Engels did nothing but give a more systematic form to the indications provided by Marx himself. Marx's relationship with Feuerbach, within the limits of the first phase of his thought, is attested to by three pieces of surviving evidence. The first consists in a letter dated 1844; the second, the references in his *Theses on Feuerbach*; and the third, *The German Ideology*, from the spring of 1845. The letter of 11 August 1844 was written by Marx in Paris when he was finishing the draft of his *Economic and Philosophic Manuscripts*. It perfectly summarises the role played by Feuerbach in the development of his ideas:

> I am glad to have an opportunity of assuring you of the great respect and – if I may use the word – love, which I feel for you. Your *Philosophie der Zukunft*, and your *Wesen des Glaubens*, in spite of their small size, are certainly of greater weight than the whole of contemporary German literature put together. In these writings you have provided – I don't know whether intentionally – a philosophical basis for socialism and the communists have immediately understood them in this way. The unity of man with man, which is based on the real differences between men, the concept of the human species brought down from the

> heaven of abstraction to the real earth, what is this but the concept of society![1]

The *Theses on Feuerbach* and *The German Ideology*, however, already critically highlight the path taken by Feuerbach towards materialism: the contraposition of concrete and sensuous reality to the abstractions of idealist philosophy and religion is limited to a valorisation of sensibility conceived of as a merely passive faculty of intuition and dependence on the external world. The latter is legitimately seen as a real and autonomous world that cannot be reduced to a mere projection of the Idea. However, what Feuerbach's only intuitive materialism does not take into account is the active nature of human beings' sensuous existence; it does not take into account labour as the practical activity of transforming the external world. As a result of this radical insufficiency, it does not see the history of material praxis and its resulting social relations as the privileged subject of interest. Instead, he proposes a merely naturalistic theory of the human essence, from which derives a rhetorical and sentimental celebration of love as the only privileged instrument of emancipation.

Marx's observations, while pertinent, are, above all from a critical point of view, so rapid and schematic that they represent Feuerbach as an incomplete materialist who abandoned the rarefied air of philosophy in order to utilise the concrete nature of life but, through this abandonment, achieved only a naturalistic rather than a historical materialism. In this form, humanity is at last conceived of as a sensuous subject, but still without any recognition of the peculiarities of its practical sensibility.

However, we are now separated by more than a century and a half of studies, of philological and critical research, from the simplicity of this canonical representation. The figure of Feuerbach can now be assessed in all its various aspects. Thus, in relation to what interests us here, we can now return to that close confrontation with Hegel's philosophy which was so important, in his agreements and dissent, in Feuerbach's thinking, and which the fairly cavalier materialistic reduction of Marx and Engels too radically pushed back into the shadows. What emerges, in my opinion, is the persistent pantheist-humanist system that dominates Feuerbach's work, at least up to the texts that are of interest due to their influence on Marx. With their fusional-totalising tendency, they have little in common with traditional materialism.

Feuerbach's break with Hegel, rather than being explained in terms of the much celebrated reversal of spirit into matter, appears to be more understand-

1 *MECW* 3, p. 354.

able in the light of the substantial lack of understanding and extraneousness that Feuerbach demonstrates, in all his work, in relation to the Hegelian circle of the presupposed-posited and the dialectical function of negation. From the very start, what distinguishes Feuerbach from Hegel, despite emphatically declaring himself to be his disciple after attending the 1825–6 lectures in Berlin, is the positing as the basis of his thought a fullness of reality that is not built up but, from the very beginning, is available to the subject as long as it chooses its most authentic nature and passes from an individualistic mode to an organic and universalist approach to reality.

This is not because in Hegel there is not also an idealistic basis to events, according to which reality is structured in terms of the levels of a progressive and more appropriate consciousness that a subject has of its identity and, therefore, on the basis of the available knowledge-based faculty that is awakened in it (sentiment or intellect or reason). However, this idealistic causation of reality in Hegel is instituted by a subject who moves from a natural-abstract modality to a dialectical-universalist modality, the more its relationship with otherness is opened up and accepted within its self. Furthermore, such a process in Hegel is constrained by a manifold and articulated series of movements that obliges such a subject not to remain within a naturalist and dogmatically finite perception of its own self.

Studies on Feuerbach have correctly identified two phases in his theoretical production: the first tending towards a profound idealistic spiritualism and, the second, marked by a radical change and based on the priority of finite and sensible experience in distinction from dematerialised and speculative spirituality. Nonetheless, despite the various philosophical emphases, Feuerbach is substantially still a unitarian thinker with an unchanging pantheistic-organicist system. The permanent basis of his thought, even when this appears as a humanism of concreteness and material needs, effectively lies in a) the reduction of all reality to the alternation, in the human being, of a mode of existence based on sensuous-bodily instances or, in other words, on a perspective of natural-individualistic interests or, on the other hand, on reason and its intrinsic ability to resolve every individualist and particular viewpoint in the universal; b) in overcoming the abstract egoistic singularity in the universality of the human species that this privileging of either reason or sensibility immediately – insofar as it is achieved in the interior nature of the individual and without any real relation to alterity – implies.

The theme of the immediate universalisation of the individual, as long as sensuous and rational life prevails in its experience, is present and remains unchanging throughout his thinking from his very first work, his Latin dissertation *De ratione, una, universali, infinita*. In this, the basis of human life is reason, which is defined as one, universal and infinite, so much so that, through this, the individual loses every one of its particularities and determinations and becomes a universal being. This is because, as an entity defined by a body and its human sensuousness, it is enclosed in a finitude that distinguishes and separates it from other entities which, above all, make it rigid and distant from other human beings. However, through knowledge and thought, human beings become infinite, become a species and participate in the community.

> Insofar as I think, I cease to be an individual and thought is nothing other than the being of universality [*cogitare idem est atque universale esse*].[2]

> In so far as I think, I can at the same time also be the other [*quoad cogito, alter ipse*] and in truth I am; my essence is also of the other; what is in my deepest interiority can and will also be part of the other's being [...]. In the act of thinking the other is inside me; I am at one and the same time myself and you; but undoubtedly not a determinate you but you in general, or insofar as a species.[3]

> Senses, sensations, in contrast to thought, remain enclosed in the particular.

> Senses, by which I am moved, deprived of thought, remain in themselves and for themselves always and only mine, tightly enclosed in the circle of my being. It is without a doubt that the word always expresses something of the universal while senses are singular. [...] For this reason, since sensitive perception distinguishes me from the other, because in this I am only myself and the other is for me another, the other cannot participate in me.[4]

Reason, on the other hand, makes individual humans participants in a whole of which, as thinking entities, they are determinations. It is, therefore, the absolute essence of the human being as a species. 'Insofar as I think, I am the human species [*cogitans ipse sum genus humanum*], not an individual person, as happens to me when I feel, live, act. When I think I am not an individual determinate person (this or that), I am no-one'.[5] Whatever the content of

---

2 Feuerbach 1981, vol. 1, p. 8.

3 Feuerbach 1981, vol. 1, pp. 12–16.

4 Feuerbach 1981, vol. 1, pp. 10–12.

5 Feuerbach 1981, vol. 1, p. 31.

thought, even if worthless, whoever the individual who thinks it might be, thought, precisely due to its form as thought, belongs to humanity in general. 'However the thoughts of any one person move in a cramped and limited space, however vacuous their content, the form of thought remains integral and untouched by this. This form is the form of the community or universality [*Est autem haec forma communitatis sive universitatis*]'.[6] Human beings are separated by sex, age, nationality, customs, and intelligence levels in terms of their physical and natural existence. But, when they think, they become members of a universal, continuous and uninterrupted essence that removes any possible difference between them.

> Thought coincides and is united with itself through the thoughts of all human beings. However widespread amongst individuals, it is continuous, perpetual, one, equal to itself, inseparable from itself. In an act of thought all human beings, however in contrast they may be for the rest, are equal to each other. *Qua* a thinking being, I am joined, or rather united, with all; or rather, I am all human beings [*ipse ego omnes sum homines*].[7]

On the other hand, the connections between thought in general and the manifold and determinate acts of its knowledge should be seen, within every individual mind, as identical to the relationship between a species and its infinite generations. Reason is effectively consciousness in the sense of self-consciousness, a totality that is in relation to itself, while knowledge is the same reason that becomes particularised, taking on every particular content of thought in the circle of its inevitable self-reference.

> Consciousness [*conscientia*] can legitimately be called a genus [*genus*] due to the fact that, in relation to itself, it is the original relationship that solely through knowledge [*cognitio*] can be generated. Consciousness, in fact, remains both in thought as in the knowledge of things, remaining eternal, uninterrupted, equal and continuous with itself through all the knowledge and determinate forms of thinking. In contrast, knowledge [*cognitio*] [...] should be called a species [*species*] of [the *genus* of] consciousness because knowledge refers only to determinate and single things that it understands by means of determinate and finite forms of

6 Feuerbach 1981, vol. 1, p. 8.

7 Feuerbach 1981, vol. 1, pp. 16–18.

> thought. Knowledge is thus, of that primary and permanent relationship with itself that is consciousness, a determinate and particular relationship.[8]

Every material and determinate act of knowledge is nothing but the specification and self-determination of the primary structure of consciousness – for Feuerbach, as mentioned, synonymous with self-consciousness. Thought, in its non-materiality and infinity, is an activity that does not depend on nor is limited by either individual subjects or individual objects. It is universal activity that can have nothing other than itself and the attestation of its universality as its object. Thus, every particular content of knowledge, every determinate and finite relationship of the knowing subject and known object, is nothing more than a specification, an individualisation of that relationship of infinite subject-infinite object that is the dual unity, the one and binary structure, of self-consciousness *qua* the thought of thought. With regard to the nature of the genus-individual relation, it is only external in the sense that the universality of the genus is provided only by the inexhaustible succession of the disappearance of single entities. In reasoning, inversely, the genus-species-individual nexus is realised in the co-presence of all the elements, given that the individual is only a particularisation, a division and diremption of the self in the universal.

> Consciousness [*conscientia*] is therefore the genus, knowing [*cognitio*] is the species of the genus which represents the same relationship diversified into several distinct elements, in some way a breakage in the relationship of the consciousness that is the simple and same relationship with itself. But knowing [*cognitio*] unceasingly divides itself into single knowledges [*cognitiones*], or, in other words, into many and diverse [sub] species and these are none other than a collection and a bringing together of the innumerable finite and single elements.[9]

Moreover, this authentically unique human act of human life that is thought never stops with finite experiences and content, so that it is thinking itself that negates and sublates its determinations. True knowledge constantly universalises the object of its interest, subtracting it from the limitations of human sensations and makes it infinite. For, if thought in its form – that is, in its

8 Feuerbach 1981, vol. 1, p. 52.
9 Feuerbach 1981, vol. 1, p. 54.

most generalised characteristics – is absolute and infinite (insofar as in self-consciousness the object is none other than the subject and, therefore, does not depend on anything outside itself), the infinite in its form cannot help but search for and claim a content that is equally infinite. 'An infinite form, such as knowledge, expects a congruent infinite matter such as knowledge of the infinite'.[10] Consequently, thought necessarily universalises all its content and subtracts it from finitude, spreading its originary universality to every one of its individual self-determinations.

> Consciousness [*conscientia*], that already possessed an infinite nature, insomuch as it was one and in itself (liberated and far away from knowledge), does not hold its own infinite nature for long but imparts and takes it into its self-determination and knowledge [*cognitionem*].[11]

This positing of concrete determination and its negation constitutes the dialectical essence of knowledge, which 'through itself is the unity of forms and matter, of itself and the other [*per se ipsa est unitas formae et materiae, Sui Ipsius et Alterius*]'.[12]

This world of the unity and harmony of the many, of the infinite generation of determinations constantly drawn back into the circle of the totality, is found only in the reason of human beings. Beyond this, there is only the natural world and the human world itself composed of bodily and differentiated individuals; in other words, the horizon of bodies and mutually external existences. Here, self-consciousness is not an essential structure of the human species but a function of the individual and empirical self who lives by removing the universal from reality and assigning it instead only to itself. This world is, therefore, that of sensuous life dominated by personal sensibilities and needs that impede, in the concentration of its individuality, any aspiration to the infinite and the recognition, on the part of the single individual, of its essence in the universality of its own species – even if this same ambit of nature and individual life, when considered in depth, already anticipates in itself the profound tendencies towards the One and the Universal. This is the case not only in the repetition in the animal generations between species and individuals, but also in human senses themselves that have just been removed from a merely utilitarian and individualistic consideration. Infinity is in fact also present, over and above

---

10 Feuerbach 1981, vol. 1, p. 60.

11 Feuerbach 1981, vol. 1, p. 58.

12 Feuerbach 1981, vol. 1, p. 62.

their finitude. Given that every sense assumes as its content only those objects that adapt themselves to its form and nature and, as a result of this identifying of form and content, due to this coincidence with itself, not dependent on anything external to itself, precisely in its being finite, it is unconditioned and infinite.

> A condition of the senses is that what they take on must be similar and suitable, and they must not apply to anything else if not to that which is congruous. The eye effectively never tries to take on the role of the ear and appropriate itself of its nature, neither does seeing tend towards something that overbears it in force and constitution and by which it would be repelled. It is for this reason that it does not perceive the limits imposed on its nature. It is precisely due to the fact that it remains in the finiteness assigned to it by nature and does not try to appropriate itself of the duties of another sense that, in its activities, it is contemporaneously infinite.[13]

But this tendency towards absolute unity is also obviously present in the powerful reaching out to the other human being characteristic of every human being's life. Friendship and love, in particular, demonstrate that the human being is not a being that has relationships with others starting from its individuality, but, rather, that by its very essence it is in communion with others.

> On the contrary, the individual, who is a single being insomuch as it excludes the other from itself and which, nonetheless, must necessarily relate to other individuals, which it also excludes, is an individual only thanks to this relationship [*relatione*] and not due to its own nature [*non essentia*].[14]

The unifying capacities of love, though, are reduced with respect to the absolute unity produced by reason, since in this there still remains a certain sentiment of difference and delimitation.[15]

---

13 Feuerbach 1981, vol. 1, pp. 60–2. On the presence of a Romantic inspiration in Feuerbach's education and first writings, on the role played by love and by a representation of nature as unity and totality, see Schott 1973, pp. 42–8, 67–70, 189–93 and Cesa 1963, pp. 25–8, 40–2, 142–4.

14 Feuerbach 1981, vol. 1, p. 82.

15 'Man, guided by an obscure feeling that his condition as a natural body, due to which he is separated from the other, is not true, tends to ardently meet with the other. But all the

Nonetheless, even physical appetite, material desire, demonstrates that the supreme law of reality, however little this may be recognised, is unity, coincidence, the harmonic interpenetration of the parts.

> Every need has its place between two things which, even if separate and distance the one from the other, coincide profoundly in the fact that the one cannot live without the other [...]. If there were not a natural link between my body and the things that it desires, it would not be affected by any suffering for their lack. It is impossible, as a consequence, that in the same desire there should not be present, in some way, the thing desired.[16]

This is the case to such an extent that underlying the fullness of the One is not lack; an absence can be conceived only as already a presence.

> I do not have appetite for anything if not for that which I can obtain. Therefore, to desire is already to be able to. I already possess (in being able) that which I embrace with desire [...]. Therefore, in desire that which is present is contemporaneously absent.[17]

*De ratione, una, universali, infinita,* of which we have summarised only the most relevant theories, is only Feuerbach's first youthful work. Nonetheless, it already introduces us to the complex, fleeting nature of a thought whose literal claims are contradicted by the theoretical instrumentalisation effectively brought into play. The early Feuerbach appears to start theorising with the difference between nature and spirit, or between existence and essence, with profoundly Hegelian overtones, on the impossibility of the individual exhausting the possibilities of the species in itself; in other words, the fact that the individual can never identify itself and coincide with the universal, as many philosophies that make individual subjectivity the principle of reality would claim. These theories, for Feuerbach, would seem to generate the irreplaceable function of mediation, as an explanation of the modes and degrees of transition of the human being from its belonging to the life of the natural-animal world

---

methods of unification, such as love, friendship, etc., are particular, imperfect and finite since in them differences are not entirely removed. This is evidenced for example precisely by love which always remains, even in the presence and in the possession of the thing beloved, a desiring, a feeling of the difference and the limitations' (Feuerbach 1981, vol. 1, p. 92).

16 Feuerbach 1981, vol. 1, p. 66.

17 Feuerbach 1981, vol. 1, pp. 66–8.

to a spiritual-rational one. However, as is possibly sufficiently clear from the few passages already quoted, it is precisely this need for mediation, central to Hegel's philosophy, which finds no space and articulation in that of Feuerbach. He appears instead to resolve the issues much more in the sense of immediacy and organic unity. The renunciation of a bodily and sensuous life, of individual existence, in order to reach the species, the unity with all human beings, is effectively consumed in the immediacy of the consciousness of the individual in question and in the alternation of its modality of existence as long as its relationship with the world passes from the prevalence of bodily-naturalistic sensibilities to those of thought and its automatic universalising virtue. An alternation of natural sensuousness and reason – the latter being, furthermore, immediate, given that the transition from one to the other has the characteristic of a *metábasis eis allo ghenos*, or, in other words, an absolutely heterogeneous passage without any mediation and without any indepth examination of the nature of their possible opposition or relationship – could be added, neither in the sense of a transcendental nexus of the faculties of Kantian criticism, nor in that of a phenomenological-dialectical development of the sensible consciousness to other figures of consciousness, in Hegelian terms. However, given that it is Hegel's idealism to which Feuerbach's text is most similar, to the point of wanting to coincide with it to the greatest possible degree – as confirmed in the letter which, in July 1828, Feuerbach sent along with *De ratione* to the master in Berlin[18] – what must be highlighted as lacking in Feuerbach's pages is, above all, the theoretical heart of what defines *Geist* in Hegel's philosophy. Hegel's *Geist* involves the attaining to a complete place of authenticity and truth (the Absolute) that is given only on condition of passing through, in a process of self-removal, all the places and configurations of existence which, due to a rigidity of vision and fear of abandonment to the fullness of life, remain in error and partiality. It is this intrinsic mediation, this turning of the negative towards oneself, this catastrophe of partiality, in the series of figures that this kind of procedure initiates, that is completely lacking from Feuerbach's vision. Feuerbach's conception is not at all disposed to such a self-reflective accentuation of difference and is immediately ready, on the other hand, to establish itself in the rediscovery and relaxation of identity. As a consequence, due to this lack in Feuerbach's pages – whose appearance of a dialectical nature and substantial distance from the Hegelian model has passed unnoticed by many interpreters, also due to the use of Latin rather than the German of Hegel's lexicon – of a vision of subjectivity based on confrontation with its own internal alterity,

18 The text of the letter is in Feuerbach 1976, pp. 5–11.

there can be no presence of a theory of the universalisation of the subject that also takes into account the confrontation with external alterity, or of that path of acknowledgement/lack of acknowledgement of the other of itself and of the production of artefacts with a progressively broader latitude of utility by means of which, for Hegel, the construction of subjectivity becomes possible. Such a subject, for Hegel, can never be presupposed but is always produced and posited. The naive dialectics of the faculties in which the subjectivity that Feuerbach conceives in *De ratione* is entirely exhausted ignores the valency of the negation that occurs when, at the moment in which such negation is internally activated against the torpid and dogmatic coincidence of subjectivity with itself, that same subjectivity turns simultaneously externally to the encounter/clash and mediation with the external to itself. Thus, what is entirely lacking is the nexus of internalising-externalising that explicates and defines the sense of the 'negative' in Hegel's dialectics. Consequently, also lacking is the vision of alterity that is central to Hegel, namely, the notion that access to the other of the self is guaranteed to the extent that it is interwoven and synchronised with the access to the other in the self.

I would recommend to the interested reader to study the entire development of 1828 dissertation (that is, beyond the passages that I have been able to quote here) in order to verify more analytically the extent to which motifs of identification – of coincidence, the fitting, the fusion and the co-penetration of the parts – prevail in Feuerbach's first work over those of differentiation, of the concrete articulation of the world of knowledge and of experience, and over a theory of the human being that contains, even if only implicitly, the founding possibility of both social and relational action and historical occurrence.

## 2 Against the Self-Foundation of the Self. *Thoughts on Death and Immortality*

Feuerbach's first work, *Gedanken über Tod und Unsterblichkeit* [*Thoughts on Death and Immortality*], published anonymously in 1830, explicitly takes into account this philosophy that has as its basic principle the difference between existence and essence. It begins, that is, with the ontological inability of the individual to contain and exhaust within itself the vastness of the species. This philosophy, contradictorily, falls back onto a theory of immediacy through the divinisation of reason as an infinite unity, present in every individual act of knowledge, by means of which the individual returns to being the immediate witness of the whole (very differently to that which occurs in Hegel's presupposed-posited circle).[19] This includes the critical supposition of the naturalness that paradoxically returns to push reason towards the disposition of a nature immanent to the human species. The content of this work was so violently hostile to Christianity that it prevented its author from continuing his professorial career begun at the University of Erlangen. The basic thesis underlying the work is that humanity will not be able to enter a new phase in the history of the world and civilisation until Christianity has been exhausted and overcome. That religion is seen as linked to the exaltation of the individual self that prevents humanity from becoming a spiritually collective subject and participating thereby in the freedom and universal nature of the human species.[20]

It is no coincidence that the most intriguing pages of this text regard the concept that Feuerbach develops of God as a mere position and projection of the self. Religious faith in a personal God derives from a human being who has separated itself from the communion of life with others, projecting its own personal characteristics and idealising them in the infinite and perfect form of a divine Being.

> If God is only conceived and defined as a person [...] then God will be conceived as a superficial essence. God so conceived is without depth, is only a smooth surface that reflects the human back to himself, is the prototype but also the exact image of human personhood. [...] The same determinations that are in God are in humans, only they are in him infinitely, in humans finitely – in other words, they are realized in God in an infinitely higher degree.[21]

This consideration on religion as an anthropological reflection naturally recalls Hegel (and also, obviously, Spinoza's criticism of a personal and anthropomorphic God). All the main concepts used by Feuerbach in this text equally appear to be derived from Hegel: the definition of Spirit as that which places itself above and beyond life, seen as passivity and dependent on the other outside itself; the criticism of the intellect as a principle of division; the resultant radical rejection of egoistic and abstract individuality; the denunciation of philosophies that, by placing the infinite outside the finite, make the latter

19 It is this incongruous outcome of Feuerbach's philosophy – the immediate infinitisation of the finite – that clarifies and explains, I believe, the sense of the sixth paragraph of Marx's *Theses on Feuerbach* written in 1845: 'But the essence of man is no abstraction inherent in each single individual' (*MECW* 5, p. 4).

20 See Casini 1974, pp. 57–72.

21 Feuerbach 1980, pp. 22–3.

not something that finishes but rather a being that is unconditionally certain of itself; and, finally, the explication of the positive sense of the boundaries and limits in determinate and finite existences as something that leads every individual entity to sublate and negate their own partiality in the horizon of the whole. However, on closer examination, what is lacking is that which we have argued to be the decisive and characteristic instance of Hegelian dialectics: the fact that an individual existence, in its abstraction from others, necessarily abstracts from an inner part of itself, consigning itself to a contradiction which, from inside, leads it to overcome that limited form of life. In Feuerbach, the process of universalisation – that is, of liberation – of a finite existence does not occur through the removal and deconstruction of identity that the generation of a relationship-confrontation with alterity opens up within the interiority of the individual, but through the immediate transition, precisely in the sense of a transition without mediation, from a perspective of life based on individualism to an organicist-participatory vision in which singularities only count as members without fractures and possible oppositions of a totality. The nature of 'essence' (as Feuerbach calls the species in this work, in contrast to individual existence or beingness)[22] is that of a universal that is not given as the result and by means of the various partial identities matured by an individual, but as the summative and fusing unification of single elements where each participates through harmonic composition and integration with others.

> If you add all single existences together, and if you integrate and compensate for that which is absent in one by that which is present in another, you will discover that all phenomena taken together constitute the adequate, pure complete existence of essence itself [...] For the existence of the single being is single existence, while the existence of essence is actuality itself, because actuality itself is not single existence for itself, but is all existence together, is everything as it is one, is the unity of all mutually compensating and integrating phenomena.[23]

The person, in its individuality, is an excluding being-for-itself. 'For the personal being as such, only as person, does not love, but only excludes and repels; the person strictly conceived as person cannot love but can only hate, divide,

22 The species [*die Gattung*] is the universal of every determinate type of existence or individuals. Humanity is the specific species of human beings. 'That which is your essence as an individual is clearly the species [*Gattung*], your species as a human, therefore, the human species [*Menschheit*]' (Feuerbach 1980, pp. 107–8).

23 Feuerbach 1980, pp. 94–5.

estrange'.[24] But beneath the individual person stands as its foundation, essence and generating principle, the universality of the species, human life *qua* universal. It is precisely the immanent working of this universal force that obliges the individual to subtract itself from its particular poverty, to die as an individual, and to turn towards a superior and creative modality of life. 'Eternal blessedness, eternal joy, exists only when the individual exists no longer, only when the individual ceases to be an individual'.[25] The positive value of death, against every faith in immortality, lies in testifying how finite bodies do not endure but finish when faced with eternity and the durability of the universal, just as their demise is already written into their birth as a body enclosed within boundaries. 'Complete and perfect can only be the One and the All, the universal, the whole, the being, the absolute'.[26] Looking more closely, however, the true death of the individual, beyond natural death, is the product of the source of reason that denies the determination of space and time, as belonging only to sensible experience. The principle of spiritual life effectively lies in the organic nature of a whole that lives in the fullness and completeness of its articulations, in a timeless perfection from which time derives and is ignited only when the Absoluteness of that essence develops in the infinite history of its creatures and finite existences.

> Inasmuch as time is distinct from essence, all that is sequential in time is one and the same time in essence. But arising and passing away are at once [*Zugleich*] in time, inasmuch as time is identical with the 'at once' [*Zumal*] of essence. Everything, therefore, the multiple, particular, finite, is one and at once in essence; thus, essence is negating unity. Conceived of solely as being-one [*Einessein*], essence is essence; but conceived of as negating being-one (as which it must be conceived, for without negating there is no unity), precisely as negating, it is time; essence is the being-one that is sequential, which is arising and passing away at once for the very reason that essence is the being-one of being that is sequential. For although arising and passing away within temporality are separated for the senses, in time itself they are inseparable. Time is distinguished from essence as negating is distinguished from negation. The essence, as it negates, is time. As negation negates, it posits and creates; that is, it posits the particular, the finite, the multiple, which is one in essence and

24 Feuerbach 1980, p. 29.

25 Feuerbach 1980, p. 52.

26 Feuerbach 1980, p. 12, translation modified.

> infinite in this unity; it posits everything that is one in essence as many, as externally divided; negating negation posits the particular as particular, the finite as finite. But to posit the finite as finite means nothing else than to posit the negated as negated. Thus, essence, negation as act [*Aktus*] of negating, in which positing and cancelling are one, is time. Time is only essence in action [*Handlung*]. As that which exists in disposition in which everything that exists at once and identically is posited in succession. So, again, time is only the positing of negation as negation. But negation is posited as negation only when that which is at once in essence, that which is negated at once, is negated sequentially, thus, only when it becomes and is succession, that is, negating in action.[27]

Very differently from Hegel, the principle of occurrence in Feuerbach is not a diminished and impoverished reality. It is, rather, an already full and complete reality that contains within itself all the world of multiplicities and the differentiated, due to the simple fact that its unity, negating multiplicity, refers nonetheless to it and, therefore, implicates it in itself. Thus, the creation of the world, the creation of the differences between individual existences, is only an externalisation, an analytical development of that which that One already synthetically contains within itself. To generate a particular – which, in effect, corresponds to a negation because the birth of something is immediately linked to its death – means, therefore, taking outside an act of denial that is already implicit within the One which, in its initial fullness, is a potential container negating all particulars. Negation itself, in Feuerbach, therefore has a clearly different sense from that which it has in Hegel. In the latter, it is effectively the negation of self, exclusion and distance from the self, which a subject achieves in its partial and lacking identifications in order to obtain more solid and certain configurations of reality. In Feuerbach, however, it is a taking outside of that which is already inside, in a nexus which is equally external and reciprocally exclusive of unity and multiplicity, of the universal and the particular, because when one is given (without time) there is no multiplicity and when multiplicity is given (in the serial nature of time) there is no synthesis of the one. In moving from a finite that makes itself infinite through an internal negation, Hegel cannot but reject pantheism as the organic and unitary composition of the multiple in which unity is given only by eliminating differences: precisely the opposite of his concept of *Geist* seen as the concrete universality of all its differences and as imposed by a theory of subjectivity established on the distance

27 Feuerbach 1980, p. 44, translation modified.

and difference from itself. Feuerbach, however, who rejects a theory of spirit as originary lack and as permanent self-negation, cannot but result in pantheism and the aporia of a negation that consistently comes only from outside. It is the serial negation that the biological species performs on the individualities that belong to it and the spiritual and organic negation that humanity *qua* species performs on individuals when these posit themselves extremely as individuals and do not comprehend themselves as members of the universal in a condition of perfect continuity.

This results in an organicism and organic teleology which, for Feuerbach, crosses the entire universe and which – with a singular, for the nineteenth century, reproposal of geocentrism – outlines a cosmology where the Earth is seen as the aim and unifying principle of everything: 'so it is absolutely certain that, in all of creation, there exists but one animated and ensouled point, and that this point is the earth, which is the soul and purpose of the great cosmos'.[28] The Earth is the natural place in which life reaches its greatest level of development and, as such, is that which orders and provides meaning to the entire history of the universe.

> Just like everything else that exists, the earth, too, must have its stages and members that mediate and make possible its existence; the earth, too, must have its background. Since the earth is living existence, is existence that contains life, the heavenly bodies, without containing life in and for themselves, are only the conditions of life, are only the presuppositions of earth, are only the preparations, the scholastic exercises, and the pre-arrangements for the earth, just as the body is only the preparation for the soul.[29]

On the other hand, the Earth remains an organic and organising measure not only of the whole universe but of all the forms of natural life that exist within it. Nature reveals on the Earth all its possible forms of life, all its infinite generating power. 'Nature develops its unlimited creative power in unrestricted multiplicity, independence, separation, severing, determining and distinguishing'.[30] Thus the Earth is the container, the universal genus [*Gattung*] which leads the multiplicities of the many varied species and infinite number of individuals back to an organic unity: 'the terrestrial nature is the universal genus

28 Feuerbach 1980, p. 62, translation modified.
29 Feuerbach 1980, p. 64, translation modified.
30 Feuerbach 1980, p. 58.

[*Gattung*] of all life, the species that has developed all the possible modes of life as they exist on the earth; then the earth itself is the only measure, the insuperable limit of all life'.[31] So the Earth is, therefore, the organic measure and organiser of natural life, a finite system that turns itself into the infinite.

However, if the Earth is the culmination of all natural history, if it is the centre from which the entire Universe takes its meaning and coherence, that in which its organic life in turn culminates is the life of the human species as a life in which the universal not only contains within itself the infinite creatures of its generating but in which, through the consciousness of each, the universal contains and possesses itself. True life, authentic life, is effectively only that of the Spirit because only here is there a conscious organicity present to itself. Only the Spirit is perfect self-sufficiency and conclusivity in itself and, as such, it cannot help but be the ambit that goes beyond natural and sensible life: 'but Spirit is the death, the destroyer, of sensible reality'.[32] One passes from natural to spiritual life, to the life, that is, of Humanity and in Humanity, since only here is achieved the conscious production of the Universal and the sublation of life by living beings of their particularistic individualities, and not by means of physical death. For love is the human being's expression of its capacity to let its own, individual persona die and to enjoy the 'Being-One': 'But love is not being-in-oneself and being-for-oneself; love is being-together, being-in-common [*Gemeinsamsein*]; therefore, you love not with your personhood or as person, but only in and with essence, which is being-together, and not being-distinct or being-for-oneself'.[33] But that which in the individual's life is *par excellence* the universal is in reality, as set out already in Feuerbach's dissertation, knowledge. In the act of consciousness, the person ceases to be an individual and is translated into the universal persona, a persona in which all people are identical, without any differences. 'But consciousness itself is purely universal: knowing is an activity of essence, of Spirit itself. Consciousness as such is self-equal, self-identical, one in all humans'.[34]

In every form of life, the observer can distinguish between that which makes it similar to its species [*Gattung*], its essence, and its individual being. But only the human being, through its self-reflective awareness of itself, can separate itself from its more contingent and ephemeral existence and divide itself into a more naturalist and particularist individual, on the one hand, and into being the evidence and function of the universal, on the other.

---

31 Feuerbach 1980, pp. 76–7, translation modified.

32 Feuerbach 1980, p. 63.

33 Feuerbach 1980, p. 29.

34 Feuerbach 1980, p. 108.

> For precisely because of this free separation and distinction, you are not just a living, ensouled essence, but also a conscious, spiritual essence. Everything that lives, indeed, everything that exists, has an essence and is divided and distinguished into existence and essence, yet every reality does not divide and distinguish itself into these [...]. That which is your essence as an individual is clearly the species [*Gattung*], your species as a human, therefore the human species [*Menschheit*]. [...] But this distinguishing and objectifying is not a particular activity and action that is distinguished from your essence, or, indeed, that is external to it, but is an activity and action of your essence itself. You distinguish yourself from your essence only by and in your essence; that you can distinguish yourself from your essence and make it into your object is itself your essence.[35]

The natural species divides from itself, in all occasions, the infinite generation of its individuals. Only the human species gives life to an individual who reproduces and returns, through thought, to make the species itself the object of its vital activity. 'The knowing person in you [...] is an absolutely self-identical person, distinguished from your distinct particularity, universal in all persons, the person of Spirit itself. More accurately, this knowing person in you is the self-consciousness of Spirit, autonomous and subsisting within itself'.[36]

Thus, only the human being consciously produces its own species and, in this liberation from a determined and physical nature, places itself as the centre and end of all physical and natural life. The de-individualisation of the person is permitted by the awakening within it, beyond sensuous and natural life, of the two faculties of love and thought, which are the organs not of an individual subject, but directly of the universal Spirit. It is undoubtedly love, but above all, thought, that beginning from self-consciousness separates the individual from its coincidence with its natural self and establishes it as a member of humanity:

> Consciousness is the absolute center of humanity; or, rather, consciousness is humanity itself, is this undivided totality in the form of knowing. Know and see the great mystery of totality and unity in consciousness. It is the absolutely complete, indestructible, immovable focal point, the sun of humanity. As well as sensible nature, consciousness is a world into which the single human enters. Like the corn in the sun, you ripen and

35 Feuerbach 1980, pp. 107–8, translation modified.

36 Feuerbach 1980, p. 110.

> mature into a person by basking in the sunlight of the eternally closed and eternally youthful consciousness of humanity that forever develops and creates within itself.[37]

Self-consciousness is the identity proper to the human race and this alone, with its self-reflectiveness, breaks the perspective of nature and introduces it to the life of the spirit. For this, the universal lives in every human being, present to itself and unlimited by any other than itself. Due to this very essence, capable of the greatest unconditional and free universality, the human species is constituted as an organically systematic foundation and the unifying element of all reality. The natural entities and the species immanent to them overcome the limits of their particular existence, unvivified by freedom, only because they become the object and reflection of the *menschliche Gattung*, as occurs, for example, in the relationship between soul and body, in which every possible heterogeneity of the natural, with respect to the spiritual, is contrasted by being only the instrument and pretext of the establishment of the latter. 'The body', Feuerbach writes, 'is the opposite and object of the soul; the soul is soul only in the continuous conquering and negation of its own opposition'.[38] And he adds in another paragraph:

> The soul is related to the body as the fire to its fuel. The body is the wick and candle, the nutritive fuel of the soul. Where there is no fuel, there is no fire. One can say that to this extent the fire is dependent on its fuel and must be bound to it; the fuel is the instrument of the fire. But insofar as it consumes and destroys the fuel, the fire is its lord and master [...]. Ensoulability, or determination for a soul, is the inner determination that is identical to the body; the soul is the realization or the actual existence of this inner ensoulability. Only that which the body is in and for itself is revealed and comes to existence in the soul.[39]

As a conclusion to this brief exposition of *Thoughts on Death and Immortality*, it is impossible to ignore just how far this fusional anthropology is from Hegel's idealism. If there is no doubt about the influence that the teachings of Hegel had on the young student in Berlin, evidenced by the famous letter of 1828 with which he accompanied his dissertation sent to the master in Berlin, other

37 Feuerbach 1980, p. 117.
38 Feuerbach 1980, p. 102.
39 Feuerbach 1980, pp. 100–1.

more determining cultural influences should not be ignored. These include, for example, the fact that Feuerbach, before this year in Berlin, was a theology student in Heidelberg and attended the lessons of Carl Daub, the speculative theologian who within the ambit of the Protestant tradition greatly valorised the idea of the renunciation of the self, as theorised in his *Studium der christlichen Dogmatik*. Commenting on the vanity of the world, Daub encouraged the 'volatile act of renunciation [*Entsagung*]' in order to access awareness of that which is true and timeless.[40] But it should be remembered, above all, just how much the thoughts of the young Feuerbach combine Hegel's philosophy of spirit with the pantheistic-mystical current of European philosophy, which runs from Böhme, via the Italian philosophies of Telesio, Campanella and Bruno to Spinoza.[41] The main categories of Hegel's thoughts are thus rewritten and given new significance in the light of an organicism and pantheism that are considerably different from their original significance. The mystical tradition of *eros*, and the concept of truth as a theoretical act which, at one and the same time, is an ethical-moral act of universal fusion, concur in outlining a philosophy of the human species in which both the noun ('species') and the adjective ('human') have a pregnant sense. Thus, if the adjective highlights the negation of the natural ambit that humankind's spirituality must enact in order to realise itself (and thus the anti-naturalism of the early Feuerbach), the noun expresses, in contrast, the weight that a dimension of naturalist organicism continues to have in Feuerbach's thought, according to which, every individual participates by birth – and therefore immediately – in the most universal characteristics of its species. As a consequence, even in the case of the spiritual species, the individual participates immediately, by means of its own act of knowing reason, in the virtues of free universality typical of a humanity considered as such precisely because of its absolute unity, as a 'species' (even as the most excellent of all possible species).

Starting with his dissertation, as I have tried to demonstrate, Feuerbach's rationalism, expressed in the principle of *cogito ergo omnes sum homines*, possesses alongside its theoretical meaning an intensely ethical-emotional value.[42] Thought is the place of such an exhaustive communication that it has the

40 Daub 1810, p. 2 et sqq. On the influence of Carl Daub on the young Feuerbach, see Schott 1971. In a letter to Carl Daub at the end of August 1824, the young Feuerbach wrote from Berlin, evidencing the teachings received from him in Heidelberg: 'If the first steps of every philosophy are the sunset of the world, how much more must the poor, feeble self of the individual suffer!' (letter published in Ascheri 1970, p. 192).

41 See Weckwerth 1996, pp. 304–5.

42 On this, see the biography by Saß 1988, p. 36.

immediate value of a universal communion, without any residual diffidence or individuality amongst human beings. It is also noteworthy how this organicist-pantheistic inspiration, according to which the persistence and autonomy of individuality constitutes the original sin of any possible ethics and ontology, will continue to stand as the fundamental criteria in the great works of philosophical historiography that Feuerbach wrote during the 1830s, such as *Geschichte der neueren Philosophie von Bacon von Verulam bis Benedikt Spinoza* (1833), *Leibniz* (1837) and *Bayle* (1838). In these works, the more properly historical theme is the progressive autonomy and universalisation of the scientific and modern rational spirit from any theological vision of the world consistently refers to, as its founding principle, the negation of any subjectivism and the capacity of the individual to become pure reason, renouncing any personal passion and interest in the cognitive analysis of the object of its research.[43]

Finally, in relation to this dominance of the theme of immediacy over that of mediation in the early Feuerbach, it is necessary to mention the schematic philosophy of history that he outlines at the start of his *Thoughts on Death and Immortality*, on the motif of the presence or lack thereof of faith in the immortality of the soul by means of the comparison of ancient, medieval and modern times. He claims that the affirmation of the immortality of the soul corresponds to the defence and valorisation of individual existence, unrelated to any of its connections or its communitarian dependency. With his claim that faith in personal immortality was only affirmed in the modern era there derives Feuerbach's historical division between the extreme individualism of modernity and its counterpart, without any mediation, in the communitarian nature of living of the ancient world (political communitarianism) and the medieval world (religious communitarianism).[44] Once again, therefore, we encounter an opposition without mediation of communitarianism and individualism, and

---

43 'This ascetical motive of the negation of the "life" and "subjectivity" in relation to "pure objectivity", to philosophy, of one's own *Selbst* for spiritual totality [...] is the main theme around which the greater part of Feuerbach's thought revolves, at least until 1842' (Casini 1974, p. 86).

44 'Within the developmental history of the Spirit of European humanity, it is possible to distinguish three main epochs in the doctrine of the immortality of the soul. The first epoch is that of the Greeks and Romans, who neither believed in nor were aware of immortality as we understand it. The Roman lived only in Rome; the Roman people were, so to speak, the one and only space that contained his soul and defined the horizon of his public life. [...] The second epoch in the developmental history of this doctrine or belief is the Catholic Christian period, the Middle Ages. [...] The individual human [...] had been received and included in the holy communion of believers, and perceived and felt himself to be redeemed, delivered, in possession of the true life, but only by being

also a very simplified and reworked re-representation of Hegel's philosophy of history, which, rather than counterposing community and individuals as values and disvalues, assumes them to be equally positive and irreplaceable values through the various solutions that the different civilisations have given to the interaction, or not, with the equilibrium or lack of equilibrium of both the unchangeable components of human existence. Feuerbach's philosophy of history is, instead, simple and mono-directional. It moves in a short space from the organicity of the ancient world to the disorganicity of the modern world, demonstrating very little interest in the complexities of history and without taking on board Hegel's fundamental indications in this sense, such as the historical role assigned by him to Christianity in the preparation of modernity and, in particular, in the valorising of people's interior life against the unchallenged hegemony of the community.

The texts extracted from Feuerbach's *Nachlass* from the period of publication of the *Thoughts on Death and Immortality*, such as the lectures he gave in Erlangen – the *Introduction to Logic and Metaphysics* [*Einleitung in die Logik und Metaphysik*] (1829–30) and the *Lectures on Logic and Metaphysics* [*Vorlesungen über Logik und Metaphysik*] (1830–1)[45] – and in a manuscript entitled *Aristoteles, Qualität, Metaphysik, Δ 14*, but also dedicated to commenting on Hegel's *Logic*, continue to provide evidence, in my opinion, of the appearance of a Feuerbach who elaborates his philosophy by remaining within Hegel's horizon, but in substance profoundly modifying its underlying principles. While, in Hegel's *Logic*, the first category considered, that of 'being', expresses an impoverished beginning of reality and thought, an absolutely empty and indeterminate start that must grow dialectically and conquer the entire world in order to gain an existence and concretion, for Feuerbach being is a complete beginning wherein the absence of determinations must be interpreted as a potential beginning with a wealth of determinations. While being in Hegel is an abstract category with almost no depth of reality, such that it needs to be removed in becoming, in Feuerbach, in contrast, being is rich in a hidden

---

included in a divine communion, [...] being in the church that constituted the essence of the individual [...] The belief in the immortality of the individual as such emerges on its own ground and without disguise only in the modern age. [...] The trademark of the entire modern age is that the human as human, the person as person, and therefore the single human individual in his own individuality, has been perceived as divine and infinite. The first shape in which the character of the modern age was expressed was Protestantism. Its highest principle was no longer the church and being in unity with the church but was belief, individual conviction' (Feuerbach 1980, pp. 6–10, translation modified).

45 See Feuerbach 1975 and 1976.

complexity that is only explained and brought to light in the world of differences and individual beings. The notion that being is originally full of all its determinations, implicit and contained within it by the fact that by being indeterminate they are negated, is clearly expressed by Feuerbach when he defines particular existence as the subtraction from and diminution of originary being.

> Being is robbed, deprived of, reduced; with this dispossession arises the concept of limits and determinations. [...] Lack of determination is removed from being, being is removed from being. [...] The limit is, therefore, insomuch as narrowing, reduction of being, concentration, contraction, oppression, constriction, and impediment.[46]

The negation that a particular existence implies of being in general is already contained in the negation that the universal being implies in itself as negation of every particular and determinate negation. However, in this way, it confirms that negation for Feuerbach is always the negation of the other and never of the self, since either it is the negation-implication that the universal being makes of a determinate existence or, vice versa, it is the negation-limitation that the latter makes of the former.

It is through this interpretation of negation that Feuerbach substantially distances himself from Hegel,[47] as well as in the resultant theory of subjectivity not founded, as in Hegel, on an initial and structural distance from the self. However, all this implies that what he defines himself as 'the art and force of dialectics',[48] seen as the ability to enforce intrinsically the finite-infinite nexus, nonetheless in his philosophy falls back into a perspective of separation and extraneousness that returns to a concept of spirit, essence, as an identity enclosed within and satisfied with itself, beyond and before becoming and difference.

> Change, in the strict sense, is not applicable to spirit, in the strict sense. In fact spirit is purely coherent, in motionless unity with itself, which

---

46 The text of this unpublished work, *Aristoteles, Qualität, Metaphysik, Δ 14*, and its Italian translation, can be found, together with another unpublished work by Feuerbach, *Übergang von der Theologie zur Philosophie*, in Tomasoni 1982 (see p. 51).

47 Cesa writes that, for the Feuerbach of the *Thoughts on Death and Immortality*, 'negation and dialectics are forms of the old world which he accepts only insomuch as they serve to leave it' (Cesa 1963, p. 135).

48 Tomasoni 1982, p. 65.

> contains within itself all the particular, the different, the opposite […]. The most profound and most internal determination of essence is unity; that of the phenomenon, difference.[49]

This is so much so that, within this perspective, the very concept of limit, which is so pregnant in the self-reflective and self-denying valency of Hegel's *Logic*, is, once again resolved in a positive sense of coincidence and harmony of that which is limited with itself.

> The limit, insomuch as it is reality, insomuch as it is identical with something, insomuch as it is its essence, represents its pleasure and its joy, its peace. It is all that which is within its limits; the limit is not, therefore, a limit for it, it is not, said in subjective terms, a torment, a suffering and an oppression.[50]

## 3 The Overturning of Subject and Predicate

While Hegel is a thinker of discontinuity and dialectical negation, Feuerbach, from his very first works, despite the affinity of language and the use of many Hegelian expressions, appears to be a thinker of continuity. Thus, the former is a thinker of synthesis as the co-presence and intertwining of heterogeneous levels of reality, while the latter is a thinker of analysis in a horizon of experience that is unable to generate otherness within itself. Furthermore, as we have seen, this relates both to the organic continuity between the species and the individual but also, when the individual presumes to prevail over the species, to the continuity between the self and God. Modern subjectivity is so centred and infinitised in itself that it can even project onto itself the value of a otherworldly continuity and a personal God who, with its attributes of perfection, does nothing more than confirm and repeat to the highest degree the attributes of the human individual.

> Thus, after the disappearance of nature and universal history, all that is truly real, universal, essential, all that which is spirit, soul and essence, and all this is massacred, dissolved into its parts, deprived of being, of

49 Tomasoni 1982, pp. 63–5.

50 Tomasoni 1982, pp. 57–9. On the thematic of these pages by Feuerbach, see Tomasoni's preface (1982, pp. 1–28).

> unity, of spirit and soul, then the individual plants on the ruins of the destroyed world the flag of the prophet, the sacred vessel of faith in its own immortality and its own beloved thereafter.[51]

It is no coincidence that in modern history, which proceeds irreversibly towards an overcoming of Christianity and the restoration of the divine to the immanence of the world and nature, Protestantism has represented the transition from Christian-Medieval religiosity based on the community of the Church and a faith founded only on the interior nature of the person. Equally, the latest versions of Protestantism, such as pietism, orthodox and rationalist morality and romantic religiosity itself, represent the apex of a form of personalism that conceals behind the devaluation of any personal interest and total humiliation before God the unconditional and absolute exaltation of personal discretion and subjective-individualistic passions.

It is precisely on the basis of this nexus of continuity between humankind and God that Feuerbach's reflections on religion during the 1830s develop. These continue, alongside his previously mentioned works on philosophical historiography that take as their underlying subject the indepth study of the great contrasts in the modern era between secular-scientific rationality and Christianity,[52] highly significant essays such as 'On Philosophy and Christianity' ['Über Philosophie und Christentum'] (1839) and 'On the Miracle' ['Über das Wunder'] (1839). The valorisation of natural sciences and the study of the great contrasts between secular rationality and Christianity are the subjects of these works but, above all, the nexus of philosophy-religion-theology stands at their centre, flanked by various investigations undertaken according to whether the

---

51 Feuerbach 1980, pp. 14–15, translation modified.

52 The interest in Jacob Böhme and the pantheism of Renaissance Italian philosophy (Telesio, Campanella, Bruno) in the unpublished *Vorlesungen über die Geschichte der neueren Philosophie* of 1835–6 (see Feuerbach 1974) are evidence of how the liberation of reflections on nature from theological conditioning is, for Feuerbach at that time, much more than the physical-mathematical science of nature, instead a philosophy of nature imbued with a profound vitalistic-mystical element (see Feuerbach 1974, pp. 28–45). Within this area of interest are some extracts discovered in Feuerbach's *Nachlaß* on the Kabbala. See Tomasoni 1992, pp. 57–67. See also Casini 1979, pp. 21–62. On the other hand, the entire *Geschichte der neueren Philosophie* of 1833 is built around the development and maturation of modern pantheism (rather than teological dualism). In Feuerbach's reconstruction, this first takes on a mystical form with Böhme, and then a still idealistic-subjective expression with Descartes, Geulincx and Malebranche. Its most complete and objective form is with Spinoza and is further extended with Leibniz to all German idealism.

first or the second term in the humankind-God relation of continuity is privileged.

The object of philosophy is knowledge, through reason, of the immanence of the universal in reality and how this works by means of a non-individualistic consciousness. The essence of theology, on the other hand, is particularism.

> Theology […] has as its basis a limited interest, full of prejudices, lacking in freedom; it has no other interest that is not that of interpreting and demonstrating, by historic or dogmatic means, that which it believes – and which it believes not for scientific reasons, because faith is not supported by any scientific principles or foundations – that which it presumes to be true, and not insofar as a scientific truth but insofar as a particular truth of faith.[53]

The nature of theology is practical since it wishes to bend all reality to the advantage of its own personal religious interests. The nature of philosophy is, on the other hand, theoretical: 'philosophy is the only science which openly represents the idea of science, that presents the spirit of science as a spirit isolated by a determinate content'.[54] Theology gives body to the discretion of the individual who, having projected its desires through the filter of divine omnipotence, cancels out the objective laws and nature of things.

> I want, this is the decisive argument: I am not interested in the content of the thing, there are no laws that bind me; I am, in fact, the master of all, I am the legislator, nothing is impossible for me. *Sic volo, sic jubeo, stat pro ratione voluntas*. Thus speaks the Lord according to the theologians.[55]

For this reason, philosophy, on a par with natural science, takes as its content reality in its necessity, while theology is concerned with miracles and the supernatural. It is sufficient to consider, in this sense, the most recent expression of modern theology represented by so-called 'positive philosophy'.[56] This, Feuerbach wrote in an essay of 1838 which appeared in the *Hallische Jahrbücher*, makes the God-person the absolute principle of reality and, in this personalising of reality, places itself beyond science. 'Its principle is none other

53 Feurbach 1981, Vol. 8, p. 240.
54 Feurbach 1981, Vol. 8, p. 273.
55 Feurbach 1981, Vol. 8, p. 292.
56 See Note 66 of Chapter One.

than personality and, precisely, personality as a concretum: God is the absolute personality and personal being. But, precisely where personality begins concretely, philosophy is at its end'.[57]

However, Feuerbach begins increasingly to distinguish theology from religion in a positive and naive sense,[58] according to the direction in which the nexus of continuity of the Self-God is viewed. Religion, in its immediacy, does not separate God from man, making it into another being with its own ontological reality, distinct from the reality of nature and mankind; theology, on the other hand, with its metaphysical pretensions, claims to separate God from man. At the origin of spontaneous religion is a complete absence of distinction between the subjective and the objective; God is only the expression of mankind's needs, emotions and fears. God is man in the manifestation of its most intimate, and intellectually unmediated, humanity, in a difference, as we already know from the *Thoughts on Death and Immortality*, that is only quantitative in the sense that divine qualities are the same as human qualities but conceived in the infinity of their species essence.[59] However, the relationship is overturned with theology. God's infinite nature is removed from its human place of generation and arbitrarily rendered an autonomous body and quality, distinct and separate from the human creature, now conceived as dependent and finite. But this overturning that translates human religion into inhuman religion is possible only due to the original ontological continuity between man and God, which established the divine only as a continuation and projection of the human. This is a qualitative continuity, which theology, by inverting the meaning and priorities of this relationship, arbitrarily transforms into a distinction of quality and essence. It is an inversion of subject and predicate, due to which the human subject is made a predicate or, in other words,

57 Feuerbach 1981, pp. 26–7. 'The persona in me is the inseparable from me, that which is not resolved in the concept, that which remains outside, that which cannot be made into an object of speculation [...]. [Jacobi] demonstrates that he did not make the absolute or divine personality an object of knowledge or of thought but the inexplicable axiom of an immediate sentiment, simply apodictic or, in other words, a purely personal truth and affair [...]. The determinations of a true rational being are not determinations of thought, but immediately personal affections that are removed from thought' (Feuerbach 1981, pp. 27–8).

58 Beginning with an essay on Bayle, Feuerbach introduced into the history of Christianity the distinction between an original and authentic religiosity and a modern-theological religiosity, very far from the true interests of the human species. On this period, see C. Ascheri 1970, pp. 147–254.

59 Feurbach 1981, Vol. 8, pp. 257–8.

a product of that predicate to which it originally gave life in order to express itself and its needs. It is through an ongoing reflection on religion, on its difference from theology, on the decadence and dogmatic and doctrinarian rigidity of Christianity as a fundamental obstacle to the progress of humanity, that Feuerbach develops a different valuation of sensibility and the emotional and bodily dimension of human life during his intense work of the 1830s (now outside the university).

The 1841 *The Essence of Christianity* explicitly theorises that religion is the product of imagination and the heart and has nothing whatsoever to do with reason. It is born of the practical and not knowledge-based needs of the individual, as Feuerbach had already argued in *Thoughts on Death and Immortality*: from the need to bind together existence and essence immediately, the singularity of the individual and the omnipotence of the species. Religion is based on the rejection of reason which is the only faculty capable of pantheism, of finding, that is, the universal not completed in a particular but realised in the infinite series of space and time, in the innumerable individualities of genus and species. However, with the difference that the immediate unity of individual and universal that religion proposes is now considered by Feuerbach less from the point of view of the arbitrary and dogmatic universalisation of an individual, but much more from the perspective of the enactment and consciousness of the reality of the universe. Religion, at its origin, is effectively to be seen as the coming to be of the consciousness of the individual of the universality of its own essence, that is, of being both individual and part of the species. However, it is a consciousness that is given, due to its naivety, still in an external manner, in such a way that this essence is represented as the other of humanity, external to it, like God.

> Religion is man's earliest and also indirect form of self-knowledge. Hence religion everywhere precedes philosophy, as in the history of the race, also in that of the individual. Man first of all sees his nature as if out of himself, before he finds it in himself. His own nature is in the first instance contemplated by him as that of another being.[60]

The essence of religion – and, in particular, of the religion *par excellence* of Christianity – is anthropology. The greater part of the chapters of this famous text are dedicated to tracing back the most characteristic mythologies of the Christian religion – from the Trinity to incarnation, from the *creatio ex nihilo* to

60 Feuerbach 2008, p. 11.

the Mother of God, from the suffering God to the institution of monasticism – to a phenomenology of the human being, marked by the three faculties of reason, the will and sentiment. However, it is reason that undoubtedly continues to be valorised as the only faculty capable of true universality. Feuerbach writes in the 'Appendix' that

> Reason is the self-consciousness of the species, as such; [...] Feeling only is my existence; thinking is my non-existence, the negation of my individuality, the positing of the species, reason is the annihilation of personality. [...]. Reason is the highest species of being; hence it includes all species in the sphere of knowledge. Reason cannot content itself in the individual; it has its adequate existence only when it has the species for its object.[61]

But imagination also, or the faculty of the soul, and passions, or the faculty of the heart, have by now their own specific statute in relation to the production of the universal which is not entirely marginal or unessential, as was instead the case in the still strongly rationalistic structure of the *Thoughts on Death and Immortality*. The soul as a faculty, not of the essence, of the universal, but rather of existence 'as an individuality's sense of itself', expresses an element of reality which, for Feuerbach, it is impossible to ignore, without, however, forgetting the consistently supreme value of the species and, amongst all species, of the human species.

Thus, if the authentic relationship between sense of self as an individual person and the sense of self as a human being is that by which each of us finds the value of our own self in continuity with the other, in the participation in the human species *qua* past, present and future humanity, it is nonetheless true that, before achieving this maturity of awareness, it must necessarily comprehend the universal in the deformed shape of an imaginatively elaborated and realised desire. It does this by removing, first of all, every limitation of time, capacity and place from its individuality, dilating it, therefore, into a perfect essence capable of every possibility which, however, in turn, is not pure and abstract universality, but again achieves concretion in a determinate figure, in the God-person.

> With the Christians God is nothing else than the immediate unity of species and individuality, of the universal and individual being. God is the idea of the species as an individual – the idea or essence of the species,

61 Feuerbach 2008, pp. 233–5.

> which as a species, as universal being, as the totality of all perfections, of all attributes or realities, freed from all the limits which exist in the consciousness and feeling of the individual, is at the same time again an individual, personal being.[62]

The sentiment of finite existence, of the limit, is something pitiful. An individual can support and positively elaborate it only by means of the culture of the 'species', but can also support it through the compensation and comfort of religious fantasy. Paganism and classical antiquity created a culture of immanence according to which the individual can satisfy its physical and spiritual needs through the real exchange and organic participation in the natural and human world. Christianity, however, created a way of satisfying needs which, however fallacious, occupies a much broader space in the emotional and imaginative life of the individual and which, even if in a naive form projected outwards, awakens in the individual's perspective the motif of the universal. Beyond this there is only theology, where the divine becomes extreme and falls entirely outside the human, and where the autonomy of divine existence prevails over the human qualities of its essence.

The significance of the sensibility and emotional life of the human being gains increasing importance in Feuerbach's philosophy. Sentiment, working together with the capacity for imagination through religion, demonstrates in itself already to be the evidence of belonging to and the resolution of individuality within the perspective of a life in which the true subject is the *Gattung*.

> The essence of religion is the immediate, involuntary, unconscious contemplation of the human nature as another, a distinct nature. [...] The beneficial influence of religion rests on this extension of the sensational consciousness. In religion man is in the open air, *sub deo*; in the sensational consciousness he is in his narrow confined dwelling-house. Religion has relation essentially, originally – and only in its origin is it something holy, true, pure, and good – to the immediate sensational consciousness alone; it is the setting aside of the limits of sense.[63]

Not only love, as stated in his first work, in the *Thoughts on Death and Immortality*, but the entire sphere of sensibility of the human being, comprised of needs, desires, imagination and dependence on all that which goes beyond the indi-

62 Feuerbach 2008, p. 127.

63 Feuerbach 2008, pp. 176–8.

vidual shows itself to have a fullness and dignity with regard to the negation of personalism and the enactment of the depth of reality of 'species'. What follows now is a dislocation of this very concept of species. From the excessively univocal cognitive and interior dimension of the rationalism of the first writings, it becomes increasingly an external expression that can never be concluded in the life of the individual, open to encountering and integrating with all species of life – humanity *par excellence* – which are part of its no longer merely theoretical horizon of existence.

> Man and woman are the complement of each other, and thus united they first present the species, the perfect man. [...] In love, the reality of the species, which otherwise is only a thing of reason, an object of mere thought, becomes a matter of feeling, a truth of feeling [...] Doubtless the essence of man is one, but this essence is infinite; its real existence is therefore an infinite, reciprocally compensating variety, which reveals the riches of this essence. Unity in essence is multiplicity in existence. [...] The other is my thou, – the relation being reciprocal, – my alter ego, man objective to me, the revelation of my own nature, the eye seeing itself. [...] That is true in which another agrees with me, – agreement is the first criterion of truth; but only because the species is the ultimate measure of truth.[64]

But what is most important for our study is that, despite these different emphases, the basic, fusional and symbiotic tonality of Feuerbach's philosophy remains unchanged. Even if the species emphasises its exteriority and, therefore, its distance from and irreducibility to the individual, these then return to join and interpenetrate their similars through a continuity and immediacy that excludes any separation and difference. The presupposed organicism of the species continues to render the establishment of individual differences and their autonomy impossible and, even where deployed in the exteriority of time and space, its unity is always the sum of various individualities, without any residues.

> But the idea of deity coincides with the idea of humanity. All divine attributes, all the attributes which make God God, are attributes of the species – attributes which in the individual are limited, but the limits of which are abolished in the essence of the species, and even in its

64 Feuerbach 2008, pp. 129–31.

> existence, in so far as it has its complete existence only in all men taken together. My knowledge, my will, is limited; but my limit is not the limit of another man, to say nothing of mankind; what is difficult to me is easy to another; what is impossible, inconceivable, to one age, is to the coming age conceivable and possible. My life is bound to a limited time; not so the life of humanity. The history of mankind consists of nothing else than a continuous and progressive conquest of limits, which at a given time pass for the limits of humanity, and therefore for absolute insurmountable limits. But the future always unveils the fact that the alleged limits of the species were only limits of individuality. [...] Thus the species is unlimited; the individual alone limited.[65]

Precisely in opposition to the intention, claimed very explicitly by Feuerbach also in this passage, of placing the impossibility of reducing the universal to the particular as the basis of his philosophising, the endurance of the concept of species reveals itself as entirely insufficient, if not contradictory, for allowing the conceptualisation of reality that can be seen as a unity of differences. To this end, it is obligatory to recall what Hegel had theorised in his *Encyclopaedia*, § 367, in relation to the concept of *Gattung*, on its inscription in a solely naturalistic context and on its structural impossibility of being used within a historic-human ambit and that of the sciences of spirit.

> The genus [*Gattung*] is in an implicit, simple unity with the singularity of the subject whose concrete substance it is. But the universal is disjunction or judgement [*Urteil*], in order to issue from this its diremption as a unity for itself, give itself an existence as a subjective universality. This process of its closing with itself contains the negation of the merely inner universality of the genus, and also the negation of the merely immediate singularity in which the living being is still only a natural being; the negation of this singularity exhibited in the preceding process (§ 366) is only the first immediate negation. In this process of the genus, the merely natural being only perishes, for, as such, it does not transcend the natural. But the moments of the process of the genus, since their basis is still not the subjective universal, still not the single subject, fall apart and exist as a plurality of particular processes which culminate, in one way or another, in the death of the creature.[66]

---

65 Feuerbach 2008, pp. 126–7.

66 Hegel 2004, p. 410 (§ 367).

Hegel sees *Gattung* as the universality of a natural species only through the serial and inexhaustible generation of a multitude of individuals. The existence of the individual in itself, in its individuality, in the natural world does not reveal or provide evident reality to the universal. The *Gattung*, as an ordering principle of nature, expresses itself only through the disappearance of the individual and its replacement with its similar: or, in other words, through that negation which Hegel calls immediate. This is in contrast to that which, in Hegel's terminology, is the negation of the negation, or mediated negation, whose function is not overcoming singularity but the opposite, of maintaining and guaranteeing it through its inclusion in a universality which is not its superior and transcendental principle. For Hegel, however, it is not the natural body that is capable of such negation, but only the spiritual-human subject who finds its identity, rather than its loss, in the other-than-the-self. A loss of identity occurs, on the other hand, for natural creatures belonging to the same species in the infinite series of births and deaths. It is precisely because of this structural characteristic of exteriority of nature that the presence of the species in the life of the single animal and natural entity is realised and manifested only as a force other than and different from its individuality.

> But the moments of the process of the genus, since their basis is still not the subjective universal, still not the single subject, fall apart and exist as a plurality of particular processes which culminate, in one way or another, in the death of the creature.[67]
>
> The inner universality therefore remains opposed to the natural singularity of the living being as the negative power from which the animal suffers violence and perishes, because natural existence [*Dasein*] as such does not itself contain this universality and is not therefore the reality which corresponds to it.[68]

Feuerbach's theoretical distance from Hegel, which is much greater than normally thought, is also measured, and here more than elsewhere, in the breaking of the prohibition that Hegel had dictated with respect to the inappropriate use of the naturalistic category of *Gattung* and in Feuerbach's dilation-transposition of it into the amibit of the human sciences. The new method of research into truth that Feuerbach claims to have introduced into philosophy,

67 Ibid.

68 Hegel 2004, p. 440 (§ 374).

the 'genetic-critical' method, focused on the anthropological reduction of religious alienation, suffers from an excess of identification and the mirroring that the continuity of the mankind-God essence assumes. It is not that the fecundity of Feuerbach's reductionism and his inclusion in the noble theoretical tradition that, moved by fear and desire, leads from religion to the psychology of the human soul, from Epicurus to Lucretius, from Seneca to Hume and, beyond Feuerbach, through Nietzsche up to psychoanalysis and Freud, should be underestimated. However, it should not be forgotten that the concept of the divine as a projection of the human,[69] of the humanistic genesis of religion, is effectively Hegel's, and that his philosophy of religion exists as a type and phenomenology of the various historical religions which are not so much broader than Feuerbach's philosophy of religion (essentially limited to Christianity), as they are more rich and complex with respect to the number of levels of reality they include. The individual and the community, psychology and political institutions, private behaviour and collective customs, according to the various figures of their possible appearance, their opposition or reconciliations, produce in Hegel the historical religions that operate according to projection mechanisms that are more articulated and complex than those of a simple and linear mirroring. It is precisely Hegel who originally connected the broad phenomenology of historical religions to the conceptual definition of religion as a still naive and anticipated consciousness, insofar as it was alienated in the figurative and imaginative thought of the real universal. This found, in the alienated-representative characteristics of religion, in its metaphorical-symbolic nature, the key to the concreteness and multiplicity of its historical variety. This connection between the consciousness of peoples and the alienated form of the real is less prominent in Feuerbach. In his works, religion, both in terms of the subject of it and humanity of its totality of the species and the empirical individual, becomes the expression of an immediately considered human who does not participate in historical mediations and differentiations. Max Stirner noted this upon the publication of *The Essence of Christianity*, accusing Feuerbach of denying God as a subject but undoubtedly not of denying and overcoming the divine predicates, by attributing them to a humanity which, in its dimension as a species, is only an abstraction that lives merely in the thoughts of those who conceive it and which, in its generic universality, cancels out the real life of the individual.[70]

---

69 On the subject of 'projection' in the Feuerbach of *The Essence of Christianity*, see Van Harvey 1995, pp. 25–66.

70 See Andolfi 1983.

> But the species is nothing and, if the individual raises itself above its individuality, this occurs precisely because it is an individual [...]. Man is nothing more than an ideal, the species exists only in thought. Being a man does not mean realising the ideal of mankind but representing itself, the individual. My task is not the way in which I realise the universal human, but how I satisfy myself.[71]

Furthermore, the distance separating Hegel from Feuerbach also lies in the latter's theory of the inversion of subject and predicate, or of subject and object, which constitutes the basic, conceptual nucleus of his genetic-critical method. This is expressed most clearly in *The Essence of Christianity*. 'Man – this is the secret of religion – objectivises its own being and then renders it an object again in this objectivised essence, converted into a subject'.[72] Or, as is claimed in another passage, 'it belongs to the *differentia specifica* of religion to render the predicate into an authentic subject'.[73] Thus, for Feuerbach, the essence of the true consists in overturning the false, in retranslating into a true subject the expression which, in false knowledge, is only made into a predicate. The truth is that of a subject that lives expressing itself in its predicates, in the objects it creates. Falsity is that of a predicate which, having been placed in the position of the subject, posits the latter in the place of a predicate, making it a predicate of its own predicates. The genetic-critical method, in which knowledge of the truth consists, does not, therefore, reformulate and never changes the terms of a problem. It leaves them unchanged, only dislocating and placing them in an inverted hierarchy of priorities. However, obviously, it does this only beginning with a subject-predicate nexus that is emanationist on an ontological level and of an analytical identity on a logical level. The subject is presupposed as originally full in order to deposit itself, without any residue, in its own productions. The judgement that translates this ontological nexus on the logical level is merely analytical, in the sense defined by Kant as a judgement where the predicate adds nothing new to that already contained in the subject, but simply allows it to emerge from an implicit to an explicit level. For Hegel, on the other hand, as is well known from the 'Preface' to the *Phenomenology of Spirit*, the identity of subject and predicate, in order to have meaning and not fall into the tautological void of an analytical judgement, must contain within itself difference, or even opposition and contradiction; in other words, it must give rise

71 Stirner 1995, p. 163, translation modified.
72 Feuerbach 2008, p. 25, translation modified.
73 Feuerbach 2008, p. 73, translation modified.

to a speculative proposition or dialectical-synthetic judgement. This can be explained for Hegel only through reference to a subject that, on an ontological level, is not presupposed in an originary fashion, but rather, lives through consistently new and more adequate identities whose greater adequacy implies a contradictory exhaustion of the preceding identities.

## 4 The Criticism of Hegel

Due to its structurally analytical nature, the genetic-critical method is a long way from the principles and goals of the Hegelian dialectic. In the theory of the inversion of subject and predicate, only a faint echo of the reversal of opposites, which Hegel assigns to the intellect, remains, and with wholly different methods. Nonetheless, it is precisely through the application of the genetic-critical method that Feuerbach tackles and liquidates Hegel's philosophy. In an essay which precedes *The Essence of Christianity* by two years, 'Towards a Critique of Hegel's Philosophy' (1839), Feuerbach had effectively taken into account and definitively left behind the Hegel who had been the maestro of his youthful years in Berlin and the main inspiration behind his transfer, against the wishes of his father, the eminent jurist Paul Feuerbach, from the faculty of theology to that of philosophy. The essay's conceptual structure also consists in applying the critical method of inverting subject and predicate to Hegel's philosophy. By now, the entire structure of Feuerbach's thought is guided by the overturning of what is originary with respect to that which is derived.

In his two preceding works, 'On Philosophy and Christianity' and 'On the Characterisation of the Text "On Philosophy and Christianity"' ['Zur Charakterisierung der Schrift über Philosophie und Christentum'], Feuerbach had begun to criticise Hegel's excessive valorisation of the Christian religion. According to Feuerbach, by seeing Christianity as the religion closest to the dialectical structure of his philosophy, Hegel had revealed himself as too inclined to find in religion more the metaphor of logical-conceptual narratives than the consciousness of the human species and its properties. However, it was precisely in his essay 'Towards a Critique of Hegel's Philosophy' that the polemic went beyond the ambit of the philosophy of religion and extended to all of Hegel's philosophy, with particular attention paid to his writings on logic.

Hegel's philosophy, Feuerbach writes, enacts the ordering and integration of the real by means of the dimension of time alone and its serial succession, rejecting, however, that of space and its capacity to attribute co-presence and co-ordination to the multiplicities of existences. At the end of the temporal development of the spirit into reality, into history, Hegel's philosophy effectively proposes itself as the perfect and ultimate realisation of the entire history of philosophy, relegating all previous philosophies to only partial and temporary episodes. This occurs according to the claim and arbitrariness that a totality, a species, can completely synthesise and realise in a single individual.

> Reason, however, knows nothing [...] of a real and absolute incarnation of the species in a particular individuality [...]. The incarnation of the species with all its plenitude into one individuality would be an absolute miracle, a violent suspension of all the laws and principles of reality; it would, indeed, be the end of the world.[74]

Every philosophy, Feuerbach continues, is born and belongs to a determinate historical epoch, with determinate presuppositions formed by the theoretical traditions that precede them. This is also valid, obviously, for Hegel's philosophy, despite its 'rigorous scientific character, universality, and incontestable richness of thought'.[75] Thus, in the *Science of Logic*, Hegel has taken on and completed the Fichtean problem of the method and nature of science, theorising the progress of philosophical science as equal to a circle in which the conclusion coincides with the beginning and where the conception of truth as an infinite, linear process is negated. 'The Hegelian philosophy is actually the most perfect system that has ever appeared. Hegel actually achieved what Fichte aspired to but did not achieve, because he concluded with an "ought" and not with an end that is also beginning'.[76] However, Hegel not only denies this derivation of his philosophy from Fichte because it absolutises its historical relativity, abstracting it from the contexts which generated it, but also, specifically in relation to the theory of truth as a circle that overturns the substantial into the secondary, that which is first and absolute into that which is relative and mediated. In the circular journey of the entire *Logic*, the presupposed, already seen from the very start as the condition of possibility of the entire process, is effectively the idea itself. The thought of the idea is the more or less tacit presupposition of the whole work, which does nothing more than set out, in various figures, that which has already been thought and known from the very start. Hegel, in the relationship between thought in the act of its production and thought in the act of its exposition-communication, thus overturns

74 Feuerbach 1972, p. 57.

75 Feuerbach 1972, p. 59.

76 Feuerbach 1972, p. 61.

the hierarchy between the two. It abstracts from the first and makes the second into the true, presumed substance of the process of knowledge.

> Hence, the forms of demonstration and inference cannot be the forms of reasons as such; i.e., forms of an inner act of thought and cognition. They are only forms of communication, modes of expression, representations, conceptions; in short, forms in which thought manifests itself.[77]

Thus, Hegel overturns and replaces that which is first and unconditioned, thought in action, with that which is derived and consequent, thought that is only expository, only formal. In this way, originary thought, thought as such, finds itself as the subordinate object of that of which it is, instead, the principle and condition. Hegel 'made form into essence, the being of thought for others into being in itself, the relative goal into the final goal',[78] and, by so doing, consigns reason to its own alienation.

> The Hegelian system is the absolute self-externalization of reason [...]. Hegel compresses everything into his presentation, that he proceeds abstractly from the pre-existence of the intellect, and that he does not appeal to the intellect within us. [...] Everything is required either to present (prove) itself or to flow into, and be dissolved in, the presentation. The presentation ignores that which was known before the presentation.[79]

For Feuerbach, therefore, mediation and dialectics in Hegel have only a formal character. They are resolved in a method of merely extrinsic exposition and are not, as claimed, an intrinsic structure of reality and thought: it can be the logic of communication but not of science. The extrinsic nature of the dialectical process in Hegel is well evidenced by the only apparent processuality both in the *Phenomenology of Spirit* and *Logic*. Hegel, throughout all this thought, moves from the presumption of absolute identity, that is, from the conception of the Absolute as an idealistic identity of thought and being, of spirit and nature and such that, in this, the object is only the subject's position and reflection. He inherited this from the idealism of Fichte and Schelling. It is, in particular, from the latter's philosophy of identity that Hegel takes the theory of

77 Feuerbach 1972, p. 65.
78 Feuerbach 1972, p. 68.
79 Feuerbach 1972, pp. 68–9.

the Absolute as the unquestioned and unconditional foundation, elaborating this too only formally. He removes the fundamental thesis of the identity of thought and being from the ambit of imagination and subjective intuition, as occurs in Schelling, and assigns it a rational, universally understandable formulation and exposition rather than a merely individual feeling and assent. For this reason, that which appears to be the beginning in the *Science of Logic* or, in other words, indeterminate being, is only an apparent beginning. The real beginning is the absolute presupposed idea, the coincidence, that is, of being and thinking, although this appears only at the end.

> What Hegel premises as stages and constituent parts of mediation, he thinks are determined by the Absolute Idea. Hegel does not step outside the Idea, nor does he forget it. Rather, he already thinks the antithesis out of which the Idea should produce itself on the basis of its having been taken for granted […]. The externalization of the Idea is, so to speak, only a dissembling; it is only a pretense and nothing serious – the Idea is just playing a game.[80]

Hegel, it is true, tries to introduce the multiplicity and multiple forms of existence to Schelling's Absolute, but his valorisation of the principle of difference or, in other words, the negation of the abstract Identity and the establishment of particular forms is, itself, only formal. He would have needed to conceive a thought capable of confronting itself with and welcoming within itself the faculty that constitutes the opposite of pure thought and which, insofar as perception or sensible intuition, is the instrument of the sensible individuals' experience. However, in Hegel, the truth of the idea, rather than legitimising itself through an exchange with the other than the self, guarantees itself by remaining within the circle of its identity. The principle and totality of the real is, for him, constituted only by pure thought, by the idea; sensible experience, on the other hand, is only appearance. Furthermore, the *Phenomenology of Spirit* also demonstrates, even if in an inverted way, that the Hegelian idea can never go out of itself, achieving an encounter with the world of concrete individuality. Here, the initial experience of sensible consciousness, from which Hegel's work takes its starting point, remains, in its unrepeatable individuality, extraneous to the whole logical-universalising game with which it is juxtaposed by Hegel. The resolution in the universal of this immediate and concrete content of experience is, in effect, argued for through the supposed de-individualising valency

80 Feuerbach 1972, p. 73.

of language. Here, Feuerbach emphasises, language is only a tool, an external means of communication, which, as such, has no intrinsic participation in the content of significant reality.

> To sensuous consciousness, all words are names – *nomina propria*. They are quite indifferent as far as sensuous consciousness is concerned; they are all signs by which it can achieve its aims in the shortest possible way. Here, language is irrelevant [...]; because otherwise we would have to feed ourselves on mere words instead of on things in life [...]. Consciousness, however, does not let itself be confounded; it holds firmly to the reality of individual things.[81]

Even the multiplication of a single sensible experience into a multitude of here and now, according to the famous Hegelian argument made in the chapter on 'sense certainty' in the *Phenomenology of Spirit*, does not consider the here and now as truly experienced but as a logical-linguistic here and now: it takes into consideration 'the idea of "this-being", *haecceitas*',[82] not a representation and a concrete content of the senses. Thus, that which Hegel resolves in the universal is not the other of thought but 'the idea of the "other-being" of thought';[83] since, rather than placing itself within the concrete experience of the senses, it has made it always and only an object of theoretical-conceptual reflection, that is, of abstraction.

The central theme of 'Towards a Critique of Hegel's Philosophy', nonetheless, as in the previous polemics about theology, remains the criticism of the arbitrary substitution of that which is presupposed with that which is posited, of that which is primary and substantial with that which is accidental and secondary. But, here too, this reconstructive method based on reversing the terms in question appears to see the enactment of a genetic-critical philosophy that does not seem to touch the heart of Hegel's thought and its problematical richness. Hegel, as I have argued, is not a thinker of the simple, of the One. He is, rather, a thinker of the binary, of that which always involves, at the very least, a relationship of duality. For this reason, he is not a thinker of empiricism, he does not believe in the simplicity of the facts of experience but in the constitutive reference of each and any identity to the other of the self. The *Phenomenology of Spirit* and the *Logic* attempt to demonstrate just this: how the simplicity of

81 Feuerbach 1972, p. 77.
82 Feuerbach 1972, p. 79.
83 Feuerbach 1972, p. 80.

empiricism is impossible because every beginning which presumes to coincide with its simple factuality immediately refers back to its structural duality. This is precisely where, in Feuerbach, the variety of Hegelian experience is consistently reduced and translated into the simple, thereby losing any peculiarity of sense. Thus, while for Hegel language is inseparable from perception and representation, for Feuerbach the representative content of sensible consciousness and the linguistic expression of the same have no intrinsic connection. In fact, while in all Hegel's works language has an essential role in the creation and structuring of the human world (it is sufficient to mention the anthropological articulation of language in the *System of Ethical Life* in gestures, bodily signs and oral discourse, the theory of the name as a consolidated sign in the 1805–6 *Lectures*, the nexus of universal being-recognition-language in the *Phenomenology of Spirit*),[84] in Feuerbach language is only a means of transmission and communication added from outside to a content of consciousness, whose experience is theorised as immediate and, for this reason, in its sensorial-representative conclusiveness, conceived as independent of language.

Thus, while for Hegel the negative is an intrinsic principle of universalisation, is that which differentiates and multiplies from inside a content of experience that is blindly coincident with itself and, therefore, is a formal principle in the sense that it gives form and development through contradictory obstacles to progressively less impoverished identifications of the subject of experience, with Feuerbach it re-acquires an analytical-Kantian sense of a form which, by adding nothing new, more clearly reveals and communicates a content that is already grasped and known, from which it distinguishes itself and to which it adds from outside only as a means of clarification. Even the meaning of dialectic in Feuerbach, with the recovery of an essentially dialogic meaning of the expression, refers to a merely expositional-demonstrative ambit of truth already possessed and undoubtedly not, as in Hegel, to the ontological level of the construction of reality and subjectivity. However, it is Hegel's philosophy in its entirety, divested of its instances of mediation and circular growth, that Feuerbach forces and extends into a linear horizontality that starts, simply and conclusively, with the presupposition of the Idea, the Absolute, as the unaffected belief of resolving all reality in thought, and which is followed by the entire development of the Hegelian system, only expository and reiterative of the initial assumption. In other words, Hegel is considered more through Schelling's philosophy of originary identity than through the original and particular nature of his idealism. Feuerbach, undoubtedly, as the good historian of

84 On this subject, see Li Vigni 1997.

philosophy that he was, knew that Schelling was not Hegel, that the transcendental intuition that Schelling makes into an instrument of the non-discursive-conceptual knowledge of the Absolute is rejected by Hegel's rationalism as a principle of arbitrary and uncontrolled imagination in relation to the reaffirmation of the value of logical-discursive knowledge. Feuerbach knows, that is, that the intellect as a faculty of differentiation and separation is re-evaluated by Hegel as a moment to be transcended but which, nonetheless, cannot be eliminated from the path of reason insofar as it is a faculty of the universal and the whole. What he continues to emphasise, however, is that, in Hegel, the intellect remains external, not mediated with reason and, therefore, as in Schelling, the reasons of difference remain outside the original principle of the Absolute.

> Although he recognized that the Absolute lacked intellect or the principle of form – both are to him one and the same – and although he actually defined the Absolute differently from Schelling by attributing to it the principle of form, thus raising form to the level of essence, the fact remains that for Hegel form [...] – simultaneously means something formal, and the intellect again means something negative.[85]

Hegel thus returns to being a thinker of the immediate. His unquestioned presupposition is the identity of being and thought and all that which follows this act of faith must only support this principle, bending and homologising its nature to it. Becoming, the concrete world of differences and individualities, the context of anthropological and ethical-political relationships that Hegel's philosophy introduces is only an appearance, a farce, because in every particular figure of its development the same initial configuration presents itself unchanged.

In reality, Feuerbach takes absolutely no account of the structure that more properly belongs to the Hegelian circle of presupposed-posited, also because, according to his preferred point of view of the nexus of subject and predicate and the realisation of the subject as a mere emanation of itself, it is impossible not to interpret and to reduce the complexities and dialectical residues of the Hegelian circle to the simplistic linearity of the inversion of the two analytically connected terms. The text of 'Towards a Critique of Hegel's Philosophy', although not lacking in perceptive reflections, is affected throughout by the fragility of this critical stance. The outcome, due to Feuerbach's being unable to deal with the problems raised by Hegel in relation to the subject, is a reduction

85 Feuerbach 1972, p. 87.

of Hegelianism to Schellingianism. It also results in passing a diminished Hegel down to the tradition (and, here, thoughts naturally turn to the young Marx). Hegel is represented in terms of a totalising presupposition and immediacy which, in fact, is nothing more than the theoretical motif that most deeply inspired Feuerbach's thinking and which, misunderstood by him in the claimed concreteness of his humanism, is projected onto this deformed figure of his critical interlocutor.

However, beyond this criticism of Hegel (which is, undoubtedly, its central theme), the interest of this 1839 essay also lies in the changes that Feuerbach's anthropology begin to reveal, the results of which have already been seen at work in *The Essence of Christianity*. Encouraged by his own polemics against Hegel's abstract universal, Feuerbach here effectively begins to valorise more explicitly than before, alongside the pregnancy of the reality of the 'species', the positivity of its individualisations: the dignity, that is, of the 'particular' and the 'determined'. 'The god of limitation stands guard at the entrance to the world. Self-limitation is the condition of entry. Whatever becomes real, becomes so only as something determined'.[86] By now, in contrast to the *Thoughts on Death and Immortality*, sensible and concrete singularity is not reality that must be negated in order to comprehend the fullness of the universal; rather, it is the indispensible condition for it truly to exist. Thus, Feuerbach emphasises with increasing force that even if the essential and generic side of the human being still continues to be thought and its universalising attitude, the universal essence of man cannot realise itself other than through concrete and determined individuals.

> It is true that the spirit or the consciousness is 'species existing as species', but, no matter how universal, the individual and his head – the organ of the spirit – are always designated by a definite kind of nose, whether pointed or snub, fine or gross, long or short, straight or bent.[87]

The determinateness of the sensible world is no longer a failing, but the context in which the activities of the species assume concreteness and reality. At the beginning of the *Logic*, Hegel posited the connection of pure thought, expressed in the category of being in general, with nothingness. But the true connection, generating a pregnant knowledge, is that between the universalising faculty of pure thinking and sensible, concrete and individual experience.

86 Feuerbach 1972, p. 57.

87 Ibid.

> Dialectics is not a monologue that speculation carries on with itself, but a dialogue between speculation and empirical reality. A thinker is a dialectician only in so far as he is his own opponent. The zenith of art and of one's own power is to doubt oneself [...]. The antithesis of being – in general and as regarded by the *Logic* – is not nothingness, but sensuous and concrete being.[88]

The unceasing critical questioning of the nature of religion up to *The Essence of Christianity* and an increasingly critical approach to Hegel's thought thus appear to lead to a profound transformation of Feuerbach's original philosophy. The increasingly emphasised distinction between the true and false nature of religion, the definition of theology as the theoretical abstraction of an initially only practical-emotive experience, the identification of theology and the Hegelian system as united in the common deception of overturning reality and, finally, the more articulated and complex understanding of the human essence, progressively lead Feuerbach to the profound change in his thought that is expressed most clearly in writings such as the *Preliminary Theses for the Reform of Philosophy* of 1842 and the 1843 *Principles of the Philosophy of the Future*. In these works, Feuerbach effectively concluded the transition from the speculative spiritualism and anti-materialism of his early writings to a philosophy of materiality and concreteness, to an anthropology based on the sensuousness and needs of the body.

'The beginning of philosophy is not God, neither is the beginning of the absolute the absolute, being as a predicate of the idea – the beginning of philosophy is the finite, the determined, the real'.[89] This is what Feuerbach now claims in his *Preliminary Thesis for the Reform of Philosophy*. Hegel's philosophy removes dignity and autonomy of existence from the finite, wanting to make it only a deduction, an emanation of the infinite. However, true philosophy is only thought of the concrete. It is ruined in abstract speculation only when it overturns the nexus between life and thought and makes thought the principle and the being of life the predicate. 'The true relationship of thought with being is only this: being is the subject, thought is the predicate [...]. Thought derives from being but not being from thought [...]. The essence of being *qua* being is the essence of nature'.[90] Feuerbach now claims that there is no difference between Hegelian philosophy and theology. 'Hegelian philosophy is the last

88 Feuerbach 1972, p. 72.

89 Feuerbach 1972, p. 160, translation modified.

90 Feuerbach 1972, p. 169, translation modified.

refuge, the last rational standpoint of theology'.[91] It is theology disguised in the rational clothing of philosophy. Its Absolute, in its reality of thought alone, is

---

91 Feuerbach 1972, p. 168, translation modified. In the *Principles of a Philosophy of the Future*, Feuerbach explicitly reduces the Hegelian idea to a Neo-Platonic God. Hegel's concept of the thought-reality nexus supposedly revives the conception of Alexandrian philosophy, according to which God generates the world without a creative act and without going outside himself by means of a procession in which the One remains, without exhausting itself, in the many that irradiate from it. For Neo-Platonic philosophy, the co-presence of the One in the many permitted, in turn, the moment of conversion [*epistrophé*], as a return of the many into the One. For Feuerbach, Hegel had only translated into conceptual language that which the Neo-Platonists had conceived of the One that is differentiated from and determined in itself with more plastic and figurative expressions. 'That which is imagination and fantasy with the neoplatonists was merely rationalised and transformed by Hegel into concepts. Hegel is not "the German or Christian Aristotle"; he is the German Proclus. Absolute philosophy is the reborn Alexandrian philosophy' (Feuerbach 1986, p. 47). It is likely that Della Volpe's reduction of Hegelianism to Neo-Platonic philosophy was triggered precisely by this passage from Feuerbach. More recently, Halfwassen (1998) has re-proposed, in a much more articulated way, a strong link between the development of Hegelian thought and Neo-Platonism. But over and above the undoubted formal analogies between the Neo-Platonic and Hegelian dialectic, it is worth remembering that, while for the Neo-Platonists the One, the pure and absolute Being is the principle, with nothing lacking and so full of every perfection that it can surpass itself – emanating, flowing and exhalting itself – thereby giving rise to the multiplicities of the real, in Hegel the principle is always a place of lack and abstraction which, precisely due to its impoverished ontology, finds itself in contradiction with itself, generating the various figures of its becoming. (For this practical-anthropological implication of the beginning in Hegel, see Valenza 1999). Undoubtedly, neither could Hegel, as a result of his theory of the intrinsic self-contradiction and negation of every partial and abstract beginning, recognise himself in the merely representative and juxtaposed formula with which the Neo-Platonists describe, in his opinion, the differentiations and multiplications of the One. Plotinus, he wrote, in his *Lectures on the History of Philosopy*, does not execute the passage from the One to the many 'philosophically or dialectically, but the necessity of it is expressed in representations and images [...]. This does not express the need to manifest itself but posits it purely as a fact' (Hegel 1995b, p. 409). And if Hegel undoubtedly grants to Proclus a capacity of imagining a concrete universal – thus binding together the One and the many ones – in a much more elevated and systematic way than Plotinus, he also accuses Proclus of having lacked, as an ancient philosopher, the principle of modern philosophy or, in other words, that of a subjectivity that negates itself and opposes itself in order to realise its absolute freedom. 'But the autonomous development of this unity is not better elevated to a conceptual necessity in Proclus than it is in Plotinus; we must definitely renounce finding here the concept of doubling' (Hegel 1995b, p. 435, translation modified). The Neo-Platonists tried to think of the Absolute as concrete or, in other words, as that which gives rise to the multiple without going outside itself, but still according to substantialist, objectivist

the rational tradition of the theological doctrine that claims that God is the creator of the world and matter.

However, differently from Hegel, the immediacy [*Unmittelbarkeit*] of nature and sensuousness should not be concevied of as the not yet mediated or, in other words, as a lower and diminished level of existence, but, rather, as that which has the fullness and positivity of existence – as that which is originally and autonomously consistent within itself precisely because extraneous to and before thought.[92]

Thus, even more clearly in his *Principles*, Feuerbach claims that the philosophy of the future will necessarily take the world of sensuousness and determinate experience as its foundation, the world of needs and sentiments to which it is connected.

> Thus, love is the true ontological proof of the existence of an object apart from our mind; there is no other proof of being but love and feeling in general. That object whose being affords you pleasure and whose nonbeing affords you pain – that alone exists.[93]

Reality is only such insofar as it is the object of the senses and sensibility is the primary function of man, whose essence is no longer self-consciousness but bodily naturalness in its entirety. If speculative philosophy has made self-consciousness the source of a thought abstracted from concrete human sensibility, the new philosophy sees in thought only a tool, an attribute of man embodied in its sensibility.

---

modes and, therefore, necessarily external to ancient knowledge. 'What can be considered true is only that which manifests itself and in manifesting itself maintains itself as the one. The Alexandrians are, in this way, concrete totality in itself and have known the nature of the spirit. But they did not take their starting point either from the profundity of infinite subjectivity and its absolute detachment, nor did they understand absolute freedom or, if we will, the abstract of the self, as the infinite value of the subject' (Hegel 1995b, p. 450, translation modified).

92 See, within this perspective, Löwith 1976, pp. 151–3. Löwith strongly valorises the undialectical nature of Feuerbach's conception of reality, even if, in his opinion, he had not managed to develop his profound intuitions into a systematic philosophy. Only the claim of a theory of reality that escapes mediation would allow one to go outside dialectics and the theological philosophy of history to which Hegel's idealism gives rise with his secularisation of Christianity. For an appreciation of immediacy and sensibility in Feuerbach, see also Saß 1972.

93 Feuerbach 1986, p. 53.

> Whereas the old philosophy started by saying, 'I am an abstract and merely a thinking being to whose essence the body does not belong', the new philosophy, on the other hand, begins by saying, 'I am a real, sensuous being and, indeed, the body in its totality is my ego, my essence itself'.[94]

The certainty on which our existence is based cannot be intellectually derived from reasoning. It must be a truth that imposes itself in an immediate way, without needing to demonstrate anything. Feuerbach now thinks that sensibility alone, with its immediacy, is capable of satisfying this incontrovertible need for truth.

> The true and divine is only that which needs no proof, that is certain directly in itself, that directly speaks for itself and convinces in itself, and in which the affirmation that it exists is directly implied; it is that that is plainly decided upon, that is certain and clear as daylight. But only the sensuous is clear as daylight; all doubt and dispute cease where sensation begins. The secret of immediate knowledge is sensation.[95]

It is as a result of this new concept and valuation of sensuousness that many of those studying Feuerbach theorise that there are two profoundly different phases to his thought: the first being marked by a strongly rationalistic humanism and the second by a humanism based on the redefinition of finitude and sensuousness. Nonetheless, despite the evident and unquestionable variation in tone, it does not seem, on closer examination, that the basic substance of Feuerbach's philosophising undergoes a profound transformation. The anti-sensuous rationalism in the early Feuerbach, as seen, is inspired within an ambit of an organicist metaphysics of the species by the primacy of the human species. It would be possible to talk about a new foundation of Feuerbach's thought only if the original ontology of species were removed and a different theme of the articulation of the real replaced it. Instead, however, the revaluation of the sensuous world maintains an unchanged ontological framework and metaphysics of the species, with its structural valencies of a symbiotic and fusional organicity.

Thus, if the nature of thought, even in the 1842–3 works, is always characterised by universality, by being immaterial and unlimited activity ('particularity and individuality, however, belong to being, whereas generality belongs to

94 Feuerbach 1986, p. 54.

95 Feuerbach 1986, p. 55.

thought')[96] and, at the same time, is always identical to itself to such a degree that, in order to escape its infinite void, it must interrupt and break itself in sensible intuition, the same, more true and precious nature of sensuousness is undoubtedly not expressed in the affirmation of limits and determinateness. If anything, sensuousness is valorised and becomes a complete part of Feuerbach's anthropology only insofar as it becomes a function of attaining to the infinite and the absolute, as in the case of art.

> The old absolute philosophy banished the senses to the realm of appearance and finiteness; and yet, in contradiction to this, it determined the absolute, the divine, as the object of art. But the object of art is [...] an object of seeing, hearing, and feeling. Thus, not only the finite and appearing but also the true and divine being is an object of the senses; namely, sense is an organ of the absolute.[97]

Very differently from that of animals, linked to an enclosed and defined context, human senses are structurally capable of universality and they are, therefore, intrinsically spiritual senses.

> The senses of the animal are indeed keener than those of man, but only in respect to certain objects that necessarily relate to the needs of the animal; and they are keener precisely because of this determination, this excluding limitation to a definite object. Man does not have the sense of smell of a hunting dog or of a raven, but only because his sense of smell is a sense embracing all kinds of smell; hence it is a freer sense which, however, is indifferent to particular smells. But, wherever a sense is elevated above the limits of particularity and its bondage to needs, it is elevated to an independent and theoretical significance and dignity; universal sense is understanding; universal sensation, mind. [...] Indeed, even the stomach of a man, which we view so contemptuously, is not animal but human because it is a universal being that is not limited to certain kinds of food.[98]

Senses live through determinate contents but their structure is that of being autonomous from determination, insofar as they are also part of the general

96 Feuerbach 1986, p. 44.
97 Feuerbach 1986, pp. 56–7.
98 Feuerbach 1986, p. 69.

and all encompassing characteristic of the human being which, as in the early Feuerbach, continues to be 'freedom'.

> Man is not a particular being, like the animals, but a universal being; he is not, then, a limited and restricted being, but rather an unlimited and free being, for universality, absoluteness, and freedom are inseparable. This freedom does not lie in a special faculty, that is, will, nor does universality lie in a special faculty of thinking, that is, reason; this freedom and this universality extend themselves over man's total being.[99]

If freedom consists in overcoming limits and in indifference to the determinate, for the Feuerbach of the *Theses* and *Principles* it is now sensibility more than thought that realises it, given that self-conscious thought is by now considered as incapable of attaining to a true universal: 'absolute thought, that is, isolated thought that is separated from sensation, will not get beyond formal identity, namely, the identity of thought with itself'.[100] However, the condition by which sensibility is able to produce the same infinitisation that was previously assigned to thought is that, in its constitution, it removes all heterogeneity between perceiving subject and perceived object, for the lack of complete continuity would return to enclose the two poles in a reciprocal limit of extraneousness and alterity. This condition of fusionality and lack of distinction is again a guarantee, as always, of the principle of the human species, since only when the object and expressions of sensuousness and their sentiment-representative forms are humanity itself, only when a relationship of man-man is established, is there the identity of subject and object that truly renders infinite the subject and translates into the concreteness of an emotional-sensuous life the coincidence of the poles that idealistic philosophy had vainly sought in the abstract topos of self-consciousness.

> Not only 'external' things are objects of the senses. Man is given to himself only through the senses; he is an object of himself only as an object of the senses. The identity of subject and object, which in self-consciousness is only an abstract idea, is truth and reality only in man's sensuous perception of man. […] Thus, empiricism rightly derives the origin of our ideas from the senses; only it forgets that the most important and essential sense object of man is man himself; it forgets that only in man's glimpse

99 Ibid.

100 Feuerbach 1986, p. 64.

> into man is the light of consciousness and understanding kindled. Idealism is, therefore, in the right when it looks for the origin of the ideas in man; but it is wrong when it wants to derive them from the isolated man determined as soul and as a being existing for itself, in short, when it wants to derive them from the 'I' without a given sensuous 'thou'. Only through communication and conversation between man and man do the ideas arise. Not alone, but only with others, does one reach notions and reason in general. Two human beings are needed for the generation of man – of the spiritual as well as of the physical man; the community of man with man is the first principle and criterion of truth and generality.[101]

Thus, in the *Principles of a Philosophy of the Future*, sensibility can also be the place of needs and dependency on the external world. However, over and above this naturalistic connotation, its most true destination is that of giving rise to the transparency of the human, to the potentially absolute continuity between the self and the world in the light of the all-pervading nature of the *menschliche Gattung*. It is possible to talk of the valorisation of immediacy, of autonomisation and the priority of the level of being and nature in relation to the idealism of thought in Feuerbach only in this sense: of an immediate which consists in itself and cannot be reduced to anything else insofar as its existence involves a dimension that is so dense with universality and of organic continuity with otherness that it is subtracted from a merely empirical and particular level of existence.

On the other hand, it is unquestionable that, in the light of the overturning and primacy of sensuousness in relation to thought in the 'second' Feuerbach, significant conceptual movements have taken place. The most significant undoubtedly lies in the fact that the species, the universal, from being an internal-speculative term, accessible through knowledge in a rationalist phase, has now become an external term, translating itself into the 'community'. 'The essence of man is contained only in the community and unity of man with man; it is a unity, however, that rests only on the reality of the distinction between I and thou'.[102] The universalisation of the individual is no longer achieved through knowledge but through a community of relationships with other human beings who, as implied by Feuerbach's exaltation of love, are primarily of a practical-emotional nature. It is undoubtedly this dislocation of the species into community that allowed many young Hegelians, amongst whom Marx and Ruge

101 Feuerbach 1986, pp. 58–9.

102 Feuerbach 1986, p. 71.

in particular, to hope for a period of time to be able to associate the name of Feuerbach with radical philosophical-political initiatives that would go as far as theorising the extreme position of communism. The species for Feuerbach, as he wrote of himself in an essay of 1845,

> is not an abstract but the thou, the others against the single I fixed in itself; in other words, in general the other human individuals existing outside myself [...], the limits of this individual are not even the limits of the others, they are not the limits of current men and, even less so those of the future.[103]

But, precisely in this new formulation, as in the early writings, the species implies a horizon and modality of immediacy. There is no limit and distinction between you and you, between you and others. There is no consistency and irreducible specificity of alterity. There is only the fusional presupposition of the human by means of which each individual can pass through and continue in the other without any difficulties or resistance. The celebration of love is nothing more than the consequent clarification of this anthropology of transparency.

The synthetic reading here proposed of Feuerbach's works, up until the years which may have influenced Marx's development more significantly, is clearly very different from the interpretations that have seen the 'second' Feuerbach as the theorist of a liberated and emancipatory sensuousness,[104] or at least as the protagonist of a decisive advance in philosophy with respect to the abstractions of Hegelian idealism. What has been said above is oriented by the sense of what F.A. Lange previously noted about Feuerbach, according to a quote from K. Löwith.

> Writing of Feuerbach, F.A. Lange somewhere remarks that he worked his way up out of the abysses of Hegelian philosophy to a kind of superficiality, possessed of more character than spirit, but without quite losing the traces of Hegelian melancholy. In spite of its numerous 'consequently's', his system hovers in a mystic darkness which is not made more transparent by his emphasis on 'sensiblity' and 'perceptibility'.[105]

---

103 Feuerbach 1970, p. 434.

104 The reference here is to the title of the book by A. Schmidt, *Emanzipatorische Sinnlichkeit. Ludwig Feuerbachs anthropologischer Materialismus* (1973). See also, however, Xhaufflaire 1975.

105 Löwith 1964, p. 67.

It should be remembered, in relation to this curvature in Feuerbach's humanism, that the basic problematical node from which Hegel's philosophy originated was, as we have tried to demonstrate, that of conceiving of the possibility of mutual self-positing of both unity and difference, the universal and the particular, not only within an ontological-theoretical ambit but also within the much more complex perspective, beyond ontology, of anthropology, culture and historical-social life; in other words, the problem of how to imagine in all the possible fields of human experience the non-conflictual conjugation of the reasons of the whole with those of the individual subject. Dialectics, as the theory and practice of the co-presence and mediation of opposites, was the fundamental instrument with which the Berlin master had tried to give birth to this non-repressive composition of differences. That Hegel had not managed to do this, that the proposed solutions were neither resolutive nor consistent, that his anthropology, just as his ethical-political philosophy, behaved and were concluded according to an asymmetry of spiritualistic dominance takes nothing away, in my opinion, from the fact that, within the vastness of this problem, within the complexity of its articulations, he had posited and originally redefined the task of modern philosophy. It is precisely in relation to this redefinition and re-problematising of philosophy that Feuerbach's thought appears, instead, to diverge and take other routes, resulting, if not exactly in a regression, then still in a significant halt with respect to the Hegelian programme, despite the appearance of anthropological openness and materialist-sensuous reaffirmation. There is no doubt that his philosophy, beginning with his original intention to free philosophy from any contact with religion, leads him to distinguish religion from theology (precisely by critically examining in depth the nature of religion). He thus comes progressively to see something positive in religion which, by expressing the deep needs and affections of human beings, is capable of a pregnancy of reality greater than philosophy itself. Equally, there is no doubt that, for Feuerbach, it is need, corporeality and love that increasingly are the basis, in contrast to theoretical reason, for the communitarian nexus of the human species. Apart from the comment that it was precisely the much criticised Hegel who sketched out, in the 1807 *Phenomenology*, the model of a dialectics intrinsic to the Enlightenment, according to which secular reason, in the end, cannot help but criticise itself and acknowledge in religion the expression of parts and values repressed from itself, it is also unquestionable that the inspiration behind Feuerbach's philosophy, despite its overturnings, remains pantheistic immediacy and fusionality. It is, in other words, something which, on closer examination, belongs to the history of pre-Hegelianism and which, because of this, is unable to inscribe and maintain itself within the horizon of the problematic inaugurated by Hegel.

In the context of such considerations, we should not underestimate the singular coincidence of the radical critique of Hegel's philosophy that Feuerbach develops in these years with the themes and conceptualisation employed by the late Schelling in his critique of his old colleague in Tübingen. It is a singular and paradoxical concordance, because Feuerbach, as we know, always expressed his disagreement with Schelling's work, sometimes even with sarcasm. However, that does not change the fact that both Feuerbach and the late Schelling, in relation to their common polemical target, employed the same critical argumentation in defending the primacy of the extra-logical over the logical, projecting onto all of Hegel's philosophy the image of a panlogicism that subordinates any autonomous consistency of life to the predetermined reasons of the concept, whether it be corporeal-emotional life for Feuerbach, or theosophical-spiritualistic life for Schelling. Furthermore, the motifs of Schelling's anti-Hegelian polemic were publicised already in 1834, in the preface to the German translation of Victor Cousin's *Fragments philosophiques*. Feuerbach had also been able to become familiar with the substance of Schelling's lectures on the philosophy of revelation, delivered at the University of Berlin from 1841, from notes on them made by H.E.G. Paulus.[106] These facts suggest that we should not reject outright the hypothesis that, despite Feuerbach's explicit rejection of Schelling's theosophy, his critical distance from Hegel, already autonomously initiated, may have found indirect confirmation in, even if it was not directly nourished by, the 'positive philosophy' of the later Schelling.[107] Beginning with his Munich lectures in 1827, Schelling had provided a very reduced and polemical version of Hegel's idealism, characterising it as a philosophy that assumes the activities of thought and the pure concept as independent of the existence of the subject who must bring them into being. 'Concepts as such', Schelling wrote, 'do in fact exist nowhere but in consciousness; they are, therefore, taken objectively, after nature, not before it; Hegel took them from their natural position by putting them at the beginning of philosophy'.[108] Before conceptual thought there is intuition, the nexus of man with nature, so that existence, life – precisely what Schelling calls the 'positive' – can never be exhausted and resolved in the abstract determinations of pure thought. Hegel's logic, in contrast, by overturning the natural order of things, was exactly the work that presumed to make the self-movement of con-

---

106 As Feurbach wrote in a letter of 25 Ottobre 1843, he read closely the text of H.E.G. Paulus, who produced a commentary and notes of over 400 pages of Schelling's course in the Winter Semester of 1840–1 on the philosophy of revelation. See Paulus 1843.

107 About a possible influence of Schelling's later thought on Feuerbach, see Frank 1992.

108 Schelling 1994, p. 146.

cepts and their dialectics an autonomous system, removed from the naturality of life – so autonomous that, once its conceptual path had been concluded, nature must be conceived of only as a deterioration and falling outside of itself.

> But according to Hegel the Logic still has nature completely outside itself. Nature begins for him where what is logical finishes. Here nature in general is for him nothing but the agony of the concept. [...] But, in the Idea there is no necessity at all for any kind of movement. The Idea could not, for instance, progress further in itself (for that is impossible, because it is already complete), but would rather have to completely break away from itself.[109]

> He [Hegel] and his followers call pure thought that which has simple concepts as its content. For him withdrawing into thought means only deciding to think about thought. But, at least, this thought cannot be called real thought. Real thought is that where something which is opposed to thinking is overcome. But, where again thought has only thought as its content and abstract thought at that, then there is nothing to be overcome in thought.[110]

Thus, philosophy rejects seeing thought as the process by means of which a living subject elaborates and translates into concepts the relationship with the natural-sensuous and supra-sensuous world that lives by the immediacy of intuition, and instead makes thought the presupposition which, beginning with itself, must posit the reality of everything.

The Schelling of Berlin, of the lectures on the philosophy of revelation that he held beginning in 1841, turns the nexus between the Absolute and the natural and human world (which, in a pantheistic and immanent key, had been the underlying theses of his first philosophy) towards an increasingly theosophical and religious perspective. The 'pure and original entity' (as Schelling now defines the Absolute) is absolutely outside rational thought, which has, furthermore, only a finite and becoming reality as its content. All rationalist philosophies (of which German idealism is also part and, therefore, in some way, also Schelling's original philosophy of identity) always claim to reduce existence to essence, that is, to reduce that which constitutes the not immediately sensuous structure and foundation of the sensuous world to the abstraction of a univer-

109 Schelling 1994, p. 154.
110 Schelling 1994, p. 146.

sal that lives only in thought. However, this approach to defining essence – an approach to which, for Schelling, his first definition of the Absolute as absolute, undifferentiated and symmetric equality of the subject and object now belongs – makes essence a content among contents, negating its Absoluteness precisely at the same time as it defines it. Pure existence undoubtedly transcends the sensuous level but, contemporaneously, goes beyond the logical level and cannot be defined and enclosed within the sphere of essence, of the concept.[111] The true entity, or God, should effectively be seen as a very special being that defies any definition. This is possible only when the being of God is conceived of as an infinite 'power of existence [*Seinkönnende*]', a pure creative power that initially exists only insofar as it is power, such that it resists any passing into being. God is pure power of being or, in other words, unwilling will that excludes in this power to be any power not to be. Creation is the actualisation of this power of being, primarily though a Trinitarian, theogonic process by means of which the generating power of the Father posits an existent (the Son) outside its original being, but whose destiny is that of overcoming its own figure as separate from the father and of returning, having defeated the power to persist in the determinate and passive conservation of being, to restore the original power of divine being as pure power of being. This God who has become, as the developed and restored unity of the divine powers, is the *Urmensch*, the original man, rightly placed by Biblical traditions, due to its immanence in the divine, in the earthly Paradise. From this *Urmensch*, with his fall and separation from the divine in the strict sense, the world itself arises. The original man can prevent himself from becoming the intermediary for the reunification of God with himself and want to posit himself not in God but as God, in place of God, thereby generating with this act of pride persistence in the world of the finite, the negative, the disorganic, which only through the persistence of its separation from the divine becomes an effectively extra-divine world.[112] Mythology, as Schelling says in his *Philosophy of Mythology*, is the representative process

111 With regard to the later Schelling's criticism of idealism and study of the limits of the powers of reason, see the comments of Donadio: 'When faced, therefore, with a history which in its unfolding from its origins to the end sees itself as the manifestation of the sole, true and fundamental reality of reason, the highest faculty and true strength of mankind, which can be ascertained through a critical reflection on the conditions of its knowledge and actions, there now arises the "*immemorial being*" [*das Unvordenkliche*] to which reason itself, in its unfolding, finds itself returned as its absolute *Prius*, the original foundation to which it does not have access and starting from which it recognises itself as posited' (Donadio 2000, p. 131).

112 See, in this regard, Bausola 1997, VII–LXXXVII.

by means of which the human species in the variety of its history and peoples enacts and becomes aware of the rupture and disaggregation of the organic unity of the divine powers and the need for their reconciliation. It is the process by means of which man, fallen of his own volition into the extra-divine world, gradually becomes aware of the need to return to the originally broken unity.

This, very briefly outlined, is the substance of the philosophy of the Schelling who, after a decade, was appointed as the successor to Hegel's professorship with the intention of overthrowing the Hegelian school's hegemony in the Prussian capital. He provided his audience with an interpretation of Hegel as a thinker who could be reduced to the metaphysical rationalism of the eighteenth century, to *Wolffianismus* as a theory of reason that always places the concept before experience and which generates its logical-deductive system of innate ideas independently from any relationship with the empirical world. It is from this perspective, both ontological and theological at one and the same time, of original Being, that he criticises Hegel's panlogicism – not from the concreteness of a naturalist or historical realism, nor from an existentialism that states the priority and irreducibility of the body over the mind and emotional and pre-reflective experience over logic and reflectiveness, but from the presupposition of Being, as the original and divine source of the senses, in which the single human must find the most authentic reason for its existence. This is certainly not the place for studying in depth the complexities of the very long and multifaceted relationship between Schelling and Hegel. However, it is sufficient to recall to what degree the presupposition of an Absolute as originally given is undoubtedly more Schelling's than Hegel's, and to what degree, on the other hand, the subject of beginning in all Hegel's works is consistently linked to a radically impoverished and destitute condition of experience or modality of thinking. Schelling's Absolute, from the *System of Transcendental Idealism* onwards, is an immediate which, in its being an identity without any residue of difference between subject and object, is outside discursivity and mediation to such a degree that its an expression only of aesthetic-transcendental intuition. It is possibly precisely this character of immediacy, outside mediation, that permits Schelling's final philosophy to think the Absolute, in its initial pantheism and Spinozism, as a personal God to whom human reason, in acknowledging its limitations, refers as to its irreducible and inexhaustible presupposition. However, contrasting a theosophy of Being with a philosophy which, as in Hegel's, had made this first category of the *Science of Logic* the expression of the poorest and most undifferentiated beginning of thought, undoubtedly meant placing it within a fairly unsuitable position for understanding the peculiarities of the concept of *Geist* which, with its idealism, had claimed to oppose the substantialist and objectivist philosophies of *Sein*. It meant rejecting finding therein a theory that explains being, nature and history on the basis of the self-representations that a subject provides of itself. In other worlds, it renounces understanding how a subject's history of becoming, through its setbacks and increasingly emancipated self-consciousness, constitutes the fundamental structure of Hegel's philosophy. Instead, it ends up representing it as the re-edition of a pre-Kantian, metaphysical rationalism that proposes the reduction of reality to an a priori system of reason without the function and mediation of subjectivity – after Kant, an unavoidable philosophical acquisition.

## 5 The Last Feuerbach

The fact that Feuerbach had never been a theorist of materialism, in the sense of claiming the precedence and primacy of nature or, possibly, of matter, with respect to the human being and the events of its sensuous-ideological-rational existence, is further confirmed, in my opinion, by what he continued to write and think during his final and fairly long phase of activity after 1842–3. These years saw the publication of works such as *The Essence of Religion* (1846), *Theogonie nach den Quellen des classischen, hebräischen und christlichen Alterthums* (1857), and *Gottheit, Freiheit und Unsterblichkeit vom Standpunkte der Anthropologie* (1866). The historiographical debate on this phase of Feuerbach's works has been equally no less varied and controversial than that in relation to the works considered so far. Part of the criticism has even seen in this later Feuerbach the overcoming of anthropocentrism and the arrival at a materialist naturalism in which the being at the basis of reality and its original meaning is seen as 'non-human' nature and the limitation and finitude that would derive from it for man – a subject no longer creator and universal but individual, finite and creatural.

Here too, it is undoubtedly true that the pages of this Feuerbach begin and are increasingly filled with ethnological and cosmological, naturalist and psychological reflections. In other words, there are increasingly broader interests in relation to the sciences of both nature and humanity, as evidenced, for example, by the unpublished extracts from the daily newspaper *Ausland* which Feuerbach put together from 1843 to 1853 on the subjects of ethnology, geography and geology.[113] Furthermore, beginning with *The Essence of Religion*, the

113 The discovery of the unpublished Munich works, and the cataloguing of these extracts, is due to the work of Tomasoni. For a description and synthetic presentation of these texts, see Tomasoni 1986, pp. 90–130.

theme of a nature that cannot be reduced to the significance and uses attributed and applied to it by the human species becomes increasingly present.

In relation to nature, Feuerbach here writes: '(All that which is outside man: light, air, heat, water, fire, earth, plants). Another being, distinct from man, not human [*Ein Anderes, vom Menschen unterschiedenes, nicht menschliches Wesen*]: light, air, fire, water, earth – in a word – nature. In fact, in nature we are, we live and we move'.[114] Religion is born of dependency, from sentiments of uncertainty and insecurity. Man was originally dependent on nature, which is now explicitly defined as 'the basis of man's existence'.[115] On the other hand, in a letter to the publisher Wigand in the summer of 1844 in relation to the publication of another of his works, *The Essence of Faith According to Luther*, Feuerbach had already said:

> I would prefer first to publish another work which, despite appearing after *The Essence of Christianity*, is, in reality, its premise. I mean a work on the being that hides behind and precedes the human being, on the being closest to and, nonetheless, the furthest from us, on the most known and, nonetheless, most mysterious being, on that most sensuous and, nonetheless, most spiritual, on nature and this insofar as it is and was the basis and object of religion.[116]

However, on a deeper analysis of the same pages of *The Essence of Religion*, what immediately leaps out, over and above naturalism and presumed materialism, is insistently and once again anthropocentrism, that is, a hierarchical reconstruction of reality in which needs, dependency, sensuousness and the empirical concreteness of individual life are only the first level of a constitution of existence that must conclude and mature in the attestation of the freedom of the human being, insomuch as it is precisely being that gives a sense to all reality only by thinking it, acting it and using it, beginning with the self. Thus, the function of religion, its essence, does indeed consist in rendering divine that which conditions and on which human neediness depends, but also in rendering it something which, from outside, unknown and uncontrollable, becomes, through the celebration and identification of the divine, something well-known, familiar, internal – in other words, something close and similar to which to turn, to bend to one's own desires and from which to receive assist-

---

114 Quotation from the first edition of *The Essence of Religion* in Tomasoni 1986, p. 179.

115 Tomasoni 1986, p. 179.

116 Tomasoni 1986, p. 133.

ance and satisfaction. Thus, the essence of religion, in this translation from the unknown to the known, from the non-human to the human, consists precisely in liberation from that which conditions the human being from outside – primarily nature – due to the coincidence of the human being with a world that once again produces and freely signifies from inside itself.

> The progress of religion consists in the fact that, while primarily the subjective depends on the objective, this relationship is even overturned and the objective is made to depend on the subjective. In other words, while man previously believed his essence, his origins to be the being of nature, he subsequently conceives his being to be rather the essence of nature since, while initially he was subjected to nature, he later and finally subjects nature to himself.[117]

The purpose of religion is, therefore, paradoxically the negation of religion – atheism – since what is matured through it is the coincidence of man with himself, the state of never finding anything outside himself that can intimidate and subdue him. Consequently, this is the affirmation of freedom and of man being his own God.

> The sentiment of man's dependency on nature is the basis of religion. However the overcoming of this, the autonomy and freedom of man from nature is the purpose of religion. In other words: the beginning, the presupposition, the basis is the relationship of man towards a being different from that which he is, the purpose of religion is the relationship of man towards a being that is undistinguishable from him, which is his own same being. If the essence of religion is defined as the sentiment of dependency, insomuch as it expresses the humiliation, the negation, the non-being of man, then it can be said that: the basis of religion is, yes, religious but its purpose is irreligious – no religion, no God. The divinity is the beginning; atheism is the purpose of religion. The beginning is the disassociation of man with himself, the disagreement between his feelings of dependency and his impulse for freedom, the purpose is the unity of man with himself. In other words, the divinity of nature is the basis of religion and every religion, including the Christian religion; therefore the divinity of man is the final purpose of religion.[118]

---

117 Tomasoni 1986, pp. 231–3.

118 Tomasoni 1986, pp. 229–31.

Need, at the moment in which it is consigned into the hands of a God, loses the alienated character of an external obligation, of non-being, and assimilates itself to that which is within the ambit of the human sphere. It transubstantiates itself, defining the field that it procures and relates no longer to lack but rather to satisfaction – that is, the ambit of reality in which man affirms and enjoys himself.

> Religion, insomuch as it is based on the feeling of dependency, is provided by two opposing elements – by a negative component and by a positive one, by the negation and the affirmation of man. And, as a lacking precedes enjoyment, need precedes satisfaction, the feeling of my non-being the feeling of my being, so also in religion, the beginning, the foundation and the start of this is the negative sentiment that man has of himself [...] [but] it is only the start, the appearance [*Schein*]; in reality it has another sense, an entirely opposite sense with respect to that presented at first sight: it is negation whose purpose is the affirmation of mankind.[119]

With respect to this reaffirmed centrality, freedom and divinity of the human being, nature undoubtedly also exists for itself, but alone, distant and extraneous, in a characterisation almost reminiscent of Leopardi ('nature is blind, cold, insensitive').[120] Nonetheless, it is identifiable in these pages by Feuerbach, in relation to its autonomy and pre-existence to man, not by means of its own independent configurations and modalities, but essentially in *via negationis* or, in other words, through the exclusion of that which, inversely, is properly of man: '[nature] in itself does not see, does not feel, does not know what it does, the direction towards which it moves'.[121] It is precisely this being without consciousness, finality and sentiment that turns it from an independent being into a dependent being – dependent on a 'conscious being that wants, sees, feels, enjoys'.[122] The presupposition of the existence of man is 'the insensitive power, the inhuman reality of nature, its lack of regard in relation to man'.[123] But the goal of the vicissitudes of man and his cultural, political and religious history is precisely that of translating the insensitive into the sensitive, the extraneous

---

119 Tomasoni 1986, pp. 227–9.

120 Tomasoni 1986, p. 301.

121 Tomasoni 1986, p. 283.

122 Tomasoni 1986, p. 277.

123 Tomasoni 1986, p. 261.

into the own, the objective into the subjective, demonstrating that 'the conscious being is the Supreme Being [*das Bewußtseiende ist das Höchste*] and, as such, the first being'.[124]

Those reading *The Essence of Religion* in full will undoubtedly perceive the insight, if not the psychological and almost pre-psychoanalytical depth, of many of Feuerbach's passages. However, here too, it is within a perspective where anthropocentrism continues with regard to the need to transcend, ultimately, the natural in the spiritual and to humanise every material dimension of life without any exclusions.

Nonetheless, rather than in a supposed theorisation of nature as a being independent of humans' lives, it is precisely in morals and ethics that Feuerbach's last reflections manage ultimately to find new and original accents. He resolutely rids himself of a vision that sees universality and freedom triumphing in the human being. This occurs mainly in his claim for morals based on the instinct for happiness that underlies his last published work (and the decade of preparatory work that preceded it), *On Spiritualism and Materialism, Especially in Relation to the Freedom of the Will*. It is only here, in a criticism of the Kantian-Schopenhauerian theory of the intelligible and unconditionally free character of the will, that the entirely determinate and consistently individual nature of human life are affirmed, excluding the existence of a common and generic reason or sensibility. 'Sensuality and individualism are effectively', he writes here, 'one and the same thing'. But this is by now sensualism that, in contrast to the strong universalistic instances theorised in the *Principles*, is concrete and circumstantial:

> I am all over, absolutely, from my feet to the ends of my hair, from the first to the last atom, an individual being [...]. I feel, want, think the same as you do. But I don't think with your reasoning or with a common reasoning but, rather, with my own that can be found in this head here. I desire, but again, not with your desires or with general desires but with my own that are enacted with these muscles here.[125]

Human existence is by now, for the last Feuerbach, firmly incarnate, made of needs, pain and pleasure rooted in corporeality. It is only possible to talk of the life of the species and common and essential universalities in order to

124 Tomasoni 1986, p. 276.

125 Feuerbach 1993, p. 101. See the editor's lucid introduction, pp. 7–41. See also Feuerbach 1981, vol. 11, pp. 53–186.

distinguish men from the other living species such as dogs and horses. This is because what is now unconditionally valid is the 'right to individuality'.[126] Human beings' essence now consists precisely in not having an essence, insofar as organic and common, but rather in each enforcing their own diversity. 'Only in relation to themselves are human individuals infinitely, essentially different the one to the other – essentially because with the elimination of their diversity, the very essence of their individuality is suppressed'.[127]

Only at the end of his work, therefore, does Feuerbach's materialism really achieve what it appeared to promise during his sensuousness turn in the years 1838–43.

However, in following the young Marx in his theoretical adventures, it is not vital to study in depth the later Feuerbach and his works that are no longer linked to the mythologising of the 'human species'. It was the Feuerbach of the early 1840s who most attracted the attention of our young hero. His apparent and deceptive materialism imparted the lesson of an absolute and divinised humanism, with its mysticism of communitarianism without divisions or conflicts.

## 6 Marx and Feuerbach

The young Marx was aware that the utilisation of Hegel's legacy was the fundamental cultural and political question of modernity and that the elaboration of this vast theoretical legacy could not be undertaken other than by continuing to rise up to the challenge of the level of the problematic inaugurated by Hegel. This challenge remained alive for him throughout all his life, re-emerging and put to work in the thinking and composition of *Capital*. However, for a long, intervening period, this thought was repressed from his consciousness and replaced, as often occurs with the mechanism of repression, by the opposite thought of having resolved and concluded that confrontation by simply eliminating and cancelling out the figure of Hegel as a theological and speculative philosopher.

The reasons for such repression, as is known, can be fairly complex and of various natures. What can be said is that probably the end of any possibility for an academic career, with the consequent acceleration of the young Marx towards an immediate political and cultural commitment – towards praxis –

126 Feuerbach 1993, p. 103.

127 Feuerbach 1993, p. 105.

predisposed him to leave aside the toil of a more rigorous theoretical task and to be more favourably disposed towards a thought whose immediacy was its main constituent part.

This thought was, *par excellence*, that of Feuerbach. It was precisely through him that a long, initial phase of Marx's work and his first theorising of communism were strongly conditioned by a tradition of pantheistic and symbiotic humanism. The entire expanse of Marx's life was needed for him to be able to attempt to free himself from its impact.[128]

The themes of the human species and its return to unity, as the ultimate meaning of universal history, had, furthermore, been one of the philosophical strands that most intensely characterised the German Enlightenment and, in particular, Kant's philosophy of history. That the human species could progressively unify itself under the universal guide of reason is a keystone of Kantianism. By means of this, the concept of the human species is reintroduced into the course of history, but without any theological and creatural references. This is the subject that makes itself progressively autonomous from the history of nature and which, within the ambit of a human history, secularly and *weltgeschichtlich* understood, is able to become the free self-producer of itself. Feuerbach's concept of the human species as the absolute subject of reality and

---

128 With regard to the humanist, rather than materialist, character of Feuerbach's philosophy, it is essential to remember the interpretation, the intelligence of which is not undermined by being somewhat dated, made by R. Mondolfo in his 1908 essay on 'Feuerbach e Marx' (in Mondolfo 1975). Despite proposing theoretical ends dissimilar to our own and consistently claiming that true Marxism was not materialism but humanism, Mondolfo was effectively able to understand, according to Norberto Bobbio, the extent to which 'the master of Marx, Ludwig Feuerbach, is not, in contrast to common opinion and Marx's critics, a materialist' (in Mondolfo 1975, p. xv). Distancing himself from the representation of Feuerbach outlined by Marx in the famous 1845 *Thesen über Feuerbach* and, to all effect, revived in Italy by Giovanni Gentile (the first editor and Italian translator of these *Theses*, placed as an appendix to his 1899 volume on *La filosofia di Marx*), Mondolfo noted that, for Feuerbach, in contrast to Marx's argument, there is no objective and sensuous world, separated and abstracted from the subject, which would consign the latter to a merely passive cognitive intuition. For, in Feuerbach, there is a connection of reciprocal implication, of continuity, between the two poles and 'experience itself […], in place of being the exclusive formation of the concept on the part of the object, is rather the continuous revelation of the power and specific characteristics of the subject' (p. 23). Thus as the same criterion of truth and a complete and real awareness are posited by Feuerbach in the community, in a continuity, here again, of theory and praxis, this allows him to claim that 'Marx owes to Feuerbach's real *Humanismus* the orientation of his vision of the world and the start of his own economic investigations' (p. 9).

the indispensable horizon of sense recalls, amongst its various and possible genealogies, this Kantian-Enlightenment matrix of the concept of *menschliche Gattung*. It does so, however, by bending the line (that in Kant's philosophy of history is more or less infinitely progressive) into a circle of immediate and readily available organicity. It is no coincidence that entirely lacking from Feuerbach's concept of the human species is the dimension of conflict and competition between individuals that structurally belongs to Kant's concept of the history of the human species and its becoming slowly but surely one, by means of the heterogeneity of the goals that, for Kant, transform the original dominion of nature (with its clash of instincts and appetites) over humanity into a rationalisation of egoisms and in a gradual extinction of conflict. Thus, Feuerbach's concept of the human species is ultimately radicalised and translates into even more fusional terms the myth of a united humanity transparent to itself that Kant had prudently posited, only as a limit-idea, at the end of history.[129]

But now let us return to the young Marx and his first systematic work of political philosophy and radical criticism of Hegel's idealism.

129 See Burgio 2000, pp. 21–75.

CHAPTER 5

# An All Too Human Communism

## 1 A Generalised Inversion

When Marx left the editorship of the *Rheinische Zeitung* on 17 March 1843, the fate of the Cologne paper was inexorably sealed. Due to the radical nature of the liberalism that inspired the paper under Marx's editorship, the Prussian government had for some time already effectively decided upon its suppression. However, officially, it was only a ministerial order of 21 January 1843 that stated that the *Rheinische Zeitung* would cease publication by 31 March of the same year. This accordingly took place, despite Marx's efforts to obtain a revocation of the government decision and the petitions submitted by the citizens of Cologne and other Rhineland cities, as well an appeal on the part of the paper's shareholders to the Prussian sovereign.[1]

The closure of the *Rheinische Zeitung* resulted in a determining change in both the public and private spheres of the young intellectual's life. He was now 25 years old. Weighty issues, both practical and theoretical, loomed on the horizon for him. The previous year, after the death of his brother Hermann,[2] difficulties arose with his mother, Henriette, who, wanting to see him take up a secure and advantageous profession, had already refused both any financial assistance and access to his paternal inheritance. On the other hand, his engagement to Jenny von Westphalen had existed since the autumn of 1836

---

1 During the discussion on this of the General Meeting of the Shareholders of the *Rheinische Zeitung*, Jung, one of the directors, declared that 'the newspaper has prospered in its present form, it has gained a surprising number of readers with astonishing rapidity' (*MECW* 1, p. 717).

2 'Not much is known about Marx's brothers and sisters. The first born, Moritz David, died soon after birth. The second was Sophie, born 13 November 1816. As far as we know, she was the only sibling with whom he had a degree of intimacy during his youth. Nonetheless, he later only just remained in contact with his sister who had married a lawyer called Schmalshausen and lived in Maastricht. Karl was born on 5 May 1818 at 1:30 in the morning. Of Karl's two younger brothers, Hermann died at the age of 23 and Eduard at the age of 11. They both died of tuberculosis, a hereditary family illness, as did the other two sisters Henriette and Karoline who died fairly young. Louise, born in 1821, married the Dutchman Jan Karl Kuta and migrated with him to Cape Town. She came to visit Marx twice in London, with her husband, and in 1853 Marx wrote several articles for *Zuid-Afrikaan*, edited by his brother-in-law. Emilie, born in 1822, married the engineer Conradi and lived happily in Trier up until her death in 1888' (Nikolaevskij and Maenchen-Helfen 1969, p. 23).

and Karl, apart from the strength of his passion, felt profoundly responsible for this young woman from a good family who, for him 'has fought the most violent battles, which almost undermined her health'.[3] It was absolutely necessary for him to find some means of support, without foregoing the cultural-political activities to which his life was, by now, irrevocably destined. Thus, the invitation from Arnold Ruge, after the Prussian government had also imposed the closure of his journal *Deutsche Jahrbücher*, was providential. He proposed co-editing a journal in German to be published abroad. Between Switzerland, Strasburg and Paris, the latter was chosen for the publication, both due to its importance and the large resident German population. As soon as the contract was signed, Marx returned to Kreuznach, where Jenny lived with her mother, Caroline von Westphalen, married and spent the initial post-wedding period there before leaving for France in October of the same year. This meant a more or less definitive departure from his native land.

Having resolved his sentimental situation and suspended the urgency of his journalistic and publicist activities, Marx passed the months in Kreuznach before his departure for France in a return to an intensive activity of concentration and study, equalled only by that in the period of his preparation for his dissertation. The most noteworthy outcome of this organic revival of his theoretical engagement is a day of reckoning with Hegel and a liquidation – for us, as will be seen, only presumed as such – of Hegelian philosophy. Marriage and the disappearance of any professional opportunities in his homeland, even of a literary and essayist nature, the move to a new country and the maturing of increasingly radically democratic political ideas, had, by now, enabled him to liberate himself from all authorities and to resolve to carry out the parricide which, with its characteristics of extremism and absoluteness, constitutes the pivotal point of his transition from idealism to materialism.

As we have seen, during the *Rheinische Zeitung* period the young Marx had experimented, above all, with being an ethical-political essayist, criticising the distance of the German public institutions from coherence with a radical and unconditional democratic state. It was precisely with regard to political philo-

3 'I can assure you, without the slightest romanticism, that I am head over heels in love, and indeed in the most serious way. I have been engaged for more than seven years, and for my sake my fiancée has fought the most violent battles, which almost undermined her health, partly against her pietistic aristocratic relatives, for whom "the Lord in heaven" and the "lord in Berlin" are equally objects of religious cult, and partly against my own family, in which some priests and other enemies of mine have ensconced themselves' (*MECW* 1, p. 399). Marx here refers to, amongst other things, Jenny's deeply conservative stepbrother, Otto Wilhelm H. von Westphalen, who was the Prussian Minister of the Interior from 1850–8.

sophy that, with the 1843 manuscript entitled by its first German editors *Zur Kritik des Hegelschen Staatsrechts* [*Contribution to the Critique of Hegel's Philosophy of Right*],[4] that the separation of Marx from Hegel was enacted. The latter is presented as the theoriser of an irrational and conservative philosophy of the state and, more generally, of an idealism now defined as mystical and abstract. With a commentary dedicated to paragraphs 261–313 of the greatest Hegelian work of socio-political theory, the 1821 *Grundlinien der Philosophie des Rechts*, Marx criticises the logic of Hegel's philosophy as a whole by means of the logic applied to the subject of the state. The notebooks of extracts from Marx's readings probably in the same period of drafting the *Critique* of Hegel – the so-called *Kreuznacher Hefte* – evidence his commitment to this task. Marx studied Machiavelli, Montesquieu, Rousseau and many texts related to the juridical-political history of modern Europe, with particular reference to the history of feudalism but, above all, to the French Revolution and Restoration. The main subjects of the extracts and annotations contained in the *Kreuznacher Hefte* concern the problems of the origins of modern states, the differentiation of modern political institutions with respect to the limited articulation of feudal society, the nature of representative constitutions and the character of state bureaucratic organisation, the relationship between legislative and executive powers: in other words, the fundamental questions concerning the organisation of the modern state, the investigation of which represents, alongside an analysis of Hegel's more specifically philosophical side, the basic fabric of the *Critique*.[5]

---

4 With regard to the history of this manuscript, refer to the 'Philological Note' in the premise to the translation of Marx's text, edited by myself and Trincia (see Marx 1983). There was already an Italian translation in 1963 (by G. Della Volpe) of this text (posthumously published in 1927; see Marx 1963). However, the strongly theoretical over-determination which this translation appears to favour (since the 1843 *Critique* was, according to Della Volpe, the work where Marx had already elaborated a materialistic logic of thought, vastly superior to Hegel's idealistic philosophising) prompted our new and, in our opinion, more suitable translation. Della Volpe's translation of the expression '*Stand*', whose meaning of 'order' or 'estate' refers to an order-based or pre-modern constitution and historical period, with the term 'class [*classe*]', is sufficient evidence of the inappropriate forcing to which Della Volpe subjected Marx's *Critique* of 1843. This was preceded by Francesco Messineo's rendering of '*Stand*' as '*classe*' in his Italian translation of Hegel's *Philosophy of Right* (see Hegel 1954).

5 The five Kreuznach notebooks, which date from July 1843, contain extracts that Marx put together from works on the history of France – the French Revolution in particular – the history of England, Germany, Sweden, Poland, the Venetian Republic and the history of the USA, as well as classics of science of the state such as Machiavelli, Montesquieu and Rousseau. The texts from which Marx took extracts of varying length, from many pages down to just

However, understanding the nature of Marx's new relationship with Hegel cannot help but make the privileged relationship that the young Marx established with Feuerbach once again of central importance. We have previously seen how Feuerbach's writings between 1839–43 defined the essence of theoretical criticism as being the ability to discover in the heart of philosophy, and in a vision of the world such as the religious one, the logical typology of the inversion of subject and predicate. The purpose of this, naturally, is that of restoring the inverted elements to their correct and original configuration of reality. The Marx of the manuscript on Hegel's theory of the state embraced this definition of criticism in its entirety and made it a fundamental theoretical lens by means of which Hegel's works could be evaluated. Thus, if the Marx of the *Rheinische Zeitung* used, above all, the positive side of Feuerbach's thoughts in stating the ontological and ethical-political primacy of the *menschliche Gattung* as the basis for his theory of *Volk* and the *Volk-Staat*, the Marx of the 1843 *Critique* used and applied the inversion model essentially for critical and polemical purposes.

Consequently, for Marx in this period, the representation of the inversion of subject and predicate explains not only religion and philosophical idealism, but also the modern nexus of civil society and the political state.

The central thesis of Marx's manuscript is effectively that the most distinctive characteristic of modern reality or, in other words, the distinction and copresence within social organisation of the two spheres of civil society and the

---

one, are, respectively: (Heft 1) C.G. Heinrich, *Geschichte von Frankreich*, Leipzig 1802–4; (Heft 2) again Heinrich (continuation), C.F. Ludwig, *Geschichte der letzten fünfzig Jahren*, Altona 1833, P. Daru, *Historie de la république de Venise* (first edition, Paris 1819), C. Lacretelle, *Histoire de France, depuis la restauration*, Stuttgart 1831, J.-J. Rousseau, *Du contrat social*, Londres 1782, J.C. Bailleul, *Examen critique de l'ouvrage posthume de M. la B. de Staël*, Paris 1818, H.P. Brougham, *Polen*, Brüssel 1831, C.-L. Montesquieu, *De l'esprit des loix*; (Heft 3) J. Russel, *Geschichte der englischen Regierung und Verfassung*, Leipzig 1825, J.M. Lappenberg, *Geschichte von England*; Hamburg 1834–7; (Heft 4) E.A. Schmidt, *Geschichte von Frankreich*, Hamburg 1835, F.-R. de Chateaubriand, *Die neue Proposition in Bezug auf die Verbannung Karls x. und seiner Familie*, Leipzig 1831, K.W. von Lancizolle, *Über Ursachen, Character und Folgen der Julitage*, Berlin 1831, W. Wachsmuth, *Geschichte Frankreichs im Revolutionszeitalter*, Hamburg 1840–4, L. Ranke, *Deutsche Geschichte im Zeitalter der Reformation*, Berlin 1839–47, *Historisch-politische Zeitschrift*, Bd. 1, hrsg. v. L.v. Ranke, Hamburg 1832, J. Lingard, *Geschichte von England seit dem dem ersten Einfalle der Römer*, Frankfurt a.M., 1827–33, E. Geijer, *Geschichte Schwedens*; Hamburg 1832–6; (Heft 5) J.C. Pfister, *Geschichte der Teutschen*, Hamburg 1829–35, J. Möser, *Patriotische Phantasien*, Berlin 1820, C.G. Jouffroy, *Das Principip der Erblichkeit und die französische und englische Pairie*, Berlin 1832, T. Hamilton, *Die Menschen und die Sitten in den vereinigten Staaten von Nordamerika*, Mannheim 1834, N. Machiavelli, *Vom Staate*, Karlsruhe 1832. The *Kreuznacher Hefte* are contained in *MEGA*, IV/2.

political state, is structured – analogously to the connection between reality and the idea in Hegel's philosophy – according to the mode of abstract universalisation. The result for modern history, therefore, is that on the one hand stands civil society, as the area of material and concrete economic life supported by individual interests and the competition of each against all the others, and, on the other, the state as the area where particular interests come together as a general, common utility and, therefore, as the sphere of a communitarian spirit.

However, for Marx, the two spheres refer to a nexus of abstraction and alienation rather than a relationship of co-existence and distinction. The effective placing of one outside the other – civil society based on a principle of individualism and the state based on dedication to the universal – makes the latter an abstract environment because, in the contrast of their respective constitutive principles, it is separate from and in opposition to civil society. It is, furthermore, an abstract sphere in the more particular sense of an alienated sphere, given that its existence, in relation to the pregnancy and urgency of the material life appertaining to civil society, is only of an ideal and fantastic nature.

The modern state is effectively an abstract ambit but, at one and the same time, it really exists insofar as its institutions, based on the principle of universal interest, possess life and space alongside civil society, which is instead moved by the opposing principle of personal egoism. However, this real abstractness is also, and more properly, unreal and imaginary given that it is the outcome, for Marx, of a process of alienation that takes place only in thought or, in other words, it is the result of an idealisation with which the members of a community, separated in their originally communitarian human nature by their economic individualism, regain the scene of their unified and supportive equality only in their imagination. It is projected, in the same way as religious alienation, outside their material and concrete existences in the institutional and superior spheres of the political community.

Hegel's great merit, Marx points out, is having appreciated that, in relation to the lack of distinction between the public and private that still strongly characterised feudal society, the substance of modernity is played out in the co-existence of civil society and the political state. He initially theorised the existence of civil society and the political state as autonomous and distinct environs inasmuch as they are subject to profoundly different constitutive criteria. He also comprehended, in particular, that the privatisation of economic life and its liberation from communitarian or political-order based limitations corresponds to the political state becoming autonomous and public.

> Hegel is right, therefore, when he says: The political state is the constitution, i.e., the material state is not political. [...] It is obvious that the political constitution as such is brought into being only where the private spheres have won an independent existence. Where trade and landed property are not free and have not yet become independent, the political constitution too does not yet exist. The Middle Ages were the democracy of unfreedom.[6]

However, Hegel's great fault, having comprehended the substance of modernity, is that of wanting to present this as rational reality: in other words, Hegel presented in his *Philosophy of Right* that which, for Marx, is the typical division of the modern between the individualism of civil society and the universality of the political state as a world enclosed in a unified and consistent perspective without lacerations and oppositions. In Marx's opinion, Hegel attempts to do this by enacting an inversion of subject and predicate. In order to give a sense to the experience which human beings initially undergo within the family and then within the work environment and that of political institutions, he does not begin, according to Marx, from the problems and characteristics that belong respectively to those determinate circles of reality – or from that which Marx calls 'the specific logic of the specific object [*die eigentlümliche Logik des eigentlümliches Gegenstandes*]'.[7] On the contrary, he begins from the horizon of the state, presupposed as universal. Hegel thus wishes to demonstrate, following his predetermined logic, how all these various areas of reality are none other than the introduction and anticipation of the communitarian and organic elements that animate the state.

In this way, within the deformed Hegelian perspective, the universality of the state ambit penetrates into every area of private and civil life and, overturning their nature, presumes to demonstrate how each of these is informed by a principle of life that is in no way particularistic and egoistic.

> Family and civil society are the premises of the state; they are the genuinely active elements, but in speculative philosophy things are inverted. [...] Family and civil society constitute themselves as the state. They are the driving force [*das Treibende*]. According to Hegel, they are on the contrary produced by the actual idea. It is not the course of their own life which unites them in the state; on the contrary, it is the idea which in the

6 *MECW* 3, pp. 31–2.

7 *MECW* 3, p. 91.

> course of its life has separated them off from itself. [...] They are entities determined by a third party, not self-determined entities.[8]

Thus conceived, it is obvious that, for Marx, this universalisation cannot help but be misleading and fallacious, on a par with, more generally and structurally, all of Hegel's philosophy. The latter – by now evaluated and reduced by Marx, according to the interpretative paradigm provided to him by Feuerbach, to mere speculative theology – anticipates and presupposes the Idea over reality. For this reason, the rational in Hegel, rather than being the explanation of the more proper and intrinsic structure of the real, is a *logos* separated from reality, which subsumes its various environs, identifying with them only externally.

According to Marx, therefore, the mystification through inversion of the order of the real achieved by Hegel is radical. The true subjects of the real, men in flesh and blood, are reduced to predicates of pure thought which, isolated from the concreteness of life, becomes the absolute Idea. Thus, thought, which is an attribute, an activity enacted by human beings, is raised from being a predicate to being a subject. This inversion of subject and predicate – Marx adds – in turn implies the false universalisation of a given element of concrete life insofar as the new subject, abstract and hypothesised, cannot be filled with content other than by drawing on the concrete life which it has reduced to an emanation of itself. However, by making it participate through this act in its universality, it is thereby legitimised and valorised in everyone's eyes:

> Reality is expressed not as itself but as another reality. Ordinary empirical fact has not its own but an alien spirit for its law; whereas the form of existence of the actual idea is not an actuality evolved from itself, but ordinary empirical fact. [...] Family and civil society are the premises of the state; they are the genuinely active elements, but in speculative philosophy things are inverted. [...] Empirical actuality is thus accepted as it is. It is also expressed as rational, but it is not rational on account of its own reason, but because the empirical fact in its empirical existence has a different significance from it itself. The fact which is taken as a point of departure is not conceived as such, but as a mystical result. The actual becomes a phenomenon, but the idea has no other content than this phenomenon.[9]

---

8 *MECW* 3, pp. 8–9.

9 Ibid.

In the same way, in Hegel's treatment of the concept of 'sovereignty', it is separated from its true subject, which, for Marx, is none other than the people in the totality of its existence. It becomes an entirely abstract and empty category which, as in Hegel's theory of monarchy, instead of being the expression of the power of all, finds its effective and paradoxical existence in the will of a single man, distinct from all the others and invested with a universal value, which is precisely the monarchy.

> Sovereignty, the essential feature of the state, is treated to begin with as an independent entity, is objectified. Then, of course, this objective entity has to become a subject again. This subject then appears, however, as a self-incarnation of sovereignty; whereas sovereignty is nothing but the objectified mind of the subjects of the state. [...] 'Political reason' and 'political consciousness' are a 'single' empirical person to the exclusion of all others; but this personified reason has no content other than the abstraction of the 'I will'. *L'état c'est moi.*[10]

Hegel does not attribute sovereignty, or decision-making will, to the true subject – namely, the people as a whole, as occurs in democracy – but to a single being. In order to legitimise this arbitrary and conservative choice, in order to justify the monarchical institution, he separates sovereignty and will from their real subjects – who are the many ones of the people – thereby translating them into abstract factors which, in their ideality and purity, organise and move the real and which, by a mystical force, are able to incarnate themselves and be symbolised in the body of a single individual. The sovereignty of the state, rather than depending on the participation and will of all its citizens, thus depends on a person chosen by right of birth or, in other words, by an entirely casual event of nature.

> Hence, instead of the state being brought forth as the supreme actuality of the person, as the supreme social actuality of man, one single empirical man, the empirical person, is brought forth as the supreme actuality of the state. This perversion of the subjective into the objective and of the objective into the subjective [...] [has the] inevitable outcome [...] that an empirical existent is uncritically accepted as the actual truth of the idea.[11]

---

10 *MECW* 3, pp. 24–6.

11 *MECW* 3, p. 39.

Similarly, Hegel's treatment of governing power and the significance that the body of state employees and functionaries assumes within it, due to their dedication to the interests and good of the public which distinguishes them, is, for Marx, nothing other than the legitimising of a strictly private and particularistic interest which is in reality the effective content of the bureaucrat's life. The culture of the civil servant, who must demonstrate his ability in public affairs by passing examinations, is, for Marx, in reality a purely bureaucratic knowledge; due to its formality, it can only place itself alongside real life, without coming into contact with it. The true moving force of this subordination to form is only the enticement of a career and promotion. Thus, that which apparently presents itself under the guise of a public and disinterested spirit is only the dissimulation of a petty and obtusely private behaviour.

> The bureaucracy has the state, the spiritual essence of society, in its possession, as its private property. The general spirit of the bureaucracy is the secret, the mystery, preserved within itself by the hierarchy and against the outside world by being a closed corporation. [...] Hence, authority is the basis of its knowledge, and the deification of authority is its conviction. Within the bureaucracy itself, however, spiritualism becomes crass materialism, the materialism of passive obedience, of faith in authority, of the mechanism of fixed and formalistic behaviour, and of fixed principles, views and traditions. In the case of the individual bureaucrat, the state objective turns into his private objective, into a chasing after higher posts, the making of a career.[12]

However, for Marx, the examination of legislative power also confirms the transcription of the theoretical set-up of Hegel's *Philosophy of Right* of the irrationality of the modern real because, here again, the inversion of concrete subject and abstract predicate leads to the legitimisation – according to its appearance of universal validity – of a content that, rather than being universal, is particular and private.

In the *Philosophy of Right*, Hegel constructs legislative power on the participation in it – beyond the other two powers of the state (the monarchical power which, in his view, makes the final decision with respect to the laws and the governing power which enjoys a consultative role) – of the third power consisting of the elements of the estates [*ständische Element*]. Power and political repres-

12 *MECW* 3, p. 47.

entation are based on the articulation of the estates, according to which, for Hegel, as for its various economic and institutional needs, modern civil society is already articulated: the 'substantial estate' linked to agriculture, the 'industrial estate' consisting of artisans, manufacturing managers and commercial traders, and the 'universal estate' composed of civil servants and state functionaries. Thus, in Hegel's concept of legislative power, if the universal estate due to the very nature of its work is concerned with the affairs of the state and, as such, is consulted for its competencies in drawing up laws, the other two orders respectively generate two legislative houses: one formed of delegates of the various elements of the industrial class and the other formed – without delegation however – by hereditary landowners who, through the hereditary right of being the firstborn, pass their land on from generation to generation. In this way, with the institution of inalienable land ownership, life is given within the heart of modern civil society (which, due to its industrial and mercantile economy, appears as highly unstable) to a social body which is, in contrast, firmly solid according to the degree to which this class does not depend economically either on public income or the changing events of alienable private property, or on the family connections which would lead to the possibility of sub-division and the dispersion, therefore, of the inheritance amongst several heirs. These characteristics, reflected at a political-legislative level, permit landowners as such to constitute the members of one of the two houses of legislative power.

For Marx, instead, the institution of a legislative house formed by landowners who participate in this as a result of hereditary privilege is the most evident sign of the fact that in the heart of the 'public' there would be the defence of the 'private' interests of the few rather than those of all. Thus, private property is that which is established as the effective foundation of the modern state: private property is taken at its greatest level of absoluteness because it is not even conditioned by the bonds of an equal distribution between inheriting children and by the possibility of its transformation into transferable wealth.

> The political constitution at its highest point is therefore the constitution of private property. The supreme political conviction is the conviction of private property. Primogeniture is merely the external appearance of the inner nature of landed property. The fact that it is inalienable cuts off its social nerves and ensures its isolation from civil society. The fact that it does not pass to their children in accordance with the 'equality of their love for them' frees it, makes it independent even of the smaller society, the natural society of the family [...]. Primogeniture is private property

> become a religion to itself, lost in itself, elated by its own independence and power.[13]

Furthermore, even the second legislative house foreseen in Hegel's *Philosophy of Right* – the corporations' house or, more precisely, of their deputies – is evidence, for Marx, of the improper and manipulative manner in which Hegel attempts to unify and mediate the modern division that exists between public and private spheres. It is impossible to overcome modern dualism by redeploying an ancient constitution such as that based on orders belonging to a period when estates and corporations had a political role that was the direct emanation of their economic-social position, in a society in which the private was immediately public.

The authentic modern constitution cannot be one based on deputations or orders, but, rather, can only be a representative one. It is undoubtedly true that, for Marx at the time, the election of representatives who will then form a separate body distanced from the daily life of those giving them their mandate confirms and explains the structural separateness of modernity's civil and political life. However, it is equally true that this division can be overcome precisely by means of its most extreme radicalisation or, in other words, with the extension to all of election rights in both active and passive senses, which, by placing those elected in a condition of substantial continuity with their electors, would remove the distance that perpetuates the separation of state and civil society.

> Civil society has really raised itself to abstraction from itself, to political being as its true, general, essential mode of being only in elections unlimited both in respect of the franchise and the right to be elected. But the completion of this abstraction is at the same time the transcendence of the abstraction. [...] Electoral reform within the abstract political state is therefore the demand for its dissolution, but also for the dissolution of civil society.[14]

---

13 *MECW* 3, pp. 98–101.

14 *MECW* 3, p. 121. On the subject of political representation, in the *Kreuznacher Hefte* Marx takes extracts from C.F. Ludwig's *Geschichte der letzten fünfzig Jahre* and from K.W. Lancizolle's *Über Ursachen, Charakter und Folgen der Julitage*. In the latter, in particular (Lancizolle was a professor in the history of law at the University in Berlin and a critic of the modern institution of representation), Marx finds the theorisation of two *Hauptfiktionen* that undermine the essence of the modern representative constitution. The first concerns the abstract nature of the people who, as a subject with the right to vote, must abstract

For Marx, who makes the French Revolution the exemplary site of modern history and the birth of the modern political state, it is legislative power, on the model of the French constituent assembly, that is the determining force in the life of a nation, the power, that is, which most strongly expresses the general will and which transforms, revolutionises and promulgates laws and constitutions.

> The legislature made the French Revolution; in general, wherever it has emerged in its particularity as the dominant element, it has made the great, organic, general revolutions. It has not fought the constitution, but a particular, antiquated constitution, precisely because the legislature was the representative of the people, of the will of the species [*des Gattungswillens*]. The executive, on the other hand, has produced the small revolutions, the retrograde revolutions, the reactions. It has made revolutions not for a new constitution against an old one, but against the constitution, precisely because the executive was the representative of the particular will, of subjective arbitrariness, of the magical part of the will.[15]

But, furthermore, even the greatest possible democratising of the fundamental power of the modern political state also continues to confirm for Marx the aporetic nucleus of modernity: the dualism of *bourgeois* and *citoyen*, of the individual enclosed within his private interest and his universalisation in the abstract heaven of politics. Through elections, despite being generalised, individuals continue even in the vastness of their numbers to act and think as individuals. As a result of Marx's humanist organicism and his metaphysics of

---

from all the differences between its members. 'The representative system [rests] on two main fictions. The first: the entirety of all the members of a state, the entire population, represents a large community, a properly juridical or mystical persona [...]. Here all the real associations and articulations completely disappear' (von Lancizolle 1831, pp. 97–9). The second concerns the connection between those mandating and the deputies that dissolves and becomes inexistent given that the former have no control over and ability to condition the latter. 'The other fiction concerns the method with which the supposed juridical persona of the people becomes visible and acts [...]. These representatives, of which each is to be considered as mandated, not of the single province or the single electoral county, but of the mystical All, could not be linked to any instruction, to any task set by those mandating but would have, inversely, unconditional power. That which they decide as a majority must be considered as the united will of the nation' (pp. 99–100). See Mustè 1981–2.

15 *MECW* 3, p. 57.

the people, the individual *qua* participant in the *Gattungswesen* is already originally the entirety and, therefore, has no need of participating in the general affairs of any transition or access to a specifically political moment of his life.

> 'All should not individually participate in deliberating and deciding on the general affairs of the state', for the 'individuals' participate in deliberating and deciding on the general affairs as 'all', i.e., within the society and as members of society. Not all individually, but the individuals as all.[16]

Thus, any possible reflection on the theory of the division of powers, just as any possible concrete articulation of the institutions of a state, is fairly distant from Marx's thought at this time. Each positive thematisation in this sense would do nothing more than confirm the existence of a political state separated from the civil society, which he wants to overcome and negate.

There is no doubt that, in the *Critique*, Marx makes an impassioned choice and evaluation of democracy that does not appear anywhere else in his works. 'Similarly, democracy is the essence of all state constitutions – socialised man as a particular state constitution. Democracy stands to the other constitutions as the genus stands to its species'.[17] In contrast to other political constitutions, the inversion of the subject and predicate does not take place in democracy. It is the self-determination of the people, of man: 'democracy starts from man and makes the state objectified man. Just as it is not religion which creates man but man who creates religion, so it is not the constitution which creates the people but the people which creates the constitution'.[18] However, if an attempt is then made to understand analytically what democracy consists in and how it is organised according to the young Marx, it is possible to see to what degree his discourse renders every concrete indication futile and his organic ontology of the 'species-people' prevents any articulation and real differentiation of its own unity. Furthermore, as we already know from the *Rheinische Zeitung*, the only possibility for Marx to conceive of a state-institutional moment beginning with the organicity of a *Volk* is that of seeing the state as the moment in which a people most becomes aware of itself and, in this mirroring, it most coincides with its universal nature. However, the role of a mirror is precisely only to reflect that of which it is a reflection. As a consequence, the assumed autonomy and the consistency of the reality of the state are dissolved in the universality of the

---

16 *MECW* 3, p. 116.

17 *MECW* 3, p. 30.

18 Ibid.

subject of which it is only the reflective instrument of self-consciousness. Thus, Marx's state, in order to avoid the abstract separateness of the modern political state, attempts, on the one hand, to maintain a specificity of existence (to be a particular moment in the life of a people, alongside the other moments, with a determinate reflexive role); but – and herein lies the *aporia* that confronts Marx's reasoning – it is a moment which in the very instant in which it is posited dissolves in the universal that it reflects.

> In democracy the state as particular is merely particular; as general, it is the truly general, i.e., not something determinate in distinction from the other content. The French have recently interpreted this as meaning that in true democracy the political state is annihilated. This is correct insofar as the political state *qua* political state, as constitution, no longer passes for the whole.[19]

In terms of organic solutions, democracy, for Marx, is here the most advanced political form of the state because here the people, the true subject of social life, imposes itself as an organic totality that does not permit its particular manifestations of life to be separated into abstract and separate institutions. Here the political state effectively coincides, for Marx, with the people itself. It is its self-representation and is distinguished from other manifestations, even if organic, of popular life only because the universalist mirroring of the people is more complete here than elsewhere. Otherwise, the political state, in its presumed and persistent separateness, has no reason to exist for Marx and should be extinguished.[20]

## 2 The Modern World as a Binary World

All Marx's criticism in the 1843 *Critique of Hegel's Philosophy of Right* is therefore based on the most profound identity that he sees reflected in the abstraction

---

19 Ibid.

20 'In democracy the political state, which stands alongside this content and distinguishes itself from it, is itself merely a particular content and particular form of existence of the people' (Ibid). Marx had already written about this subject in the *Rheinische Zeitung*: 'Representation must not be conceived as the representation of something that is not the people itself. It must be conceived only as the people's *self-representation* as a state action which, not being its sole, exceptional state action, is distinguished from other expressions of its state life merely by the universality of its content' (*MECW* 1, p. 306).

of the Hegelian idea and the abstraction of the modern political state. The relationship of the state with the material and concrete reality of civil society is structured according to a process that is entirely equal to that of Hegel's idea in relation to the real and sensuous world, which is articulated through these four moments:

1) The constitution of the universal as subject and abstract hypostasis as opposed to the world of particulars;
2) The filling of the universal, due to its constitutional emptiness, with the content of these particulars;
3) The reduction of particulars to predicates – or, in other words, to mere emanation and incarnation of the universal;
4) But, at the same time, their legitimation and absolutisation through the transition and translation of their immediate and unreflected reality into the form of the universal.[21]

21 This is the outline that Della Volpe also extracts from Marx's 1843 text, summarising the essential passages of what he sees as Marx's already fully materialistic logic in the following: 1) superseding Hegel's idealism through Feuerbach's criticism of the inversion of the concrete subject into abstract subject taken as the idea; and 2) surpassing the limits of Feuerbach's criticism of Hegel through the discovery not only of the inversion of the concrete into the abstract but rather, and more so, of the abstract into the concrete, since, in contrast to Feuerbach, Marx in his *Critique* had discovered the way in which ideal abstraction, once made the subject (which is as far as Feuerbach goes) is then filled, misleadingly, with concrete material empirically and historically. This interpretation of Marx's logic can be countered by the objections that: 1) the critical model of misleading legitimisation of an empirically given content through the juxtaposition of universal form had already been identified by Hegel himself, beginning with his early writings; and 2) Feuerbach had already denounced, over and above the inversion of the concrete into the abstract, the spiritualisation and legitimisation of the resultant empiricism. See, in this sense, the following passage from Feuerbach's essay of 1839, 'Towards a Critique of Hegel's Philosophy': 'The Hegelian system is the absolute self-externalization of reason, a state of affairs that expresses itself, among other things, in the fact that the empirical character of his natural law is pure speculation (for example, he even concludes with the rights of primogeniture!)' (Feuerbach 1972, p. 68). On the other hand, the theme of the dogmatic infinitisation of a finite had been at work in Feuerbach's reflections since the 1830 *Thoughts on Death and Immortality*, where every historical-cultural and theological-religious pathology of the human being refers back to the ontological sin of the individual who wants to absolutise its singularity in contrast to its participation in and integration with the human species. The fundamental limitation, in my opinion, of Della Volpe's interpretation of Marx thus lies in not having seen, precisely with respect to the subject of false ideological legitimisation, the dependency of Feuerbach and Marx

Beginning from the structural elements of his concept of the Idea, Hegel thus passes, according to Marx, into the specific field of social and political philosophy, reconciling and rationalising as a coherent unity the modern lacerations between civil society and the political state that, for Marx, instead characterises the modern world in an absolutely incongruous and irrational way. The fundamental contradiction of modernity, for Marx in this period, is not to be found within the economic sphere that refers to civil society, as it will soon become in the development of his thought, but rather can be identified in the contrast that exists between civil society and the political state. This is because he sees the substance of modern history as consisting in the formation and construction of the state, just as in the contemporaneous creation of civil society and its autonomisation from the state.

Medieval society and pre-modern estate-based society were characterised by a polycentricism of powers: that is, by the existence of orders and corporations equipped with an autonomous jurisdictional capacity that had hindered, on the one hand, the formation of a sovereign unified state power and, on the other, with their communitarian structure, the emergence of economic individualism and free private initiative.[22] Only with modern society are civil society and the political state contemporaneously generated, that is, there is a reduction to the private sphere, without jurisdictional power, of the economic, work and contemporary institution of the public spheres as a place of universal legislation that promulgates laws and rights that are valid, without exception, for all. For Marx, this distinction of the modern into two fundamental areas – one regulated only by private rights and one regulated only by public rights – with the elimination of all privileged and corporative legislation is a crucial event eponymous with modern history and represented above all by the French Revolution.

> The real transformation of the political estates into civil estates took place in the absolute monarchy. The bureaucracy maintained the notion of unity against the various states within the state. Nevertheless, the

on Hegel, and in not having investigated to what degree the claim of materialism in Marx's early writings, of the world of sensibility and the concreteness of men in flesh and blood, effectively refers to the metaphysical idea of the *menschliche Gattung* (or man as a natural-generic entity), which Marx takes from Feuerbach and in which the human being is conceived of as a subject whose individuality is immediately universal and whose corporeal-sensible finitude is only the instrument of objectivising and realising the infinite. On this, see my essays Finelli 1991 and 1995.

22 See Schiera 1992.

> social difference of the estates, even alongside the bureaucracy of the absolute executive power, remained a political difference, political within and alongside the bureaucracy of the absolute executive power. Only the French Revolution completed the transformation of the political into social estates, or changed the differences of estate of civil society into mere social differences, into differences of civil life which are without significance in political life. With that the separation of political life from civil society was completed.[23]

The works of history and politics that Marx read and summarised in the *Kreuznacher Hefte* are sufficient evidence, beyond the 1843 *Critique* itself, of the centrality of his interest in the French Revolution seen as a watershed of history, due to its establishment of a fundamentally different meaning of that which is properly 'political' and that which is properly 'civil'.

However, if the modern society that emerged from the French Revolution forcibly expelled the universal from the ambit defined as civil society, positing it solely within the ambit of the political state, it must necessarily, according to Marx, result in a schism in the foundation of modernity; or, in other words, in the opposition between one sphere of life regulated only by private and individual interests and another ambit destined to be concerned solely with universal interests. The foundation of the modern is, therefore, a distinction between civil society and the political state that is radicalised up until opposition as a consequence of the extreme polarisation that the public and private undergo in their inevitable process of separation. This is the basic thesis that Marx derives from his study of modern history. Two further central theories of the 1843 *Critique* also derive from it:

1) The arbitrary and amorphous character of modern civil society insofar as it lacks the universal that is located entirely and only in the political state and, therefore, lacks its own structure and its own intrinsic order;
2) Consequently, in a mirror image, the entirely only formal character of the modern political state as the horizon of a universality which, leaving the sphere of material and concrete life of civil society outside itself, is of a merely apparent and decorative nature.

If, as a result of the differentiation and liberation of the political state that is the reason for its creation, modern civil society is deprived of any form

23 *MECW* 3, pp. 79–80.

of universalisation or any beginning of a structure that goes beyond private interests, it follows that its sole principle is that of egoism and individualism. 'Present-day civil society is the realised principle of individualism; the individual existence is the final goal; activity, work, content, etc., are mere means'.[24] Once the private individual has established itself as the foundation of modern civil society, it must not contain any stable organisational method. Its articulations are fluid, variable and arbitrary because they depend on constantly varying inclinations and interests of the individual. Nor, on the other hand, is there any structuration by ordering, as occurred in pre-modern society, whose divisions were created by a precise distinction between needs, work and social roles. Modern differences arise only on the basis of 'money' and 'culture', that is, according to criteria that may also possess a reality beyond the individual but whose nature, by definition, are mobile and lacking in any stable objectivity.

> The estates of civil society likewise were transformed in the process: civil society was changed by its separation from political society. Estate [*Stand*] in the medieval sense continued only within the bureaucracy itself, where civil and political position are directly identical. As against this stands civil society as civil estate. Difference of estate here is no longer a difference of needs and of work as independent bodies. The only general, superficial and formal difference still remaining here is that of town and country. Within society itself, however, the difference was developed in mobile and not fixed circles, of which free choice is the principle. Money and education are the main criteria [...]. The estate of civil society has for its principle neither need, that is, a natural element, nor politics. It consists of separate masses which form fleetingly and whose very formation is arbitrary and does not amount to an organization.[25]

Thus, for the young Marx, it is neither need, nor labour, nor politics that constitutes the organisational criteria of modern civil society, in contrast to estate-based society where the differences between orders and professions was articulated in a stable manner in accordance with these principles. The very performance of labour has now ceased to be the characteristic of some orders when compared with others since it has become a general horizon and,

24 *MECW* 3, p. 81.

25 *MECW* 3, p. 80, translation modified.

therefore, undifferentiated, of creating and destroying differences between individuals. Nor did the performance of labour organically link the subject in question to a community of men, as still took place in the system of corporations and orders. Since in modern society, Marx noted, using a play on words between *Stand* as synonymous with order (or estate) and *Stand* as synonymous with condition, the performance of any profession or work can be indifferently connected to very differing levels on the social scale. The foundation of modern civil society is, therefore, entirely extra-social and, in this sense, reverts to being merely naturalistic: it is simply the individualist principle of pleasure alone. This occurs to such an extent that the members of civil society become men – that is, subjects capable of a relationships and social participation – only as citizens, namely, when they abandon their locations in civil society and think of themselves as members of the political state.

> Only one thing is characteristic, namely, that lack of property and the estate of direct labour, of concrete labour, form not so much an estate of civil society as the ground upon which its circles rest and move. [...] The present-day estate of society already shows its difference from the earlier estate of civil society in that it does not hold the individual as it formerly did as something communal, as a community [*Gemeinwesen*], but that it is partly accident, partly the work and so on of the individual which does, or does not, keep him in his estate, an estate which is itself only an external quality of the individual, being neither inherent in his labour nor standing to him in fixed relationships as an objective community organised according to rigid laws. It stands, rather, in no sort of real relation to his material actions, to his real standing. The physician does not form a special estate within civil society. One merchant belongs to a different estate from another, to a different social position. For just as civil society is separated from political society, so civil society has within itself become divided into estate and social position, however many relations may occur between them. The principle of the civil estate or of civil society is enjoyment and the capacity to enjoy. In his political significance the member of civil society frees himself from his estate, his true civil position; it is only here that he acquires importance as a human being, or that his quality as member of the state, as social being, appears as his human quality. For all his other qualities in civil society appear inessential to the human being, the individual, as external qualities which indeed are necessary for his existence in the whole, i.e., as a link with the whole, but a link that he can just as well throw away again. (Present-day civil society

> is the realised principle of individualism; the individual existence is the final goal; activity, work, content, etc., are mere means).[26]

For this Marx, therefore, basing himself on a theoretical approach that is a long way from what will become his future thought, the individual is the principle of modern civil society, to such an extreme and radical degree that all social links rather than constituting the essence of the individual (as he will theorise a few years later in his sixth thesis on Feuerbach) instead are only the most external and incidental side that the individual can leave aside and take up again according to their needs and choices. On the other hand, it is the modern state that becomes the container of the universal, of that relationship between human beings that is excluded from civil society as an environment dominated by individualism. However, at the same time, the universal nature of the state can only be formal or, in other words, apparent and unreal, because, due to belonging to another sphere, to another ontological domain constituted by a different principle, it is unable to penetrate into the environment which opposes it in any way. It is reduced, by this limited extension, to an only partial universal being – that is, to a universal which is not really such and which, due to its lack of reality, inevitably returns to being concerned and filled with a content consisting only of particular and private interests (as seen in Marx's critical comments on sovereign, government and legislative powers).

Thus, as the modern state is intrinsically formal, all its characteristics must also be formal. Among these are equality and common ownership of rights and duties that are extended to all its members, not as private individuals [*bourgeois*] with their distinguishing economic conditions that render them unequal in civil society, but rather as citizens [*citoyens*] and members of equal standing in the political state. Just as the Christian religion unites and makes all men brothers not on earth but only in heaven, thus the modern state renders individuals equal – although remaining unequal in the material and concrete life of civil society – only in the abstractions and exceptional nature of political life.

> This political act is a complete transubstantiation. In it, civil society must completely give itself up as civil society, as civil estate, and assert an aspect of its essence which not only has nothing in common with the real civil existence of its essence but stands in opposition to it. [...] Hence, in order to behave as an actual citizen of the state, and to attain political

26 *MECW* 3, pp. 80–1.

> significance and effectiveness, he [the individual] must step out of his civil reality, disregard it, and withdraw from this whole organisation into his individuality; for the sole existence which he finds for his citizenship of the state [*Staatbürgertum*] is his sheer, blank individuality, since the existence of the state as executive is complete without him, and his existence in civil society is complete without the state.

Thus, for Marx in the *Critique*, the universal nature of the modern state is formal in two distinct but related senses: on the one hand, because that which supposedly constitutes the public interest is revealed as consisting of private interests and, on the other, because the equality of citizens, as members of the state, is located only on the margins, leaving their inequalities as members of civil society intact. Consequently, this formalism generates two ideological effects: the dissimulation of a content of private interests through the form and container of public interests and the repression of the differences between private subjects through the enactment of an equality that lives not in the reality of daily life but only in heaven and on the Sunday of politics. The young Marx's theory of state formalism, it must be added, has nothing to do with the classic liberal concept of the state as the 'form' according to which (it is sufficient to think of Locke and Kant) the activities of the state must coincide with a merely regulatory role from outside the activities of all individuals who are, in themselves, private and unquestionable (given that the main and fundamental value of the modern world is the freedom of the individual). In the tradition of the political philosophy of liberalism, the state must never intervene to assign content and sense to the life choices of its citizens – since, in this case, it would become a paternalistic and authoritarian state – but can only prevent the life choices of an individual from limiting and damaging the choices and possibilities for existence of all others. Beginning with the primacy and uniqueness of the value of freedom, classical liberalism thus theorises the legitimacy of a merely formal and negative state, in the sense that it does not say what must be done but only that which must not, and in the sense that, by not intervening regarding the content of individual ways of living, it only ensures that the form of its negative provisions will have universal extension and validity precisely through the form of law.

It is clear that, beyond the traditions of juridical-political formalism, the young Marx inaugurated his own concept of the state as form: a form that is not a juridical-negative form (in the sense of the liberal state and the guarantee of individual freedom), but a form that is dissimulating and repressing (in the sense of the confirmation of the inequalities and asymmetries of real civil life). The modern political state, for Marx, is the ambit of mere form because it is unable to carry out a real universal elaboration of the substance of civil society's life. Dissimulation and repression as the only possible figures of the contemporaneous presence of the two environments explain (given the absence of a single point of real and positive mediation and integration) even more the fact that the nexus between civil society and the political state are only those of extraneousness and opposition. For Marx, in his 1843 *Critique*, a radical division thus characterises the modern world,[27] which Hegel in his *Philosophy of Right* had instead presented as a world of organicity and the harmonic co-presence of different spheres. Hegel's political philosophy is thus characterised according to Marx by two theoretical acts of profound misrepresentation of reality: the claim to be one that which, on the contrary, is marked by division, and the identification of that one and its presumed organicity with the historical institutions of the Prussian state which is thus celebrated as the rationality of the modern state as such.

---

27 Colletti (1974, p. 70) quotes a passage from Marx's 1843 *Critique* as an example of real opposition, where the opposites are supposed to be real entities or forces, without any relationship with the vagueness of dialectics: 'Real extremes cannot be mediated precisely because they are real extremes. Nor do they require mediation, for they are opposed in essence. They have nothing in common, they do not need each other, they do not supplement each other' (*MECW* 3, p. 88). He thereby proves nothing more than how an empiricist point of view, such as his own, creates huge misunderstandings of Marx's text. For the opposites to which Marx refers in the quoted passage are not at all entities of an empirical-factual nature but rather *essences* [*Wesen*] whose nature is absolute and universal. It is only the uniqueness and unconditional nature of essence, its absolute consisting of itself, that effectively permits Marx in these pages to claim that every opposite (*qua* essence) includes in itself all the conditions of its possibility of existence and, as such 'the one does not have in its own bosom the longing for, the need for, the anticipation of the other' (ibid.). Thus, in contrast to Colletti's interpretation, which does not perceive the metaphysics of the essence (or of species) on which all Marx's reasoning is based in the quoted passage and in the entirety of the *Critique*, the real opposition of essence is not, for Marx here, the absence of contradiction but, rather, the greatest contradiction possible (due to the fundamental, absolute heterogeneity, the one excluding the other) that exists between two universals. For Marx, what happens to modern reality is absolutely contradictory, despite Hegel's efforts to bring it back to unity, precisely because it exists between civil society, whose essential principle is individualism, and the political state, whose essential principle is universalism. On the other hand, the distance between the early Marx and that of *Capital* can be measured by the theory of contradiction which, from the division between individual and species and the organic metaphysics to which this refers, later becomes a theory of the labour power as the subject of right and *contemporaneously* as the deprivation of the same. On Colletti's interpretation of Marx's works, I refer to my essays Finelli 1990a and 1991.

From this summary, despite its schematic nature, the premise presented at the beginning of this chapter should, I hope, be sufficiently apparent: in other words, that the logic used by Marx in writing his anti-Hegelian pages in 1843 is none other than the genetic-critical logic (in the sense of the inversion of subject and predicate) theorised by Feuerbach. The 1843 *Critique* consists in extending the concept of alienation used by Feuerbach in investigating the nature of religion and Hegelian philosophy to the analysis of the modern state. Furthermore, just as Feuerbach had bound together (according to the unity of his critical method) the alienation of the Hegelian Idea and the alienation of a theological God, thus Marx binds together in his criticism the separateness from concrete reality of both Hegel's Idea and the modern state. In the image created by Marx at this time, the modern state is an institution whose universality is entirely abstract, just as is Feuerbach's God. It is created by the atomistic fragmentation of a community of species which, having lost consciousness of its unity, cannot help but project and deposit this same unity in a power that is both foreign and in contrast to itself. Civil society and the political state, the individual and the universal, are divided and opposed in the same way that real life and the life of the Idea are in an estranged and opposed relationship in Hegelian philosophy.

The state is, therefore, a hypostasis fallen into reality, a universal nurtured by humanity's alienation, and which, due to the abstract quality of its nature, stands as a dominating and authoritarian pole in opposition to the concrete life of human beings. We will see later the contradictions and theoretical difficulties within which Marx's discourse becomes enveloped in relation to this real abstraction. For now, it is sufficient to note that this need to follow Feuerbach's logic leads Marx to a paradoxical theory that the modern world multiplies into two worlds animated by two absolutely heterogeneous logics: that of civil society, based on the most extreme form of individualism; and that of the political state, based on a universalism that entirely ignores the individual (although it then fills itself in the void of its abstract purity with solely private and partisan interests). The modern world thus breaks up and divides into the opposition of two spheres that have no point of contact or mediation and which Hegel had only presumed to reconcile and recompose as one.

At this stage, it is clear that our path cannot avoid an encounter with Hegel's *Philosophy of Right* and his theorisation of the nexus of civil society and the political state as the particular and original characteristic of modernity. It is indispensible to dwell on this a little in order to evaluate the validity of Marx's parricide and also the type of economic and political theory that the young Marx in this way gave to the tradition of modern culture.

## 3 Hegel and Modern Civil Society[28]

As is known, it was Hegel who first introduced and made famous the distinction between civil society and the political state while, generally speaking, before his work, the concept of *societas civilis* coincided with that of political society insofar as it was distinct from and in contrast to *societas naturalis*. However, with his 1821 *Philosophy of Right* (and the second edition of his 1827 *Encyclopaedia*), Hegel introduces the concept of civil society [*bürgerliche Gesellschaft*] (in the section of objective spirit dedicated to 'ethics') as an autonomous part of his theoretical system and as a sphere of society clearly distinct from, on the one hand, the family and, on the other, the political state. What should immediately be pointed out with respect to our subject is that, in contrast to Marx's arguments, for Hegel the fabric of modern civil society is not limited to the single principle of individuality but, rather, also requires for its existence a dimension beyond the individual, which Hegel here defines as the principle of universality.

> The concrete person, who as particular is an end to himself [...] is one of the principles of civil society. But the particular person is essentially connected with others. Hence each establishes and satisfies himself by means of others, and so must call in the assistance of the form of universality. This universality is the other principle of civil society.[29]

It was not that Hegel had not already, in his early works in the Jena period, meditated and written on the economic and moral role of the *bourgeois* and that area of reciprocal and general interdependency which he saw as constituted by the market and exchange system of modern society. His 1802 essay 'Über die wissenschaftlichen Behandlungsarten des Naturrechts' ['On the Scientific Way of Treating Natural Right'] already refers to the sphere of the 'difference of wants and work' that exists 'in the rights and justice of possession and property',[30] just as the so-called *System der Sittlichkeit* of 1802–3 takes as its subject the 'system of needs', defined as a 'system of universal physical dependence on one another'.[31] The two lecture series of the Jena period – of 1803–4 and 1805–6, respectively, on the *Naturphilosophie und Philosophie des Geistes* – should also be remembered.

---

28 The text of this section repeats, with some modifications, Finelli 1999.

29 Hegel 2005, p. 96 (*PR*, §182).

30 Hegel 1971, p. 105. See Hegel 1975b.

31 Hegel 1979, p. 165.

However, what is lacking in all these works is Hegel's theorisation (which is present only beginning with the *Philosophy of Right*) of the capacity for self-reproduction and self-regulation of such an ambit of social life as a structural possibility, autonomous from the actions of government and political institutions, of guaranteeing to its components, through specific automatisms and specific forms of administration and organisation, well-being and security of existence. The autonomy that *bürgerliche Gesellschaft* progressively achieves during Hegel's work is intrinsically connected to the way in which its environment is determined as based on specific legalities which, be they of a causality that is natural-unintentional or ethical-intentional, attribute consistency and coherence to that determinate (and relatively enclosed in itself) sphere of sociality and the problems that are generated within it.

The *bürgerliche Gesellschaft* as a distinct environment consistent with reality is articulated in the *Philosophy of Right* according to a tripartite division: a) the system of needs; b) the administration of justice; and c) the police and corporations. Now, what must be briefly examined here is to which form of legality each of these sub-totalities refers, and the extent to which and in what way their multiplicities can effectively form a unitary and non-contradictory logic of the entire sphere of life and institutions, which Hegel so clearly saw as distinct from the family and the political state.

### 3.1 *The System of Needs and Classical Political Economy*

The *System der Bedürfnisse* [system of needs] is defined by Hegel in §188 of the *Philosophy of Right* as the area of reciprocal satisfaction of needs through work and, more precisely as 'the recasting of need, and the satisfaction of the individual through his work, through the work of all others, and through the satisfaction of their needs. This is a system of needs'.[32] This means that, within this ambit, the principle of social integration coincides with the market, with the exchange of goods between single producers and private owners and that, within this perspective, Hegel accepts and welcomes the peculiar legality that political economy has defined and fixed as belonging to modern mercantile society. 'Economy' is obviously understood here as a new science and no longer in the traditional and classical sense of the expression, as the science of the *oíkos*, linked to the administration of the house. Modern political economy is a science that refers to the human community beyond the family; precisely because it refers to the polis, it is political economy. 'It is the task of political science [...] to detect the laws governing the movement of the masses in the

32 Hegel 2005, p. 100 (*PR*, §188), translation modified.

intricacy of their qualitative and quantitative relations. This science has sprung from the soil of modern times'.[33]

On the page quoted above, Hegel refers to Smith, Say and Ricardo as the fundamental authors of this new science. However, it should be remembered that, while there are no other references to the latter two economists in any of Hegel's other works (thus, we might doubt whether Hegel had first-hand knowledge of their works), his direct knowledge of *The Wealth of Nations* is documented in the Jena Lectures of 1803–4. In these lectures, in the section dealing with the division of labour and, in particular, with the famous example of pin manufacture, there appears in the margin the name 'Smith' citing the page number of the original text by the Scottish author ('Smith. p. 8').[34] References to Smith's example of pin manufacture, furthermore, are widespread throughout Hegel's works. They reappear in the Jena Lectures of 1805–6 and in the Lectures on the Philosophy of Right of 1817–18, 1818–19, 1819–20, 1822–3 and 1825–6, even if Adam Smith's name is not always explicitly quoted.[35]

It is precisely the concept of the division of labour – in the twofold meaning assigned to the term by Smith, and used by him indiscriminately, of social division (as the distribution of individual labour activities between the members of an entire social body) and technical division (as the parcelling out of functions within a single labour process) – that constitutes the essential horizon within which Hegel theorises civil society as a system of needs. It is thus the importance that the Scottish thinker assumes in Hegel's economic and social philosophy, precisely through his concept of the division of labour, that obliges us to consider carefully the basic foundations of Smith's more specifically economic works.

Adam Smith's theory of modern mercantile society, in *An Inquiry into the Nature and Causes of the Wealth of Nations* (1776), is essentially analytical. He begins from an originary principle, namely, the propensity that man apparently naturally possesses – 'the propensity to truck, barter, and exchange one thing

33 Ibid, translation modified.

34 Düsing and Kimmerle in their notes to Vol. 6 of Hegel's *Gesammelte Werke*, containing the *Jenaer Systementwürfe I*, convincingly argue that Hegel's citation refers to the English edition of Smith's *Wealth of Nations* present in Hegel's private library and not to the German translation by C. Garve (Breslau 1794–6).

35 For the Jena *Vorlesung* of 1805–6, see Volume 8 of the *Gesammelte Werke*, p. 224. For the other citations, see, respectively, Hegel 1983a, p. 127; Hegel 1976, Vol. 1, p. 314; Hegel 1983b, p. 159; Hegel 1976, Vol. 3, p. 609; Hegel 1976, Vol. 4, p. 502. On Hegel's relationship with English political economy, see Waszek 1986a and 1986b.

for another'.[36] From this principle, he deduces the genesis and establishment of society, conceived of as the outcome of the multiplication and generalisation – precisely through a process of sub-division and analysis – of this initial presupposition.

Therefore, the fundamental structure of society can be found in the division of labour, as the distribution and social integration of various labour activities and also as the technical organisation of the labour processes within each of them. Beginning from his natural propensity – and, therefore, from a cogent and inevitable modality of being – man, open and inclined to barter, determines and specifies his labour activities and at the same time participates in the social nexus, not for altruistic and moral reasons, but through the exchange of his products with those of others. Thus, through the market and exchange, in which each turns the egoism of the other to his own advantage, the division of labour leads according to Smith to the most rationally possible organisation – without waste or injustice – of both society as a whole and the activity of each of its individual members. Exchange, based as it is on the confrontation and connection of individual egoisms, is by definition the exchange of equivalents and, therefore, is such as to guarantee the greatest articulation of the productive structure without the creation of hierarchies and asymmetries.

This model of social integration holds both 'in the rude ages of society' (when the only factor of production is labour and where relative prices are determined by the amount of labour undertaken),[37] and in modern society, characterised by the private appropriation of land and the accumulation of capital, where the exchange value of a commodity must evidently guarantee, alongside remuneration for labour, also an income of profit and revenue. However, over and above the difficulties which Smith's thoughts encounter in formulating a coherent theory of the price of commodities and the distribution of income in modern times and over and above the problems opened up by the different quality of exchange in a pre-modern society based on incorporated labour and that of a modern society based, instead, on commanded labour,[38] the market agreement remains for the Scottish economist the unquestionable horizon of modern socialisation. It is a place where the various individual functions solidly identify with each other to generate a co-operation and a social body that is structurally and naturally just: because, on the one hand, these are composed by means of market automatisms in which, as each depends on all the others

36 Smith 1835, p. 53.
37 Smith 1835, p. 85.
38 See the chapters dedicated to Smith in Napoleoni 1970 and 1976.

and on no-one in particular, decisions (or the fixing of prices) are balanced and impersonal; and, on the other, because they are historically developed and multiplied expressions of an original propensity that assigns to all its realisations the harmony and order of the necessity of nature.

The market, as a social synthesis of commodities, services and productive roles diversified according to the division of labour, is therefore the place of a general will realised by the participation of all in which no-one is *extra pares*. For this reason, whilst establishing the market as a horizon going beyond the will and consciousness of the individual, the general interest that is generated in it cannot contradict individual interests. The market is thus the ambit in which, due to a lack of significant asymmetries, care for individual good achieves, on the basis of itself alone, care for the good of all.

It is precisely in this way that Smith attempted to resolve – through the lack of differences between individual and general interests – the possibly most radical *aporia* of the entire natural law tradition, consisting in the problem of how and why it is possible and necessary to pass from a non-social condition, of nature, to a profoundly different social and institutional condition; in other words, to a condition of culture. The natural law and contractualist tradition, both in the absolutist and in the liberal-democratic versions, has always been profoundly troubled when faced with the difficulty of explaining how, from the necessity (unavoidable by definition) of a law of nature, it is possible to establish the cogency of civil law – whether the latter is established by the authority of one or of all, or whether (*qua* a civil order) it must overcome and transform or only reproduce and guarantee natural order, or whether such a natural order has value as a historical antecedent or as a merely logical antecedent that can nevertheless be proposed to the present as a regulatory value and idea.[39]

When faced with the dualism of natural law with regard to the distance between nature and culture, Smith, however, by positing social being immediately in natural being, aims to remove all problems of transition and mediation: the social nexus is not established through a project or act of will that goes beyond the natural interest of each person in their own survival, since they are rather the explanation and analytical articulation of natural propensities rather than their negation or overcoming.

Human activity is aimed solely at personal well-being. General well-being, as the outcome of the interweaving of individual goods, is an automatic effect, lacking in intentionality and conscious regulation, according to the mechanical nature of a naturalistic order. Should it be objected that, for Smith, a balanced,

39 On this, with particular reference to Rousseau, see Reale 1983.

competitive market is achieved only in the presence of a precise order of public institutions, it should also be remembered that 'the three duties of great importance' that he entrusts to the tate are not in contradiction with an economic system based on individual advantage and *laissez-faire*, because these roles circumscribe precisely the ambit of that which private actions could never undertake and profitably sustain.[40] Thus, that the state should safeguard through the administration of justice the rights of ownership, should provide for national defences and construct and maintain determinate public works is only the guarantee that the market, for its part, without any political intervention, should be balanced in its automatic mechanisms as a 'simple system of natural liberty'.[41]

It should ultimately be emphasised that with his theory of modern mercantile society as an automaton of nature, as well as trying to resolve with the identical natures of natural and social laws the *aporia* of the doctrine of natural law, Smith profoundly participates in the realisation of one of the prime examples of Enlightenment culture inspired by Descartes: that of extending to the ambit of historical and social events the cognitive method of an exact science which, *par excellence*, is that of nature. Thus, if the Cartesian method proposes (in contrast to the cognitive Aristotelian-Scholastic method of proceeding by deduction and definition through genera and differentiae) the connection of analysis and synthesis as the decomposition of a given element into its simple, clear and evident elements – in order to recompose these fundamentals that cannot be further dismantled into a fabric of a new unity of the given element which is now re-designed according to constant and regular, mathematically codified connections – and if, overall, the Enlightenment can be read as an attempt to generalise this methodology within an entire cognitive perspective,[42] then Smith in *The Wealth of Nations* profoundly participates in this project. That is, he participates in the gnoseological-cultural project, inaugurated by Hobbes, of giving a rational reading of life, history and human society, which by means of an analytical capacity to identify first, clear and distinct elements (such as, for example, the segments of social division and labour methods) claims to render the whole as transparent and intelligible, as a mechanical and objective composition (or, in other words, without arbitrariness and personal interventions) of connections with the structure and regularity of law, just as mathematics and physics has done and does for the life of nature.

40 Smith 1822, p. 42.

41 Ibid.

42 See Cassirer 1970, the first chapter in particular.

### 3.2 *The Forms of Modern Socialisation*

In the 1821 *Philosophy of Right*, Hegel fundamentally accepts Smith's concept of a mercantile society established on the social and technical division of labour, but mediates and re-elaborates it in the light of his concept of dialectics, removing it from the analytical inspiration of the classical economist. The substance of this re-elaboration consists in the fact that, for Hegel, if modern society as a 'system of needs' is based on the automatisms of the division of labour and the market, that which is valid in it is not only the principle of particularity (with its actions and interests limited to the individual self) but also that of universality, in the sense that the social nexus must possess a form and method of specific existence that cannot be reduced to the mere repetition and sum of individual interests. Beginning from his concept of totality as the whole endowed with its own particular reality that cannot be reduced to the mere aggregation of the parts, Hegel accepts from Smith that the principle of modern civil society is the existence of individuality which, originally free and autonomous from others, gives life with them, for its own advantage, to the articulation and equivalence of exchange. But he must then also emphasise, with force and originality in relation to the various theories of political and social thought based on empiricism and utilitarianism, that the method of modern socialisation possesses its own logic, which imposes specific forms of elaboration and new modalities of existence on individual praxis.

This logic rests on the becoming a historical institution and an element of reality of that which, for Hegel, is the most fundamental characteristic of intellectual activity: abstraction. Modern socialisation, for him, is effectively synonymous with abstraction. This means that all the individual's private activity, in order to have social visibility and recognition, must conform to an abstract form and measure of existence that, by removing every concrete and individually differentiated element, renders it comparable and interchangeable with the activity of others. In fact, if exchange is the principle of social integration and generalisation, it cannot be established by means of a comparison of details: it must take place through the assumption of characteristics that, not coinciding with anyone's specific activities, must be those of an impersonal objectivity. Neither, as occurs with Smith, can the common measure of commodities and particular labour be only the effect of calculation and accounting: it must, therefore, be only the result of a habit and mental practice, however diffuse and collective it might be. Logical-intellectual abstraction, the outcome of a merely mental generalisation of the world of the multiple and the particular, must become for Hegel a real abstraction or, in other words, one that constructs and organises reality independently of thinking and the abstraction of the individual. The sub-sections of 'the system of needs' in Hegel's *Philosophy of Right* dedicated to 'Need and its Satisfaction' and 'Labour' try to explain how this occurs.

In modern civil society, needs are no longer within that immediate connection of limited needs, labour and satisfaction that are generally factors of every society that still has a strongly naturalistic dimension and are not centred on the mechanism of exchange. In the reciprocal confrontation and recognition inherent in a mercantile perspective, these multiply and particularise and, in this decomposition and particularisation, they become more abstract: just as the means and methods for their satisfaction are specified.[43] However, for Hegel, it is above all labour in civil society, through its social and technical division, that acquires the characteristic of abstraction from personal modalities and behaviour. Through training, labour practices and processes with what would we would call today a high level of standardisation are generalised.[44] Labour becomes abstract precisely when put to work, that is, within the ambit of labour processes in which their divisibility arrives at such a stage as to generate such mechanical and automatic functions that they can be replaced by the automatism of machines.[45]

In order to resolve the fundamental problem of modernity – that is, how to envisage sociality and personal autonomy together – Hegel thus radicalises Smith's concept of the invisible hand and its impersonal nature in the direction of abstraction. The unintentional nexus of the general connections of many members of society – their common and universal interests – are established only as long as they take on a particular mode and physiognomy of existence which is that of abstraction. For Hegel, the principle of the modern world, in contrast to the community-based and undifferentiated ethics of the ancient

43 'The animal has a limited range of ways and means for satisfying his limited wants. Man in his dependence proves his universality and his ability to become independent, firstly, by multiplying his wants and means, and, secondly, by dissecting the concrete want into parts. The parts then become other wants, and through being specialized are more abstract than the first' (Hegel 2005, p. 102; *PR*, § 196).

44 'Practical training, or training by labour['s] [...] action is limited partly by the nature of the material, but chiefly by the caprice of others. It involves an habitual use of skill acquired by practice and implying objective conditions' (Hegel 2005, p. 104; *PR*, § 198).

45 'The universal and the objective in work is to be found in the abstraction which, giving rise to the specialization of means and wants, cause the specialization also of production. This is the division of labour. By it the labour of the individual becomes more simple, his skill in his abstract work greater and the amount he produces larger. [...] Moreover, the abstraction of production causes work to be continually more mechanical, until it is at last possible for man to step out and let the machine take his place' (Hegel 2005, p. 104; *PR*, § 198).

world, is that of the value of individual subjectivity. In modernity, individual interests and general interests can coexist only if the latter takes on an identity and procedures that are configured as external to and beyond the person: that is, as endowed with a specific, abstract and impersonal reality.

However, the exteriority of a determination of the real with respect to the other, exteriority and juxtaposition between individual and universal, are synonymous in Hegel's thoughts with 'nature' in the entirely peculiar sense that this expression has been seen to take on in Hegel's philosophy. Nature does not mean here, as in natural law in general, the place of origin and beginnings, be they then to be maintained and examined in depth or rejected and abandoned, but rather the ambit of reality in which each body, by not accepting in the definition of its own self that alterity which, nonetheless, nurtures and supports it, but seeing in the other only the confines of its own being, is obliged to accept the shape of the whole that surrounds it as only a mechanical and external limitation.

According to this understanding, the life system that comprises civil society is a 'state based on needs':[46] because the relationship that links the one to the others, although consubstantial, is experienced only as an external compulsion and obligation. It is thus that socialisation based on abstraction reproduces in the heart of modern society the ontological statute of nature, implying, consistently with Hegel's design, that this can produce the events that are equal to an overturning of physical nature and, as such, are blind and not immediately controllable.

In the 1802 *System of Ethical Life*, where exchange is also still limited to the mere exchange of excess products of the production of each individual, Hegel writes that in the system of needs people cannot provide for themselves, 'for the totality of [their] needs [...]. Whether the surplus that [they possess gives them] a totality of satisfaction depends on an alien power [*Macht*] over which [they have] no control'.[47] To the individual, the market appears as 'the unconscious and blind entirety of needs and the modes of their satisfaction'.[48] It happens that, as in nature, a balance (here of supply and demand) is achieved only through imbalances of greater or lesser intensity. 'Natural influences bring it about automatically that sometimes the proper equilibrium is maintained with insignificant oscillation, while at other times, if it is disturbed more seriously by external conditions, it is restored by greater oscillations'.[49] Thus, the abstract

46 Hegel 2005, p. 97 (*PR*, §183).

47 Hegel 1979, p. 165, translation modified.

48 Hegel 1979, p. 167, translation modified.

49 Hegel 1979, p. 168.

and impersonal nature of mercantile socialisation generates a richness that is merely quantity which, as such, can be accumulated in the extremes of unbounded wealth or be reduced to that of extreme poverty.

> Great wealth, which is similarly, bound up with the deepest poverty [...] produces on the one side in ideal universality, on the other side in real universality, mechanically. This purely quantitative element, [...] is the unmitigated extreme of barbarism. [...] The mass of wealth, the pure universal, the absence of wisdom, is the heart of the matter [*das Ansich*]. The absolute bond of the people, namely ethical principle, has vanished, and the people is dissolved.[50]

By using Smith's theory of the division of labour, the nexus that Hegel sees between modern socialisation and abstract universalisation is expressed with even greater clarity in the 1803–4 Jena Lectures. The division of labour – that is, the impossibility of any producer to satisfy autonomously their own needs – establishes a form of labour that, by satisfying the needs of all, is universal.

> In other words his labour, *qua* labouring of a single [labourer] for his own needs, is at the same time a universal and ideal [factor of public life]; he satisifies his needs by it certainly, but not with the determinate thing that he worked on; in order that that may satisfy his needs, it must rather become something other than it is [...]. Between the range of needs of the single [agent], and his activity on their account, there enters the labour of the whole people, and the labour of anyone is in respect of its contents, a universal labour for the needs of all, so as to be appropriate for the satisfaction of all his needs; in other words it has a value.[51]

However, by becoming universal through the division and specialisation of labour, labour becomes abstract because, once sub-divided, it involves a single role and ability:

> The universality, into which private need, and labour, and its aptitude to satisfy need are all elevated, is a formal one [...] they are simplified, but their simplicity is formally universal abstract simplicity, it is the lying-apart of the concrete [order of nature], which in this external separate-

50 Hegel 1979, p. 171.

51 Hegel 1979, p. 247.

> ness becomes an empirical infinite of singularities; and while man subjects nature to himself in this formal, and false, way, the individual only increases his dependence on it.[52]

In other words, specialist ability increases to the detriment of intelligence and labour becomes mechanical and lacking in subjectivity: 'labour becomes much deader, it becomes machine work, the skill of the single labourer is infinitely limited, and the consciousness of the factory labourer is improverished to the last extreme of dullness'.[53]

Furthermore, modern socialisation based on the freedom of subjects in civil society implies for Hegel a nexus of abstract universalisation. This is confirmed by the nature and functions of money.

> This manifold labouring at needs as things must likewise realise their concept, their abstraction; their universal concept must become a thing like them, but one which, *qua* universal, represents all needs; money is this materially existing concept, the form of unity, or of the possibility of all things needed.

Thus, the fact that the conditions of modern freedom imply that the social nexus lies outside the individual can mean that this separation-abstraction becomes an objective and impersonal mechanism that consistently tends to elude human control.

> Need and labour, elevated into this universality, then form on their own account a monstrous system of community and mutual interdependence in a great people; a life of the dead body, that moves itself within itself, one which ebbs and flows in its motion blindly, like the elements, and which requires continual strict dominance and taming like a wild beast.[54]

Again, in the Jena Lectures of 1805–6, where, for the first time, there is the theorisation of a social ambit integrally constituted on the generalisation of exchange (no longer limited only to excess), alongside the reproposal of the identical nature of socialisation and abstraction, Hegel continues to consider the problematical nature of the modern market (as a form of mediation with

52 Hegel 1979, p. 248.
53 Ibid.
54 Hegel 1979, p. 249.

an impersonal reach) in terms of exhaustively guaranteeing the reproduction of the existence of the entirety of its members.[55] In this text, there is not just the general polarisation of wealth and poverty, but also, Hegel adds, the tendency of wealth to be concentrated and accumulated in the same place.[56]

From this point of view, there is no doubt that Hegel's explanation of *bürgerliche Gesellschaft* in the text of 1821, in comparison to the Jena manuscripts written between the end of 1802 and 1806, is certainly more organic and less asymmetrical in the sense that, due to the autonomy and, above all, relative conclusiveness that are now assigned to the ambit of civil society (in its location between the family and the state), the imbalances and difficulties in the reproduction of civil society as a whole are less accentuated and radicalised. However, at the same time, it is also certain that the structurally naturalistic condition assigned to civil society is confirmed: that is, the locating outside individual subjectivity of the modes and typologies of socialisation and, with this, the possibility that this difference will be extended to such an extent as to become the opposition between the individual and the whole and the contradiction of the whole with itself. This is confirmed in the famous paragraphs 244 and 245 of the *Philosophy of Right* on the exclusion of individuals and entire social groups from the circuit of labour and exchange.

> When a large number of people sink below the standard of living regarded as essential for the members of society [...] a pauper class arises, and wealth accumulates disproportionately in the hands of a few. [...] There arises the seeming paradox that civil society when excessively wealthy is not rich enough. It has not sufficient hold of its own wealth to stem excess of poverty and the creation of the rabble [*Pöbel*].[57]

---

55 'This is subject to all the tangled and complex contingency in the [social] whole. Thus a vast number of people are condemned to a labor that is totally stupefying, unhealthy and unsafe – in workshops, factories, mines, etc. – shrinking their skills. And entire branches of industry, which supported a large class of people, go dry all at once because of [changes in] fashion or a fall in prices due to inventions in other countries, etc. – and this huge population is thrown into helpless poverty' (Hegel 1983c, p. 139).

56 'The contrast [between] great wealth and great poverty appears: the poverty for which it becomes impossible to do anything; [the] wealth [which], like any mass, makes itself into a force. The amassing of wealth [occurs] partly by chance, partly through universality, through distribution. [It is] a point of attraction, of a sort which casts its glance far over the universal, drawing [everything] around it to itself – just as a greater mass attracts the smaller ones to itself. To him who hath, to him is given' (Hegel 1983c, p. 140).

57 Hegel 2005, p. 127 (*PR*, § 244), translation modified.

The fact is that the principle of integration in the system of needs is externalisation [*Entäusserung*]: the capacity of the individual to become other than their unrepeatable and incomparable singularity by conforming to forms of universalisation that are visible to and recognisable by all. However, externalisation in Hegel's philosophy implies in itself, as one of its possible constitutional outcomes, alienation [*Entfremdung*]: the possibility that the being-for-another is not the medium for returning to oneself – for being in oneself and for oneself – but hardens itself in an alterity that becomes absolute and without mediation. *Geist* in Hegel's thoughts is the spiritual subjectivity that circles round on itself through a double negation: the negation of its immediate and particularist existence in being-for-another and, in turn, the negation of this *Andersein*, of this depending on the other, in the recovery of an identity enriched by this path of mediation. This circular subjectivity coincides with the speculative use of 'reason'. Diversely, the 'intellect' is the faculty and function that keeps the determinations of reality separate. Civil society, as a system of needs, just as the subjectivity that corresponds to it, belongs to the intellect. It is the modality of the latter, therefore, that guarantees the freedom of the modern, that is, the freedom that does not occur as in ancient Greece where '*each* [*individual*] is custom, [and thus is] immediately one with the universal. No protest takes place here, each knows himself *immediately* as universal – i.e., he gives up his particularity, without knowing it as such, as this Self, as the essence'.[58] However, it is precisely this specific modality of the modern, very differently from that of ancient times, of guaranteeing singularity through exteriorisation, that is not the immediate conservation and reproduction of the same, since this can also lose itself in bad infinity or, in other words, in a process of alteration from which there is no return because alterity here does not, in its turn, negate itself in order to become the medium of subjectivity but rather maintains itself, absolutely, as the other.

### 3.3 *Ethics in Civil Society*

Civil society, *qua System der Bedürfnisse*, is thus, for Hegel, an organic system, as Adam Smith had conceived, but with a profoundly different understanding of what nature is from that of the scientific naturalism adopted by the traditions of the Scottish Enlightenment. In Hegel's interpretation, the system is reproduced by means of the greatest exteriority and reciprocal indifference of each member to the others. This structural character necessarily leads to mechanicism, to individual times and modes, for better or worse, of a great automaton outside

58 Hegel 1983c, p. 159.

the controls of humanity. *Rechtspflege* [juridical apparatus] on the one hand and the *Polizei und Korporation* [Police and Corporations] on the other – the other two sub-wholes which, together with the *System der Bedürfnisse*, constitute the more general whole of *bürgerliche Gesellschaft* – have the role of introducing different logics from that of mechanical automatism. In this way, they limit the hard and objective legality of the system of needs and, at the same time, refer to the translation of action (of being encouraged by external forces to move according to self-determination) in which, for Hegel, the fullest freedom of the human subject consists and, equally, the true functions of the state. The juridical apparatus carries out this task by intervening in social life in relation to form, while the police and the corporations intervene in relation to content.

The administration of justice in modern civic society is called upon to apply universally valid legislation that is extended without any privileges to all the members of the social body, thereby defending the good of all from the damage that can be done by the arbitrariness and violence of the individual. For what renders a law visible – with respect to remaining confined within the interests of the *System der Bedürfnisse* – is precisely the reality and the value of that which is common to all and which, precisely because it is common to all, is that which, as the fabric of the whole, guarantees the well-being and satisfaction of each person's private life. The law does that, not by intervening in the content of social action as if it were, for example, wanting to translate the common being into a being-in-common, but through the pure form of itself, which in its obligatory nature is extended to all, imposing on all, over and above the historical circumstances over which it legislates, the awareness of a universal.[59]

The visibility that the law by means of the generalisation of duties and prohibitions without exception gives to the universal and the defence, thereby, of behaviour equal for all against the egoism of the individual, explains why the discussion of 'Abstract Law', or private law, was placed by Hegel at the start of the *Philosophy of Right* and considerably precedes the section dedicated to *Rechtspflege*. The administration of justice in civil society effectively assumes, as we have already discussed, the interest of the community as the fundamental interest of its codification, in which *Abstrakte Recht* has taken as its specific object the links and possible conflicts between single and private

59 'The objective actuality of right consists partly in existing for consciousness, or more generally in its being known, and partly in having and being generally recognized as having, the validity and force of a reality' (Hegel 2005, p. 110; *PR*, § 210).

owners. The main interest of private law, for Hegel, is the question of the *utilitas singolorum* or, in other words, the nexus between the individual, property and the use of nature or, rather, in Hegelian language, of the nexus between 'person' and 'thing'. It is no coincidence that the concepts of person, property and thing constitute the fundamental heritage that Roman law left to modernity, defining human freedom as the will and capacity to establish itself in the face of the natural world of things.[60] Thus, private law fundamentally determines the superior nature of man in becoming the master of nature ('That which is defined as different from the free spirit is both in its own nature and also for this spirit the external. It is an object, something not free, impersonal and without rights');[61] at the same time, it defines the freedom of ownership as abstract because the possession of a thing that belongs exclusively to a single person, although it establishes its persona, it also excludes and isolates it from those who are similar to it. For Hegel, the 'person' and the 'subject' are different.[62] The subject is the human individual in the multiplicity of its determinations and relationships, while the person is an abstraction from this concrete and articulated subject. It is, in the etymological and Latin sense of the expression, only a mask behind which is hidden the concrete and differentiated individual. It refers solely to the faculty, undifferentiated for all and, therefore, formal and abstract, of becoming the owner and possessor of things.

The *Rechtspflege* does not contradict *abstrakte Recht*. With regard to content, it limits itself to enforcing respect for the regulations of private law that regulate the relationships between men as owners of property rights and the exchange of things (insofar as they are members of the *System der Bedürfnisse*). However, at the same time, it subjects abstract law to an *Aufhebung*, because, with the certainty of law guaranteed by statutes, with the public nature given to legislation and the entire administration of justice, with the institution of the judge and trial procedures, it explains how this private and particular content has validity and sense only on the basis of the universal fabric and perspective of connections and, how, therefore, rather than a mechanical and invisible consequence but as a clear and unmoveable foundation of the individual's care

60 'A person in his direct and immediate individuality is related to a given external nature. To this outer world the personality is opposed as something subjective. But to confine to mere subjectivity the personality, which is meant to be infinite and universal, contradicts and destroys its nature. It bestirs itself to abrogate the limitation by giving itself reality, and proceeds to make the outer world visible existence its own' (Hegel 2005, p. 3; *PR*, § 39).

61 Hegel 2005, p. 5; *PR*, § 42.

62 See Ritter 1983, pp. 139–61.

and interests, it is none other than the existence and organisation of general interests and well-being. With the administration of justice in civil society, the subject of legislation is no longer the person of abstract law, fundamentally qualified by its relationship with property and possession in the natural world, but humanity, the universal person whose horizon of reference is other men and the equality that is established on the basis of a generalised participation of all in labour and exchange.[63]

Nonetheless, it is effectively a fact that, within *Rechtspflege*, justice, insofar as its content is concerned, limits itself to defending existing property. It is, as we have seen, a vector of merely formal universalisation in the sense that its statutes impose knowledge (awareness) on all of the universal, but not the certainty that the will of the individual assumes the pursuit of the collective good within the effective reality of their life.

However, the mechanism of socialisation through abstraction also guarantees only the possibility and not the real guarantee of coincidence between individual interests and general wealth. The contingency, with regard to the fate of the individual, is intrinsic to a civil society structured on the modern market and, for this reason, for Hegel it is necessary to introduce – beyond the universal by means of abstraction belonging to the economic field and beyond the universal by means of juridical statute and formalisation – effective and real vectors of universality in which the ends of collective benefit are assumed and pursued integrally by individual will, without being obtained *a posteriori* (as occurs with the economic universal) or only on a formal-cognitive level (as occurs with the juridical universal). *Polizei* and *Korporation* are the institutions that Hegel sees as the most appropriate for the creation of the further dimension of civil society.[64]

63 'It is the essence of education and of thought, which is the consciousness of the individual in universal form, that the I should be apprehended as a universal person, in whom all are identital. Man must be accounted a universal being, not because he is a Jew, Catholic, Protestant, German, or Italian, but because he is a man' (Hegel 2005, p. 109; *PR*, § 229, note).

64 'In civil society [...] right [...] refers merely to the protection of what I have. To right as such, happiness is something external. Yet in the system of needs well-being is an essential element. The universal, which is at first only right, has to spread itself over the whole field of particularity. Justice, it is true, is a large factor in civic society. The state will flourish, if it has good laws, of which free property is the fundamental condition. But since I am wholly environed by my particularity, I have a right to demand that in connecting myself with others I shall further my special happiness. Regard to my particular well-being is taken by the police and the corporation' (Hegel 2005, p. 122; *PR*, § 229, addition, translation modified).

Hegel's *Polizei* has very little in common with the modern institution aimed at the prevention and repression of crimes. Undoubtedly, in Hegel, 'police' activity can also limit the freedom of the individual in order to safeguard and maintain the public spirit. However, his concept sees the essential functions of this institution as fundamentally linked to the role played by the *Polizei* in the territorial principalities of the German Empire between the sixteenth and seventeenth centuries. Within this context, the meaning of this expression, maintaining its classical etymology (the Greek *politeia* and medieval *politia*), refers to the entire order and complexity of all state functions; more precisely, those state functions that coincided with the strengthening of the power of the territorial prince with respect to prerogatives and powers that until then had belonged either to imperial authority or the polycentrism of a society organised and marked by the articulation of estates.

The *Polizeistaat* refers to the construction of a legislative and administrative structure in which the state's role is seen not so much or solely as guaranteeing order – as occurs in classical liberal doctrine – as that of procuring and maintaining the well-being of its subjects. *Ordnung und Wohlfahrt*, order and well-being, constitute the values that must direct the actions of the prince and his government, paternalistically encouraging the happiness and good life of his subjects. Thus, the *Polizeistaat* is not only a formal state, in the sense of not limiting itself, only negatively, to prohibiting the damage created by an excess of freedom of the individual over the freedom of the others – as was theorised in general by liberal doctrine and, in particular, Kant's *Metaphysik der Sitten*, which is entirely aimed at assigning a merely formal-negative nature to the state with respect to the prioritised and fundamental value of the freedom of initiative and action of the individual.[65] Rather, the *Polizeistaat* is properly speaking an ethical state, in the sense that precisely by means of a paternalistic and patrimonial concept of the state, the state is tasked with positively intervening with legislation and administration in the concrete praxis of the individual's life. It must promote, through codification often so detailed as to become mere pedantry, behaviour and customs that are coherent with the good of the entire community. The prince's command, with his work of unification and centralisation of power, extends, over and above the traditionally assigned functions of the state (such as the defence of territory and the creation of a stable army, the formation of a body of public officials, the imposition and collection of taxes), to include activities such as the control on weights and measures, on drinks and food stuffs, the surveillance of prices and markets, the

65 See Sasso 1965, pp. 5–45.

safety and viability of commerce, the definition of precise methods of labour processes, control over corporation statutes, as well as the surveillance of the quality of medicines and the health of livestock.[66]

Beginning from this peculiarly German ethical-political tradition – but removing it from a context of enlightened despotism with a privately oriented and patrimonial concept of the state – Hegel conceives of the *Polizei* within the horizon of *bürgerliche Gesellschaft* as the institution providing for the needs of common utility with actions that are put in place as a result of aware and direct choices, without the intentional and natural mediation of the division of labour and generalised exchange.

On a par with the *Polizei* and thus at a distance from the reality of an impersonal universal that is imposed through the abstraction of the market or through the pure form of the law is the other institution which, in civil society, works in accordance with an immediate and explicit aim of universality – the corporation. This is an association of trades that is also typical – with its hierarchical consistency of the wage earners and masters and with its right to its own statutes – of pre-modern and estate-based society. However, in the *Philosophy of Right*, there is an association of trades that is, in some way, modernised, particularly due to the fact that Hegel, on the one hand, removes it from any prerogative of secrecy with respect to the knowledge about and performance of labour processes and, on the other, attributes to it an essentially ethical-spiritual role of legitimising and valorising the existence of an individual through their rooting in a totality (although circumscribed) of members united, as well as by the same trade, by reciprocal care and assistance. The individual, unused to concerning itself with the good of others within the horizon of the market or sensitive to the universal only in the form of mere equality and juxtaposition of all before the law, effectively manages with the corporation to place within itself the passion and care of the universal, in however still limited a way. It finds in this a 'second family' where reciprocal common interests moderate the extremes of poverty and wealth since, within this ambit, labour is recognised not in relation to its abstraction of economic and monetary value but rather – to use modern terms – in relation to its 'use value', that is, in relation to the form of life on which it is based insofar as it is characterised by the technical capacity, honesty and honour derived from it.[67]

66 See Schiera 1968; Maier 1980, esp. pp. 39–91.

67 'If the individual is not a member of an authorized corporation [...] he has no class-honour. By limiting himself to the self-seeking side of trade and his own subsistence and enjoyments, he loses standing. [...] In the corporation the assistance received by poverty

### 3.4 *Civil Society and the State*

This complex articulation of levels, this interweaving of economic markets in the strict sense with institutions of an ethical-professional, juridical and political-administrative nature, this mediation and tempering of various needs renders Hegel's civil society an organic system of reality. It is organic in the sense that it is not compromised by a structural impotence in terms of the needs for the satisfaction of which it was created, and it is thus able to provide for the reproduction of itself, of all its members and each of its functions. Its completeness as a system lacks only one element, which, for Hegel, is discriminatory, which enables it to create a fully self-sufficient (or, in other words, absolute) reality. It is the awareness that, in this complex system of economic and institutional practices, each person, despite being limited to acting within its own specific ambit, acts to generate the universal good, utility for all. This is why, in Hegel's philosophy, the space of the state opens up, beyond that of civil society. Thus, the main characteristic of the political state is the establishment, organisation and production of this consciousness and intention: that is, that each person assumes the universal interest as the content and interest of their own being in a way that is now explicit and conscious.

The specific production of the modern political state is, therefore, that destined to produce a universal consciousness. It must, that is, generate, reproduce and consolidate in the individual the consciousness and habits of the universal. This is achieved through the fundamental division of powers, which entrusts the capacity to define the universal (with the formulation of laws) to the legislative power; the capacity to subsume particular cases under the universal of the law to the governmental power; and the capacity to embody and guarantee with any private arbiter the sovereignty of the whole to the monarchical power. In other words, Hegel does not attribute any properly material role to the political state other than that of defence in relation to other states given that, as mentioned, civil society is entirely destined for material reproduction. The state must occupy itself, more or less solely, with spiritual affairs, turning into consciousness that which in civil society is realised unconsciously or, in other words, translating into intentional will the reciprocal functioning between individual utility and universal interest that is realised automatically and unintentionally. The aim of the political state – and, here, Hegel returns to solidarity with the traditional doctrine of natural law – is the overcoming

---

loses its lawless character, and the humiliation wrongly associated with it. The opulent, by performing their duty to their associates, lose their pride, and cease to stir up envy in others. Integrity receives its due honour [*Ehre*] and recognition [*Anerkennung*]' (Hegel 2005, pp. 130–1; *PR*, § 252).

of natural society to the degree to which modern civil society is still contained within a naturalistic order, in Hegel's concept of the expression. The political state is only concerned with removing human activity from the constrictions of need and thereby leading it into the sphere of free will, through its education and cultivation of a universal consciousness.

## 4 Mental Abstraction and Real Abstraction

We have provided a fairly rapid overview of the wide-ranging question of what civil society and the political state represent in Hegel's philosophy, one which was clearly weighted more towards an analysis of the former than to that of the institutions and articulations of the latter. This is in contrast with Marx's reading in 1843 *Critique*, which is almost entirely dedicated to providing a critical commentary of the paragraphs of Hegel's *Philosophy of Right* related to the state. However, this is an intended discordance because, although the mature Marx makes civil society and its economic ambit the single and determining foundation of modernity, here, in an opposed and reductive way, the importance assigned to the structure of modern civil society is greatly limited.

It is clear from this, in my opinion, that it is precisely the interlinking of the various levels of *bürgerliche Gesellschaft* that Hegel attempts to resolve and which for him constitutes the fundamental *quaestio* in which the essence of modernity is enclosed. He formulates and proposes, at the highest level of maturity, the ethical (but also theoretical) question that historically runs through and substantiates the entire course of Hegel's work: namely, how to guarantee that the value of modernity, consisting in the discovery of subjectivity and its freedom, does not conflict with the equally vital value of ancient ethics represented by the bonds of solidarity and common belonging which, more or less idealised, connote the perspective of the ancient *polis* for Hegel. Precisely in order better to appreciate the terms of the relationship between the young Marx and Hegel – according to the paradox of a more spiritual Marx and a more materialist Hegel – it is necessary to emphasise strongly how and to what extent the resolution of this decisive issue is located for Hegel above all within the horizon of the *bürgerliche Gesellschaft*.

We have seen that Hegel's response is essentially concerned with the contemporaneous organisation of modern civil society on the basis of the market, on the one hand and, on the other, of the pre-mercantile institutions of an estate-based and pre-modern society (as evidenced, furthermore, in Hegel by the social organisation of *Stände*, or, in other words, the pre-modern organisation of estates into agricultural, industrial and bureaucratic-general orders).[68] Thus, if socialisation by means of abstraction is indispensible for there to be free choice of life by the individual and the autonomous creation of the 'private', it is also true that this type of social integration through abstraction undoubtedly implies, due to its very structure, radical dangers for every member of civil society. It is, therefore, necessary to refer, in Hegel's view, to the presence of direct and unmediated institutions of universality or, rather, institutions that do not pass through the mediation of commodities and money but relate to practices of virtue and to emotional links, or that take on the interests and care in which all, without any distinctions, can participate. It is no coincidence that the corporation plays an irreplaceable role within these institutions ('As the family was the first, so the corporation, grounded upon civil society, constitutes the second ethical root or basis of the state').[69] Within this is realised, as also in the family, without the mediation of money or abstract institutions, the recognition of the individual on the part of others, which for Hegel from the early days in Jena onwards is the mainstay of his anthropological dialectics.

The recognition, the confirmation (or lack thereof) on the part of others, as the most profound basis of identity, is furthermore the distillation in Hegel's practical philosophy of his definition of *Geist* as the subjectivity achieved through alterity. The entire articulation of modern civil society as a 'system of needs', 'the administration of justice' and 'police and corporations' is ordered according to the progression of forms of recognition, which, from an abstract and impersonal typology, gains in concreteness to the point of guaranteeing, precisely through the corporation, a form of socialisation that, as a concrete universal in a logical-cognitive context, does not abstract from the particular but welcomes and acknowledges it, maintaining it in its individuality.

On the other hand, it is undoubtedly true, at least in my opinion, that Hegel's proposed solution raises more problems than it resolves. The contemporaneous presence of different times – of the modern time of the market and the pre-modern time of an estate-based society – cannot but open up the aporia of

---

68 As to how Hegel's attitude to the fundamental institutions of a society based on orders – the 'estate [*Stand*]' and 'corporations [*Zunft*]' changed from his youthful writings through to his mature socio-political works, I refer to my work *Mito e critica delle forme. La giovinezza di Hegel. 1770–1801* (Finelli 1996a, p. 262). On the role in the mature Hegel of these institutions' mediation between economic individualism and social ethics, see Kersting 1986, pp. 373–82; Cullen 1988, pp. 22–41. On the distinction and resulting impossibility of equation between Hegel's medieval 'corporations' and modern 'unions', see Waszek 1989, pp. 355–63.

69 Hegel 2005, p. 131 (*PR*, § 255).

a radical ontological and historical dualism within a social context that should be unitarily consistent. Given such dual temporality and the subsequent contemporaneous presence of two social formations that are profoundly heterogeneous, it is perhaps not irrelevant to question the degree to which Hegel's solution managed to remain at the considerably high level at which his historical intelligence had posed the question of modernity through the introduction and conceptualisation of civil society as a system of needs.

However, the most surprising fact, for our purposes, is that this fundamental difficulty in Hegel's philosophy of right entirely escapes Marx's attention in the 1843 *Critique*. Of course, it could not be otherwise, given that his attention was entirely concentrated on and absorbed by another form of dualism – that of civil society and the political state – and the resultant structural inversion of reality, for which every moment of human experience loses its concrete meaning and is constantly given a new significance on the basis of a code of abstract and universalistic spiritualism.

What Marx, at the time, effectively still does not consider at all – very differently from what takes place in his mature works – is the valency of abstract universalisation in terms of praxis in the material constitution of modern civil society that Hegel, however, had achieved with profound theoretical awareness in the *Grundlinien der Philosophie des Rechts*. This had made the essence of modernity coincide to such a degree with individual freedom that it necessarily resulted in a socialisation lacking in any relationship or community-based connotations that might precede and influence the freedom of the modern subject, liberated from any assumed conditioning. It is precisely socialisation by means of universalising and impersonal practices that is the solution that appears to Hegel the most able to guarantee the unconditional principle of individual freedom. In a similar way, the central role that socialisation assumes in Hegelian modernity, realised through abstract practices and institutions, implies that Hegel, in order to contain its asymmetries, must refer to solidarity-based institutions and habits of a different historic-political era and to that tradition of *Polizeistaat* that is constituted in a context far removed from classic European liberalism and the absoluteness of the value of individual freedom that liberal traditions see as the only and irremovable principle.

It is in terms of this way of resolving the nexus of *liberté-égalité-fraternité* in Hegel's ethical liberalism – again, by means of the juxtaposition of profoundly heterogeneous socio-political systems – that it should have been possible to raise the question of dualism and Hegel's enforced unification of irreconcilable expressions. However, to the young Marx, the heroic haste to commit the parricide and make himself heard as the one who has become superior to the great spirit of contemporary philosophy rapidly makes him blind to the richness and complexity of the figure he hopes to bypass and to criticise. In order to dispute Hegel's ideas, it was necessary and sufficient, in the young Marx's opinion, to affirm the pregnancy of the concrete against the vagueness of the abstract, to posit from the life of men in flesh and blood and their reality against the life of ideas alone and a reality transfigured by speculation. He thereby repressed the most profound problematic in Hegel in relation to the 'modern' and the extent to which the Swabian philosopher had attempted to bind together various forms of realisation of subjectivity, in particular with the tripartite articulation of *bürgerliche Gesellschaft*: from the economic-juridical individualism of the state of rights to the social individuality of the ethical state. He did not appear to appreciate that only on the basis of such a question is it possible then to pose the question of the state, the nature of the bureaucratic-corporative constitution that Hegel had assigned it and the type of non-democratic-liberal representation that distinguishes it.

Furthermore, if the human being, conceived as participating in the organicity and richness of its species, becomes the principle and presupposition of all reality in an assumed ontological exhaustiveness, abstraction, as occurs in Marx's humanism of the time, can only have the meaning of an act of alienation: in other words, an ontological caesura where an individual, due to arbitrariness and individual error, separates itself from its universal container, suffering all the effects of such an individualistic radicalisation – in the first instance, that of finding outside itself, and deformed into a different and hostile reality, the root of universality that it has repressed from itself.

It is only that, within this context, abstraction-alienation – as error and arbitrary forcing with respect to the continuity and unitary compactness of the species – necessarily has a solely individualist-mental genesis and nature. As a consequence, if a solely subjective and mental genesis and function is attributed to abstraction, as occurs in the young Marx, this results in the impossibility of conceiving of it also as a function that is real and objective or, in other words, valid not in the mind of the individual, but as a principle of practical and impersonal organisation of social reality, in accordance with Hegel's conception of modern civil society.

The extension of the meaning of the category of abstraction, the deepening and extension of its polysemy, is one of the most original and innovative aspects of Hegel's philosophy. Alongside its traditional, logical meaning, in the sense of the extraction of common and general elements from a multiplicity of particulars, abstraction in Hegel refers to an ideological meaning as the merely external juxtaposition of the universal and the particular, with the consequent absolutisation and legitimation of the particular, as well as a practical meaning as the nexus of socialisation that models and informs the modalities of individual labours according to general rules of behaviour.

The young Marx substantially appropriated the meaning and ideological function of the concept of abstraction and made it the mainstay of his interpretation of the contemporary world, of his *Critique*, both in institutional-political and culturally and philosophically critical terms. On the basis of a universal subject such as the human species, he interpreted and defined as abstract all those realities in which the universality of the real subject, negated and repressed, are projected and merely juxtaposed to any particular content which, in this ideological operation, take on the representation and the symbolic (surplus) value of the whole. It is in this critical analysis of the processes of the individual and collective imagination, in this analysis of the ideological representations arrived at through an investigation of mental mechanisms of repression-displacement-projection enacted by abstraction *qua* alienation, that he undoubtedly demonstrates all the creative potential of his thoughts. Undoubtedly, he achieves the extreme accuracy and profundity previously inaugurated and developed by his teacher Hegel in the discovery and criticism of processes of the false infinitisation of the finite.

It was Hegel, as we have seen, who first discovered, when faced with the lack of a real and concrete universal, the presence and role in the human soul of the workings of abstract universalisation as compensatory and symbolic. If the subject claims to coincide with a partial identity of itself by abstracting from the relationship with alterity that constitutes its truest identity, the same nexus of relation and universalisation – which cannot be suppressed and cancelled due to its priority and ontological consistency – is translated into the ideological and symbolic function of false universalisation: that ubiquitous and transcendental function of the human mind, alternative to but nonetheless contemporaneously present with the function of truth, which can be attributed to the identification of the subject in question with the praxis of that which for Hegel is *Geist* in the proper sense of the term. Marx, despite denying its paternity, takes this original instrument entirely from Hegel, an indispensible instrument for the criticism of the ideological imaginary. The meaning of the reflections in his 1843 manuscript that remain valid and stimulating even today are inscribed under its banner. Despite the excessively organicist and fusional presupposition of his concept of the people, Marx's analysis of the manner in which the private hides and dissimulates in the form of the public, of the way in which the particular disguises itself in the image of the universal, opens up an entirely new perspective on the formalism of the modern state. The other formalist tradition of modern constitutional rights, the liberal and negative tradition we have previously discussed, cannot avoid a confrontation with it.

However, it is precisely the centrality, if not the ubiquitous nature and repetitivity, assigned in this first phase of his thought to abstraction as ideological and symbolic alienation that ensures that Marx is completely unable to perceive the valency of abstraction not as the organising principle of the world of imagination but of the world of materiality and real praxis.

It is precisely this repression of Hegel enacted by Marx's parricide that reveals that he does not possess the maturity of a detachment and autonomy that has been truly acquired and elaborated.[70] This repression and blindness, with respect to a determination essential for an understanding of modernity, together with the presupposition of a subject that has been excessively naively and generically defined (at least with respect to the complexity of subject formation in Hegel), are the result of the young Marx still being too close to

70 Although Benedetto Croce seriously misunderstood Marx's *Capital*, in my view, he did discern the excessive rapidity and self-assurance of the young Marx's 'inversion' of Hegel, defining it as being of a more psychological than theoretical-philosophical nature. 'As the reader knows, Marx, when discussing the relation between his opinions and Hegelianism employed a pointed phrase that has been taken too often beside the point. He said that with Hegel history was standing on its head and that it must be turned right side up again in order to replace it on its feet. For Hegel the idea is the real world, whereas for him (Marx) "the ideal is nothing else than the material world" reflected and translated by the human mind. Hence the statement so often repeated, that the materialistic view of history is the negation or antithesis of the idealistic view. It would perhaps be convenient to study once again, accurately and critically, these asserted relations between scientific socialism and Hegelianism. To state the opinion which I have formed on the matter; the link between the two views seems to me to be, in the main, simply psychological. Hegelianism was the early inspiration of the youthful Marx, and it is natural that everyone should link up the new ideas with the old as a development, an amendment, an antithesis' (Croce 2001, p. 201; Croce 1914). It should also not be forgotten that Croce, in a much later text of 1937, *Come nacque e come morì il marxismo teorico in Italia* [*How Theoretical Marxism in Italy was Born and Died*], seems to have understood well the spiritualistic nature of concepts like 'humanity' and 'human species', which are fundamental for the thought of the young Marx. 'Neither here should we forget what could be called the religious origins of historical materialism, not unknown to those familiar with the history of the Hegelian left. After it had destroyed Christianity with its radical critique and affirmed atheism, it found before it the religious element of "humanity". It seemed to the Hegelian left that "humanity" was offended in its purity and prevented from undertaking its free expansion by the class divisions and contrasts (that is, by history), while the demand of communism would have actualised the true liberty, the true world of humanity' (Croce 2001, p. 294). On Croce's interpretation of Marx and Marxism, in its totality, and on the important influence it has had on the history of Italian politics and culture, another study of a different systematic nature would be necessary.

and dependent on Hegel: the more he feels their relation truly intimately as such, the more violently and externally does he attempt to negate it. Marx, at this time, is still profoundly subaltern to Hegel, so much so that all his most significant conceptual instruments, beginning with the definition of what a 'critique' is, derive directly from Hegel, or indirectly through Feuerbach's mediation. However, it is precisely this that Marx, in the fiery days of his youth, is unable to acknowledge and accept.

The attempted parricide is thus substantially a failure. The young Marx must now conquer the fundamental principle for the criticism of the ideological world, thereby nurturing his thought during the rest of his life. It was means of this path that he arrived at, for example, the critique of the illusory and formal nature of the equality of citizens in the modern state when faced with their real differences in civil life and the importance of this dissimulating nexus of reality-fantasy in the reproduction of modern life. However, these intelligent and original observations on contemporary social reality remain in a framework of great theoretical naivety that, in order to criticise Hegel, incongruously arrive at a theory of the division and multiplication of the contemporary world into two absolutely heterogeneous worlds governed by two entirely opposing principles: civil society resolved completely in the principle of egoistic individuality, and the political state in that of universality. This occurs, however, without Marx having any awareness of the problems and the modes, over and above dualism, of their unity and reciprocal functions in the reproduction of a society such as the modern one that lives as a whole.[71]

71 The person in Italy who had already in the 1930s appreciated the substance of the relationship between the young Marx and Hegel, much earlier than the over-determination that Della Volpe imposed on the 1843 *Critique*, was Giuseppe Capograssi (see Capograssi 1959, pp. 45–69). According to Capograssi, Marx 'mechanically' applied 'the game of substituting the subject with the predicate and the predicate with the subject' (1959, p. 50). Feuerbach's influence was negatively determining for the young critic. Marx claimed to base his criticism on the fact that Hegel implemented 'a split between the logic of the idea and the logic of the concrete' (ibid), while Hegel's idealism precisely intended to 'trace the logic of the concrete, the logic of the absolute idea throughout the concrete world' (ibid). The young Hegelians were profoundly unjust to their master. 'Even more unjust as it happens, because they owed him everything. In all this criticism, Marx is moved by nothing but Hegelian intuitions and insights: to arrive at the precise determination of a particular idea, to capture the intrinsic reason of the historical fact, to discover the rational meaning of a reality in which there is only concrete and objective reason, is precisely Hegel's teaching'. However, for the conflation of the Hegelian Idea, including the dimension of immanence, with the Platonic idea, we can return to what Giovanni Gentile wrote in 1899 in his book on Marx (see Gentile 1955, esp. p. 39 and p. 127).

There remains, of course, the value of the ideological connection that the Marx of the 1843 *Critique* saw as a functional relationship between civil society and the political state, in the twofold sense of the state as the place where the species as a community of equal citizens is located (in opposition to the inequalities that inversely denote civil society) and state institutions as the place of the transformation and symbolic translation of that which is private into the public by means of the form of the universal. However, this connection puts into play a subject that is not the same as that which Marx posited as the principle of modern civil society. This discontinuity of discourse is further evidence that in the theoretical structure of the 1843 text the dualism of civil society and the political state, conceived as the co-presence of two opposing worlds, remains structurally and aporetically divided and unreconciled. The subject who gives life in the ideological scenario to the representation of the unity of the species in the community of equal citizens or to the inappropriate projection of the universality of the species repressed into particular institutions or individuals is a subject whose roots refer either to a civil society riddled with differences or to a rootedness of the species. In both cases, it is a subject whose identity is immersed in a relational context. The subject on whom Marx constructs modern civil society in these pages, on the other hand, is the individual abstracted from relations and closed within its own egoism; an egoism which, because it is conceived of atomistically, is, *qua* atom, without any difference with respect to all the other, equally atomistic, individuals.

In this Marxian work of 1843, there is thus constantly at work, obviously without any awareness on the author's part, an exchange of subjects: from the subject based in the species or in relations, who becomes the protagonist of events of the ideological universal, to the atomistic subject closed within itself that has nothing whatsoever to do with the universal. Through the use of the former, Marx constructs a critical analysis of the ideological effect of the modern state; through the use of the latter, he constructs a critical analysis of Hegel's *Philosophy of Right* and, from this, of all Hegel's philosophy. However, in order to radically refute Hegel, this second type of criticism assumes a form of subjectivity – namely, the atomistic-abstract subject – that leads Marx's thought into radical difficulties. For, if we assume that society is composed of many ones, it is not possible to see how, from this multitude of equal individuals, there can emerge a society similar to that of modern civil society consisting of relations and differences, and which then consigns any socialising and integrating link only to the other and opposite sphere of the political state.

Furthermore, it should be noted that it is not that Marx does not mention the lack of congruency linked to the co-presence of two profoundly different and incompatible historical and institutional epochs in Hegel's notion of the state: on the one hand, a socio-political organisation marked by estates, and on the other, the modern state animated by a public spirit of universality without distinctions. The entire central part of Marx's manuscript is effectively dedicated to refuting the artificiality of the fusion of public and private that Hegel attempts to bring about with respect to the institution of representation, with the political element of the estates; in other words, through the delegation with which, according to Hegel, a civil society structured according to estates participates in legislative power. The young Marx was thus well aware that an estate-based society belonged to a historic period in which, in the absence of the universal horizon of the modern political state, each part of society saw politics merely as a defence of its own particular interests.

> Their whole existence was political. Their existence was the existence of the state. […] The general legislative effectiveness of the estates of civil society was not at all an attaining to a political significance and effectiveness on the part of the civil estate […] it was rather their attaining to matters of wholly general concern as a civil affair, their attaining to sovereignty as a civil estate.[72]

Marx clearly understood that in giving reality and a role to the division into estates both within civil society and in the legislative power of the state, Hegel does nothing more than attempt to resolve the radical opposition of spheres (civil society and the political state as essences based on irreducible principles), concealed and negated by him at the very moment when he originally discovered and theorised them. 'Hegel wants the medieval-estates system, but in the modern sense of the legislature; and he wants the modern legislature, but in the body of the medieval-estates system! This is the worst kind of syncretism'.[73] Nonetheless, far from understanding the real motives that forced Hegel to mitigate the harshness of the modern with pre-modern communitarian instances, Marx in the 1843 *Critique* did not investigate the nature of Hegel's syncretism and juxtaposition. He rather looked only at the letter of the work, limiting himself to reiterating, in a highly figurative and expressive style, the critical motif of the magical transubstantiation that Hegel was assumed to make of the particular into the universal, of the private into the public. The purpose of this is supposed to be the concealing, in a reconciled reality subsumed into the

---

72 *MECW* 3, pp. 72–3.

73 *MECW* 3, p. 95.

Idea, of the ontological division that in Marx's simplifying and reductionist vision exists in the modern world between the unfettered individualism of civil society and the merely ideal and separated universality of the political state. It is clear that, once again, the superimposition of Plato over Hegel or, in other words, of the former's 'idea' over the latter's 'Idea', deriving from Feuerbach's anthropocentrism, renders Marx's vision opaque and lacking in depth, forcing him into an inversion of Hegel's discourse that only superficially grasps its significance.

The theoretical setback that Marx suffers due to this parricide, so intensely desired but so aporetically missed, lasts for a long time. The ghost of Hegel, unwelcomed and buried under the *pietas* of an insufficient understanding of his complexity, will plague the mind of our hero for several years, preventing him from achieving the discovery of his true self with the serenity of a clear break. It was only through the loss suffered in the defeat of the European revolts of 1848, and the destruction of the facile delusions of radicalising social conditions and the explosion of revolution, that Marx, with his exile in London and a return to a period of profound meditation and study, was able to view the person who had been his spiritual father with greater serenity, thus enabling him to push his parricide to a true conclusion and thereby strive to achieve his own maturity.

## 5 A Fusional and Symbiotic Communism

It was starting from the presupposition of the human subject as the organic and harmonious principle of life and history that Marx wrote the two essays that appeared in 1844 in the single published issue of the *Deutsch-französische Jahrbücher*. They are unanimously identified by interpretative traditions as the documents that provide the first explicit evidence of Marx's transition to the concreteness of materialism on the level of general interpretation of historical and human life, and to the theorisation of communism on the level of social and political struggles. At the end of this reconstruction of the young Marx's thought, it is impossible not to consider them synthetically in order to ascertain the degree to which, even in Marx's undoubted theoretical-political radicalisation during his move from Germany to France, his thoughts remained within the ambit of a metaphysics of the human subject. Humanistic spiritualism, in other words, continued profoundly to condition even the first steps of his assumed materialism and his political transition to socialism.

At the end of September 1843, the 25-year-old Marx left Kreuznach and Germany to move to Paris, the city that, after the revolutions of 1789 and 1830, had become the moral and intellectual capital of the world, and the place where all unconventional and radical souls came together.

> And so – to Paris, to the old university of philosophy – *absit omen*! [May it not be an ill omen] – and the new capital of the new world! What is necessary comes to pass. [...] But whether the enterprise comes into being or not, in any case I shall be in Paris by the end of this month, since the atmosphere here makes one a serf, and in Germany I see no scope at all for free activity. In Germany everything is forcibly suppressed; a real anarchy of the mind, the reign of stupidity itself prevails there [...] It therefore becomes increasingly obvious that a new rallying point must be sought for truly thinking and independent minds.[74]

The closure of the *Rheinische Zeitung* had not been an isolated episode of the Berlin government's repression. The entire group of young Hegelians and their various intellectual and editorial activities had been hit for a number of reasons by the Prussian state. As a consequence, Marx and Ruge decided to create a new magazine that could be published on French soil, taking advantage also of the vast number of Germans, labourers and artisans above all, present in the French capital. Marx published two essays in the *Deutsch-Französiche Jahrbücher* which were, respectively, 'Zur Judenfrage' and 'Zur Kritik des Hegelschen Rechtsphilosophie Einleitung', which are considered as the fruit of rapid transition of the young intellectual's thought from a position of radical democracy, as expressed in the *Rheinische Zeitung*, to one increasingly open to materialism and communism. In particular, concepts and theoretical figures such as 'praxis' and the 'proletariat' seem to inaugurate new fields of philosophical and historical-political meaning in Marx's vision. It is thus worthwhile, at this point, as a conclusion to this excursus into the work of the young Karl Marx, to consider briefly how much the metaphysics of the generic subject, as the presupposed and implicit principle of history and social analysis, continued to condition profoundly the first steps taken by Marx between the end of 1843 and the beginning of 1844 towards a theory of the liberation of humanity in which 'the criticism of heaven turns into the criticism of earth'.[75]

In the first of the articles in question ('On the Jewish Question'), Marx, in discussing Bruno Bauer's theories on the problem of the Jews, again criticises, through Bauer, what he sees as the persistently intellectual-abstract approach

74 *MECW* 3, p. 142.

75 *MECW* 3, p. 176.

of the *Junghegelianer*. The latter continued to make criticism of religion their main activity, seeing in the secular emancipation of the state from every type of religion a fundamental step for modernity. However, modern political emancipation, the equality of all citizens, without any differences or privileges before the law, Marx observed, does not facilitate but rather contradicts the true freedom of the human being. Political equality is effectively only formal equality that exists in the heavens, separate from politics, leaving unchanged all the differences that connote civil society. It is an equality that, just as religion makes everyone the equal children of God, is in its ideological compensation a function of the inequality of civil society. The emancipation of political democracy that establishes a free and equally sovereign citizen, Marx observes in a manner which now goes beyond the democratic radicalism of the *Critique*, is contrasted with a human emancipation that must revolutionise modern civil society and its divisions, recomposing the communitarian and generic nature of human beings.

> The limits of political emancipation are evident at once from the fact that the state can free itself from a restriction without man being really free from this restriction, that the state can be a free state a without man being a free man. [...] The state abolishes, in its own way, distinctions of birth, social rank, education, occupation, when it declares that birth, social rank, education, occupation, are non-political distinctions, when it proclaims, without regard to these distinctions, that every member of the nation is an *equal* participant in national sovereignty, when it treats all elements of the real life of the nation from the standpoint of the state. Nevertheless, the state allows private property, education, occupation, to *act* in *their* way – i.e., as private property, as education, as occupation, and to exert the influence of their *special* nature. Far from abolishing these real distinctions, the state only exists on the presupposition of their existence; it feels itself to be a political state and asserts its universality only in opposition to these elements of its being.[76]

Thus, the alienation of religion, or the losing of man in a God created by himself, over and above the rational and philosophical criticism of religion and the merely political claims of the secularism of the modern state, will only truly cease when real alienation ceases, or, in other words, when there is an end to that which expropriates the individual in the daily running of economic

76 *MECW* 3, pp. 152–3.

and civic life, tears it away from any communitarian relationship, from any identification of species, and abandons it to the war of all against all. Modern civil society, it is repeated here again, has as its principle egoism, the private individual.

> It is no longer the essence of *community*, but the essence of *difference*. It has become the expression of man's *separation* from his *community* [*von seinem Gemeinwesen*], from himself and from other men – as it was originally [*ursprünglich*]. It is only the abstract avowal of specific perversity, *private whimsy* [*Privatschrulle*], and arbitrariness.[77]

Furthermore, it is now money, with a passage that is more explicit and resolute than the vague indications contained in the pages of the *Critique*, that is placed for Marx at the centre of modern civil society, imposing with its real abstraction a type and quality of the alienation of man from man of which the alienations-abstractions of thought, in philosophy, religion and law, represent significant but subordinate reflections (given that they take place only in the imaginary life of the mind).

> Money is the jealous god of Israel, in face of which no other god may exist. Money degrades all the gods of man – and turns them into commodities. Money is the universal self-established value of all things. It has therefore robbed the whole world – both the world of men and nature – of its specific value. Money is the estranged essence [*das dem Menschen entfremedete Wesen*] of man's work and man's existence, and this alien essence dominates him, and he worships it.[78]

---

77 *MECW* 3, p. 155.

78 *MECW* 3, p. 172. As mentioned, in this text Marx discusses Bruno Bauer's theory according to which the emancipation of the Jews could only come about through emancipation from their religion and the recognition of the human spirit's universal nature. Marx argues, however, that the problem is not religious or political but rather practical and material-social in nature, since what is in question is the relation of subordination between 'Judaism' and 'money'. It is worth highlighting the harshness and simplification used by the young Marx in representing and criticising Judaism in its sordid attachment to the world of trafficking and money, not dissimilar to the most widespread and unsophisticated stereotypes of the Christian tradition. This is confirmed, furthermore, by other elements in his works, such as passages in the *Neue Rheinische Zeitung* and many other letters, which testify, in their excesses, to the very difficult relationship of negation and repression that Marx had, throughout his life, with the Jewish world in which his family roots were so

The alienation of humanity in money thus adds a fourth area to the system of alienations that the young Marx had considered until now (respectively, alienation in religion, in philosophy, in law and in the political state). At the same time, it reorganises it in terms of priority and principle. Money is the abstraction whose existence is established on the level of each person's real and practical life. As a consequence, it is the objective and fundamental abstraction of modern times that precedes, in terms of importance for the construction of historical and social reality, any other type of abstraction. However, this abstraction that is assumed to be practical, real and no longer merely mental and ideal, it should be noted, refers to the same generating act and the same metaphysics of the subject which, for Marx, underlies the previous types of alienation. It still consists in an inversion due to which the true subject, which gives sense and principle to things, finds itself subordinate to and dependent on that which it has created but which has become progressively autonomised and abstract for it to such an extent that it has become an independent and other principle of the human being. In this type of economic abstraction-alienation, the discourse also moves from the fullness of a presupposed subject, whose inversion from subject into object or whose emptying out from full into empty through the deposition of its own wealth in another than itself cannot help but lead to an inversion of the inversion, due to the irrepressible impulse for restoring the original, violated and repressed fullness. Even in the passage from its theoretical completion to the conceiving of the abstractions of the philosophical Idea, of God and the state, to that economic-practical concept of the institutions of money, the functioning of the alienating mechanism remains the same: the projection of the value of the universal on some particular, so that the latter enjoys a symbolic (suplus) value that derives, in its excess, from the emptying of value of all the other particulars. There is not even the most embryonic germ of capital, labour power and the theory of labour value in this philosophy of money based on a hydraulic-mechanical theory (of the emptying out and filling up) of the human being.

The Marx of 1843 did not arrive at this first theory of money as the alienated essence of humanity by means of his first engagement with economic theory, upon which he embarked in Paris and which, after a short period, rapidly res-

---

deeply embedded. On the other hand, not as a justification but to explain his schematic approach, at least in part, it should be seen that what he was most anxious to demonstrate in 'On the Jewish Question' was, above all, the superior nature of his theoretical arguments and deductions in relation to the concepts of the young Hegelians considered by him as ideological. On this, see Blumenberg 1962, pp. 57–9. Interesting points but with excessively reductionist, psychological overtones, can be found in Künzli 1966.

ulted in the drafting of the so-called *Economic and Philosophic Manuscripts of 1844*.[79] Rather, it was most probably through reading Moses Hess's essay 'Über das Geldwesen' ['The Essence of Money']. Hess, previously a fundamental intellectual of the *Rheinische Zeitung* group, wrote the essay in 1843 for publication in the *Deutsch-Französische Jahrbücher*, but it was subsequently published only in 1845 in the *Rheinische Jahrbücher zur gesellschaftlichen Reform*. Hess was

79 The *Deutsch-Französische Jahrbücher* came out as a double issue (nos. 1–2) at the end of February 1844. Marx's two essays that compose them, 'Zur Judenfrage' and 'Kritik des Hegelschen Staatsrechts. Einleitung', were, therefore, written between the end of 1843 (Marx's arrival in Paris with his wife Jenny occurred in October 1843) and the start of 1844. The study of political economy that Marx began in Paris is evidenced by seven notebooks of extracts in which Marx studied the works of Adam Smith, Jean-Baptiste Say, Frédéric Skarbek, Xenophon, David Ricardo, James Mill, J. Ramsay McCulloch, A. Destutt de Tracy, Carl Wolfgang Schüz, Friedrich List, Heinrich F. Osiander and Eugene Büret. These studies, of which the *Economic and Philosophical Manuscripts* (May/June–August 1844) constitute the natural outcome, must have been begun coincidentally with or immediately after the failure of the magazine and the break, due to deep theoretical disagreement, with Ruge. They occupied, from an intellectual point of view, the greater part of the Parisian period, which lasted through to the end of January 1845. (The expulsion order signed by the Guizot government, as a result of his collaboration on another anti-Prussian magazine *Vorwärts*, was dated 11 January 1845). At the start of this Parisian period, Marx continued to dedicate himself to the gigantic study of the French Revolutionary texts that he had started in Kreuznach. According to Ruge's testimony to Feuerbach, his aim was to dedicate himself to a history of the Convention. 'Marx wants to write the history of the Convention. To this end he has accumulated material and has made some very interesting interpretations. [...] He wants to use his period in Paris for this work' (letter of 15 May 1844, in Ruge 1886, p. 345). Another letter from Ruge to K.M. Fleischer of 9 July 1844 claims that Marx wants 'to write the history of the Convention and, to this end, he has read enormously' (Ruge 1886, p. 362). Again, on 6 February 1845, the radical *Trier'sche Zeitung* wrote, in relation to Marx's enforced departure from Paris to Brussels, that he has moved there 'in order to finish his history of the Convention' (*MEGA*, IV/2, p. 725). The transition from studying history to economics is evidenced, furthermore, by the composition of one of the *Pariser Hefte* in the first six pages of which Marx transcribed extracts from the works of the Jacobin René Levasseur, dedicated to the French Revolution (*Mémoires*, vol. 4, Paris 1829–31), to then continue, in the following pages, with extracts from the French edition of the work by Adam Smith, *Recherches sur la nature et le causes de la richesse des nations*, Paris 1802. Marx's residency and studies in Paris, where his first daughter, Jenny, was born on 1 May 1844, were guaranteed by a donation of one thousand thalers which his friends from the *Rheinische Zeitung* had collected and sent from Cologne. As we have seen, since the summer of 1842, Karl had been denied any support and access to his paternal inheritance by his mother Henriette, with whom deep divisions had arisen regarding his life choices (see the letter of Marx to Ruge of 25 January 1843, *MECW* 1, p. 396).

also a philosopher of action, believing in the possibility of eliminating the particularism that estranges one man from another, not by means of theory but through practical action, since the Enlightenment of the conscience is only internal and cannot touch an individualist social order. A *Junghegelianer*, profoundly influenced in his formation by Rousseau's optimistic naturalism and by Herder's organic doctrine of history,[80] he combined Spinoza's philosophy and Jewish Messianism with the theories of Fourier and Babeuf, seeing communism as the advent of the New Jerusalem in which the human species would overcome the egoistic life that assigned it to the natural world and replaced the universality of the species with that of money. Egoism is the reciprocal alienation of the human species; the society of money represents the highest level of this alienation. Only the transformation of social praxis, with the abolition of private property, of hereditary rights, with the removal of money from its central place in modern society, permits the elimination of the fundamental causes of social inequality and the reaffirmation of harmonious life based on the equality of goods which, as written in his 1837 work, *Die heilige Geschichte der Menschheit von einem Jungers Spinozas* [*The Sacred History of Humanity by One of Spinoza's Pupils*] characterised humanity in the period of its infancy and before the advent of Christ.[81]

Similarly, for Marx, the emancipation of the human being is also achieved through the dismantling of civil society based on private property. Theoretical criticism continued to be important inasmuch as, in order to liberate oneself from oppression, it is necessary to be aware of it, but, nonetheless, 'the weapon

80 See Kanda 1996, pp. 183–5.

81 On the criticism of money and modern society in Hess, see Avineri 1985, pp. 115–58. On the figure of Hess, see also Vaccaro 1981; Na'aman 1982; Bensussan 1985; Bongiovanni 1987, pp. 20–3; Bazzani 1987, pp. 59–93. Hess's philosophy of history, set out in the *Heilige Geschichte*, was based on an accumulative and non-dialectical theory of the progressive expansion and realisation of the human species' universality. The seasons of history are effectively marked, in a development that does not negate but accepts and expands the preceding moment, by Moses's people (characterised as man-nature) and by a primitive community of goods, by the people of Christ (distinguished as man-spirit) and by the predominance of love and, ultimately by man-man who, beginning with Spinoza, inaugurates the most complete divinisation of humanity recognised in all its universal fullness. In this work, Hess explicitly refers to Cieszkowski's philosophy of praxis and, in 1843, planned a *Philosophie der Tat* of which, however, he wrote only the introduction (see Hess 1961, pp. 210–26). An anastatic reprint of the original edition of the *Heilige Geschichte* (Stuttgard 1837) was published by Gerstenberg, Hildesheim 1980. For an Italian translation of Hess's work, see Heß 1988.

of criticism cannot, of course, replace criticism by weapons'.[82] Furthermore, the tireless study of social, constitutional and political history that Marx continued to pursue in Paris, on the transition from a feudal-estate based, pre-modern society to the French Revolution and the establishment of the bourgeoisie, increasingly convinced him that the divisions between civil society and the political state could no longer be resolved through 'true democracy' (as he still believed in the 1843 *Critique*) which would return to the sovereignty of the people all those powers that had become abstract and separate. It would rather be resolved through the negation of modern civil society as such which, because internally established on the principle of private property, is primarily divided in itself and, therefore, separated, secondarily, from the political state, to which only apparent and illusorily functions of recomposition are attributed. The broadening of his reflections to include the constitution of the United States also led him to consider that political revolution – the completion, that is, of the modern democratic state – which no longer binds, as in the past, the political rights of the citizen to their condition in economic-civil society, confirms, precisely by means of such separation, the unlimited movement of private property and modern industry.

As a consequence, the solution no longer lies in achieving a democracy, as Marx still believed in the *Critique* (by generalising the active and passive right to vote, for example), that does not take into account the pre-modern divisions of estate, income and property; rather, the solution consists in the identification of a new subject capable of promoting, instead of political revolution, a more radical emancipation of the human being.

Thus, in Marx's second essay published in the *Deutsch-französosche Jahrbücher*, 'A Contribution to the Critique of Hegel's Philosophy of Right, Introduction', the subject of revolutionary action is by now explicitly identified, no longer in the people-species as in the *Critique*, nor, furthermore, in a group of intellectuals such as the *Junghegelianer*, but in the proletariat as the only class capable of a generalised emancipation of society as a whole.

A partial revolution, a solely political revolution, that does not modify the condition of division and human alienation, Marx now writes, takes place when a class of civil society achieves political power, universal power, without renouncing any of the determinations and property that render it a particular class distinct from any other. A solely political revolution consists, therefore, in the false universalisation of a particular class that makes itself a general representative without permitting that its specific civil conditions are truly gen-

82 *MECW* 3, p. 182.

eralised in the life conditions of all. The true revolution, that which implies universal human emancipation, needs to be achieved by a class whose particular nature consists in not having any particular nature and property and in being, as a consequence, a universal class. This absolutely negative class, in the sense that it has no positive characteristics and property to defend, is the proletariat: or, in other words, the class excluded from any property, from any positive relationship with reality. It is the object, due to its poverty, only of the most extreme and annihilating human alienation. The response to the possibility of an authentic revolution lies, that is,

> in the formulation of a class with radical chains, a class of civil society which is not a class of civil society, an estate which is the dissolution of all estates, a sphere which has a universal character by its universal suffering and claims no particular right because no particular wrong, but wrong generally, is perpetuated against it; which can no longer invoke a historical but only a human title; [...] a sphere, finally, which cannot emancipate itself without emancipating itself from all other spheres of society and thereby emancipating all other spheres of society, which, in a word, is the complete loss of man and hence can win itself only through the complete rewinning of man. This dissolution of society as a particular estate is the proletariat.[83]

Thus, only the proletariat is a historical-social subject or, more precisely, a human subject that is both particular and universal which finds the basis and objective reason for becoming a universal subject precisely in the particularity of its existence. It is only with the proletariat that revolution loses any moral and intellectual character, in the sense of being a promise of emancipation preached by a few enlightened intellectuals to a people that is merely an external object of their activity. It becomes, instead, an objective and necessary movement since the values and claims advanced by this social class are of an analytical nature; in other words, they do nothing more than explain, bring to light and generalise the conditions of life that are already present and immanent in the proletariat:

> By proclaiming the dissolution of the hitherto existing world order the proletariat merely states the secret of its own existence, for it is in fact the dissolution of that world order. By demanding the negation of private

83 *MECW* 3, p. 186.

> property, the proletariat merely raises to the rank of a principle of society what society has made the principle of the proletariat, what, without its own co-operation, is already incorporated in it as the negative result of society.[84]

Thus the research project from which the young Marx set out, starting with the preparatory notebooks for his dissertation, seems to be momentarily resolved and concluded. The problematical nexus of philosophy-world – or, in other words, the question of how and where to find a truly real universal – results in the identification of a human subject capable of a full universalisation, without residues. This subject is the proletariat, whose identity lies in its etymology. A possessor solely of its own offspring (from the Latin *proletarius*), the proletariat has no relationship with property of any kind and, therefore, is, by definition, a non-egoistic subject. Its positive identity lies precisely in the negative absoluteness of its existence, in its exclusion from social relationships relating to property and the entire context of the human species. Radically excluded from private property, it need do nothing more than generalise its own condition and thereby achieve social relationships communally centred on reciprocal participation. 'By demanding the negation of private property, the proletariat merely raises to the rank of a principle of society what society has made the principle of the proletariat, what, without its own co-operation, is already incorporated in it as the negative result of society'.[85] In this negativity that is immediately positivity, because it is exclusion from the private and egoistic, lies the originally communist virtue of the proletariat and the legitimacy of its being the sole and authentic universal class. The proper demand of philosophy, of conquering and making real the principle of the universal, has found its real subject at long last: no longer a mere abstract and speculative idea or the expression of the consciousness of a few intellectuals, but the collectivity of men in flesh and blood, which authorises and announces the paradoxical thesis that the proletariat is the only and true realiser of philosophy.

> As philosophy finds its material weapons in the proletariat, so the proletariat finds its spiritual weapons in philosophy [...]. The *head* of this emancipation is *philosophy*, its *heart* the *proletariat*. Philosophy cannot realize itself [*sich verwirklichen*] without the abolition [*Aufhebung*] of the

84 *MECW* 3, p. 187.

85 Ibid.

> proletariat, and the proletariat cannot abolish itself without the realization of philosophy.[86]

However, as is evident, even in the completion of philosophy's becoming worldly, in the priority that praxis has attained over critical theory, just as in radical democracy's flowing over into increasingly revolutionary and communist instances, the paradigms and metaphysics of the species continue to be strongly active in the young Marx's thought. Its most aporetic, philosophical-anthropological implication consists in the immediate unity of the individual and the universal.[87] It is starting from this presuppostion that Marx effectively continues to interpret modern civil society in the two *Deutsch-französosche Jahrbücher* essays, or, more precisely, in the negation and rejection of such organicism of the species, given that here too modern civil society is described and conceptualised as the opposite of the species, with its extreme disaggregation in the principle of egoism and individualism. 'Practical need, egoism, is the principle of civil society, and as such appears in pure form as soon as civil society has fully given birth to the political state'.[88]

Thus, at a level of historiographical analysis, Marx here continues to define modernity, in accordance with Hegel's teaching, as marked by the co-presence of civil society and the political state. As a consequence, he also theorises that civil society is a peculiarly and originally modern sphere. He comprehends, that is, the degree to which pre-modern, feudal-estate based society was characterised by corporative and economic-estate groupings that had meaning and political power immediately and as such. He thus sees that there was not a distinction between the ambit of economic-civic life and a purely political one.

> The character of the old civil society was directly political – that is to say, the elements of civil life, for example, property, or the family, or the mode of labor, were raised to the level of elements of political life in the form of seigniory, estates, and corporations. In this form, they determined the relation of the individual to the state as a whole – i.e., his political relation, that is, his relation of separation and exclusion from the other components of society. For that organization of national life did not raise property or labor to the level of social elements; on the contrary,

86 *MECW* 3, p. 187, translation modified.

87 On this subject I would like to refer to my contribution in Finelli and Trincia 1982, pp. 186–207.

88 *MECW* 3, p. 172.

> it completed their separation from the state as a whole and constituted them as discrete societies within society.[89]

Marx, therefore, understands to what degree pre-modern society was, on the one hand, structured according to a polycentrism of powers that reduced the presence of an eventual state power to that of a particular power alongside a multiplicity of other powers ('As a result of this organization, the unity of the state, and also the consciousness, will, and activity of this unity, the general power of the state, are likewise bound to appear as the particular affair of a ruler, isolated from the people').[90] On the other hand, he sees how the economic-social organisation into estates inscribed the individual's activities within a horizon of necessarily collective obligations and behaviour. As had already occurred with his analysis of the French Revolution in the *Critique*, here Marx also claims that the birth of both the modern political state and civil society refers to a single historical event in which one ambit is the reciprocal condition of the other. 'The establishment of the political state and the dissolution of civil society into independent individuals – whose relation with one another on law, just as the relations of men in the system of estates and guilds depended on privilege – is accomplished by one and the same act'.[91]

However, again, as in the *Critique*, the outcome of this historical process is the polarisation of absolute individualism in civil society and the absolute universalism of the political state with the consequence that modern civil society is once more a non-structured and unorganised place based on the movements of individual egoism.

> Throwing off the political yoke meant at the same time throwing off the bonds which restrained the egoistic spirit [*den egoistischen Geist*] of civil society. Political emancipation was, at the same time, the emancipation of civil society from politics, from having even the semblance of a universal content. Feudal society was resolved into its basic element – man, but man as he really formed its basis – egoistic man.[92]

The disappearance of feudal-estate based society, of the coincidence between socio-economic roles and specific political rights and obligations, liberates the individual from any presupposed belonging to groups and communities and

---

89 *MECW* 3, p. 165.

90 *MECW* 3, p. 166.

91 *MECW* 3, p. 167.

92 *MECW* 3, p. 166.

posits it, as an egoistic being abstracted from a structural relationship with those who are similar to it, as the principle of modern society.

> The political revolution [Marx refers here, in particular, to the French Revolution] [...] necessarily smashed all estates, corporations, guilds, and privileges, since they were all manifestations of the separation of the people from the community. The political revolution thereby abolished the political character of civil society. It broke up civil society into its simple component parts; on the one hand, the individuals; on the other hand, the material and spiritual elements constituting the content of the life and social position of these individuals. It set free the political spirit, which had been, as it were, split up, partitioned, and dispersed in the various blind alleys of feudal society. It gathered the dispersed parts of the political spirit, freed it from its intermixture with civil life, and established it as the sphere of the community, the general concern of the nation, ideally independent of those particular elements of civil life. A person's distinct activity and distinct situation in life were reduced to a merely individual significance. They no longer constituted the general relation of the individual to the state as a whole.[93]

The historical constitution of modern civil society imposes, with the clear separation between that which is public and that which is private, the expulsion and collocation of all public-universal dimensions, of all elements of generic integration, within the sphere of the political state. As a consequence, only individuals, on the one hand, and the ambits of their actions and existence (money and culture, Marx had written in the *Critique*), on the other, connote modern civil society deprived of any organic function of socialisation: egoistic individuals and material and cultural elements of their existence that are connected only extrinsically and accidentally in a nexus that appears to be instrumental for their needs and the pleasure of the individual but which, precisely because it exists between the individual and methods of socialisation without any internal logic or order, inverts and alienates the freedom of individuals in their unregulated and unrestrained movements. 'The liberty of egoistic man and the recognition of this liberty, however, is rather the recognition of the unrestrained movement of the spiritual and material elements which form the content of his life'.[94]

---

93 Ibid.

94 *MECW* 3, p. 167.

Marx accomplishes his first mature theoretical position in his writings for the *Deutsch-französosche Jahrbücher*. The issues that had already enthused the young Marx at the time of his dissertation here find their first systematic conclusion. How to reconcile philosophy and the world in a more intimate way than in Hegel's idealism? How to find a subject which, more than Hegel's idea, is a vector of universalisation and integration of the real? How to combine theory and praxis, intellectuals and the people, over and above the abstract subjectivity and intellectualism of the *Junghegelianer*? The universal subject is the proletariat, whose historical and political journey towards communism does not derive, Marx argues, from a presupposed theoretical system or the acceptance of a 'must' or, in other words, does not derive from a moral choice or the wisdom of an external intellectualism, but is all one with its existence. This is because, as the proletariat's life practices are an inverted form of existence, a critical praxis that puts back on its feet that which has been forcibly and arbitrarily overturned and stood on its head must necessarily be created and developed.

> By proclaiming the dissolution of the hitherto existing world order the proletariat merely states the secret of its own existence, for it is in fact the dissolution of that world order. By demanding the negation of private property, the proletariat merely raises to the rank of a principle of society what society has made the principle of the proletariat, what, without its own co-operation, is already incorporated in it as the negative result of society.[95]

The exclusion of the proletariat from the community of the human species – since the human species in the completeness of its organic nature is the foundation and fabric of reality – opens up a radical division in the history of the present, assigning it a statute of contradictions, incompleteness and ontological insufficiency, in the sense of a level of reality that is and at the same time is not.

Excluded radically from the ambit of history and the human community, the proletariat is the human that is negated as human and therefore, with the practical overthrowing of the current society and its foundation in private property, claims not particular rights, belonging to a particular estate – as has happened in all the previous revolutionary transitions in history – but, rather, the right to humanity as such and to the universality that this in itself implies.

95 *MECW* 3, p. 187.

Thus, the praxis that belongs to such a subject (far from possessing a close connection of meaning with labour as a transforming praxis on the part of a subject of natural objectivity) is synonymous solely with revolution; that is, of inverting a world which, with the negation and division of the human essence, is already inverted in itself. There is no problem of forming and educating this revolutionary subject, given that it will take its strength immediately from the very process of violent inversion – only changing its sense and direction – that had claimed to bend to its own ends the originary nature of reality. Thus, every difference, every distance and every possible need for mediation between the particular self and the universal self (whose dialectic constitutes, as we have seen, the underlying motif of Hegel's philosophy) is lessened in the proletariat, as it is a part that is immediately all.

But it is precisely in this concept of praxis as revolution, in this first Marxian formulation of social contradiction, as the inconsistency of the *menschliche Gattung* with respect to itself that explains the degree to which this first systematic theory of Marx is dominated and invalidated by a metaphysics of the subject. Overturnings, divisions, contradictions, projections, unitary and communitarian recompositions are generated by having presupposed the organicity of the human species during the course of human life and history. Every human being, over and above its unrepeatable individuality, over and above, that is, its physical-corporeal nature, possesses a universal nature common to humanity, and by participating in which it is a non-individual but organic and generic subject. However, when 'practical needs' – needs, that is, limited to the interests and reproduction of the single individual – replace the centrality and essential nature of the more precisely human need to participate in the community and life of the species – when, that is, the individual wants to replace the species with itself – human and social life is degraded. It is no coincidence that the Marx of 'On the Jewish Question', with a formula that appears paradoxical with respect to the centrality of the practical and material needs of his subsequent writings dedicated to the theory of historical materialism, identifies 'practical needs' *tout court* with 'egoism', defining this as that which opens 'the conflict between man's individual-sensuous existence and his species-existence'.[96]

The modern Judeo-Christian world, which has tried to 'put egoism and selfish need in the place of these species-ties, and dissolve the human world into a world of atomistic individuals who are inimically opposed to one an-

96 *MECW* 3, p. 174.

other',[97] developed this division between individual and species in an extreme way, leading the human being to the greatest 'self-estrangement' from its own essence. It is communism's task to remove the human being and all humanity from this naturalistic self-misunderstanding, from this falling into a representation of the self based on merely physical needs, and to propose, in a previously unachieved historical maturity, the fullness of common being. Communism is humanity's accomplishment where any difference and distance between human beings is removed, once the corporeal-naturalistic separations have been overcome, and where each sees in the other not alterity but the perfect continuity and integration of its own being. From this fusional-communitarian point of view of the young Marx, with apocalyptic-palingenetic implications, it is possible to refer to various sources of inspiration: to Feuerbach or, we have seen, to a strongly spiritual version of rationalism and Enlightenment universalism with strong traces of Romantic organicism, or the Messianic bent of Moses Hess's version of Spinoza, or the human and social world's overdetermination of meaning with respect to the devaluation of 'nature' by means of which Marx has accepted and radicalised Hegel's lessons (as seen in the 1841 dissertation).[98] What must be more urgently highlighted, however, is the degree to which Marx's first contact with communism was underwritten by a strongly fusional and symbiotic, anthropological conception within the ambit of which there is no space for the value of individual existence, distinct and autonomous from others. Communism is without individuals, since the human species that is its basis does not allow discontinuities and interruptions of essence into the organicity of its ontological fabric.[99] Furthermore, the revolutionary praxis which should establish it is a praxis which, rather than being radically practical, is, instead, profoundly saturated with abstract and strongly idealised thought in its claim to overcome the limits of idealism, linked as it is to the subject becom-

97 *MECW* 3, p. 173.

98 On the way in which the extracts Marx takes in Kreuznach from Rousseau's *Social Contract* give rise to the devaluation or, rather, the negation of any value or consistency that can be attributed to nature in comparison to the exhaustive nature of meaning belonging to the social fabric of human life, see Trincia 1985.

99 In the genesis of the young Marx's radically anti-individualist orientation, the anti-personalistic polemics (only briefly mentioned in this study) of the young Hegelians against the personalistic concept of God in religion and the monarchical sovereignty of the state should not be forgotten. It is sufficient to remember that a moderate Hegelian such as Michelet claimed in 1841 that the discussion of the 'personality of God has dominated the history of philosophy over the last ten years' (Michelet 1841, p. 7). On the reconstruction of this debate, see Breckman 1999, pp. 1–19.

ing thaumaturgical, the subject who, precisely in its most radical impotency, finds the source and form of its omnipotence.

Obviously, human existence has also a concrete, flesh and blood form for the young Marx. But concrete existences, considered in their immediate aspect, in that which does not make them common and identical the one to the other, are only nature. In other words, they belong to a merely and reductively biological level of existence in which they are linked solely to the physical needs of their reproduction. History, on the other hand, is beyond nature and constitutes the rightful ambit of the realisation of the human species, because only in history are there the universal institutions by means of which humanity, *qua* generic being, can overcome its naturalistic egoism and mirror itself in the objectivisation of its own free, creative and universal essence. In contemporary history, the human species, *qua* universal subject, is now translated and personified by the proletariat for the young Marx. As a consequence, communism, which constitutes the most rightful destiny of the proletariat, automatically receives all the characteristics of undifferentiated fusionality belonging to the human species.

The young Marx thus arrives at communism and a practical-revolutionary concept of subjectivity directly by marrying history and the metaphysical anthropology of the 'species' well before beginning his studies of political economy. The mythology of the organic subject and the resultant philosophy of history, marked by the objective inevitability of the initial increase and subsequent recomposition of the divisions and lacerations of human community, thus form the initial theoretical 'container' by means of which he began to compose his first economic manuscripts and to elaborate his later materialist conception of history. The transgressive enthusiasm of the young Marx lives, in this period, in an abstract conception of collective subjectivity, of its immanence and, ultimately, invincible strength of opposition, accompanied by an objective vision of historical movement and its final destination. The overdetermination of the presupposed subject that allows no space within itself to individuality, and the theory of history as the mechanical alternation of the time of unity and the time of disaggregation (save being unable to explain how and why the one could fall into the other) go together. As a result, the fate of all his future works will depend on how much and in what way he can manage to include in this theoretical container new theoretical material and interpretative perspectives that will mitigate, when not happily break, the tendency and shape of an extremely fecund system of thought, but one still fossilised in the mythology of the 'human species'.

# Bibliography

Adams, Henry Packwood 1972, *Karl Marx in His Earlier Writings*, New York: Atheneum.

Albanese, Luciano 1984, *Il concetto di alienazione*, Rome: Bulzoni.

Althusser, Louis 1969, *For Marx*, translated by Ben Brewster, London: Allen Lane.

——— 1970, 'Sur le rapport de Marx à Hegel', in *Hegel et la pensée moderne*, Paris: PUF.

Andolfi, Ferruccio 1983, *L'egoismo e l'abnegazione*, Milan: Franco Angeli.

Ascheri, Carlo 1970, *Feuerbach 1842. Necessità di un cambiamento*, Florence: Sansoni.

Avineri, Shlomo 1985, *Moses Hess: Prophet of Communism and Zionism*, New York: New York University Press.

Bauer, Bruno 1960, *La tromba del giudizio universale contro Hegel, ateo ed anticristo. Un ultimatum*, in *La sinistra hegeliana*, edited by Cludio Cesa, Bari: Laterza.

——— 1989, *The Trumpet of the Last Judgement against Hegel the Atheist and Anti-Christ. An Ultimatum*, Lewiston: Edwin Mellen.

Bausola, Adriano 1997, 'La collocazione della Filosofia della Rivelazione nel contesto della filosofia posthegeliana', in *Filosofia della Rivelazione*, by Friedrich Wilhelm Joseph Schelling, Milan: Rusconi.

Bazzani, Fabio 1987, *Il tempo dell'esistenza. Stirner, Heß, Feuerbach, Marx*, Milan: Franco Angeli.

Bedeschi, Giuseppe 1972, *Alienazione e feticismo nel pensiero di Marx*, Bari: Laterza.

Bellofiore, Riccardo and Roberto Finelli 1998, 'Capital, Labour and Time: The Marxian Monetary Labour Theory of Value as a Theory of Exploitation', in *Marxian Economics: A Reappraisal*, Vol. 1, edited by Riccardo Bellofiore, London: Macmillan.

Bensussan, Gérard 1985, *Moses Hess. La philosophie. Le socialisme (1836–1845)*, Paris: PUF.

Blumenberg, Werner 1962, *Marx*, Hamburg: Rowohlt.

Bobbio, Norberto, Nicola Matteucci and Gianfraco Pasquino 1992, *Dizionario di politica*, Turin: UTET.

Bongiovanni, Bruno 1987, 'Introduzione', in *Quaderno Spinoza (1841)*, by Karl Marx, edited by Bruno Bongiovanni, Turin: Bollati Boringhieri.

Breckman, Warren 1999, *Marx, the Young Hegelians and the Origins of Radical Social Theory: Dethroning the Self*, Cambridge: Cambridge University Press.

Burgio, Alberto 2000, *Strutture e catastrofi. Kant Hegel Marx*, Rome: Editori Riuniti.

Capograssi, Giuseppe 1959, 'Le glosse di Marx ad Hegel', in *Opere*, Vol. 4, Milan: Giuffrè.

Casini, Leonardo 1974, *Storia e Umanesimo in Feuerbach*, Bologna: Il Mulino.

——— 1979, *Feuerbach postumo. Il panteismo delle lezioni di Erlangen*, Florence: Sansoni.

Cassirer, Ernst 1970, *La filosofia dell'Illuminismo*, translated by Ervino Pocar, Florence: La Nuova Italia.

Cesa, Claudio (ed.) 1960, *La sinistra hegeliana*, Bari: Laterza.

——— 1963, *Il giovane Feuerbach*, Bari: Laterza.

——— 1972, *Studi sulla sinistra hegeliana*, Urbino: Argalìa.

Cieszkowski, August 1839, *Du crédit et de la circulation*, Paris: Treuttel et Wurtz.

——— 1979, *Selected Writings of August Cieszkowski*, edited and translated by André Liebich, Cambridge: Cambridge University Press.

——— 1997, *Prolegomeni alla storiosofia*, edited by Massimiliano Tomba, Milan: Istituto italiano per gli Studi Filosofici-Guerini e associati.

Cingoli, Mario 2001, *Il primo Marx (1835–1841)*, Milan: Unicopli.

Colletti, Lucio 1974, *Intervista politico-filosofica*, Bari: Laterza.

——— 1976, *Il marxismo e Hegel*, Bari: Laterza.

Cornu, Auguste 1971, *Marx e Engels dal liberalismo al comunismo*, translated by Francesco Cagnetti and Mazzino Montinari, Milan: Feltrinelli.

Croce, Benedetto 1914, *Historical Materialism and the Economics of Karl Marx*, translated by Christabel Margaret Meredith, New York: Macmillan.

——— 2001, *Materialismo storico ed economia marxistica*, Naples: Bibliopolis.

Cullen, Bernard 1988, 'The Mediating Role of Estates and Corporations in Hegel's Theory of Political Representation', in *Hegel Today*, edited by Bernard Cullen, Gower: Aldershot.

Daub, Carl 1810, *Einleitung in das Studium der christlichen Dogmatik aus dem Standpunkte der Religion*, Heidelberg: Mohr und Zimmer.

De Toni, Gian Antonio (ed.) 1981, *Annali di Halle e Annali tedeschi (1838–1843)*, Florence: La Nuova Italia.

Della Volpe, Galvano 1969, *Logica come scienza storica*, Rome: Editori Riuniti.

——— 1972, 'Le origini e la formazione della dialettica hegeliana. 1. Hegel romantico e mistico (1793–1800)', in Galvano della Volpe, *Opere*, vol. 1, Rome: Editori Riuniti.

Diogene Laerzio, *De clarorum philosophorum vitis*.

Donadio, Francesco 2000, 'L'eredità luterana nell'interpretazione schellinghiana della storia' in *Dalla materia alla coscienza. Studi su Schelling in ricordo di Giuseppe Semerari*, edited by Carlo Tatasciore, Milan: Guerrini e Associati.

——— 2002, 'Introduzione', in Christlieb Julius Braniss, *Religione filosofia e filosofia cristiana*, Catanzaro: Rubbettino.

Duichin, Marco 1982, *Il primo Marx. Momenti di un itinerario intellettuale (1835–1841)*, Rome: Cadmo.

Eßbach, Walter 1988, *Die Junghegelianer. Soziologie einer Intellektuellengruppe*, Munich: Fink.

Ferreri, Dino 1990, *Identità e colpa. Saggio sul giovane Hegel*, Rome: Bagatto.

——— 1994, *Sulla negazione. Un saggio di filosofia della psicoanalisi*, Rome: Astrolabio.

Fetscher, Iring 1965, 'La concrétisation de la notion de liberté chez le jeune Marx', in *Annali Istituto Feltrinelli*, VII, Milan: Feltrinelli.

Feuerbach, Ludwig 1972, *The Fiery Brook: Selected Writings of Ludwig Feuerbach*, translated by Zawar Hanfi, Garden City: Anchor Books.

——— 1974, *Vorlesungen über die Geschichte der neueren Philosophie. Von G. Bruno bis G.W.F. Hegel 1835–1836*, edited by Carlo Ascheri and Erich Thies, Darmstadt: Wissenschaftliche Buchgesellschaft.

——— 1975, *Einleitung in die Logik und Metaphysik (1829–30)*, Darmstadt: Wissenschaftliche Buchgesellschaft.

——— 1976, *Scritti filosofici*, edited by Claudio Cesa, Bari: Laterza.

——— 1980, *Thoughts on Death and Immortality, From the Papers of a Thinker*, translated by James A. Massey, Berkeley: University of California Press.

——— 1981, *De ratione, una, universali, infinita*, in *Gesammelte Werke*, Vol. 1, edited by Werner Schuffenhauer, Berlin: Akademie Verlag.

——— 1982, *Aristoteles, Qualität, Metaphysik, Δ 14*, in *Feuerbach e la dialettica dell'essere*, edited by Francesco Tomasoni, Florence: La Nuova Italia.

——— 1986, *Principles of the Philosophy of the Future*, translated by Manfred H. Vogel, Indianapolis-Cambridge: Hackett Publishing Company.

——— 1993, *Spiritualismo e materialismo, specialmente in relazione alla libertà del volere*, edited by Ferruccio Andolfi, Bari: Laterza.

——— 2008, *The Essence of Christianity*, translated by George Eliot, Mineola-New York: Dover Publications.

Fichte, Immanuel Hermann 1834, *Die Idee der Persönlichkeit und der individuellen Fortdauer*, Elberfeld: Büschler.

Fichte, Johan Gottlieb 1970, *The Science of Knowledge*, Cambridge: Cambridge University Press.

Finelli, Roberto 1987, *Astrazione e dialettica dal romanticismo al capitalismo. Saggio su Marx*, Rome: Bulzoni.

——— 1989, 'Some Thoughts on the Modern in the Works of Smith, Hegel and Marx', *Rethinking Marxism*, 2, 2: 111–31.

——— 1990a, 'Marx e l'intelletto hegeliano. Note sulle interpretazioni di L. Colletti e E. Severino', *La ragione possibile*, 1: 26–42.

——— 1990b, 'Dal paradigma del lavoro al paradigma della forza-lavoro. Sulla trasformazione dei concetti di "storia" e "dialettica" nel Marx della maturità', in *Trasformazione e persistenza*, FrancoAngeli: Milan.

——— 1991, 'Il marxismo italiano fra Della Volpe e Colletti', *Democrazia e diritto*, 1–2: 95–115.

——— 1995, 'Della Volpe e la "Kritik" del 1843 di Marx', in *Galvano Della Volpe. Un altro marxismo*, edited by Guido Liguori, Rome: Fahrenheit 451.

——— 1996a, *Mito e critica delle forme. La giovinezza di Hegel*, Rome: Editori Riuniti (germ. ed., *Mythos und Kritik der Formen. Die Jugend Hegels: 1770–1803*, Peter Lang: Frankfurt a. Main).

——— 1996b, 'Logica analitica e logica sintetica', *Trimestre*, 29: 12–27.

——— 1998, 'Al di là di una logica del sì e del no', *Psicoterapia e Istituzioni*, 1: 61–76.

——— 1999, 'La bürgerliche Gesellschaft nell'opera di Hegel', in *Storia, filosofia e letteratura. Studi in onore di Gennaro Sasso*, edited by Martha Herling and Mario Reale, Naples: Bibliopolis.

Finelli, Roberto and Francesco Saverio Trincia 1983, 'Nota filologica e Commentario', in *Critica del diritto statuale hegeliano*, by Karl Marx, translated by Roberto Finelli and Francesco Saverio Trincia, Rome: Edizioni dell'Ateneo.

Frank, Manfred 1992, *Der unendliche Mangel am Sein. Schellings Hegelkritik und die Anfänge der marxschen Dialektik*, Munich: Fink.

Friedenthal, Richard 1981, *Karl Marx. Sein Leben und seine Zeit*, München: Piper.

Gentile, Giovanni 1955, *La filosofia di Marx*, Florence: Sansoni.

Gielkens, Jan 1999, *Karl Marx und seine niederländischen Verwandten*, Trier: Karl-Marx-Haus.

Guastini, Riccardo 1974, *Marx: dalla filosofia del diritto alla scienza della società. Il lessico giuridico marxiano (1842–1851)*, Bologna: Il Mulino.

Habermas, Jürgen 1987, *Knowledge and Human Interests*, Cambridge: Polity.

——— 1990, *The Philosophical Discourse of Modernity*, Cambridge MA: MIT Press.

Halfwassen, Jens 1998, 'Die Bedeutung des spätantiken Platonismus für Hegels Denkentwicklung in Frankfurt und Jena', *Hegel-Studien*, 33: 85–131.

Harvey, Van A. 1995, *Feuerbach and the Interpretation of Religion*, Cambridge: Cambridge University Press.

Hegel, Georg Wilhelm Friedrich 1948, *Early Theological Writings*, translated by Thomas Knox, Chicago, IL: University of Chicago.

——— 1954, *Lineamenti di filosofia del diritto*, translated by Francesco Messineo, Bari: Laterza.

——— 1970, *Lo spirito del cristianeismo e il suo destino*, edited by Edoardo Mirri, L'Aquila: Japadre.

——— 1975a, *Logic: Part One of the Encyclopedia of Philosophical Sciences*, translated by William Wallace, Oxford: Oxford University Press.

——— 1975b, *Natural Law*, Philadelphia, University of Pennsylvania Press.

——— 1976, *Vorlesungen über Rechtsphilosophie 1818–1831*, edited by Karl Heinz Ilting, Stuttgart-Bad Cannstatt: Frommann Holzboog.

——— 1977, *Phenomenology of Spirit*, translated by Arnold V. Miller, Oxford: Oxford University Press.

——— 1979, *System of Ethical Life and First Philosophy of Spirit*, translated by Henry Harris and Thomas Knox, Albany: SUNY.

——— 1983a, *Vorlesungen über Naturrecht und Staatswissenschaft. Heidelberg 1817–18*

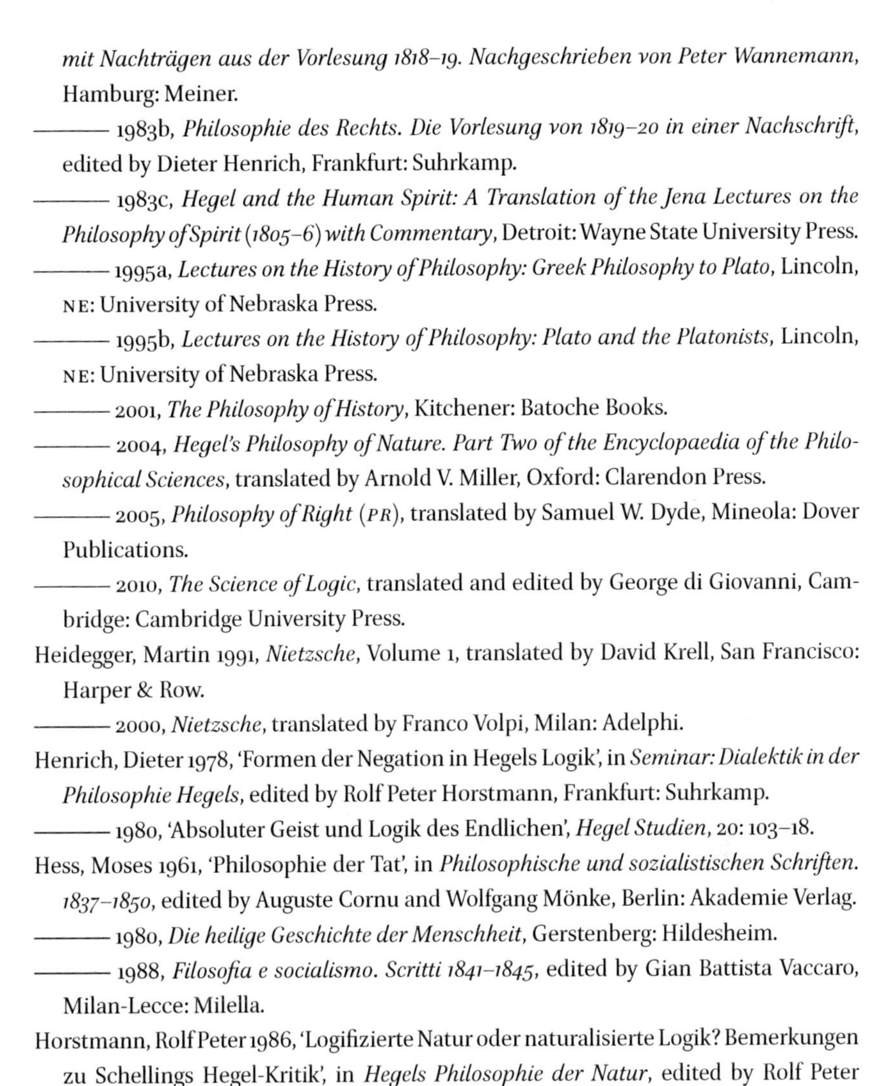

*mit Nachträgen aus der Vorlesung 1818–19. Nachgeschrieben von Peter Wannemann*, Hamburg: Meiner.

——— 1983b, *Philosophie des Rechts. Die Vorlesung von 1819–20 in einer Nachschrift*, edited by Dieter Henrich, Frankfurt: Suhrkamp.

——— 1983c, *Hegel and the Human Spirit: A Translation of the Jena Lectures on the Philosophy of Spirit (1805–6) with Commentary*, Detroit: Wayne State University Press.

——— 1995a, *Lectures on the History of Philosophy: Greek Philosophy to Plato*, Lincoln, NE: University of Nebraska Press.

——— 1995b, *Lectures on the History of Philosophy: Plato and the Platonists*, Lincoln, NE: University of Nebraska Press.

——— 2001, *The Philosophy of History*, Kitchener: Batoche Books.

——— 2004, *Hegel's Philosophy of Nature. Part Two of the Encyclopaedia of the Philosophical Sciences*, translated by Arnold V. Miller, Oxford: Clarendon Press.

——— 2005, *Philosophy of Right* (*PR*), translated by Samuel W. Dyde, Mineola: Dover Publications.

——— 2010, *The Science of Logic*, translated and edited by George di Giovanni, Cambridge: Cambridge University Press.

Heidegger, Martin 1991, *Nietzsche*, Volume 1, translated by David Krell, San Francisco: Harper & Row.

——— 2000, *Nietzsche*, translated by Franco Volpi, Milan: Adelphi.

Henrich, Dieter 1978, 'Formen der Negation in Hegels Logik', in *Seminar: Dialektik in der Philosophie Hegels*, edited by Rolf Peter Horstmann, Frankfurt: Suhrkamp.

——— 1980, 'Absoluter Geist und Logik des Endlichen', *Hegel Studien*, 20: 103–18.

Hess, Moses 1961, 'Philosophie der Tat', in *Philosophische und sozialistischen Schriften. 1837–1850*, edited by Auguste Cornu and Wolfgang Mönke, Berlin: Akademie Verlag.

——— 1980, *Die heilige Geschichte der Menschheit*, Gerstenberg: Hildesheim.

——— 1988, *Filosofia e socialismo. Scritti 1841–1845*, edited by Gian Battista Vaccaro, Milan-Lecce: Milella.

Horstmann, Rolf Peter 1986, 'Logifizierte Natur oder naturalisierte Logik? Bemerkungen zu Schellings Hegel-Kritik', in *Hegels Philosophie der Natur*, edited by Rolf Peter Horstmann, Stuttgart: Klett-Cotta.

Ilchmann, Achim 1992, 'Kritik der Übergänge zu den ersten Kategorien in Hegels Wissenschaft der Logik', *Hegel Studien*, 27: 11–25.

Jakubowski, Marek Nikodem 1992, 'Hegel and "the End of Philosophy" in the Polish Philosophy of Action of the 1840s', *Hegel-Jahrbuch*: 155–61.

Jäschke, Walter (ed.) 1992, *Sinnlichkeit und Razionalität. Der Umbruch in der Philosophie des 19. Jahrhunderts: Ludwig Feuerbach*, Berlin: Akademie Verlag.

Johnston, William M. 1967, 'Karl Marx's Verse of 1836–1873 as a Foreshadowing of his Early Philosophy', *Journal of the History of Ideas*, 28: 259–68.

Kanda, Junji 1996, 'Vom Spinozismus zum Junghegelianismus. Moses Heß und sein Weg zur Philosophie der Tat', in *Philosophie, Literatur und Politik vor den Revolutionen von 1848. Forschungen zum Junghegelianismus*, edited by Lars Lambrecht, Frankfurt: Peter Lang.

Kant, Immanuel 1992, *Theoretical Philosophy 1755–1770*. Cambridge: Cambridge University Press.

Kersting, Wolfgang 1986, 'Polizei und Korporation in Hegels Darstellung der bürgerlichen Gesellschaft', *Hegel-Jahrbuch*: 373–82.

Koselleck, Reinhart 1988, *La Prussia tra riforma e rivoluzione (1791–1848)*, translated by Marco Cupellaro, Bologna: Il Mulino.

Künzli, Arnold 1966, *Karl Marx. Eine Psychographie*, Vienna: Europa Verlag.

Lancizolle, Karl Wilhelm von 1831, *Beiträge zur Politik und zum Staatsrecht*, Berlin.

Landucci, Sergio 1977, *La contraddizione in Hegel*, Florence: La Nuova Italia.

Lange, Erhard (ed.) 1983, *Die Promotion von Karl Marx. Jena 1841. Eine Quellenedition*, Berlin: Dietz.

Laufner, Richard and Rausch, Albert (eds.) 1975, *Die Familie Marx und die Trierer Judenschaft*, Trier: Karl-Marx-Haus.

Leibniz, Gottfried Wilhelm von 1628, *Opera omnia*, edited by Louis Dutens, Geneva.

Léonard André 1974, *Commentaire littéral de la logique de Hegel*, Paris: Vrin.

Li Vigni, Florinda 1997, *La comunanza della ragione. Hegel e il linguaggio*, Milan: Guerrini e Associati.

Lobkowicz, Nicholas 1976, *Theory and Practice: History of a Concept from Aristotle to Marx*, Notre Dame, IN: University of Notre Dame Press.

Longato, Fulvio 1977, 'Note sul significato del "principio d'identità e di contraddizione" nella formazione del pensiero hegeliano', in *La contraddizione*, edited by Enrico Berti, Rome: Città Nuova.

Löwith, Karl 1964, *From Hegel to Nietzsche*, New York: Columbia University Press.

——— 1976, 'Vermittlung und Unmittelbarkeit bei Hegel, Marx und Feuerbach', in *Ludwig Feuerbach*, edited by Erich Thies, Darmstadt: Wissenschaftliche Buchgesellschaft.

Lübbe, Hermann and Saß, Hans-Martin (eds.) 1975, *Atheismus in der Diskussion. Kontroversen um Ludwig Feuerbach*, Munich: Kaiser-Gruenewald.

Maier, Hans 1980, *Die ältere deutsche Staats- und Verwaltungslehre*, Munich: Beck.

Marx, Karl 1983, *Critica del diritto statuale hegeliano*, translated by Roberto Finelli and Francesco Saverio Trincia, Rome: Edizioni dell'Ateneo.

Marx, Karl and Friedrich Engels 1927, *Historisch-kritische Gesamtausgabe* (*MEGA*[1]), Frankfurt a.M.: Marx-Engels-Archiv Verlaggesselschaft.

——— 1975–2005, *Marx Engels Collected Works* (*MECW*), London: Lawrence and Wishart.

——— 1976–, *Gesamtausgabe* (*MEGA*), Berlin: Dietz Verlag.

Matassi, Elio 1991, *Eredità hegeliane. Da Cieszkowski e Gans a Ritter*, Naples: Morano.

Mazzone, Alessandro (ed.) 2002, *MEGA*[2]. *Marx ritrovato grazie alla nuova edizione critica*, Rome: Mediaprint.

McLellan, David 1973, *Karl Marx: A* Life, London: Macmillan.

Michelet, Carl Ludwig 1841, *Vorlesungen über die Persönlichkeit und Unsterblichkeit der Seele*, Berlin: Dümmler.

Mirri, Edoardo 1977, 'Introduzione' to *Lo spirito del cristianesimo e il suo destino*, in *Scritti teologici giovanili*, by Georg Wilhelm Friedrich Hegel, edited by Edoardo Mirri, Naples: Guida.

Mondolfo, Rodolfo 1975, 'Feuerbach e Marx', in *Umanismo di Marx. Studi filosofici 1908–1966*, edited by Norberto Bobbio, Turin: Einaudi.

Monz, Heinz 1973, *Karl Marx. Grundlagen der Entwicklung zu Leben und Werk*, Trier: Hoffmann und Campe.

Monz, Heinz, Konrad Krosigk and Georg Eckert 1973, *Zur Persönlichkeit von Marx's Schwiegervater Johann Ludwig von Westphalen*, Trier: Karl-Marx-Haus.

Mustè, Marcello 1981–2, 'Le fonti del giudizio marxiano sulla rivoluzione francese nei "Kreuznacher Hefte"', *Annali dell'Istituto italiano per gli studi storici*, 7: 55–85.

Na'aman, Shlomo 1982, *Emanzipation und Messianismus. Leben und Werk des Moses Hess*, Frankfurt: Campus.

Napoleoni, Claudio 1970, *Smith Ricardo Marx*, Turin: Bollati Boringhieri.

——— 1976, *Il valore*, Turin: Isedi.

Nikolaevskij, Boris and Otto Maenchen-Helfen 1969, *Karl Marx. La vita e l'opera*, Turin: Einaudi.

Paulus, Heinrich Eberhard Gottlob 1843, *Die endlich offenbar gewordene positive Philosophie der Offenbarung oder Entstehungsgeschcichte, wörtlicher Text, Beurtheilung und Berichtigung der v. Schellingischen Entdeckungen über Philosophie überhaupt, Mithologie und Offenbarug des dogmatischen Christenthums im Berliner Winterkurs von 1841–42*, Darmstadt: Wilhelm Leske Verlag.

Pepperle, Ingrid 1978, *Junghegelianische Geschichtsphilosophie und Kunsttheorie*, Berlin: Akademie Verlag.

Pöggeler, Otto 1986, *Hegel. L'idea di una fenomenologia dello spirito*, Naples: Guida.

Popper, Karl 2011, *The Open Society and Its Enemies*, Volume 2, Abingdon: Routledge.

Raddatz, Fritz 1975, *Karl Marx. Eine politische Biographie*, Hamburg: Hoffmann und Campe.

Reale, Mario 1983, *Le ragioni della politica*, Rome: Edizioni dell'Ateneo.

Riedel, Manfred (ed.) 1975, *Materialien zu Hegels Rechtsphilosophie*, Frankfurt: Suhrkamp.

Ritter, Joachim 1983, 'Persona e proprietà', in *Metafisica e politica*, edited by Gerardo Cunico, Genoa: Marietti.

Rockmore, Tom 1989, 'Hegel's Circular Epistemology as Anti-Foundationalism', *History of Philosophy Quarterly*, 6: 101–13.

Rodano, Franco 1986, *Lezioni di storia impossibile*, Genoa: Marietti, Genoa.

Rose, Margareth A. 1978, *Reading the Young Marx and Engels: Poetry, Parody and the Censor*, London: Croom Helm.

Rosenzweig, Franz 1976, *Hegel e lo Stato*, translated by Remo Bodei, Bologna: Il Mulino.

Rossi, Mario 1977, *Da Hegel a Marx, III, La Scuola hegeliana. Il giovane Marx*, Milan: Feltrinelli.

Ruge, Arnold 1886, *Briefwechsel und Tagebuchblätter aus den Jahren 1825–1880*, Vol. 1, Berlin: Weidmann.

——— 1960, 'I nostri ultimi dieci anni', in *La sinistra hegeliana*, edited by Claudio Cesa, Bari: Laterza.

——— 1975, 'Die Hegelsche Rechtsphilosophie und die Kritik unserer Zeit', in *Materialien zu Hegels Rechtsphilosophie*, edited by Manfred Riedel, Frankfurt: Suhrkamp.

——— 1981, 'La filosofia Hegeliana del diritto e la politica del nostro tempo', in *Annali di Halle e Annali tedeschi (1838–1843)*, edited by Gian Antonion De Toni, Florence: La Nuova Italia.

Sabetti, Alfredo 1962, *Sulla fondazione del materialismo storico*, Florence: La Nuova Italia.

Saß, Hans Martin 1972, 'Feuerbachs Prospekt einer neuen Philosophie', *Revue internationale de Philosophie*, 26: 255–74.

——— 1998, *Ludwig Feuerbach*, Hamburg: Reinbek.

Sasso, Gennaro 1965, *Introduzione* all'*Antologia degli scritti politici di Emanuele Kant*, Turin: UTET.

Savigny, Friedrich Carl von 1837, *Das Recht des Besitzes. Eine civilistische Abhandlung*, Giessen: Heyer.

Schelling, Friedrich Wilhelm Joseph 1994, *On the History of Modern Philosophy*, translated by Andrew Bowie, Cambridge: Cambridge University Press.

Schiera, Pierangelo 1968, *Dall'arte di Governo alle Scienze dello Stato. Il cameralismo e l'assolutismo tedesco*, Milan: Giuffrè.

——— 1992, 'Società per ceti', in *Dizionario di politica*, edited by Norberto Bobbio, Nicola Matteucci and Gianfraco Pasquino, Turin: UTET.

Schmidt, Alfred 1973, *Emanzipatorische Sinnlichkeit. Ludwig Feuerbachs anthropologischer Materialismus*, Munich: Ullstein.

Schott, Uwe 1971, *Die Jugendentwicklung L. Feuerbachs bis 1825 und ihre Bedeutung für seine spätere Religionskritik. Inaugural-Dissertation*, Heidelberg.

——— 1973, *Die Jugendentwicklung Ludwig Feuerbachs bis zum Fakultätswechsel*, Göttingen: Vandenhoeck & Ruprecht.

Siegel, Jerrold 1978, *Marx's Fate: The Shape of a Life*, Princeton: Princeton University Press.

Smith, Adam 1822, *An Inquiry Into the Nature and Causes of the Wealth of Nations*, Vol. 3, London: G. Walker.

——— 1835, *An Inquiry Into the Nature and Causes of the Wealth of Nations*, Vol. 1, London: Charles Knight and Company.

Stahl, Friedrich Julius 1830–3, *Die Philosophie des Rechts nach geschichtlicher Ansicht*, Heidelberg.

Stirner, Max 1995, *The Ego and Its Own*, edited by David Leopold, Cambridge: Cambridge University Press.

Strauss, David Friedrich 1835, *Das Leben Jesu kritisch bearbeitet*, Tübingen.

——— 1838, *Streitschriften zur Verteidigung meiner Schrift über das Leben Jesu*, III, Tübingen.

Stuke, Horst 1963, *Philosophie der Tat. Studien zur 'Verwicklichung der Philosophie' bei den Junghegelianern und den Wahren Sozialisten*, Stuttgart: Klett.

Tomasoni, Francesco 1982, *Feuerbach e la dialettica dell'essere*, Florence: La Nuova Italia.

——— 1986, *Ludwig Feuerbach e la natura non umana, Ricostruzione genetica dell 'Essenza della religion' con pubblicazione degli inediti*, Florence: La Nuova Italia.

——— 1992, *Materialismus und Mystizismus. Feuerbachs Studium der Kabbala*, in *Sinnlichkeit und Razionalität. Der Umbruch in der Philosophie des 19. Jahrhunderts: Ludwig Feuerbach*, edited by Walter Jäschke, Berlin: Akademie Verlag.

Tomba, Massimiliano 1997, 'Politica e storia nel *Vormärz*: August von Cieszkowski', in *Prolegomeni alla storiosofia*, by August Cieszkowski, edited by Massimiliano Tomba, Milan: Istituto italiano per gli Studi Filosofici-Guerini e associati.

——— 2002, *Crisis e critica in Bruno Bauer. Il principio di esclusione come fondamento del politico*, Naples: Bibliopolis.

Trincia, Francesco Saverio 1985, 'Marx lettore di Rousseau (1843)', *Critica marxista*, 5: 97–127.

Trincia, Francesco Saverio and Finelli, Roberto 1982, *Critica del soggetto e aporie della alienazione. Saggi sulla filosofia del giovane Marx*, Milan: Franco Angeli.

Vaccaro, Gian Battista 1980, 'Hegelismo e liberalismo tra Eduard Gans e Arnold Ruge', *Annali della fondazione Luigi Einaudi*, 14: 331–77.

——— 1981, *Socialismo e umanesino nel pensiero di Moses Hess (1837–1847)*, Naples: Bibliopolis.

Valenza, Pierluigi 1999, *Logica e filosofia pratica nello Hegel di Jena*, Padua: Cedam.

Wandschneider, Dieter and Vittorio Hösle 1983, 'Die Entäußerung der Idee zur Natur und ihre zeitliche Entfaltung als Geist bei Hegel', *Hegel-Studien*, 18: 173–99.

Waszek, Norbert 1986a, *The Scottish Enlightenment and Hegel's Account of Civil Society*, Dordrecht: Kluwer.

——— 1986b, 'Hegel's account of the market economy and its debts to the Scottish Enlightenment', *Hegel-Jarbuch*: 57–73.

——— 1988, 'Eduarrd Gans und die Armut. Von Hegel und Saint-Simon zu frühgewerkschaftlichen Forderungen', *Hegel-Jahrbuch*: 355–63.

——— 1992, 'La tentation parisienne d'un hégélian juif de Berlin', *Hegel-Jahrbuch*: 31–9.

Weckwerth, Christine 1996, 'Der Gedanke einer Generalreformierung der Gesellschaft beim jungen Feuerbach', in *Philosophie, Literatur und Politik vor den Revolutionen von 1848*, edited by Lars Lambrecht, Frankfurt: P. Lang.

Weiße Christian Hermann 1833, *Die philosophische Geheimlehre über die Unsterblichkeit des menschlischen Individuums*, Dresden.

Xhaufflaire, Marcel 1975, 'L'évangile de la Sinnlichkeit et la théologie politique', in *Atheismus in der Diskussion. Kontroversen um Ludwig Feuerbach*, edited by Hermann Lübbe and Hans-Martin Saß, Munich: Kaiser-Gruenewald.

Zanardo, Aldo 1966, 'La teoria della libertà nel pensiero giovanile di Marx', *Studi storici*: 3–70.

# Index of Names